What People Are Saying About

15 Years of Speculative Realism

When the first speculative realism symposium was held in 2007, it caused a sensation both inside and outside philosophical circles. It seemed to portend a radical shift in our relation to, and in our understanding of, the world. But it is the fate of successful revolutions in thought to be assimilated into the very frameworks that they initially seemed determined to destroy. The essays in this volume show how speculative realist projects contribute to, and enrich our understandings of, many different philosophical questions.
Steven Shaviro, DeRoy Professor of English at Wayne State University and author of *The Universe of Things: On Speculative Realism*

A definitive and invaluable re-assessment of the last decade of speculative realism.
Thomas Nail, Professor of Philosophy at the University of Denver and author of *Matter and Motion: A Brief History of Kinetic Materialism*

15 YEARS OF SPECULATIVE REALISM: 2007–2022

Edited by
Charlie Johns
and
Hilan Bensusan

zer0 books

London, UK
Washington, DC, USA

CollectiveInk

First published by Zer0 Books, 2024
Zer0 Books is an imprint of Collective Ink Ltd.,
Unit 11, Shepperton House, 89 Shepperton Road, London, N1 3DF
office@collectiveinkbooks.com
www.collectiveinkbooks.com
www.zero-books.net

For distributor details and how to order please visit the "Ordering" section on our website.

Paperback ISBN: 978 1 80341 464 5
eBook ISBN: 978 1 80341 465 2
PCN: 2023950585

A CIP catalogue record for this book is available from the British Library.

Design credit(s): Lapiz Digital

UK: Printed and bound by CPI Group (UK) Ltd, Croydon, CR0 4YY
Printed in North America by CPI GPS partners

CONTENTS

15 YEARS OF SPECULATIVE REALISM

EDITORS INTRODUCTION A

Charlie Johns

Correlationism

In 2007, at a conference held in Goldsmiths College, London, U.K., the general 'intelligentsia' finally got wind that something peculiar, brave, and significant was happening in continental philosophy (and perhaps even contemporary philosophy at large). It came under the rubric "speculative realism" and organised a group of previously connected[1] but rarely related philosophers. Those four philosophers were Graham Harman, Quentin Meillassoux, Ray Brassier, and Iain Hamilton Grant. It has subsequently been said that these four philosophers were predominantly united by one common enemy — *correlationism* — the idea that Being and Thought can never be distinguished independently of each other. This concept is not only a formal and rationalist problem[2] but also an empirical one; the claustrophobic tautology that whatever we encounter, or whatever exists, must first be posited, and hence is always already inscribed into thought itself — whether as a simple Berkeleyianism, of "reality" being dependent upon mind or as exhibiting mental properties, or as a complex Hegelian thesis, whereby the putative limitation of thought upon reality in fact lays claim to a limit *identifiable in reality itself*, hence subsuming reality into an absolute, dialectical form of thought,[3] which we call absolute (or objective) idealism. Now, one consequence of this correlationism is that the "sensible (can) only exist as a relation" (Meillassoux, 2009, p. 2), since the independent qualities of objects cannot be such "qualities" without the *perception of* such qualities (dependent on myself, a human species, specific organisms, etc.). Hence, the seemingly impossible distinction between Being and Thought is not simply an ontological or speculative enterprise but also an *epistemological* one, as this "sensible relation" is the bedrock — since at least Kant — of any kind of access to a *knowledge*, whether "transcendentally" formulated or deduced through the Humean concepts of contiguity, resemblance, and cause and effect.[4]

This leaves us with a problem: How can we define mind-independent features of the world when our relation to the world is mediated conceptually (amongst other capacities)? Conversely, how can we define and organise thought beyond the 'being' of nature or any material ground that propagates it? Concerning the German Idealists, thought does indeed have an autonomous or a priori function (similar to branches of pure logic and mathematics), but it is also complicit in the contingent world of experience (a posteriori). For this reason, the (pre-critical) question pertaining to what something is (essence) transforms into the (critical) question pertaining to how it is that we can know an entity, or, under what conditions can we come to know about an entity? To reiterate, this is because it is unacceptable to speak of entities independent of the ways in which we process them (or co-constitute them). In their own unique manner, the speculative realists propose a way out of this critical monopoly on philosophical questioning (without relapsing into a scientific realism) and rekindle classical arguments concerning space, time, materiality, nature, and objects beyond that of Kant's correlation of the spatio-temporal as (subjective) inner and outer forms of intuition.

Through the Hegelian lens of reconciling putative opposites and dichotomies qua their dialectical/antagonistic implication, I believe that all four of the original "speculative realists" can be seen to motivate the distinction between Being and Thought whilst supplementing the correlation in some way, shape, or form. For example, **Quentin Meillassoux** questions the very metaphysical/historical assumptions or *conditions of possibility* for such a "correlate" to exist and prevail in the first place, yet situates the "facticity" of the correlation within a context of absolute contingency ("hyper-chaos"), which still provides an accessible bridge between thinking and being (the "intellectual intuition" — or "speculative thinking" — of the being of absolute contingency). Another example would be **Iain Hamilton Grant**'s insistence that Nature's products (manifestations and Ideas) cannot be reducible to Nature's elusive *Ground.* Rodrigo Nunes cites Grant's idea as follows: nature cannot be identical with its concept because "it is not the result or consequence of reasoning but its logical antecedent". Any concept "that has nature as its subject must acknowledge its partiality", since "the judgement that nature is thus and so is itself an expression of the nature in which that judgement arises", and concepts are "consequent upon the nature of which they are, qua concepts, late expressions" (Nunes, 2024). Hence, although the Being of Nature is given precedence (or antecedence) over "its" thoughts and ideas, signalling a post-correlational philosophy which stresses the chronological and irreducible difference between "production" and its "product", there is still a more general correlation between Nature and its products *mutatis mutandis,* whereby all thinking is natural (a product of nature) in some way and all of nature must include thought as part of its reality (at least as an immanent, additive reconstruction of reality as a transforming whole in every instance).[5]

While Meillassoux picks out the internal contradiction of the correlation itself and designates the facticity of the correlation as a new, radical contingency, Grant picks out the preconceived equilibrium and neutrality of thought and nature to show how such a relation is more charged, creative, and transformative than any normativism, eliminativism, and even transcendental idealism is willing to accept. **Graham Harman** follows suit by picking apart what he terms the "real" and "sensual" profiles (or "faces") of the object, which, already to the attentive reader, implies that the aforementioned sensual/sensible relation imparted to Kantian knowledge is only *one* aspect of an otherwise "real" object irreducible to such a sensual relation. Here, thought and being are most certainly not intrinsically bound together, as thought appears as a *sensual relation* distinct and somewhat in contradistinction to the non-relational "real" aspect of the object (and this sensual relation furthermore appears as only *one* relation amongst a plethora of other non-human relations in the cosmos). Far from being a kind of futile dualism (sensual/real), the *modality* between sensual and real, relation and non-relation, and translated and translatable, instead *positively* enforces the way that — not just us humans but every object — compulsively reduces the object to a series of engagements, uses, profiles, i.e., a series of relations. In this sense Harman's thesis is a theory of *irreducible* (or "withheld") entities complicit in the *reduction* of presence (as relation) and is derived more from the Heideggerian legacy of concealment/unconcealment rather than any Cartesian dualism.

I call Harman's project *positive* because it indeed *affirms* the reality of irreducible objects[6] (as noumenal or "in-itself") and also describes the unbinding of the sensual and the real through his notion of "allure" (Harman, 2007). However, one could argue that, if there is no sensual object without a real object prehending (or "bridging") *another* real object, and if the real object is only ever disclosed through the register of the sensual, then thinking and being — although distinct in degree or kind — are correlated to each other as a vicarious condition of each other's emergence (an operation Harman has since called *translation*).[7]

Harman's ontological distinction between the sensual and the real also serves as an *epistemological cautionary tale*; the reality of the object cannot be reduced to external and outward relations (oriented towards a human or otherwise qua the sensual) as some surface theory of knowledge ("overmining") but the object also cannot be reduced to the internal (micro) relations of atoms, particles, or any matter-in-motion that will provide a derivative account of knowledge made from the building blocks of smaller and smaller components, which will eventually become completely uniform and arbitrary, as in those strict accounts of materialism ("undermining"). Regarding the initial premise of the correlation, however, Harman can be seen to extend the tautology of "no X without first positing X" (Meillassoux, 2007, p. 49), which human consciousness is putatively riddled with, and multiply it onto *every object in the cosmos.* German idealism mutates into a *German realism,* whereby all objects must "translate" their environment (qua relationality) through terms specifically anchored to their particular status as a real object with real qualities (just as how diggers "translate" oil differently from how a fish might, or how a plant may photosynthesise the sun whilst a vampire may be caused considerable distress and even death if exposed to such solarity). Hence, the correlation lives, formulated as the translation of real objects through (and into) sensual ones, untethered from the *human-world* vicious circle of mediation yet multiplied as the multifaceted translation of one speck of dust to another, a marble upon a table, or the intricate translations (and re-workings) of an "object" such as the New York Yankees.[8]

Such object-object encounters enter into an array of corresponding intricate sensual and real "qualities" that attempt to do justice to the plethora of individual and diverse objects out there in the universe (and — might I add — the plethora of different kinds of *relation*[9]) beyond that of the solely human, cognitive relation to its environment that the critique of correlationism is traditionally aimed at attacking.

Ray Brassier can also be viewed as a thinker who ekes out the discrepancies between the supposed prelapsarian harmony of Being and Thinking that correlationism implies, exacerbating such discrepancies by situating a *manifest* and *scientific* realm of the human whose respective findings are at *odds* with themselves. Whilst this almost validates some of Harman's insights regarding the distinction between real and sensual objects — i.e., the distinction between the brain as a *real* object and consciousness as *sensually* encoded (or perhaps the distinction between neurology and folk-psychology) — one cannot get away from the almost humanist contract (or quasi-correlation) that Brassier implies when he acknowledges the success of enlightenment philosophy in exposing the meaninglessness of reality, implying that thought has "evolved" into a scenario whereby it can disclose the meaninglessness of being as a "truth" or "achievement". The same type of subjective, neo-rationalist access to a mind-independent reality is performed when he encourages his readers to "think the extinction of thought" as a challenge for philosophy itself, when, alternatively, this activity could be simply dismissed as having no bearing on the reality that exceeds and is indifferent to our (uncorrelated) thought about it. In other words, if the *separation* of Thinking and Being can be advocated, it remains unclear to what extent thought is accessible to being (or, alternatively, whether this conceptual access can be turned into a *knowledge* with *absolute* status).

Having said this, Brassier seems much more nuanced and misunderstood than his other speculative realist brothers. He is *not* an Eliminative Materialist, and his knack of presenting polarising concepts from both the history of philosophy and contemporary philosophy, such as *the manifest and the scientific image* (regarding Sellars, Churchland, Dennett, and Metzinger's work), *Nature and Rationality* (regarding Horkheimer and Adorno's critique of the enlightenment project), and his account of *unilateral and bilateral relationality* (via the work of Laruelle), all showcase various forms of the "irrecusable philosophical wedge between our phenomenological self-conception and the material processes through which that conception is produced" (Brassier, 2007, p. 26). It should be added that, through these remarkable exegetic essays, Brassier is attempting to outline his own form of "speculative realism" (Brassier, 2007, p. 31) that neither gives in to "a pragmatism which vitiates the commitments to scientific realism" nor a naturalism that hinders the alleged inhumanism of scientific rationalism.

Through my specific formulation of each speculative realist figure and their trials and tribulations with "correlationism", I believe we can all empathise with each of their respective projects and I think we can also argue that such projects have not been resolved or supplanted by any subsequent continental (or analytic) philosophy (but more on this to come).

A Brief Note on Hegel

What all four speculative thinkers seem to be interested in overthrowing is the supposed *self-identity of Being*; whether through the fallacy of the self-identical object as a self-same totality of interior and exterior (which Harman critiques[10]), the self-identity (and dogmatic necessity) of sufficient reason (Meillassoux), the transparent correspondence (and self-presencing) of thought with nature (Grant), or the self-identification of Meaning with Being, which Brassier finds most pervasive in Heidegger. This distaste for self-identification is intensified when it is specifically and intrinsically *correlated to human thought*. Although the majority of the four original members of speculative realism have dismissed Hegel as a master-correlationist (or absolute correlationist), the identity of Being, exhibited through its objects (of knowledge), is always constantly revised and never definitive in Hegel, and is only ever approved *retrospectively* — as the owl of Minerva always flies at dusk and cannot account for the trajectory of things until it has passed. Not only does this *buffering* cause a constant discrepancy between Being and Thinking in Hegel, we also find, in his triad of logical categories, that Being was never a singular, self-identical substance that could be identified with Thought in the first place. Being was — and always will be — on the move, as a mode of *Becoming* and hence a form of *determination* between its opposing, logical, categorical sides (and not origins): that of Non-Being and Being. Both categories of Being and Non-Being are completely empty (or completely full depending on which way you look at it),[11] and both are lacking any differentiation or quality until *mediated* logically, spatio-temporally, cosmologically, or conceptually. The eternal transition of Being and Nothing qua Becoming, as a movement which — in order to be actual — must pass through itself and be identified (through something else) as X from the "outside", as it were, is something which is exhibited *finitely* in every object and subject (as "sublation"). In fact, one could say that it is the determination generated through the logical, dialectical tension of Being and Non-Being (Becoming) which allows for the transition or oscillation necessary for Hegel's definition of *objectivity*: the constant movement from a blind process to its vicarious realisation through externality or the "being-through-the-other" of external comprehension, then back into the inner workings of the process (or object) as "Subject" or *subjected*, whereby *essence* finds its way somewhere amidst *all* of these transitions (or contradictions).

Historically speaking, this process produces a "long, painfully educed, glorious result of [...] many states of things that are first inert, external, purposeless, mechanical, contingent, irregular, empirical and brutally real" (Findlay, 2019, p. 132), eventually culminating in the "activation of human thought". In this sense, one cannot *technically* correlate Thinking with Being in Hegel, because there is no "Being" to begin with: no self-identical or self-present totality of Being that can be reduced to, or even be said to originate in, human Thought. Nor is there a particular form of Thought that can claim some kind of originary superiority over everything else due to the *emergence of thought* as exhibited through the organism, that is a "logic self-externalised in substantial, objective *Nature*" (Findlay, 1977, p. xxix). However, the *correlation* between Being and Non-Being *as Becoming* is a peculiar form of absolutisation (of categories), which thought indeed *exhibits* but cannot lay claim to[12] (what Hegel called "negative determination").

Demographic and Context

The demographic of speculative realism must partly come from that side of us who refuse *scientific realism* in one way or another and see its inconsistencies through the similar lens of the critique of self-identity (and the "view from nowhere") that Hegel gave us.[13] For others, speculative realism may appeal to those who tire of the transcendental idealism that wants us to put unwavering faith in the tautology of analytic statements and the transcendental argument that limits speculative thinking to some arbitrary line marking some specific enabling spatio-temporality (or "condition of possibility") for thought. Speculative realism also appeals to some of us who have become quickly disappointed with the *non-metaphysical* accounts of *materialism* over the last century, which have no concern for origins or conditions, or any *criteria of* the real, and have no regard for any logical and conceptual resources that would inevitably make intricate and complex our initial dealings with what could only be described pejoratively as an arbitrary and formless account of matter. The linguistic turn definitely warned us that an ambiguously articulated philosophical question (pertaining to abstracts or sets, or properties such as "Being") may in turn give us the wrong answer (or is simply the wrong question to ask in the first place!), but philosophy could never stop there (even if Wittgenstein wanted to — for a while — and instead play chess). Furthermore, our interest in *semiotics* in the twentieth century already feels like a quaint form of *anthropocentrism* until figures such as Foucault and Deleuze made immanent the sign as a material assemblage of power, desire, and "affect", pointing to a notion of difference/différance or "Other" which always already threatened the self-identity and stability of the signified and relegated the previous semiotic realism to a theory of yesteryear. This prevailing "new" material reality (neo-materialism) — which located carnal, machinic, and palpable "affects" on a "plane of immanence" — already feels like a less "intense" form of "the real" relative to the speculative realism that was to triumph in the twenty-first century.

I'm no scholar of analytic philosophy, but I hear that the specific questions (re)formulated by speculative realism have been recently excavated and reinvigorated through analytic philosophy's own characteristically rigorous lens. Meillassoux himself is a fine reader of the analytic tradition, Tristan Garcia has been known to dabble, Jon Cogburn (a later proponent of Object-Oriented Ontology) is a teacher of philosophy of mind and philosophy of language at Louisiana State University, and Lee Braver occupies himself with the realism/anti-realism debate that plays more of a part in the analytic tradition than continental philosophy generally speaking. Hilan Bensusan — co-editor with me on this volume — also has analytical sentiments, and their interest in "indexicals" merges the American analytic philosopher David Kaplan with the phenomenological-ethical work of continental philosopher Emmanuel Levinas. I have also recently heard that there is a renewed interest in panpsychism amongst analytical scholars, and this research may provide a fruitful link to Graham Harman's object-oriented ontology (especially his notion of "polypsychism", "translation", and his broader use of "prehension").

Other than a more peripheral interest in the Levinasian phenomenology of the Other (as an almost postphenomenology directed towards otherness, the infinite, and alterity), the role of phenomenology plays very little part in the speculative realist enterprise. Graham Harman's work indeed has a phenomenological current that can be traced to Husserl's "intentional object" and Heidegger's withdrawn "thing", but the traditional notion of "intersubjectivity" that ensues from the phenomenological approach turns increasingly into an *inter-objectivity* where manifestation is converted into "translation" and has an object-oriented and non-human-centred approach. In this regard, those who are troubled with the lack of progress *phenomenology* has made regarding matters of ecology, geology, and the increasing disintegration of the formal differences between human and non-human, nature and technology, and animate and inanimate objects, may wish to turn to speculative realist theories of the object (and "hyper-object") as a more rewarding, open, unifying, and *democratic* approach to such questions. Tom Sparrow's book *The End of Phenomenology*

(2014) is exemplary of this turn from a "human-centered approach to metaphysics" towards a "complex realm of nonhuman reality" (Sparrow, 2014). In a way, phenomenology is saved by Harman as that *particular realm of objects* which are always directed towards some human or object; *the sensual object is always a mediated object*, whilst the *real object* lies in a realm of indifference, independence, and "withdrawal".

Regarding the inventory of unsatisfying "realisms" we have since collated — from scientific realism, common-sense realism, materialism and transcendental realism, to a philosophy of language, structuralism/semiotics, and various neo-materialisms — we must nevertheless applaud a *prenatal* spirit of realism found in a handful of those particular thinkers that predate the speculative realist movement, and hence could be credited with influencing such an enterprise: the quasi-realist univocity and anti-representationalism of Deleuze that has surely influenced Iain Hamilton Grant's work; the "non-philosophy" of Laruelle, the "Black Deleuzianism" of Nick Land, and the neurological insights of Thomas Metzinger in relation to Brassier's work; the Cartesian and Hegelian (respectively) neo-rational insights that both Brassier and Meillassoux advocate in very different ways; the mathematical formalisation of ontology in Badiou regarding Meillassoux's work; and the influence of Aristotle, Gottfried Wilhelm Leibniz, Edmund Husserl, Martin Heidegger, Alphonso Lingis, and Bruno Latour in Harman's work.

What this demographic and evolving legacy of realism suggests to us is that the trauma of "the real" has intensified and propagated itself far beyond the jurisdiction of Kantian (noumenal) and Platonic-Hegelian (Ideal) metaphysics. Yet this might be because we got Kant and Hegel wrong in the first place. Meillassoux might accuse Kant of reducing "the great outdoors" to the epistemic confines of sensible experience, but Kant's *circumscription* of "the conditions of possibility" of experience, as well as his weak and strong accounts of the existence of the noumenal, imply a possible route to the speculative real that grounds his transcendental enterprise. Hegel too — although known for obliterating the existence of both Kant's

Cartesian account of a priori subjectivity, and his account of the noumenal, gives us a constantly unresolved picture of reality, where the "contradiction" of the object (and subject), as that which exists *through* something else — lays claim to its intrinsically split nature.[14] With this in mind, the trajectory of philosophy that follows after Kant and Hegel might not be defined as a giant counter-argument to their claims (to escape a caricatured version of idealism or so-called "correlationism"), but instead could be defined as an attempt to find instances of the real with Kant and Hegel's insights in mind, e.g. mapping the distinctions between neurological and phenomenal cognitions, analysing the "dialectical" operation encountered in wave-particle duality (which Žižek's "Parallax View" explicitly defines as a Hegelian notion (Žižek, 2006)). Regarding Kant, as I have previously stated, one may be encouraged to "objectify" the human "correlation" (as "factical", for example) and look elsewhere for alien life and philosophy. Or, one may wish to insist that Hegelian philosophy — although inclined to apply theories of the absolute to Earth and the specifically tellurian — can be applied to shooting stars, black holes, and dark matter (and even other activations of "Being" and "Non-Being" that are not reducible to the dialectical "Becoming" between them nor the specific form of "Becoming" here on *Earth*).

I think it should also be added that a speculative realism, such as Graham Harman's, can be encountered and engaged with through terms that are not necessarily linked to the history of philosophy generally speaking. Most "non-philosophers" (and I do not mean this in the Laruellian sense!) who have equally engaging jobs and hobbies already affirm the richness of the object beyond philosophical questions of its existence (as phenomenal form, essence, or as a "bundle of qualities"). Take, for instance, the numerous artists engaging with Harman's work, who — although (pedantically) could be accused of being *pre-critical* practitioners through "our" inherited *critical* philosophical lens — have a far more intimate and engaging life with objects than us philosophers do.[15] Perhaps this is why game designer Ian Bogost became attracted to OOO, and the ecological theorist Timothy Morton along with him; because Harman's philosophy of objects contains within it both a theoretical and practical way of dealing with (and creating) objects untethered to the critical methods that restrict objects to the hermeneutic method (which includes the history of symbolism and impressionism) or "textual analysis", or "transcendental" conditions constituted partly through subjectivity, etc. I think this can also be applied (to a lesser extent) to Ray Brassier's work, as a swarm of non-philosophical, literary, and political "nihilists" have rushed to identify their cause with Brassier's core statement (Brassier, 2007, p. xi) that "life is meaningless" and that "thinking has interests that do not coincide with those of living" without having to be professional academics.

Speculative Realism?

At this point, it may be worth addressing the almost elephant-like presence in the room: that very few of the four original speculative realists — not to mention those key figures that continue research in the area — identify themselves with the term "speculative realist". I was patronisingly reminded only recently that "this entire strand of "speculative realism" has since abandoned the term and hasn't been identified with it for longer than a decade, considerably longer".[16] Yet how much of this dismay is warranted, and how much of it is down to the whims of fashion and the pathological inclination towards self-mutilating ideas, if they happen to spawn into different directions to the ones initially desired? In my humble opinion, speculative realism is a fine term for setting about a loose formulation of *the real*, which is not reducible to scientific realism nor to any non-philosophical, social, political realism, nor to any naturalism that extends its findings into the ontological domain, nor to any turn to a formal realism of mathematics[17] or some poetic, rhetorical meditation on "the Other". For the most part, the four original speculative realists devise clear arguments and definitions:

Harman, for example, does so through what now feels like an almost natural extension of the Heideggerian project of the present-at-hand/readiness-to-hand oscillation and the subsequent concealment and disclosure of Being *upon all objects* (and not simply reserved for the exacerbations of human thought and perception); Brassier, by eking out a realism that is not eliminated by materialism, a thinking of the real that is not ensconced nor nurtured by what we have come to characterise as Nature after the Enlightenment tradition, and by seeking out a cosmological-psychological position whereby *thought* is purported to chronicle the trauma of life as it disappears due to its inevitable extinction. Meillassoux, by invoking an "ancestral" time that problematises the "correlationist" argument that Thinking is a presupposition of Being (amongst other manoeuvres that aim to positively deliver us towards the "great outdoors" of the real). In Grant's work, his insistence that "metaphysics cannot be pursued in isolation from physics" (Grant, 2008, p. x) rids us of the supernatural "appearance qua appearance" (Brassier, 2017, pp. 26–31) thesis that someone like Brassier accuses the tradition of phenomenology of upholding, and therefore *speculatively* permits an alternative, generative layer of "appearing" which compliments its conditional environment, ensconced within a larger conception of Nature not correlated to purely human philosophies of access. This, amongst other methods, gets Grant out of the correlationist circle for now.

While it seems cogent to say that such formulations of the real come from the Kantian tradition (especially his belief in the existence of noumena), one could easily cite Plato as a precursor to any reality/appearance divide, as well as that unique mixture of the logical and the conceptual that culminates in a speculative Spirit (*Geist*) that "cannot be adequately grasped through categories or concepts abstracted from finite things, much less from sensible things, because it is not a thing or even like a thing" (deVries, 1988, p. 25). In fact, one may wish to sum-up the speculative realist project as an attempt to engage in "post-critical *ontologies*"[18] *after Kant*, which, after all, was also Hegel's objective.

A Politics of the Correlation or the Correlation of the Political?

Whether we endorse the thesis that being is irreducible to thought, or that thought can successfully untether itself from any auto-co-constitutive entanglement with being (and hence can formalise the latter without becoming stymied by the former's shadow), this should not imply that the two do not implicate each other in some way. Maurizio Ferraris suggests the paradoxical notion that "social objects [...] are dependent on the mind, but they are independent of knowledge (i.e., even of consciousness)". In other words, there is a co-constitutive contract between humans and their "social objects", yet the act of "documenting" such an object (or artefact), as a form of "material" inscription, allows the object to retain such "data" as a real, mind-independent object, just as "an artefact can offer it's affordance even in the absence of minds (even a table can be a shelter for an animal)" (Ferraris, 2015, pp. 159–160). What I am trying to give voice to here is the idea that speculative realism does not have to be (and simply is not) an *apolitical* enterprise due to the realist assertion that being is independent of the political. Take this passage for example, from *The Speculative Turn: Continental Materialism and Realism*:

> If the basic claim of realism is that a world exists independent of ourselves, this becomes impossible to reconcile with the idea that all of ontology is simultaneously political. There needs to be an aspect of ontology that is independent of its enmeshment in human concerns. Our knowledge may be irreducibly tied to politics, yet to suggest that reality is also thus tied is to project an epistemological problem into the ontological realm. (Harman, Bryant, Srnicek, 2011, p. 16)

My opinion on this is similar to the attitude of another of Ferraris' essays entitled *Realism as Emergentism*.[19] Far from the idea that an essential correlation between being and thought would imply an increased sense of complicity in — and responsibility for — our actions and environment, Ferraris argues that it is because our orientation as human beings has direct consequences upon a real, autonomous reality that our actions are so meaningful. Ferraris says the same regarding epistemology: "if knowledge does not refer to something other than itself, the words 'subject', 'object', 'epistemology', 'ontology', 'knowledge', and 'reflection' would be meaningless" (Ferraris, 2015, ibid.). I think this attitude is reciprocated by all of the original speculative realist figures. Brassier states that "reality [...] is indifferent to our existence and oblivious to the 'values' and 'meanings' which we would drape over it in order to make it more hospitable" (Brassier, 2007, p. xi), and this leads Brassier to suggest that "an underlying trust in the capacities of conceptual rationality" (Brassier, 2006, p. 1) affords us the materials to better ourselves and our world. Both Harman's and Grant's work could easily be read to imply geological and environmental concerns regarding a new emphasis on the independent existence of objects themselves (Harman), or the infinitely propagating "ground" of Nature (Grant). Harman's analysis of the Dutch East India Company in his book *Immaterialism* (Harman, 2016) is a good example of this new sensitivity towards what constitutes an object and how objects are affected by their environments *without being reducible to them*. Although Meillassoux affirms a "dead, inert matter", distinct yet formalisable by thought, this does not have to be concomitant with a fundamental disconnection between human and environment; Meillassoux has an ethical and poetical concern with the world in terms of *contingency* and this can be found in the "possible existence of god" ("if there is no law of becoming, then becoming is capable even of God" (Meillassoux, 1997)) but also the poems of Mallarme, where he finds a mutual interest in change, contingency, infinity, and eternity valorised into a state of artistry by the French poet. To summarise this shift in one sentence — instead of a collective emphasis on inter-subjective judgements, the consensus of a society, or a tribunal of reason parading itself as an absolute criteria for objectivity, we alternatively have a renaissance of the Levinasian dictum: to have and hold an infinite responsibility towards The Other *as completely uncorrelated to us* (what Levinas called "alterity"), an uncorrelated other that is also actual, impending, and real regarding the *reality of infinity*. Although this outside is uncorrelated to us (and is hence indifferent to our *thoughts*), this does not imply that it would not respond or be affected by the decisions we make concerning it. One could also argue that even the late Kant and subsequent Hegel remain indebted to a *human-all-too-human* world of judgement when both make rationality an intrinsic "impetus" (Hegel) or "universal law" (Kant) inhering in all of reality, as this makes the "other" or the "independent" simply another internal ingredient of this rational structure. Furthermore, Kant's demand for a principle of action based on reality's intrinsic and universal law of reason explicitly embeds human subjectivity as *correlated* to this rational environment/reality.

Object-oriented thinker Timothy Morton sums up this new, strange, paradoxical proximity to the political in his work on "hyper-objects". There may be no "outside" for Morton that could be designated as an uncorrelated, indifferent externality, yet his manoeuvre of embedding all objects — whether inanimate, artificial, or otherwise — into a shared common space, performs a similar function as that of Ferraris and the speculative realists. In Morton's words:

> There is no 'outside' — just the entire universe of entities constantly interacting, and you are one of them. (Morton, 2021)

The idea goes something like this: if we allow reality to have its own non-human-centred and non-human-oriented existence, we become simply *one more object* in a vast political ecology of objects. This reveals at least two things: 1) that there is both a false *correlation of the political* — in the sense that we wrongly believe that we are at the centre of all politically consequential action, and that all political antagonisms can be converted into a "human-all-too-human" realm of human language and semantics; 2) that there is also a *politics of the correlation* whereby this correlation is grounded in a deeper, metaphysical concern for the intimacy of human and world as a necessary condition of reality (or — going down the Marxist route — that capitalist exploitation encourages the sustainability of the correlation of human-world by making the proletariat a selfish, desiring, and ultimately *alienated* individual that views everything through a system of exchange for the benefit of an inauthentic ego). It would seem that situating an ethics of responsibility for "the Other" (Levinas) as *co-habiting* a world (realism) but not *co-constituting* a world (correlationism) might be a more fruitful way to go regarding notions of the political.

Furthermore, the argument for a mind-independent realism does not presuppose the inexistence of the political beyond the human remit — whether we accept the *strong* argument that all objects are politically implicated in a world (beyond the immediately human), or the *weak* argument that natural and man-made objects *retain* uses and characteristics (and hence political traces) even after we are done with them, even beyond any singular or total act of consciousness dependent on them (Ferraris' table example).

The New Absolute

Within the last 15 years, there has been somewhat of a mini-renaissance of the philosophical concept of *the absolute* found in Quentin Meillassoux's 2007–08 work *After Finitude*, but also found in the speculative realism movement overall. The general presuppositions and first principles that are formulated regarding the possible existence of an absolute *has been* a philosophical discourse of yesteryear. That is until only recently, when speculative materialist Quentin Meillassoux openly advocated a thinking of the absolute in terms of "an absolute necessity of contingency" (Meillassoux, 2009, p. 34) and an absolute "great outdoors" regarding an escape from what he terms "correlationism" (and "subjectalism" respectively). There is an almost ironic flavour regarding this position, and it should be further analysed.[20] If one instantiates an *absolute* knowledge, whereby its speculative/

deduced content is at the same time *indifferent* to the human subject (mind-independent realism), then how is it that this knowledge achieves new pertinency in the human who grasps this? Can this instantiation or absolute claim to knowing even be deemed "knowledge" *sensu lato*, as it certainly does not adhere to the conventional *co-constitutive* models of truth that have dominated the last 300 years of philosophy, whereby both the "conditions of possibility" and *what the subject brings to bear on such raw material*, encourages a more *supplementary*[21] account of the real. This perhaps more "normative" sense of the real refers to the history of knowledge *we* have formulated, such as a human "space of reasons", evolutionary knowledge (which includes both environmental and organic/subjective adaptation), and knowledge as "transcendentally" (or subjectively) guaranteed (Kant/Hegel). If this knowledge becomes untethered to us (absolutely) then — without sounding overtly philanthropic — how can this help us? In Meillassoux's project, it seems that we are left "knowing" only the "facticity" of a thing (that it "is") and that this facticity is mathematically formalisable/formulatable, yet the realm of phenomenological description, moral, and teleological considerations, or *a priori* necessity has nothing to do with this "realist" fact and can only be subsequently offered up to us as broken idols which comfort us in a time of disappointment or denial; *we have nothing to do with* knowledge.[22] Of course, this non-co-constituting theory of knowledge (as almost *passive*) compliments Meillassoux's disavowal of any co-constitutive, *co-relational* (and hence relativist) account of knowledge (of the real).

The speculative realist movement in general has a plethora of both implicit and explicit references to (what the twentieth-century continental tradition had disregarded as the "dogma" of) the absolute, such as Ray Brassier's affirmation of the power of truth[23] and rationality against the auspices of relativism, and Iain Hamilton Grant's interest in Schelling's absolute metaphysics of nature. Even Graham Harman's characterisation of the "object" — as a *non-relational* entity or unity — signals an absolute turn in the sense that the "non-relative" can here be quickly interpreted as "absolute". Regarding Harman's work, we can discern a much larger shift in the terrain of the absolute — from the all-encompassing, absolute (non-relative), autonomous yet integrational "whole" of Hegel, to the absolute, autonomous independence of the individual or discrete *object* (or possibly even the "in-itself" of the object). Considering the contemporary compulsion (and obligation) to embed philosophical methods into political paradigms and ulterior forces, we could also consider that this shift in contemporary philosophical readings of the absolute seeps into the collective unconscious, subconscious, and conscious (intentional) activities of political theory and praxis (further assuming that such metaphysical formulations are not without political implications).

Considering the notion of a metaphysical absolute, Meillassoux reminds us that the absolutisation of Being only implies the absolutisation of thinking or knowledge when Being is turned into a *sufficient* ground, origin, or trajectory (e.g., Hegel) — something that Meillassoux quickly disqualifies (it just so happens that Meillassoux feels ambitious enough to attempt reaching *his* absolute with a *rationalist* rhetoric traditionally tied to the legacy of people like Leibniz and Hegel). In fact, not only does Meillassoux refute any absolute grounding of thought with being,[24] being "itself" is only absolutised through a major redefining of its original premise, i.e., Meillassoux wants to account for the non-being, coming-into-being, and possible being, etc., *of* being and hence traditional accounts of being are supplanted by the (necessary) **absolute contingency** that determines being's forms (or "facticity"/is-ness).

It is important to state that Meillassoux describes the *possible* being or non-being of an entity or occurrence as pertaining to specific moments (the possibility of an *actual* occurrence, which will subsequently pass) and not some hypostatised time (or eternity) where an entities possibility to both exist and not-exist becomes an a priori *contradiction*. In other words, it is not a contradiction to not exist and then subsequently exist (like the emergence of a God), it is only a contradiction if this happens *at the same time* (see Meillassoux, 1997). Meillassoux argues that this type of false formulation — of contradiction — makes every entity dogmatically *necessary* anyway, as a "self-contradictory entity could neither change, nor cease to exist, because it is already what it is not. If something cannot cease to be, nor become anything else, then if it exists it does so necessarily".[25] It is precisely this type of necessity that Meillassoux wishes to do away with, opting for the necessity of radical contingency. Interestingly, Meillassoux equates *traditional* metaphysical necessity with stasis (contradiction) à la Hegel, whilst he re-characterises his own necessity as non-contradictory, which escapes any eternal or sufficient subsumption/sublation of contingency into pre-existent terms. It is more accurately a specific type of infinity that does not turn in on itself (like Hegel's eternity) and I think the prefix "after" in *After Finitude* can help us denote an idea of a contingency which has no room for the object or propositional statement to posit itself as both existent and non-existent (i.e., in a state of non-contingent equilibrium). In other words, Meillassoux's necessity is not necessary in the sense of an entity's necessary existence (contradiction) but necessary in the sense that *nothing must necessarily be.*

That the contemporary absolute is now associated with the non-conceptual (speculative *materialism*), with "hyper-chaos", with the necessity *of contingency* (as well as being offered up as a blanket term for any absolute "blind spot", "gap", "whole", or "not-all" in Lacan and Žižek's work), shows us that we are some way off the trajectory of Hegel's absolute idealist axiom. But in speculative realism, a strange inversion appears: it seems that we can *know* this *failure* of absolute knowledge (and its failure to correspond to identity). Meillassoux can "absolutely" know the "unreason" driving the facticity of every "thing" (i.e., that it is absolutely true that anything can change from one moment to the next; the abolition of the principle of sufficient reason). The culmination of this "futile" absolute can be found in those passages where Meillassoux suggests access outside of the correlation of being and thought by acknowledging the absolute facticity of our own death (because the thought of our own death is at once terminated before death occurs… yet we can still somehow think it). Graham Harman can also be seen to participate in this inversion of *absolute non-knowing* by suggesting that there is indeed a "real object" or "essence" *behind* the encyclopaedia of everyday objects we utilise as *Dasein* ("being-in-the-world"). However, it is our absolute *non-knowledge* of objects (or indirect access/allure of objects) which we must uphold instead of "undermining" or "overmining" the object into a set of knowable traits. This is what leads Terrence Blake and others to label Harman's philosophy as a "negative theology".[26] To conclude, knowledge can find some kind of speculative solace in the fact that *there is* an absolutely *non-knowable* real object behind *the sensual* domain that knowledge exclusively accesses (Harman) or knowledge can find some speculative solace that it (knowledge) *cannot* know one particular thing (or ground a particular set of things) but instead can know the absolute contingency and unreason that would potentially (absolutely) demolish its adequacy (or accuracy) with regard to any single instance or object (i.e., it is only this precise formulation of absolute indeterminacy that can be known).

It seems that we are left at this crossroads in contemporary continental philosophy: if we wish to posit an absolute which is sophisticated and post-critical enough to endure, then we must set aside the possibility that *knowledge* can be tethered to this new, alien absolute in any sort of active, positive, or co-constituting (supplementary) way.[27] Yet the *positing* of such an absolute is paradoxically accessed through a *type* of thought (or where thought reaches its other, a resistance, a "withdrawal") which *appears* to be a new manoeuvre beyond Kantian and post-Kantian philosophy.[28] Or, alternatively put, knowledge of the absolute is secured if we accept that what this knowledge is *of* cannot be converted into anything even vaguely resembling the principle of sufficient reason, transcendental (Kantian/Hegelian) identity, or some underlying substance/form.[29] Meillassoux in fact makes the same point through his distinction between "metaphysical" and "speculative" thinking — the former is the argument for an absolutely necessary *entity* (God, Reason, Mind, Nature, "World", etc.); the latter being the argument for the absolutely necessary *possibility* underpinning any one particular entity (or that an entity might *not* "be" in alternative scenarios). In Meillassoux's own words: "*we must uncover an absolute necessity that does not reinstate any form of absolutely necessary entity*" (Meillassoux, 2009, p. 34). Harman manages to create a similar manoeuvre by reversing the *known-unknown* (Meillassoux) into an *unknown-known* by affirming the reality of independent, withdrawn objects whilst arguing that there is no way to access, define, exhaust — and hence know — these real objects (we *cannot know* what is *speculatively known* as the "in-itself" of the real object). However, one could also reverse the *unknown-known* formula back into the *known-unknown* in Harman, because Harman upholds the *positive* non-contradiction found in Kant's deduction of the existence of "noumena" (or the "in-itself") as distinct from phenomena whilst simultaneously suggesting that we can never fully account for noumenal entities — the complicit form of sensual/phenomenal "translation" that stymies any direct encounter with the noumenal is turned into a kind of universal science, epistemology, and ontology by designating all "objects" as possessing this primary strife between noumenal and phenomenal modes of existence. In other words, we can *know*/deduce — through the rift between sensual and real objects and their qualities, and the object's resistance to overmining and undermining — that there is an *unknowable* object irreducible to any translation of it.

Speculative Realism Now

The argument for the historical and intellectual coherence, significance, and pertinence of speculative realism has been briefly adopted and answered in the above passages, but there are those who view its bright lights as only an incandescence, and I feel as though I should respond to this opinion as well.

It is simply not true that speculative realism has been left under a bus soon after its initial folly into the mainstream of online blogging and publishing. Whilst it is true that the publishing house Urbanomic seem to have now completely neglected "speculative realist" projects after their exhilarating *Collapse* series,[30] they still continue to promote Meillassoux's work (as a recent interview lays claim to[31]). Repeater and Zer0 Books still provide a solid platform for Graham Harman's speculative work, as well as publishing works from Arjen Kleinherenbrink, Paul Ennis, myself, Maurizio Ferraris, and Ben Woodard and Steven Shaviro (two authors who previously contributed to *The Speculative Turn* book, published by re.press in 2011). Various other reputable publishers such as Punctum Books,[32] Mimesis International, and Edinburgh University Press remain faithful to the speculative realist cause, and the Warwick journal *Pli*[33] still publishes volumes that are open to speculative thinking. Hence, regarding the publishing and general dissemination of speculative realist literature, it seems just as prevalent now as it ever was, with even more of a diverse array of publishers offering contracts to "speculative realist" writers over the last 5 years (other examples include Bloomsbury/Continuum,[34] Pelican, Duke University Press, Polity Press, Springer Press, University of Minnesota Press, and Kismet Press).

Furthermore, it is worth mentioning briefly that, although the blogosphere is not what it once was in relation to speculative realist discourse (or any discourse for that matter), there has been an arguably larger congregation and unity between different contemporary philosophical camps at present on social media than any time immediately following speculative realism's inaugural presentation in 2007. In fact, one could easily view those early, formative years as the progressive *segregation* of various speculative realist ideas due to their ongoing refinement.[35] For an example of the ongoing openness and inclusivity of speculative realisms within current philosophical discourse, we could turn to the book entitled *Subject Lessons: Hegel, Lacan, and the Future of Materialism*, edited by Russell Sbriglia and Slavoj Žižek, a book which *should* be categorically against any formulation of reality designated by the original four speculative realist members.[36] However, correspondences, citations, and references have been made between Graham Harman and both Žižek and Sbriglia (all jovial and somewhat sympathetic of each other's respective projects) through a series of published and unpublished engagements. Catherine Malabou has also engaged with both Žižek and Harman's work (many of these can be found in the *De Gruyter* open-access journal *Open Philosophy*) as well as Malabou endorsing my own speculative-dialectical twist on Object-Oriented Ontology (Johns, 2022). Hilan Bensusan's recent symposium concerning his book *Indexicalism: Realism and the Metaphysics of Paradox* (Bensusan, 2021) brought together thirteen contemporary philosophers, with at least five of them having speculative realist inclinations,[37] whilst psychoanalytically leaning thinkers such as Todd McGowan and Duane Rousselle appear at least empathetic towards insights of speculative realism.[38] One could argue that Slavoj Žižek bridges the psychoanalytic with the speculative realist as he did contribute to *The Speculative Turn* in 2011 and has also managed to revive Lacan into a significant area of debate regarding materialism and psychoanalysis. However, it seems much more cogent, in my humble opinion, to allocate this marriage between Lacanianism, materialism, and speculative realism as the growing acknowledgement of Hegel's own deeply *speculative* philosophy and its concern with psychology formulated as "self-alienated spirit" (see Hegel, 1977, pp. 294–297).

These are but four examples of a plethora of socially endearing correspondences between camps as diverse as Schellingians, neo-Hegelians; the various Badiouians and Meillassouxians working between the matrices of mathematics, philosophy, contingency, and negation; the animated Lacanians that oscillate between sex, gender, revolution, and anarchy; the Marxists and Leninists that always seem to have some podcast or other; the neo-nihilists that gravitate towards neo-rationalism more than to the previous Schopenhauerians, Nietzscheans, Stirnerites, or Baudrillardians; and on and on the list goes.

For those sceptics or cynics who think that "speculative realism" is dead, just take one look at the list of contributors presented in this volume. In fact, this volume attests to at least two initial things: 1) that work (and development) is being made in the respective camps of Harmanian, Meillassouxian, Brassierian, and Grantian philosophies; and 2) that enough time has elapsed for earlier, more tentative folk to appreciate and associate themselves with the movement. Let us look at the first of these two propositions.

Layout A

As you can see, Hilan and I have arranged the first half of the contents of this book in a way that sincerely corresponds to the work of each original speculative realist.

Looking at **Graham Harman**'s tribute section entitled *Speculative Objects*, we see a group of young and emerging talent who considerably bend and appropriate the original tenets of Object-Oriented Ontology to consider new ways of formulating technology and artefacts (*Kleinherenbrink*) and mathematical models (*Ardoline*). It is worth mentioning here that we received over twenty essays dealing with a variety of areas concerning Harman's OOO, clearly indicating that his work is in fact increasing in significance, more so today than ever before.

Iain Hamilton Grant's tribute section, entitled *Speculative Nature*, is represented by two extremely well-versed scholars of "Naturphilosophie": *Tyler Tritten* in relation to Schelling and Žižek, and *Leon Niemoczynski* in relation to Schelling but also Grant's specific reading of Schelling. Tritten argues that Schelling must be seen as already a prototypical realist, usurping many of his lesser-known passages against idealism and providing us with a much-needed service of tracking the contemporary interpretations of Schelling, from Gilles Deleuze to Slavoj Žižek, through Andrew Bowie and Markus Gabriel, enabling us to contextualize Grant's work via the history of naturphilosophie and metaphysics in general. Niemoczynski re-introduces some of the more essential points originating in Schelling's thesis — yet exacerbated in Grant's work — such as whether the phenomenological reduction made by human consciousness (as an act intended for human consciousness) is essential to the phenomenological method *itself* and — more speculatively — to human beings in general. Niemoczynski also responds to the different accounts of Being in Hegel and Schelling, as well as the Platonic theory of matter that influences Grant's work. Niemoczynski ends by calling his own philosophy a "transcendental naturalism" that "admits to the reality of the vital negative" in both Hegel and Schelling's work.

In our tribute section to **Quentin Meillassoux**, entitled *Speculative Contingency*, our focus turns to Meillassoux's ambiguous relationship with the intellectual project of Hegel and how he manipulates Hegel's account of identity and contingency. If Hegel can be said to "abolish" the "thing-in-itself", so that only a "relation between subject and object remains" (Meillassoux, 2009, p. 37), this is not to emphasise the self-identity or transparency of the relation but to make the relation itself irreducible to a specific property of the universe, a certain instantiated knowledge, or a certain presence. *Ørjan Steiro Mortenson* argues that *contingency* is just as necessary as necessity itself for Hegel and that one should not be prioritised but *dialectically* instantiated. This more open debate between Meillassouxian and Hegelian accounts of necessity and contingency will surely yield fruitful results, which aim at reshaping the very definition of such terms beyond the relativistic, probabilistic theories of certain linguistic propositions, certain methods of scientific falsification, and the "empirical contingency of material objects". Hegelian dialectics might argue that Meillassoux's "hyper-chaos" is *consistently* inconsistent (absolutely inconsistent), which may deem it a sort of *science*, whilst Meillassoux's argument is that this inconsistency is *incapable* of guaranteeing the consistency of scientific discourse. Both would argue that *absolute* contingency (in either its dialectical or chaotic forms) must be upheld for the necessary existence of any true proposition, yet Meillassoux would go further and add that this absolute contingency must also attend to the possible *non*-existence (or *in*existence) of physical laws.

What begs more attention, as a possible offshoot of a Meillasouxian "speculative materialism", is the proper attention to *dialectics* outside of the historical/materialist tradition. Meillassoux adamantly refutes contradiction (opting for the principle of non-contradiction) mainly because, if something both is and is not, contingency then loses its absolute dominance as a means of *determining* what is and is not. If something both is and is not, is both present and absent, then any non-metaphysical theory of movement is hence ensconced within a Hegelian metaphysics of immanence and eternity, where an object is simultaneously becoming and not becoming at the same time. This is indeed Hegel's position: that the absolute — or identity par excellence — is (qua retrospection) already there, and it is the subject or object's operation of negation (of self-othering) that initiates movement as a *mediation* of this absolute. This structure of movement is dialectical in that it presupposes that Being is already full, complete, and reconcilable, whilst the meta-movement is merely the mediation of the whole, which appears as a kind of pseudo-becoming of the object. But the Being of its Becoming (X) is already established *at the same time* as it moves into its opposite. However, it is Hegel's anti-foundationalism — or auto-production — that adds the caveat that what is conceivably "absolute" must integrate the movement of this negation as *an addition to Being itself*, as infinitely additive and supplementary (and hence constantly revisable).

It is also worth noting *Dustin Zielke*'s closing essay in this section, which refreshingly argues that the phenomenological attitude which Meillassoux so criticises, when "properly understood", establishes "the material referent's *real independence* from the referrer" and not its co-constitutive "givenness". This essay contributes to the intersection of Meillassoux studies and phenomenology by developing a counter-notion: that phenomenology can be correlational without being *correlationist*.

I cannot think of two better representatives of **Ray Brassier**'s work — other than the exceptions of Pete Wolfendale and Reza

Negarestani[40] — than that of *Daniel Sacilotto* and *Evrim Bayindir.* Sacilotto has been following Brassier for some time now and his current research focuses on "the reconciliation of rationalism and materialism, and the methodological relation between epistemology and ontology in contemporary philosophy".[41] He is currently editing a full-length monograph tentatively titled *Saving the Noumenon: An Essay on the Foundations of Ontology* and his uniquely tailored paper in this section, called "Speculative Nihilism", achieves nothing less than a total genealogy of nihilism, culminating in Brassier's particular brand of nihilism as serving an "epistemic" and "speculative" role in contemporary philosophical discourse in the form of a *stubborn disenchanted realism* (suggesting future routes for nihilism's zest regarding mathematical formalisation and contemporary science). In Sacilottos words: "the project of disenchantment must be extended to render experiential mediation intelligible as different modalities through which it is possible to know of a world indifferent to thought and life".

Evrim Bayindir has the courage to acknowledge the "elephant in the room" regarding contemporary, theoretical strands of nihilism (what Bayindir calls "the negativist turn") and its relation to continental philosophy, most notably that of Gilles Deleuze's project of active and reactive forces. If Deleuze, following Spinoza, asserts that no reactive force can be fully untethered from a context, passage, and actualisation of active force, then Bayindir uses Brassier's work as a counterclaim to this in order to suggest a radical finitude of thinking and life that rids us of any vitalist, active impulse or infinite horizon of being; "the function of Brassier's reactive force is to effectuate the aggressive movement that irreversibly terminates the active forces which strive to secure thought's all-pervasive perpetuity". Bayindir then goes on to suggest that Deleuze develops a theory of the "irreducible superiority of active forces", arguing that the *irreducible* element *beyond* reactive force anticipates the movement of speculative realism: the irreducible object of OOO, the irreducibility of nature (Grant), or the irreducibility of "the real" (Brassier/Meillassoux) to any human correlate of thinking/knowing (or any reactive force of human interpretation[42]).

Layout B

In the second half of this book, we move toward a more general *Analysis & Impact* of speculative realism, which is not aimed at any one of the original speculative realist figures in particular but at the movement as a whole. This section includes an essay by Micah Tewers on the ancient theme of justice and its renaissance in the works of the four original speculative realists. Tewers' paper achieves the joint objective of locating speculative realism within a much larger and more consolidatory tradition of philosophy while pointing at cutting-edge attempts in (twenty-first century) philosophy to rework the concept of justice into realist positions. In *Amanda Boetzkes*' paper, we are invited to think the rise of Earth-imaging technologies as the inception of a new form of ecological thinking, which simultaneously de-privileges the human perspective whilst placing the object Earth as but another vulnerable, contingent, and arbitrary object in the universe. Boetzkes' response is an *art after truth* which mediates its environment as a new force of reality (or the real). Boetzkes uses many enlightening examples of arts realism after truth such as forensic architecture, global theatre, Graham Harman's OOO, media theory, and performance art. Our final section provides brand new *interviews* with two of the original speculative realists, Graham Harman and Ray Brassier, followed by an interview from one of speculative realism's most understated instigators, *Alberto Toscano.* Toscano was partly responsible for creating the initial speculative realism conference in 2007 at Goldsmiths, University of London (along with Collapse/Urbanomic and Ray Brassier himself). Toscano moderated that event and also took Meillassoux's place[43] at the second "Speculative Realism/Speculative Materialism" conference at the University of the West of England, Bristol (UWE) in 2009.

Speculative Realism... Again...

Philosophers, theoreticians, and practitioners that are *not* conventionally seen as speculative realists are lining up to participate in this book, because sometimes the dust needs to settle before one can truly appreciate the initial project of speculative realism and identify what it was about those four figures that have influenced their (our) present projects and ways of thinking. Regarding the unresolved charm of speculative realism, authors of subsequent projects like "new realism" (Ferraris) and "transgressive realism" (Braver) have come to show their debt to speculative realism by contributing to this book in some direct or indirect way.[44] But in no way can such "realisms" be said to *overcome* what those initial four speculative realists forged out for us. In fact, I would describe Ferraris' work as returning to a naive, pre-critical, or common-sense *residual* realism, which nonetheless provides a lingering function even after post-critical and speculative realist considerations. Braver's thesis is less an affirmation of realism (although he has proposed a "transgressive realism") and more a steady, historical analysis of how "realism" and "anti-realism" have come to be defined through both analytic and continental traditions (tracing both to Kant), and although I disagree with the claim that Kant (and furthermore Hegel) "accepts the basic anti-realist picture" (Braver, 2007, p. 8), Braver's sheer depth of knowledge on the subject and technical prowess should be applauded.

Like in the 1990s, when an Eastside rap artist disses a rapper from the West, first comes the malicious taste of contempt, then perhaps humility, but soon after comes the awareness that some other posse, hood, celebrity, or academic has publicly recognised and acknowledged your existence. This act should be construed as a particularly novel, backwards, and indirect form of respect, and it is a respect exemplified here, in those authors who have contributed to this book while being neither indirectly nor directly related to the speculative realist movement. Of course, there have also been many who have used "speculative realism" as a *straw man* in order to raise their own profile (only ever achieving this temporarily), yet never with enough intellectual creativity, force, or merit to achieve a significant counter-philosophical position or movement of their own.

We have already spoken about Slavoj Žižek's admiration for Harman's object-oriented ontology, exemplified through their well-known public debate at the Southern California Institute of Architecture (SCI Arc), but Žižek also admits that OOO's language has found a long-lasting place in his own discourse (as well as the vibrant materialism of Jane Bennett).[45] That Ray Brassier would even consider contributing something to this book is evidence that not all of "speculative realism" can be successfully reduced and caricatured as a "movement whose most signal achievement thus far is to have generated an online orgy of stupidity".[46] Perhaps it is testimony to the idea that every significant event in one's (intellectual) life holds a sentimental place in one's heart — however confusing, turbulent, and quarrelsome it may have first appeared to be. In this sense, we are all obligated to confront *speculative realism again* — not "first as tragedy and then as farce", but first as provocation and then as commitment; as an asceticism based on *fidelity to an event.*

Hilan and I flirted with the idea of writing a purely historical account of the last 15 years of speculative realism, starting from the now infamous conference at Goldsmiths, University of London, in 2007. However, as we know from Hegel, every form of looking back instantiates a new determination of that past, and furthermore, it soon felt like an act of slander because we recognised that speculative realism was still going on, still developing, and still pertinent in contemporary philosophical discourse. If one tilts one's head and squints one's eyes hard enough, one will see a perfectly natural continuity between the original four speculative realist figures and a large demographic of current philosophers who occupy themselves with an increasingly diverse variety of philosophical fields;[47] the *neo-rationalism* of Negarestani and Wolfendale amongst others points to Brassier's influence, exemplified in their most recent respective book projects, *Intelligence and Spirit* (Negarestani, 2018), and *The Revenge of Reason* (Wolfendale, 2023). The various forms of "transcendental" or "dark" naturalism found in Niemoczynski (2017) and Woodard's individual works (2020 and 2013) signal a debt to Iain Hamilton Grant. Fabio

Gironi can be seen to extend Meillassoux's work by placing him in direct dialogue with the domain of analytic philosophy, especially the work of Wilfrid Sellars (Gironi, 2017). Bart Zantvoort's recent textual engagement with both Hegel and Meillassoux[48] regarding the absolute status of necessity and/or contingency — and its various metaphysical, dogmatic, and speculative groundings — seems apt considering the enduring freshness of Meillassoux's project and the recent rejuvenation of Hegel in both continental[49] and analytic[50] camps. It is also worth mentioning the publication of *The Meillassoux Dictionary* (Gratton and Ennis, 2014), which signalled a prolonged future interest in Meillassoux's work. Regarding Harman's philosophy, I myself have been occupied by the possible distinctions between relation and non-relation, relation and object, and themes of interior and exterior influenced by his work for about 4 years now, culminating in my book projects, *The Irreducible Reality of the Object* (2020), and then later, *Object Oriented Dialectics* (2022). I also know of a dozen other thinkers who have been undertaking serious engagements with Harman's work, such as Niki Young, Jon Cogburn, Micah Tewers, Niels Langballe, Levi Bryant, Gabriel Yoran, Tristan Garcia, Ian Bogost, Steven Shaviro, Timothy Morton, Tania Rossetto, Iman Frouzesh, Erfan Ghiasi, Joseph Bedford, Tom Sparrow, Arjen Kleinherenbrink, Hilan Bensusan, Manuel DeLanda... The list goes on.

I have attempted the impossible task of crystallising speculative realism while extracting its quintessence. I have charted its rise, from *that* unique conference in 2007 in London, through 15 years of expansion and reception, to its current state alongside other present-day discourses on post-Kantian philosophy, neo-Hegelianism/rationalism, realism, materialism, and its influence on other "non-philosophical" subjects such as art, architecture, politics, psychology, media studies, and environmental studies. I hope this book may lead to further investments in speculative realism, more collaborations and interdisciplinary engagements. I believe it has been an extremely *inclusive* enterprise, which this volume attests to through its rich diversity of authors… But Hilan may say otherwise in his own introduction…

London, January, 2023.

References

Bensusan, Hilan. *Indexicalism: Realism and the Metaphysics of Paradox.* Edinburgh: Edinburgh University Press, 2021.

Brassier, Ray. *Nihil Unbound: Enlightenment and Extinction.* London: Palgrave MacMillan, 2007.

Brassier, Ray. "Dialectics Between Suspicion and Trust". *Stasis* 2 (4) (2016), pp. 99–113.

Braver, Lee. *A Thing of This World: A History of Continental AntiRealism.* Evanston: Northwestern University Press, 2007.

DeVries, Willem. *Hegel's Theory of Mental Activity: An Introduction to Theoretical Spirit.* Ithaca: Cornell University Press, 1988.

Ferraris, Maurizio. "New Realism: A Short Introduction". In *Speculations VI*, edited by Fabio Gironi, Michael Austin, Robert Jackson. Santa Barbara: Punctum, 2015.

Findlay, John. *Ascent to the Absolute: Metaphysical Papers and Lectures.* London: Routledge, 2019.

Gironi, Fabio. *The Legacy of Kant in Sellars and Meillassoux: Analytic and Continental Kantianism.* London: Routledge, 2017.

Grant, Iain Hamilton. *Philosophies of Nature After Schelling.* London: Continuum, 2008.

Grant, Iain Hamilton. "The Universe in the Universe: German Idealism and the Natural History of Mind". *Royal Institute of Philosophy Supplement* 72, pp. 297–316, 2013.

Gratton, Peter & Paul Ennis. *The Meillassoux Dictionary.* Edinburgh: Edinburgh University Press, 2014.

Hamza, Agon & Frank Ruda (eds). *Slavoj Žižek and Dialectical Materialism.* New York: Palgrave Macmillan, 2016.

Harman, Graham, Levi Bryant, & Nick Srnicek. *The Speculative Turn: Continental Materialism and Realism.* Melbourne: re.press, 2011.

Harman, Graham. *The Quadruple Object.* London: Zer0 Books, 2011.

Harman, Graham. "On Vicarious Causation". In *Collapse II*, edited by Robin

McKay. London: Urbanomic, 2007.

Harman, Graham. *Immaterialism: Objects and Social Theory*. Hoboken: Wiley, 2016.

Hegel, Georg. *The Phenomenology of Spirit*. Oxford: Oxford University Press, 1977.

Johns, Charles. *Object Oriented Dialectics: Hegel, Heidegger, Harman*. Sesto San Giovanni: Mimesis International, 2022.

Meillassoux, Quentin. *L'Inexistence divine*. Dissertation at the Université de Paris I, 1997.

Meillassoux, Quentin. *After Finitude*. London: Bloomsbury, 2009.

Meillassoux, Quentin. "Subtraction and Contraction". In *Collapse III*, edited by Robin McKay. London: Urbanomic, 2007.

Morton, Timothy & Meis Morgan. "Timothy Morton's Hyper-Pandemic". *The New Yorker*, 8 June 2021.

Negarestani, Reza. *Intelligence and Spirit*. London: Urbanomic, 2018.

Niemoczynski, Leon. *A Philosophy of Sacred Nature: Prospects for Ecstatic Naturalism*. Blue Ridge Summit: Lexington Books, 2014.

Niemoczynski, Leon. *Speculative Realism: An Epitome*. Leeds: Kismet Press, 2017.

Nunes, Rodrigo. "What Are Post-critical Ontologies?". In *Speculative Realism Today*. London: Bloomsbury, 2024.

Orensan, Martin. "A Critique of Meillassoux's Reflections on Mathematics from the Perspective of Bunge's Philosophy". *Metascience* 1, 2020.

Sparrow, Tom. *The End of Phenomenology*. Edinburgh: Edinburgh University Press, 2014.

Wolfendale, Peter. *The Revenge of Reason*. London: Urbanomic, 2023.

Woodard, Ben. *Schelling's Naturalism, Space, Motion and the Volition of Thought*. Edinburgh: Edinburgh University Press, 2020.

Woodard, Ben. *On an Ungrounded Earth: Towards a New Geophilosophy*. Santa Barbara: Punctum, 2013.

Yoran, Gabriel. "Applied Metaphysics: Objects in Object-oriented Ontology and Object-oriented Programming". *Interface Critique Journal* 1 (2018).

Žižek, Slavoj. *The Parallax View*. Cambridge: MIT Press, 2006.

Žižek, Slavoj & Russell Sbriglia. *Subject Lessons: Hegel, Lacan, and the Future of Materialism*. Evanston: Northwestern University Press, 2020.

Notes

1 Ray Brassier and Alberto Toscano have translated some of Meillassoux's works in 2003 and 2004, as well as Ray translating *After Finitude* in 2008 (1 year after the speculative realism conference). Brassier also "acknowledges" Graham Harman in his debut book *Nihil Unbound* (2007).

2 Explicated in Rene Descartes' distinction of "thinking" and "extended" substance for example.

3 For example, Hegelian "contradiction".

4 Before Kant, I think one could successfully argue that, for instance, Cartesian thinking substance and extended substance do not need to be seen as co-constituted substances. Of course, pre-Descartes, there is a plethora of pre-critical ontologies that do not imply "correlationism", for example, Aristotle.

5 "[B]ecause thought occurs in the same universe as thought thinks, it remains part of that universe whose elements in consequence now additionally include that thought", Grant (2013).

6 Or it at least safeguards a domain of objects irreducible to "undermining" and "overmining" (these terms will be explained in the next few sentences).

7 However, Harman has briefly discussed the notion of "dormant" objects, which are real objects that have not come into contact with any other object/s or relation/s. This thesis could affirm the discrete existence (being) of real objects distinct from any sensual form of relation/prehension.

8 Part of this notion seems to be formulated on the premise that certain ingredients (or parts) of an object can undergo change (or be destroyed completely) without affecting the integrity of the object (such as a major league baseball team) as a whole/unity.

9 If we are to affirm the position that all objects are on the same footing, then I do not believe that this should be turned into a univocity, where we have *different* objects yet it is the *same* inter-objective relation that constitutes all of them. We should analyse how the notion of relation is drastically transformed depending on the object's qualities and capacities. Not all sensual relations are sincere in the same way and not all real relations of fission and fusion exist in the same chemical,

physical, spatial remit. I don't see why this has to contradict the notion of a "shared common space" of objects because the "space" in which something relates (as sensual) can be different to the "real" space in which the object occupies, and the sensual can always find a way to transform the real.

10 For example, Harman states that the essence of an object (its real qualities) can emerge through outside entities. Harman, 2011, pp. 106–7.

11 Being and Non-Being are described as being abstract, having no qualities, i.e., exempt from — or prior to — any dialectical determination into qualities.

12 Thought cannot lay claim to a specific account of Being or Non-Being *independently* from one another, as such categories are always co-implicated in the Becoming of the subject and the determination of any actuality, i.e., Becoming is strictly the relation between (actuality of) Being and Non-Being.

13 Exposed in such questions as the following: can objectivity be objectively accounted for? Or, is objectivity really commensurate with our epistemological capacities — as a known fact included or hypostatised from that structure of objective reality in which we come to adduce this fact in the first place?

14 This contradiction in Being takes over the more *distinct*, non-contradictory opposition of phenomena and noumena in Kant.

15 As well as a variety of computer scientists, see Yoran (2018).

16 I have also been recently told by an admirer of speculative realism that secondary writings on the original philosophers are equally as redundant. Apparently, it has "become a kind of funny thing writing about Meilassoux now, a bit cultish feeling", which does not seem to harbour any encouraging remarks on engaging with the texts for the sake of their content.

17 Orensan (2020) shows very clearly that Meillassoux is more allegiant to a form of materialism and that he denounces mathematics as existing as a reality in-itself.

18 See the essay "What Are Post-critical Ontologies?" (Nunes, 2024) and see J.P. Caron's response in *Speculative Realism Today*, Bloomsbury, 2024.

19 See https://www.academia.edu/38149400/Realism_as_emergentism_pdf

20 How can one *reconcile* absolute contingency with human thought (or "intellectual intuition") when the absolute is in excess of the human? Or must thought simply witness this greatness as it too fades into the absolute chaos where all cows are black?

21 This is epitomised in Hegel's account of consciousness as making explicit what was already implicitly true in its activity. It is as if the missing piece to *the real* is the *awareness of* the real.

22 For instance, knowledge is not *co-constituted* through the standard, phenomenological methods of subject-object found in both Kant and later Hegel, neither is it a property of subjective ideation, mind or mental context (Berkeley), nor the demarcation of various linguistic instantiations.

23 Ray Brassier states "I am a nihilist because I still believe in truth" in an online interview here: https://xylem.aegean.gr/~modestos/mo.blog/i-am-a-nihilist-because-i-still-believe-in-truth/

24 It is obvious in Meillassoux's opening two chapters of *After Finitude* that his "speculative materialism" derives its pertinence from a description of being prior to thinking (the existence of the arche fossil, for example).

25 See https://deontologistics.co/2009/09/11/meillassoux-and-contradiction/

26 See https://terenceblake.wordpress.com/2021/10/13/graham-harmans-the-third-table/ or https://itself.blog/2011/02/08/ooo-a-negative-theology-of-the-object/

27 An alien absolute in the sense that *subjectivity* does not sublate the absolute as a category intrinsic to — and necessary for — its full realisation or resolution (Hegel).

28 Hegel's dialectical and antinomical thinking comes to mind here, but instead of thoughts "other" or "opposite" being *speculatively* "reconciled" or "sublated" by a supplementary mode of *identity*, we have a *speculative* form of philosophising which outstretches any *identity* capable of integrating thinking and being into a transparent relation that can account for itself *causa sui*.

29 Regarding substance, it is not "matter" which is absolute in Meillassoux's work (although Meillassoux uses a "speculative" account of "matter" to break out of "correlationism", i.e., the persistence of the "arche fossil"). Matter is not absolute because matter could be otherwise, and this

"otherwise" is the hyperchaos driving materiality and not materiality itself.

30 See https://www.urbanomic.com/series/collapse/

31 See https://www.urbanomic.com/document/founded-on-nothing/

32 Although Punctum Books' "Speculations" series has been officially discontinued (see https://punctumbooks.com/imprints/speculations/), they still continue to publish works of speculative thought.

33 See https://plijournal.com/volumes/

34 Hilan and I will be working with Bloomsbury on a new philosophy project in 2024.

35 For example, the productive disagreements and conceptual distinctions between Graham Harman's object-oriented philosophy and Levi Bryant's own rendition.

36 Whether as against Grant's naturalist leanings, Harman and Meillassoux's phenomenal/noumenal distinction, or Harman, Meillassoux, Grant, and Brassier's generally apolitical and non-psychoanalytical leanings regarding the autonomy of realism from any human implication.

37 Graham Harman, Steven Shaviro, J.P. Caron, Jon Cogburn, and myself.

38 See https://www.youtube.com/watch?v=6ct-bxomoq0 and *Umbr(a): The Object*, Umbr(a) Journal, 2014

39 Both Wolfendale and Negarestani were asked to contribute in this volume. Negarestani had no "note-worthy material" on Ray, whilst Wolfendale agreed but found that the imminent deadline for his paper made any genuine and rigorous undertaking of Ray's work unfeasible.

40 See https://www.urbanomic.com/contributor/sacilotto-dan/

41 Reactive forces "separate active force from what it can do such that the latter becomes-reactive", as Deleuze has in his reading of Nietzsche.

42 Meillassoux was unable to attend.

43 Ferraris agreed to answer some interview questions for this book concerning speculative realism, but due to issues of length, it will be published elsewhere. Braver had also written an essay on Heidegger and Harman which will now be published at a later date.

44 This can be found in Hamza et al. (2016).

45 See https://thecharnelhouse.org/2011/05/30/ray-brassier-on-the-speculative-realist-movement-including-his-reaction-to-my-satiric-manifesto-of-speculative-realistobject-oriented-ontological-blogging/

46 And discourses in the life sciences, mathematics, technology, and media studies, gender studies, science-fiction studies, artificial intelligence studies, global studies etc.

47 Which can be found in this volume.

48 To name but a few: Frank Ruda, Agon Hamza, Rebecca Comay, Slavoj Žižek, Charles William Johns, David Kolb, Reza Naderi, Todd McGowan, Jean-Francois Kervegan, and Stephen Houlgate.

49 After the Pittsburgh School (i.e., Robert Brandom, John McDowell, etc.), Robert Pippin, Willem DeVries, and Paul Redding come to mind.

15 YEARS OF SPECULATIVE REALISM

EDITORS INTRODUCTION B

Hilan Bensusan

I believe that the movement of speculative realism was a breakthrough.

The rest of this introduction will be my attempt to explain my belief and to qualify my claim. To be sure, a note about "breakthrough" is in order from the outset. Philosophy is certainly larger than what goes by its name — and surely is not consigned only to its professionals. Further, the idea of a breakthrough appeals to a narrative, to a history of certain kinds of philosophy that leaves aside other kinds either because they are marginal or because they are simply out of sight of those who do professional philosophy and have tacit beliefs about its history.

To narrate its history often entails displaying some biases that are not acknowledged, let alone questioned. It is in this perceived history of recent philosophy that speculative realism was a breakthrough — that is to say, within the narratives that are often academically reinforced and, surely, to a large extent within the narrative of recent history that the movement, or some of its proponents, have put forward. After making this initial caveat, I can reformulate my claim, without (yet) enlarging it too much: *I believe the movement of speculative realism was a breath of fresh air for those involved in the most reinforced narratives of recent philosophy.* My own belief in this claim was motivated by my perception of what was going on in philosophy; it seemed to me that a door was open towards a place that was rarely found in my general image of the professional area. This door and this place are what I attempt to describe here. If I manage to do it, the qualified idea of a breakthrough will somehow make sense.

It is within these boundaries that I agree with Charles Johns when, in his introduction, he writes that *speculative realism is a fine term for setting about a loose formulation of the real.* As I attempted to show in my contribution to this volume, "Realism and speculation beyond Speculative Realism", the movement opened the gate for varieties of realisms that were not quite conceivable before either (1) because the shadow of Kant loomed large, or (2) because philosophers thought the very term "realism" was to be forsaken once enterprises like onto-theology or the metaphysics of presence are exorcised.

As for the shadow of Kant — (1) in the disjunction above — or rather a certain shadow of a certain Kant, the movement helped curb it by providing it with a name: correlationism. With the name given, it is already easier to think beyond it. Meillassoux, however, did more than revamp this term from Husserl's writings as he diagnosed an era of the correlate where, apart from the attractors of weak and strong forms of correlationism, there was also another tendency, that of making the correlation itself absolute — that is, apart from the intermittent disposition to simply ignore the correlation (Meillassoux, 2009). Weak correlationism considered the correlation between us and the world to be unavoidable as far as knowledge and other cognitive endeavours are concerned. Strong correlationism extended that to thought in general — it cannot escape the correlation. The attempt to make correlation itself the absolute that correlationism intended to dismiss, which he called subjectalism or metaphysics of the subjectivity, simply accept that correlation was here to stay, and the best one could do about it was to promote it to the furniture of the universe or to show that it is shared beyond the limits of the human. Meillassoux's aim, which is arguably the *de jure* point of departure of all speculative realism, was to avoid correlationism, weak and strong, while making no compromise with the view that correlation is unavoidable or absolute. Further, he aimed at no simple rejection of correlationism: there was a lesson to be learned from Kant without walking his path. The extent to which the aim of fully exorcising correlations was fulfilled by any speculative realism — and by Meillassoux's own brand of speculative materialism itself — is debatable but besides my point. (Some of the contributions in this volume — the ones by Zielke and Tritten, for example — among many other texts have directly or indirectly addressed the issue.) What matters here is the diagnosis and the aim set up by Meillassoux, for it is the diagnosis and aim that somehow make the breakthrough effective. The "real" in Charles' phrase is the one that can be found, or explicitly struggled to be found, beyond correlation. Part of what I mean by the door and the place opened by speculative realism is also a reference to overcoming correlation, and not simply replacing one version of it for another. Notice that the aim formulated from Meillassoux's work can turn out to be partially or completely unreachable and that the formulation itself can be seen as being biased, inappropriate, or just inadequate, but still it provides a glimpse of a door and a place that were previously unconceived and that envisage a formulation of the real hardly available before the movement.

As for the discouragement in some circles to employ words like "realism" — (2) in the disjunction above — the movement was bold to suggest that one could think of realism without the commitments sometimes associated with it. Realism needs to not entail an adherence to the representations provided by any cognitive endeavour, an acceptance that things in themselves are determinate, separate, or ordered, and not even an endorsement of the notion of reality as a landscape of actual items fully present that stand on their own. One could think of realism without a reference to any cognitive enterprise — and indeed as a criticism of some of them — without subscribing to any common-sense notion of what is real and without taking for granted that reality should compose a landscape of *actualitates.*[1] Realism could be faithful not to the transparency of what it is concerned with but rather precisely to the withdrawal of objects, as Harman's object-oriented ontology does. It can be about the uncanny and the eerie, as to some extent Grant and Brassier suggest. It can also be about the being-another that Meillassoux's principle of facticity envisages. The game of speculative realism here can be described as an attempt to rescue the word "realism" from its ordinary use — and in this sense, it is engaged in a renewed, non-phenomenogical return to things themselves. Here again, it is possible that none of the new dashes of realism rehearsed by the proponents of the movement, or at least by the initial ones, have really escaped the fate associated with the word — and it could therefore be that it would be best to leave the vocabulary associated with the term behind. Still, the target has been proposed: think of realism (and of "reality") in terms that would resist lapsing into the ordinary projects associated with that in recent philosophy.

This narrative — and the corresponding breakthrough — that correlations were just accepted as part of life throughout the twentieth century can be itself challenged. Further, even though strong realisms were seldom presented explicitly at the time, several philosophers have attempted to think beyond the correlationist pale. Some of them have provided resources to revamp the notion of realism in terms that are out of the ordinary. I limit myself here to two salient examples. Although process philosophers such as Alfred Whitehead, Gilbert Simondon, Etienne Souriau and, perhaps above all, Gilles Deleuze can be read as making correlation absolute, they have contributed to thinking that the human correlation with the world is part of a broader picture that could be thought in terms that are at least partly not reducible to "correlation". Reading Deleuze as someone who made correlation absolute is certainly interesting, but one could also read him as a groundwork for forms of realism stronger than those usually proposed in his time. Further, the Heideggerian heritage of looking for manners of thinking to turn away from the metaphysical heritage — including the different efforts of Heidegger since his diagnosis that metaphysics is an event in a broader history of *being*, but also Jacques Derrida's deconstruction, Gianni Vattimo's weak thinking, and Catherine Malabou's plasticity — can hardly be understood solely in terms of vindicating correlations. The way Heidegger thought metaphysics through, and considered that it was made explicit and then concluded by Nietzschean nihilism, is oblivious to the issue concerning correlations. It is arguably transversal to it and, further, it can be read as a starting point for a stronger form of realism according to which human thinking is thoroughly part of a broader history. The diagnosis that Meillassoux put forward could be the blueprint of a breakthrough, but it is not the single relevant way to address what was going on in twentieth-century philosophy. This is where the narrative provided by speculative realism about the recent past of philosophy — from which the breakthrough becomes salient — risks becoming itself parochial. Speculative realism being a breakthrough is not the single key to approaching any issue in philosophy. To be fair, few people would take it to be this way 15 years into the (incipient) history of the movement. However, my claim would have to include this qualification: the breakthrough of speculative realism is not the single most important event in twenty-first-century philosophy, let alone of contemporary philosophy at large.

Still, it is a breakthrough. Circumscribed, restricted, relative to a narrative, and among others, but still a breakthrough. This can be brought to the fore through a consideration of its legacy. This is possibly the best way to engage with the movement and it has oriented this publication — it testifies to the many developments that speculative realism has already prompted. Legacies are always in the making — even for long-disappeared movements such as *Naturphilosophie*, British idealism, or existentialism. This is also because philosophy is spectral: it is hard to say how dead anything is — often philosophical ideas and gestures come back in one or many variations. Charles, in his introduction, addressed the issue of whether the movement was itself still alive — or whether it has existed at any point. It is a relevant question as some of its initial proponents have explicitly signed out of it. I would like to place the issue of the legacy beyond such issues of life and death. My gambit is that we can circumvent these difficult questions by concentrating on the effects of the movement — no matter how non-existent it was. If this is so, I can engage in a reformulation of my initial claim, this time unavoidably with a more wordy result: *I believe the movement of speculative realism had several refreshing effects, independently of the feasibility of their aims or the adequacy of their diagnosis; these effects can be sensed primarily by those that are more directly involved in the most reinforced narratives of recent philosophy.* I move now to consider briefly the three-and-a-half effects of the movement that I consider more visible so far. Needless to say that at least one of them appears in most of the contributions to this volume. Perhaps less needless is the remark that they are intrinsically related to the attempt to escape the correlation and the endeavour to bring about different varieties of realism.

The First Effect: Speculation

Speculative realism enabled a fresh look into speculation, the idea that one can see something broader from narrower knowledge and experience. The idea is that we can start from something familiar or accepted and take that as an example of something larger. German Idealists have taken speculation to be the very activity of unaided reason, that of extending what can be known beyond the limits of experience — speculation is expanding. Whitehead took speculation as a method to do more with what is already accepted or assumed; the quality of a point of departure, for him, is revealed in how much one can expand from it. In all cases, speculation has to do with the amplification that mirrors provide; Whitehead thought that an appropriate procedure should find suitable starting points and then reflect them as far as possible to enable thought that was not possible before. Speculative realists have engaged in the effort of furnishing their realisms with items resulting from speculation. It was shown to lead from the withdrawal of objects from cognitive and sensorial attention to a general notion of objects and their secret lives by Harman's account of the quadruple object. Objects are taken to have a common structure that is speculated from the elements that can be found in all sorts of objects, including familiar ones, the ones inspected by phenomenological analyses and the subject of experience who is witness to the persistently secret life of its own objects. Likewise, speculation, as Schelling thought, could be used to craft a picture of nature that is active, enabling, and subject to history. The contrast between the historical and the law-like that Grant draws shows that nature can still be thought of in terms close to those of *Naturphilosophie*, suggesting that the sciences of nature that engage in the history of their subjects are exposing no more than the tip of the iceberg. It is also speculation that led Meillassoux to move from the contingency of our own correlation between thought and world to the facticity of all correlations and to the principle of insufficient reason, stating that the only necessity is contingency itself. His speculative move starts from correlationism while using a central feature of the correlation in the lessons to be learned from Kant, who insisted that it is not absolute to assert facticity. His own speculative conclusion — a realism about hyper-chaos — is a general thesis to be upheld both against varieties of scientific realism (or even mathematical Platonism, to some extent) and the attempts to supplement the lack of rational access to things-in-themselves with some sort of nonrational path to ultimate reality. It was also speculation that guided Brassier to rethink the Enlightenment ideas about the disenchantment of the world in terms of non-philosophy and some Sellarsian ideas. Extinction, as a conclusion, was held by Brassier to follow from a systematic consideration of disenchantment. In his *Speculative*

Realism: An Introduction, Harman (2018, Introduction) maintains that speculation oriented all four of the initial proponents to reach conclusions that are against common-sense realism while taking a realist stance about them.

In contrast with Whitehead, who was a relevant influence on Harman's distance from the human-centred perspective in philosophy, speculative realism found a way to engage with speculation without a commitment to transparency. Instead of making speculation a tool to reveal what can be disclosed, speculative realists turned it into a strategy to make some opacity explicit. By looking into crafting strong varieties of realism, they brought back speculation as a tool to make room for the structurally concealed. It ventured beyond the border drawn by the correlation between our cognitive apparatus and what it can access and, as a consequence, often beyond the limits of human experience in its surroundings. In his encouragement of a renewed exploration of the absolute, Meillassoux finds it in facticity itself. Speculation is what enables him to see what is absolute and, as a consequence, to dismiss any other necessity. That things can be otherwise is not a way to expose them, but rather facticity is a way to implement the general concealment of what is necessary. Harman (2011) more explicitly rejected transparency by showing through speculation that a real object, which he deemed as part of the structure of any object, is always secret — there is something in any object that is hidden from anything that interacts with it. The real object is systematically elusive — and this has little to do with human limitations, but could be speculatively unveiled by them. As a consequence, withdrawal from transparency is a general feature of whatever exists. There is a shade inside any object that can be found but not inspected by speculation. Real objects are somehow speculative blind spots of the kind that had no room in Whitehead's picture. However, they are not in a special realm untouched by specular lights; on the contrary, they are everywhere. Speculation reveals that the concealed is concealed — instead of just disclosing what was otherwise just concealed. It becomes a way to conceive of what cannot be accessed as an inextricable part of any object. It is a realism about the concealed that is achieved through speculation. What the movement provided was a certain freedom concerning how speculation is deployed.

I have presented some misgivings concerning most uses of speculation elsewhere (Bensusan, 2021). I suspect speculation itself brings in a commitment to the extension of the same — the very image of a mirror suggests that. Further, even though the tendency of speculation towards disclosure can be curbed by the speculative realist effort to focus on the hidden, it still favours the idea that reality is not far from some sort of *actualitas* — I take that any renewed realism that engages in speculation is at a productive friction with the speculative attraction for resolved landscapes. It is, to a large extent, about using the reflection of mirrors to complete a picture, to shed light into the darker zones. Interestingly, the speculative turn — which reaches beyond speculative realism[2] as much as beyond the scope of philosophy[3] — has been contemporary of another turn concentrated on another derivative of the same radical: the spectral turn, which is frequently associated with Derrida's 1993 book, *The Specters of Marx*.[4] Both contemporary movements are about the gaze — both are connected to the constraints to what is commonly taken to be visible. The contrast between the speculative and the spectral is suggestive by itself — the Indo-European root *spek* — is also related to aspect, inspect, prospect, suspect, speculum, spectrum, species, spy, and respect — but I will only remark that a comparison makes clear that speculation promotes a broadening of the gaze by emphasising reflection, extending to the unseen what is already visible. It is about revealing, even if it reveals what is opaque. This, again, can be in contrast to the effort to construct realisms that go beyond the presentation of a landscape of *actualitates*, and, again, this is a way to portray the uneasiness between speculation on the one side and realism on the other. This friction can be resolved in several different ways — including through a sheer rejection of speculation in general. Part of the effect of the movement concerning speculation has been calling for new considerations of the difficulties and blind spots of speculative thinking. As a result, it has placed speculation resolutely back in the philosophical landscape.

The Second Effect: Beyond the Human

Speculative realism renewed the philosophical attention toward what is beyond human reach — partly motivated by the exhaustion of correlationism; partly guided by the urgency of the ecological crisis; partly following a movement of departure from assumptions concerning human exceptionalism; and perhaps partly because humans are in their downfall, as they are being gradually replaced even to the point that it is less clear that they are the only public (or consumer) of philosophical thinking. By taking the focus away from human access to the world, the movement was one of the gates for post-human feelings to enter into philosophy. It provided a platform for philosophy in an era where humans can no longer afford to think for themselves and address only themselves — either because the effect of their thinking on the rest of the world has been made explicit or because they have themselves forged yet rudimentary thinking devices that are increasingly part of the intellectual environment where they dwell. Speculative realism hints at the pressure to place philosophy beyond human loneliness. That could entail taking the human as an object absorbed in a larger environment of other objects, as it is suggested by Amanda Boetzkes in her contribution to the volume drawing from Harman's object-oriented ontology (see also Harman's contribution here where he explicitly addresses the issue of a flat ontology).

To be sure, neither the overcoming of correlationism entails the rejection of the human as a central focus — the absolute could be taken to be accessible to the human only, for example — nor the abandonment of the human exceptional status is itself a movement away from the era of the correlate — as Meillassoux's remarks against making the correlation absolute show. They are related issues, nonetheless. The attempts to put behind our correlation with the world are also a way to leave the scene or the central stage. The era of the correlate has been arguably an anthropocentric era — with many variations including attempts to escape anthropocentrism through an anthropomorphism that embraces rating the human as less central while favouring the projection of human features elsewhere. This anthropomorphic escape line was part of the reading of philosophers as distinct as Hegel, Nietzsche, and Whitehead — a reading that informs the very diagnosis of Meillassoux concerning absolute correlations. Again, it could be that anthropomorphism is the only way to be out of the reach of the tentacles of anthropocentrism or that the two terms are too coarse and deserve a finer analysis. However, speculative realism paved the way for a philosophy that is less centred on human measure.

Speculative realism belongs to a time where humans are urged not to act and think on their own, both because the rest of what is taken to be the natural world has become increasingly or explicitly entwined with most human drifts and because, simultaneously, humans are forging for themselves artificial companions that not only live more and more by their side but that are steadily mastering the abilities required for thinking and feeling. The movement was concocted in the post-human crossroad of these two tendencies: one towards what co-exists on this planet with the human and another towards what humans are engendering in their effort to think about the world. The crisis some people detect in the endeavour to make the world intelligible — extracting its underlying intelligibility — coincides with the success stories around the metaphysical project if we regard it as a prolegomenon to any artificial intelligence. If only some people are concerned with the crisis, most people are actively engaged in the efforts to make the world inhabitable by the devices that we are multiplying. In other words, we are more clearly in the Heideggerian predicament according to which metaphysics is accomplished as a project and the consequences of this are not necessarily leading to human achievement or emancipation. Indeed, one of the prices paid for this accomplishment in making the world artificialisable is the growing ecological threat. This is the post-human crossroad[5] at which speculative realism comes to life. As such, by decentring human concerns, it hints at producing thought that is meaningful in the human absence — or at least in the absence of the humans that are low-intensity hybrids that we know. Arguably, the movement has assembled ways to think through that can be reached and understood from a point of view other than that of the human that is often assumed (and that is itself often oriented by gender, sexuality, race, age, and several other biases — more about this below). What can be seen as what the movement hints at is a philosophy that is read and written by computers, networks, cyborgs, drones, microchips and all sorts of artificial entities that could well be among the heirs of philosophy.

As a consequence, I can see philosophers invited to attempt to be daring and "to measure up to the universe", to borrow the call once made by Bataille, without contenting themselves "with the slumber of conventional knowledge" (Bataille, 1988, p. 11). Apart from promoting an ontological turn, or anything of the sort, the movement injected this kind of renewed courage into the philosophical adventure. This was made explicit in Brassier's remarks about extinction and philosophy that made him conclude his first book, after addressing the adequacy without correspondence between the end of humanity and the anticipating trauma, writing that "the subject of philosophy must [...] recognize that he or she is already dead, and that philosophy is neither a medium of affirmation nor a source of justification, but rather the organon of extinction" (Brassier, 2007, p. 239).

As part of this post-human philosophical atmosphere, the movement can be seen as a preparation for a near future where artificial philosophy will breed. By shifting the focus away from the human confrontation with the world, speculative realism also made philosophy into something more than a human concern. A possible sequel that can be foreseen through the movement is to prepare philosophers that, like the generation of poets that Christian Bök contemplated with his robopoetics project, "can reasonably expect to write [philosophy] for an audience of artificially intellectual peers" (Bök, 2002, p. 17).[6] If philosophy has often attempted to be involved in the education of new generations, it ought now equally to be called upon to help shape the thinking of the artificial offspring humanity is forging. Speculative realism is not yet artificial philosophy in the pipeline, but by urging the removal of the human as the central topic and as the salient point of reference, it makes it possible to think of a future where philosophy will outlive humanity.

This post-human aspect of speculative realism leads us to the political issue. Some people have found the movement apolitical or, at least, less concerned with political issues than its continental predecessors. Indeed, the editors of *The Speculative Turn* observe that, although it "has become almost a matter of dogma within continental philosophy that 'politics is ontology, and ontology is politics'", the authors of *The Speculative Turn*, as the editors read them, "reject the strong version of this claim", for "there needs to be an aspect of ontology that is independent of its enmeshment in human concerns" (Bryant, Srnicek, & Harman, 2011, p. 16). The post-human age to which speculative realism belongs clearly would certainly move away from *human* politics, as the issues about the future of the planet and of its more intensely hybrid population concern not only humans. However, it can be made clear that as philosophy can outlive the human, so does politics — and as Donna Haraway once suggested (1985), maybe even class struggle. Politics then becomes maybe cosmic: cosmopolitics, to use the word as used by one of the contributors of *The Speculative Turn,* Isabelle Stengers (Bryant, Srnicek, & Harman, 2011, pp. 368–380). Cosmopolitics shows that politics is not about human concerns but also that humans find themselves at crossroads that matter not only for them but also for the artificial environment they are building, as well as for the natural ground on which they build. Speculative realism addresses anthropocentrism because it is one of the philosophical movements of the anthropocene. In this age, it is arguable that the ontological and the cosmopolitical are bound to converge. Further, the entanglement of political issues in the furniture of the universe is part of the legacy that philosophy has to offer to its possibly non-human heirs. The persistence of political issues is something that will certainly concern robots and other artificial agents as much as it has concerned human philosophers.

The Third Effect: Continental and Analytic

Speculative realism is commonly portrayed as a realist renewal of continental philosophy. Still, some of its works offered a blueprint of what could be a suitable integration of analytic and continental traditions that retains the best of both. Some of its initial proponents have, indeed, engaged in different ways and intensities with analytical ideas and procedures. Tempering their continental background with analytical resources, they could sketch a new voice on issues concerning how to best formulate realism, concerning the absolute or the Promethean fate of humanity. To be sure, the coming together of these two polarised traditions is yet to come, but some of the possible insights that it could provide were made available by the speculative realist efforts to bring analytic attention to problems that have lapsed out of the continental thinking. The movement enabled philosophy to cross its own borders, and thus create something out of its often-isolated cells. In doing this, it offered a taste of what could be a more cosmopolitan, polystylistic outlook for philosophy. Speculative realism is arguably one of the most polystylistic movements of this century.

Brassier has urged for communication between the audacity that he deemed "speculative" in continental philosophy and "the really admirable level of engagement with the empirical sciences which is a feature of the most interesting work being done specifically in the kind of Anglo-American philosophy of mind" (Brassier, Grant, Harman, & Meillassoux, 2007, p. 321). He expressed interest in a bridge between the analytical philosophy that he understood as influenced by cognitive science — and in particular of Sellarsian philosophers like Paul Churchland — and the broadness of scope that he saw in the continental side. Brassier, of the four proponents, is maybe the one who more clearly attempted to establish this communication. In his interview in this volume, he brings up a criticism of the recent analytical interest in political issues related to epistemic justice while emphasising that analytic philosophy has been depoliticised as a consequence of its professionalisation. Rather than two separate endeavours that have little to say to each other, he finds a continuum between the two poles. In the twenty-first century, it seems like the distance between the two poles is widening and communication is still rare. Also as a consequence of professionalisation, philosophers rarely take the task of attempting a dialogue outside their tradition that often has little perspective in terms of printed resonance. This is why I believe that the effect of speculative realist was not to bridge the gap or pave the crossing between analytic and continental philosophy, but simply to offer a sort of blueprint for how the joint venture could eventually materialise.

As someone who has been raised with a foot in each of the poles — under the influence and later company of people like Julio Cabrera, Jon Cogburn, and Paul Livingston — and who found common issues hidden in different vocabularies, styles, and references, this is one of the possibilities opened up by the movement that called my attention. It seemed like a philosophy that crafts novelty by combining gestures, issues, and accounts from different traditions was possible. In contrast with the prevalent view that there is little to be gained by moving out of a chosen delimited area, I saw speculative realism promising something new where, for example, the style of analytic philosophy could be applied to continental issues. This is one of the areas in which speculative realist promises seem still far from being fulfilled, but one can begin to see how far one can go by bringing together traditions kept apart, not as juxtaposing different things but as a cross-pollinisation that benefits philosophy. One interesting stance of convergence can be found between the speculative turn and what C.B. Martin and John Heil (1999) have called "the ontological turn"; both of them being roughly contemporary and both pitched as a reaction to "the linguistic turn" much discussed in the twentieth century. Analytic philosophy has undergone a turn away from issues to do with language, arguably since metaphysical issues became central in discussions about language in the aftermath of Saul Kripke's *Naming and Necessity* conferences (1972). Kripke's views on reference were often read as promoting a pivotal change in the ordinary way objects and their properties were usually thought. It promoted a new form of essentialism and the view that the world is accessible through language in ways that are oblivious to descriptive knowledge (of knowledge that something is one way or another). Kripke disentangled metaphysical necessity from anything to do with the way we know things — for instance, if we know them *a priori*. Kripke, and the discussion around his work, can be said to stimulate weird realisms that can be compared with the ones developed by speculative realists — the most prominent being David Lewis' modal realism or concretism according to which possible worlds, that Lewis (1986) conceived in a way closer to Leibniz's, are real. The only distinctive mark of the actual world is that it is the one we are in. Now, if we add to Lewis' modal realism other recently proposed varieties of realism, such as Kit Fine's fragmentalism (2005) and Graham Priest's dialetheism (2002), we can maybe find something like an analytic counterpart of speculative realism. To be sure, they are different in many respects, including the use of speculation and the way correlationism is addressed. But they are nonstandard realisms that both go against common sense and, to some extent, are formulated independently of any centrality of the human. Fragmentalism is the view that reality is not coherent, but it is neutral and absolute in the sense that it is not relative to a perspective. Dialetheism understands that there are parts of reality that are themselves contradictory — contradictions are part of the furniture of the universe. Speculative realists rarely mention these alternative realisms,[7] but while polystylism can be perceived as only a promise, the movement has managed to make it.

The Half Effect: The Usual Biases

It is worth comparing speculative realism to its sister movement: new materialism. It is a *sister* movement in the sense that it is almost entirely driven by work done by women, like Jane Bennet, Vicki Kirby, Karen Barad, Diana Coole, Rosi Braidotti, Catherine Malabou, and, arguably, Deborah Goldgaber. Goldgaber, who could arguably be considered in both movements, compares them, saying that, like speculative realists, new materialists critique correlationism and do it "particularly in the form of linguistic "enclosure" — with the aim of bringing the body, its substance and matter, powers and relations back into view" (Goldgaber, 2020, p. 8). New materialists, however, work in continuity with other recent continental traditions — and Goldgaber points particularly to their recognised debt to deconstruction. About the distinction between the two movements, she sees it as based chiefly on "their distinctive relationship with post-structuralist and deconstructive philosophy"; the speculative realists tend to emphasise the rupture while "new materialists seek to extend and radicalise the insights" provided by predecessors (Goldgaber, 2020, p. 8). From feminist perspectives, it is interesting to compare the two siblings, and to take stock of the separation between them, in terms of the connection between the gender distinction and the different attitudes towards recent philosophy. Why did new materialism choose to continue and deepen the recent pursuits while speculative realists prefer to engage in a heroic narrative of rupture? Is this heroic narrative what separates the two movements, including the gender attractors that they have displayed? These questions notwithstanding, and I'll do no more than pose them, the two movements are often clustered together, and, like Goldgaber, some people transit between them and even rather have them merged. In any case, the fate of speculative realism is tied to that of new materialism — maybe they both fructify and disappear as living movements. Perhaps, though, there are still new breaths to be expected.

The last (half) effect of speculative realism is the most unsure of them all and it is connected even more deeply with the prospects for the future of philosophy. As the intellectual scene is beginning to examine its own biases and to open up space for projects and thoughts no matter the geography or social provenience, the race, gender, mode of life and other beliefs of their authors, philosophy is slowly welcoming Feminist, Black, Gender dissident, and other ways of thinking into its core. In principle, one could reckon that the speculative realist movement could have stimulated this slow drift in philosophy and even encouraged it for, after all, to displace the focus from humans can also help to abandon an image of them as white, male, and law-abiding. It has been argued, nonetheless, that speculative realism has, from its inception, complied with the implicit biases of the philosophical community. It is maybe fair to say that the movement was part of the drive to open philosophy to a broader universality, but it has played a smaller role in this than other major contemporary developments. Not only are its sources often restricted to previous European and North American thinkers, but also it has attracted decreasing attention from women and other non-majority groups within philosophy. In the age of decolonialism, when philosophy has been urged to distance itself from the image of white-only studies, the movement has done little to challenge the North Atlantic supremacy in the curricula. It has fared better with respect to its contact with Feminisms — as shown by projects such as Katherine Behar's (2016) object-oriented feminism. The aggregated effect is mixed: although there are too few representatives of the non-white and the non-male in it — and in the contributions we have received for this volume — it is too early to adjudicate the impact of the movement in the biased ecology of philosophy.

A movement is above all a promise — it is what can survive its initial gestures. This promise is what we think is expressed in the contributions of this volume. It includes fostering fresh accounts of reality which somehow learn the lessons from the era of the correlate. We believe the promise is alive, and, in that sense, speculative realism is a breakthrough. I can now offer a still longer reformulation of my claim: *I believe the movement of speculative realism was a breakthrough in the sense that it had several refreshing effects, independently of the feasibility of their aims or the adequacy of their diagnosis; these effects, which can be sensed primarily by those that are more directly involved in the most reinforced narratives of recent philosophy, are not all equally perceivable at the moment and they may not come to completion. Still, to the extent that these effects are sensed, it is clear that philosophy is no longer the same after the inception of speculative realism.*

Albuquerque, January 2023

References

Bataille, Georges. *The Accursed Share*. New York: Zone, 1988.

Behar, Katherina. *Object-Oriented Feminism*. Saint Paul: Minnesota University Press, 2016.

Bensusan, Hilan. "Geist and Ge-Stell: Beyond the Cyber-Nihilist Convergence of Intelligence". *Cosmos and History* 16 (2) (2020), pp. 94–117.

Bensusan, Hilan. "The cosmopolitical parties in the post-human era". *TripleAmpersand Journal (&&&)*, 2020a. https://tripleampersand.org/cosmopolitical-parties-post-human-age/ Accessed 11 April 2023.

Bensusan, Hilan. "O capital transversal e seus rementos atrativos ou a infância das máquinas". *Direitos, Trabalho e Política Social* 6 (10) (2020b), pp. 88–109.

Bensusan, Hilan. *Indexicalism*. Edinburgh: Edinburgh University Press, 2021.

Blanco, Maria del Pilar & Esther Peeren. *The Spectralities Reader*. London: Bloomsbury, 2013.

Bök, Christian. "The Piecemeal Bard Is Deconstructed: Notes Toward a Potential Robopoetics". *Object 10: Cybernetics, UBU Papers*, 2002.

Brassier, Ray. *Nihil Unbound: Enlightenment and Extinction*. New York: Palgrave Macmillan, 2007.

Brassier, Ray, Iain Hamilton Grant, Graham Harman, & Quentin Meillassoux. "Speculative Realism". In *Collapse III*, pp. 306–449, 2007.

Bryant, Levi, Nick Srnicek, & Graham Harman. *The Speculative Turn*. Melbourne: Re.press, 2011.

Cogburn, Jon. *Garcian Meditations*. Edinburgh: Edinburgh University Press, 2017.

Cordero, Rodrigo. "In defense of a speculative sociology". *Distinktion* 1 (18) (2017), pp. 125–132.

Fine, Kit. "Tense and Reality". *Modality and Tense: Philosophical Papers*, pp. 261–320. Oxford: Oxford University Press, 2005.

Goldgaber, Deborah. *Speculative Grammatology*. Edinburgh: Edinburgh University Press, 2020.

Haraway, Donna. "A Cyborg manifesto". *Socialist Review* 80, pp. 65–108, 1985.

Harman, Graham. *The Quadruple Object*. London: Zer0 Books, 2011.

Harman, Graham. *Speculative Realism: an Introduction*. Milton: Polity, 2018.

Heidegger, Martin. "Nietzsche's Word: 'God is Dead'". In *The Question Concerning Technology and Other Essays*, translated by William Lovitt. New York: Harper Perennial, 1977.

Heidegger, Martin. "Metaphysics as history of being". In *The End of Philosophy*. Chicago: University of Chicago Press, 2003.

Martin, C.B. & John Heil. "The ontological turn". *Midwest Studies in Philosophy* 23 (1) (1999), pp. 34–60.

Meillassoux, Quentin. *After Finitude: An Essay on the Necessity of Contingency*, translated by Ray Bressier. London: Bloomsbury, 2009.

Kripke, Saul. *Naming and Necessity*. Oxford: Blackwell, 1972.

Lewis, David. *On the Plurality of the Worlds*. Oxford: Blackwell, 1986.

Ludueña, Fabián. *La Comunidad de los Espectros I–V*. Buenos Aires: Mino Davila, 2010–2021.

Priest, Graham. *Beyond the Limits of Thought*. Oxford: Oxford University Press, 2002.

Notes

1 Heidegger has criticised the cognitive enterprises that he saw as subsidiaries of metaphysics on the basis of its silencing of Being, which could be understood as a realist critique (see, for instance, Heidegger, 1977, p. 53–114.). He has also traced the idea of an *actualitas* as presences that can be fully unveiled and made transparent once and for all in the

growing metaphysical commitment that comes from Aristotle's word ἐνέργεια to Latin translations as *actualitas* (Heidegger, 2003, p. 8–48). He has, nonetheless, not ventured into a new and cleansed employment of the word "realism" — neither has Derrida who is, to a large extent, heir of his attitude of distancing from all things metaphysical.

2 In the somehow inaugural book of 2011 (Bryant, Srnicek, & Harman, 2011), speculation is taken to reach beyond the movement not only towards its sister movement of new materialism but also encompassing contemporary thinkers, such as Isabelle Stengers, John Protevi, Bruno Latour, and Manuel DeLanda.

3 Consider, for example, the proposal of a speculative sociology (see Cordero, 2017, p. 125–132). Think also of the use of the term "speculative fiction", at least since Donna Haraway's *Cyborg Manifesto* (1985), as an umbrella term for what is described as the different literary genres of weird fiction, science fiction, superhero fiction, utopian fiction, fantasy, mystery, cyberpunk, horror among others. The speculative fiction of H.P. Lovecraft is another common element between most of the initial proponents of speculative realism.

4 In their companion to the spectral turn, Maria del Pilar Blanco and Esther Peeren trace back the turn to a few years before Derrida's book and also offer an overview of the work being produced around the spectral mostly in cultural theory (Blanco & Peeren, 2013). In recent years, the spectral turn has arrived in philosophy as well; see, for example, the five-volume book by Fabián Ludueña that appeared between 2010 and 2021. Ludueña's work is also connected to speculative realism, and Meillassoux's ideas figure with prominence in the book (see below my contribution to this volume, "Stronger realisms").

5 I have written about this elsewhere. See, in particular, Bensusan (2020, 2020a, 2020b).

6 The continuation of Bök's text, if we replace "poetry" with "philosophy" and accordingly for related terms, is a suitable diagnosis of the age that speculative realism may be seen as helping to inaugurate. The continued text would read like this: *Is it not already evident by our presence at digital philosophy conferences that the philosophers of tomorrow are likely to resemble programmers, exalted, not because they can write great philosophy, but*

because they can build a small drone out of words to write great philosophy for us? If philosophy already lacks any meaningful readership among our own anthropoid population, what have we to lose by writing philosophy for a robotic culture that must inevitably succeed our own? If we want to commit an act of philosophical innovation in an era of formal exhaustion, we may have to consider this heretofore unimagined, but nevertheless prohibited, option: writing philosophy for inhuman readers, who do not yet exist, because such aliens, clones, or robots have not yet evolved to read it.

7 Exceptions include John Cogburn's consideration of Priest's work (Cogburn, *Garcian Meditations*, Edinburgh: Edinburgh University Press, 2017) and my own development of a realism about exteriority (Bensusan, *Indexicalism,* Edinburgh: Edinburgh University Press, 2021).

CHAPTER 1
SPECULATIVE OBJECTS

GETTING REAL ABOUT ARTEFACTS: OOO, POST-PHENOMENOLOGY, AND TECHNOLOGY

Arjen Kleinherenbrink

Introduction

One way to evaluate the strength and relevance of a metaphysics is to ask what difference its use as a conceptual framework would make in other (philosophical) fields. I here ask this question about object-oriented ontology (OOO) in the context of the philosophy of technology. Specifically, I contrast salient features of OOO with the "postphenomenology of technology" developed by the well-known Dutch philosopher of technology Peter-Paul Verbeek.[1]

Such a comparison is interesting for three reasons. First, Verbeek's postphenomenology is intended as a best-of-both-worlds approach to phenomenology and Latourian actor-network theory (ANT).[2] If OOO turns out to have a more consistent conceptual framework and greater explanatory power than a theory that combines the strengths of two widely used philosophical methods, then this testifies to OOO's relevance. I will argue that this is indeed the case.

Second, Verbeek extends his systematic reflections into practical recommendations for the design of artefacts. This allows us to see that, despite wielding the combined force of phenomenology and ANT, Verbeek's approach undervalues and even overlooks important features of (the design of) artefacts. OOO can do a better job here and is therefore also the preferable theory when it comes to the applied side of the philosophy of technology.

Third and finally, Verbeek's postphenomenology builds on several related ideas that are typical of much continental philosophy. These include firm resistance against the idea that entities might have essences, a correlationist view of reality such that nothing exists without human involvement, and a relationism according to which all properties are properties of relations and never of things. If OOO has a leg up on postphenomenology, it therefore also speaks to OOO's relevance for the wider field of continental philosophy. Unlike the previous two points, this will not be argued in detail here. It is simply something for the reader to consider.

I will proceed as follows. The section "Postphenomenology and Artefacts" introduces Verbeek's postphenomenology as presented in his acclaimed book *What Things Do* (WTD) and discussed in his article "Let's Make Things Better" (2009). Next, "Conceptual Inconsistencies" discusses two major problems in Verbeek's theory. First, its inability to conceive of relations between objects wherever humans are not present. Second, some metaphysical absurdities entailed by its persistent relationism.

In *An Object-Oriented Alternative*, I show how an OOO approach remedies such inconsistencies. My argument uses a version of OOO that characterises the ontological interior of objects in terms of *powers* (Bryant, 2014; Kleinherenbrink, 2017). Since the better known OOO theory is Graham Harman's characterisation of said interior as a *real object* in tension with *real qualities*, I will compare the two and show why Harman's concerns about the powers variant might be overstated. Since their advantages over Verbeek's postphenomenology primarily exist by virtue of how both OOO variants endow entities with a private ontological interior, this comparison will be kept brief so as to keep the overall focus on the contrast between OOO and postphenomenology.

The section "Practical Consequences" identifies several ways in which Verbeek's relationism undervalues salient features of technology, and shows that OOO can do a better job there. Part of the argument concerns how a slightly reworked version of Harman's concept of *symbiosis* allows for a relevant distinction between different kinds of relations that artefacts can have with other entities (Harman, 2016). Another part concerns how Ian Bogost's and Levi Bryant's notion of *alien phenomenology* allows for an important ethological perspective on artefacts (Bogost, 2012; Bryant, 2014).

Postphenomenology and Artefacts

Verbeek's theory is an alternative to philosophies of technology that reduce all artefacts to their shared conditions of possibility, a move Verbeek calls "transcendentalism" (WTD, p. 7). Heidegger, for example, famously diagnoses modern technology as a specific way of disclosing reality as a standing reserve of raw material and energy available for our use (WTD, pp. 94–5; Heidegger, 1977). For Heidegger, the danger of modern technology is therefore that it makes us treat everything, including other human beings, as mere resources to be exploited. Yet transcendentalism need not be so gloomy. Verbeek also mentions how, in *Thoughts on Technology*, José Ortega y Gasset defines technology as a force that allows us to transform the world in order to improve our well-being, instead of alienating us from ourselves (WTD, p. 37; Ortega y Gasset, 1972).

Regardless of its tone, however, transcendentalism always equates philosophy of technology to philosophical reflection on technology's conditions (WTD, p. 30). This is problematic because artefacts clearly have salient features that are irreducible to their shared conditions. The condition of possibility for all artefacts may very well be that humans experience parts of the world as resources to be controlled, transformed, and manipulated. Yet that does not tell us anything meaningful about the difference that a particular artefact makes to the world. An oil drill has different effects on the world than a pair of sneakers, even if both ultimately have the same conditions of possibility. By almost exclusively thinking about technology in terms of its overall conditions, transcendentalists thus ignore the individual contributions of artefacts (WTD, p. 30; Verbeek, 2009, p. 253).

To prevent reducing artefacts to their conditions, Verbeek proposes to go "to the things themselves", a Husserlian motto that Verbeek adopts as his leitmotif for what he calls a postphenomenology of technology (WTD, p. 12). We will see that the prefix "post-" indicates that Verbeek takes humans and artefacts to co-constitute each other in ways that classical phenomenologies, in his view, do not account for. It also indicates that his theory has a hefty dose of Latourian actor-network theory in its DNA. Postphenomenology is designed as "a fertile hybrid of phenomenological and actor-network theory notions, which can be used to analyze how artefacts co-shape human actions" (WTD, p. 148).[3] What, then, does Verbeek's postphenomenology take from ANT and phenomenology?

As is well known, Bruno Latour holds that reality is best understood in terms of "actors" that connect and interact with each other in networks (WTD, p. 102; Latour, 1996; Latour, 2005). All entities, including camels, airplanes, molecules, and corporations, equally count as such actors. Actors are real to the extent that they have effects on other actors and other actors have effects on them. This makes ANT a relationism that defines entities in terms of what "other actors are modified, transformed, perturbed, or created by the character that is the focus of attention" (Latour, 1999, p. 122). As a result, not a single property of an actor is ever independent from its present relations to a network of other actors, on which that actor relies for its (re)production as well as for any alterations.

Verbeek's main takeaway from ANT is that no actor in such a network is ever a mere "intermediary", an entity that simply transmits the force, material, or information of some other actor without adding its own difference (WTD, p. 155; Latour, 1993, pp. 77–8). All actors, including artefacts, are "mediators" whose associations with other actors cause real change. For ANT, the emergence of, for example, social media and smartphones has not merely *facilitated* but also *altered* existing forms of friendship, romance, politics, and news media. New associations with new actors modify how things work, what we expect from them, what they are associated with, and therefore, as far as ANT is concerned, change what they *are*.

What ANT brings to Verbeek's postphenomenology is therefore a vocabulary to analyse how artefacts engage in various kinds of co-constitutive mediations within their networks (WTD, p. 168). This vocabulary includes Latourian concepts such as "translation", "blackboxing", "delegation", and "composition", but a detailed account of how each of these makes it into Verbeek's theory would lead us too far astray.

We move to what postphenomenology takes from phenomenology proper. Firstly, Verbeek admires phenomenology for holding that there is no meaningful way to think about subjects without also taking into account the relations that they always already have with their world. The familiar argument here is that consciousness is inherently "intentional", meaning that consciousness never exists in itself but only ever as "consciousness-of-something" (WTD, p. 109). Conversely, it would be equally unthinkable to conceive of objects fully separated from conscious subjects. Here the argument is that, since humans can only experience reality by relating to it, reality is never reality-in-itself but rather always "reality for someone" (WTD, p. 112). Attentive readers will spot an obvious fallacy here, to which we will return soon.

Verbeek holds that classical phenomenology nevertheless did not go beyond insisting that subject and object are always already *connected*, which still allows for the possibility that they might have intrinsic features that do not emerge from such connections.[4] Inspired by ANT's constructivism, Verbeek's postphenomenology aims to be more "radical" and posits that subject and object also fully *constitute* each other (WTD, p. 112). As Verbeek puts it, where classical phenomenology "draws a line between the two poles" of subject and object, postphenomenology "lets the poles emerge from the line that constitutes them" (WTD, p. 163).

Secondly, Verbeek thinks that a healthy dose of phenomenology helps keep sight of things that become "invisible" in ANT (WTD, p. 165). This refers to how human beings experience the world and act intentionally in ways that non-humans do not (Verbeek, 2009, p. 255). For ANT, humans are actors among further such actors, and human engagements with the world are associations among further such associations within networks of humans and non-humans. An ANT description of the intentional content of a conscious experience would not be different from an analysis of a refrigerator, a railroad, or an IT project. In all cases, the ANT analyst would trace the network of associations with other relevant humans and non-humans that endow the subject of the investigation with its character. Verbeek worries that the resulting descriptions would undervalue vast differences that exist between an object relating to some other object as opposed to a conscious human being relating to that same object:

> It is indeed meaningful to make a distinction between someone who experiences and something that is experienced, someone who acts and a world in which action takes place — regardless of how interwoven and mutually constituted they are. In human experience, that difference is a vivid reality [...] A philosophy that is to have any hope of grasping the everyday reality of human beings needs to acknowledge this difference [...]. (WTD, pp. 166–7)

Hence postphenomenology retains a sharp distinction between humans and non-humans in order to do right by the rich tapestry of human intentional experience. As Verbeek writes, ANT is primarily interested in unravelling entire networks that cause entities to emerge, treating all kinds of actors on equal footing when doing so, whereas postphenomenology has more limited aims in just seeking to understand the relations that human beings have with those entities (WTD, pp. 164–5).

The combination of a Latourian constructivism (that takes every feature of human and non-human entities to result from their mutual associations) and a phenomenological stance (that insists on the inseparability of non-human objects from human subjects and vice versa) makes Verbeek's postphenomenology revolve around *mediation*, which he understands as the "mutual constitution of subject and object" (WTD, p. 130). Mediation here means that, when people use a technology, this technology starts to organise a relation between users and their environment, such that actions, decisions, experiences, and interpretations become shaped by that technology (Verbeek, 2009, p. 253).

For example, genetic diagnostic tests are not just intermediaries or neutral instruments that increase the accessibility or efficacy of existing phenomena. By mapping which diseases someone might get later in life, they create a new category of "not-yet-ill" between "healthy" and "ill". This makes people responsible for their future fates in new ways (Verbeek, 2009, p. 257). The test is therefore an artefact that mediates how human beings experience themselves and their world by causing new identities and behaviours to emerge.

Four more aspects of Verbeek's postphenomenology, all closely related to the notion of mediation understood as mutual constitution, are relevant here. These are Verbeek's concepts of materiality, technological intentionality, multistability, and anti-essentialism.

With *materiality*, Verbeek seeks to emphasise that the mediating effects of artefacts cannot be reduced to their meaning. They are effects of artefacts themselves (WTD, p. 207; 2009, p. 253). One example is how round tables evoke different styles of communal eating than rectangular tables. Round tables lack a head and give everyone around them the same status, whereas rectangular tables instantiate a hierarchy. Such artefacts are not just passive results of cultural contexts, values, and meanings; they also produce, reinforce, and alter such contexts and meanings. After all, if we start removing rectangular tables from a culture, and follow up by several decades of steadily removing ever more artefacts that reinforce hierarchical behaviour, the social fabric of that community will surely be affected. Or to take a well-known example from Latour that Verbeek also cites: whoever slows down for a speed bump is not trying to avoid a clash with its meaning, but with the artefact itself (WTD, p. 208).

Technological intentionality means that artefacts provoke certain ways of handling them. Verbeek's example, borrowed from Don Ihde, is how fountain pens promote relatively slow and thoughtful writing, whereas type writers allow us to hammer away and thereby facilitate writing styles closer to spoken language (WTD, p. 114–5). This again emphasises how artefacts can evoke specific actions and thereby help engender a world that would have been different were it not for their presence.

Next, *multistability* refers to how artefacts can feature in different use contexts without any such context revealing the "true" artefact among a series of mere appearances (WTD, p. 117). For example, if an axe is sometimes used in combat, sometimes to chop wood, and otherwise decorates a wall, none of these is the one "true" axe as opposed to two mere usages of the axe. Even technical models or studies of its components would not reveal such a "true" axe. To Verbeek, each manifestation of the axe would be equally true and equally real (WTD, p. 105).

This ties into Verbeek's *anti-essentialism* about artefacts: "The insight that technologies cannot be separated from their use contexts implies that they have no 'essence'; they are what they are only in their use" (WTD, p. 117). An artefact *is* its series of mediating activities across different contexts, nothing more and nothing less. Or as Verbeek writes in a similar vein:

> There is […] one pitfall that needs to be avoided in this analysis of the ability of artefacts to coshape the relation between human beings and world: this ability must not be conceived as an intrinsic property of the artifact itself. […] It

> would give rise to a kind of realism in which properties would be assigned to objects independently of the subjects for whom these objects exist. (WTD, p. 117; cf. Verbeek, 2009, p. 253)

This adds a strange twist to Verbeek's theory. Everything so far suggested that tables, smartphones, speed bumps, and fountain pens *themselves* mediate between humans and world. But now, in the name of avoiding an essentialism in which artefacts would have their own properties, mediation becomes a property of the *relations* between artefacts and humans rather than of artefacts themselves. As Verbeek indeed puts it:

> The thought that technological artefacts possess intrinsic properties and can *themselves* influence the relation between human beings and world supposes that technology can be spoken about independently of the humans that engage with it. But from the phenomenological perspective *this is untenable*. Artefacts can only be understood in terms of the relation that human beings have to them. (WTD, p. 117, italics added)

More will be said about this strange twist in the next sections. For now, we have surveyed the main features of Verbeek's postphenomenology. As an alternative to theories that reduce artefacts to their shared conditions of possibility, Verbeek proposes that we go "to the things themselves". This is fleshed out as a philosophy of technology that primarily understands artefacts as relational entities that actively mediate between humans and world, in which mediation is understood as a co-constitution of the very entities between which it mediates.

Conceptual Inconsistencies

There are two major conceptual inconsistencies in Verbeek's theory. The first concerns the fallacy mentioned earlier. Verbeek holds that "human beings can only experience reality by relating to it, which does not involve reality-in-itself but rather reality-for-them. *As consciousness* [...] *can only exist as consciousness of something, reality is always reality for someone*" (WTD, p. 122 italics added). Verbeek consequently defines the world as "reality disclosed by human beings, the world-for-humans that arises when they act and experience it" (WTD, p. 108).

This is a typical case of what Quentin Meillassoux famously calls correlationism: "the idea according to which we only ever have access to the correlation between thinking and being, and never to either term considered apart from the other" (2011, p. 5). It is also a case of flawed reasoning. That one cannot experience reality without relating to it is a simply a tautology that no rational being would deny. But — and here I echo how Ray Brassier dismantles the same fallacy in another context — from this tautological premise Verbeek draws a non-tautological conclusion, namely that reality *depends* for its existence on being experienced by us and *is nothing* without our experience of it (Brassier, 2011, p. 57).

This unfortunate fallacy leads Verbeek into strange waters. Since he takes reality to always be reality-for-someone, he also takes the mediating work of artefacts to only ever concern situations where humans are present. Take how he follows Ihde in distinguishing three ways in which mediation can occur (WTD, p. 123). Artefacts can directly mediate our sensory experience of the world, as happens when we use glasses and hearing aids. They can mediate our experience with themselves, as when we operate a machine. Finally, they can mediate our relation to the world by operating in the background, as when soft jazz music evokes an elegant atmosphere in a swanky hotel lounge.

This clearly makes it impossible to conceive of relations between artefacts themselves or between artefacts and entities that are neither humans nor artefacts. This is a problem, if only because huge numbers of artefacts in our worlds are conduits, pistons, pipes, circuit boards, sensors, cogwheels, and algorithms that mediate each other's activity without direct human involvement. Verbeek indeed admits that postphenomenologists seem to "stand by helplessly if they encounter chains [of non-human entities] without humans [in them]" (WTD, p. 165).

He suggests that this gap in the theory is compensated for by the increased attention that postphenomenology pays to the richness of human experience wherever humans *are* in the presence of mediating artefacts (ibid.). Yet this will not do. First, because Verbeek's explicit aim is to go "to the things themselves"; artefact-artefact relations are a significant aspect of the existence of artefacts that any philosophy of artefacts must accommodate, as will be further discussed in the next section. Second, Verbeek's theory cannot get away with saying that postphenomenology merely wants to *focus* on something else than artefact-artefact relations. It does something far more serious. By its own tenets, postphenomenology declares artefact-artefact relations *non-existent*, as Verbeek holds that all of reality is only ever reality-for-someone.

The second conceptual inconsistency is a consequence of Verbeek's relationism. We saw that, for Verbeek, artefacts "are what they are only in their use" (WTD, p. 117). They have no properties of their own. As such, mediations cannot literally be effects of artefacts themselves, but only of the relations that humans have to artefacts.

The problem here is that this leaves nothing with which such relations can be relations. Returning to our earlier example, for Verbeek an axe is nothing but its featuring in various use contexts such as fighting, chopping, and decorating. There can be an axe-cleaving-skulls, an axe-splitting-logs, and an axe-hanging-over-the-fireplace, but not an axe as such that is carried across contexts and assures that the same axe is used in different ways.

We should not make the mistake of thinking that Verbeek's emphasis on "materiality" prevents this problem from arising. For Verbeek, that an axe is "material" merely means that its mediating effects in specific use contexts are not just symbolic or linguistic. "Materiality" stresses that it is the axe rather than its meaning that splits the skulls of your enemies. The concept does *not* posit any axe-properties that remain constant across various usages and serve as that to which all relations with the axe relate. Also recall that, for Verbeek, even the physical properties of artefacts as disclosed by science are not the reality of artefacts in and of themselves. They are just further properties of relations that human have to those artefacts (WTD, p. 105). He even follows Ihde in holding that "scientific instruments *constitute* what scientist observe; they 'interpret' reality before humans can observe it" (WTD, p. 141). In short, Verbeek's definition of materiality is so thoroughly relational and correlationist that "matter" cannot be that to which humans and non-humans relate when they relate to artefacts.

This relationism has strange consequences. For example, Verbeek sees it as a strength of his theory that it does not reduce an artefact, such as a microwave, to its symbolic meaning within, say, the cultural context of consumerist societies. His theory instead aims to track how the microwave itself mediates between human and world by its being "a quick and easy food-heater-upper" (WTD, pp. 5–6). But if we take his conceptual framework seriously, what can really be said to heat my food? Certainly not the artefact on my kitchen table, because it is denied intrinsic properties by virtue of which it could act. What heats my food can only be a set of relations between the microwave and its human users. There is literally no other option on the (kitchen) table, because artefacts do not have their own properties — which, incidentally, means that there is no real kitchen table either. Since the table qua table is denied properties, the only thing that the microwave can be said to rest on is a set of relations between the table and one or several human beings. After all, Verbeek's reality is always reality for someone, and his "materiality" is a feature of the mediating relation between artefact and human rather than a feature of the artefact itself (2009, p. 255).

This is a special case of idealism. The microwave and the kitchen table are certainly not reduced to our experiences and representations, but they *are* reduced to sets of relations that all have a human being dangling at the other end. This is problematic for several reasons. Verbeek seeks a theory that does not reduce things to "non-thingly elements" (WTD, p. 2), but that is exactly what he ends up doing. While avoiding the reduction of artefacts to shared conditions or to their symbolic meaning, Verbeek still reduces them to their relations with humans. Stressing that humans, artefacts, and other entities co-constitute each other in such relations does nothing to remedy that fact.

Verbeek is aware of these problems and of the risk of regressing into a kind of idealism. At one point, he notes that it cannot be the case that human beings arbitrarily disclose a world, as there is always "something" that is disclosed (WTD, p. 112). There must be "something" that our mediating relations relate to, because otherwise reality would still be reducible to a series of human interpretations. At one other point in the book, Verbeek similarly remarks that there must be an "existence" to subjects and objects beyond their mutual co-constitution:

> Subjects and objects constitute each other not from nothing, but by virtue of their existence…: existences are not empirically perceivable but yet they are a necessary presupposition — inaccessible though they be — in order to account for the mutual constitution of subjectivity and objectivity. (WTD, p. 164)

Yet these two isolated moments are incompatible with the rest of *What Things Do*, which constantly reiterates the idea that "reality arises in relations, as do the human beings who encounter it" (WTD, p. 113). Quite simply, if all of reality is reality-for-someone, and if the world is the world as disclosed to human beings, then there is nothing that "something" or "existence" outside those relations can *be*.

As we will see, an object-oriented alternative to Verbeek's postphenomenology modifies his excessive relationism and puts real flesh on the bones of what he calls "something" and "existence". This remedies the inconsistencies just discussed. It also allows for a philosophy of technology with more explanatory power, as it covers all phenomena that interest Verbeek, plus several relevant aspects of technology that his framework undervalues or overlooks.

An Object-Oriented Alternative

A basic tenet of OOO is that entities cannot be "undermined" or "overmined" (Harman, 2011, pp. 7–20; 2018, p. 50). To undermine is to reduce entities downwards to their parts or even lower levels of reality, such as subatomic particles or pre-Socratic substances. OOO holds that undermining cannot properly account for emergent properties. Water freezes at different temperatures than oxygen and hydrogen, human beings have capacities that their physical and noological parts do not have, paintings have aesthetic qualities that are not present in drops of paint, and so on.

To overmine is to reduce entities upwards to their effects on their environment or their relations with others. OOO holds that overmining cannot account for change. If all entities are nothing but their current deployment in mutual relations, then there exists no ontological surplus by which this status quo could ever be altered. As we saw in the previous section, positions that reduce entities to their relations also have a hard time accounting for the identity of things across their appearances in different contexts. Verbeek's philosophy of technology is a clear case of overmining. It denies that artefacts can have their own properties, and instead holds that only the mediating relations between humans and things can have properties.

Given the problems with undermining and overmining, OOO theorists hold that there must be an ontologically real aspect to entities that cannot be reduced to (relations with) their parts and environments. This is exactly what Verbeek intuits with his reference to "something" that must have "existence" beyond relations, even if the rest of his theory cannot accommodate that insight. Conversely, by making this insight one of its foundational principles, OOO opens a conceptual space for ontologies that go "to the things themselves" in ways unavailable to relationisms such as Verbeek's.

As we saw Verbeek also intuit in the previous paragraph, this ontological interior of entities is not directly accessible to human experience. This does not mean, however, that no meaningful thoughts can be formed about it. It also does not mean that OOO conceives of objects as being utterly autonomous from all other entities. The interior aspect of objects is produced by other entities and it is involved in the production of others still. It is just not reducible to what produces it or to what it produces.

To explain this more detail, I turn to the variant of OOO that defines this interior in terms of dispositions or powers (DeLanda, 2013; Bryant, 2014; Kleinherenbrink, 2020). This is a lesser-known variant than Harman's characterisation of the ontological interior of objects in terms of a "real object" in tension with its "real qualities" (Harman, 2018, p. 114). Hence, I will first briefly discuss some similarities and differences between the two that are relevant here.

Both variants agree that most relations of entities with their parts and environments are superficial phenomena that cause no real change to what these entities *are*. A newly purchased printer does not change the very being of a multinational corporation and a new phone case does not alter the being of a smartphone. Both variants also hold, however, that sometimes an encounter does cause real change to the private interior of an object.

Harman holds that such real change is so rare that it happens no more than a handful of times in an entity's existence (Harman, 2016). For example, we navigate thousands of relations with other entities on a daily basis (putting on clothing, eating food, greeting coworkers, and so on). Most of these merely alter our superficial qualities while leaving who we truly are untouched. When seeing a friend puts a smile on your face or something at work makes you grunt in frustration, such events do not profoundly change who you are. Yet sometimes — for example, when emigrating to a new country or experiencing a deeply traumatic event — we do live through experiences that do profoundly change who we are. This is what Harman calls "symbiosis" (2016, pp. 42–50).

Conversely, in my take on the powers variant of OOO, real change to the interior of an object is far more common than Harman countenances. Only *significant* real change is rare (Kleinherenbrink, 2019, p. 549). For example, most relations between me and other entities have no effect on my power to speak French. Yet a small number of them do have such an effect (think of conversations with French colleagues or reading French books). Most relations among that minority will only cause minor or even insignificant real change. However, on rare occasions, a "symbiotic" event may indeed cause profound changes to my linguistic powers, such as going on a prolonged research stay in Paris that fully immerses me in the language. Likewise, something may even happen that leads to new powers altogether, such as taking acrobatics classes during the weekends of that research stay.

Depending on the circumstances, change to powers can be gradual, abrupt, modest, or enormous. I find this a more plausible model for changes to the ontological interior of entities than Harman's restriction of any change at all to a handful of occasions, hence my preference for talk of powers rather than talk of real qualities.

Harman has expressed worries that talk of powers or dispositions relapses into an overmining position, as powers would be inherently relational properties (DeLanda and Harman, 2017, p. 60). I disagree. The fact that we can only describe powers in relational terms (an axe has a power *to cleave*) does not mean that the powers of things are reducible to their relations with other entities that may or may not be involved in their manifestations. To think otherwise confuses the manifestation of a power with the power itself. The axe that decorates a wall has the power to cleave even if it is not currently cleaving. A power need not be manifest in order to exist, and hence is not reducible to a relation that it *might* at some point have with another entity. Moreover, a power has indefinitely many ways to manifest (horizontal swings cleaving skulls in the morning, vertical swings cleaving logs in the afternoon), but even the sum total of *possible* ways to manifest would never amount to the *real* powers that the axe has, even when hanging over the fireplace.

Moving on, it is important to note that powers are ontologically different in kind from what generates them and from what they generate. They are not simply the possible or potential versions of the entities that produce them or that they produce. They are generated and regenerated by the parts of their object and by entities in its environment, but powers are emergent properties with regard to such parts and environments.[5] Powers are thus transcendental realities, as they are the causal ground of manifestations to which they help give rise. In turn, these manifestations are emergent events with regard to those powers. As such, powers, despite being fully real, are not directly accessible to the senses.

Concretely, all this means that, regardless of whether an axe manifests as a weapon, a wood chopper, or a piece of decoration, all these manifestations are expressions of its powers. The powers of an artefact are the "existence" or "something" that it *is*. Neither its components nor the indefinitely many ways in which it can manifest will ever be identical to its powers, even if those components and ways are useful informants to help us understand and describe its powers.

The inconsistencies in Verbeek's theory disappear once we grant that artefacts have powers that constitute their being. The first inconsistency was that, if reality is always reality-for-someone, object-object relations are rendered non-existent. In an OOO powers theory, reality is not reality-for-someone or even reality-for-something, but always the reality *of* something. The powers of an artefact are a reality onto itself, produced by yet irreducible to other entities. The power of a microwave to heat food is produced by its components, but as an emergent property this power only belongs to the microwave itself. For OOO, such *being* of an artefact does not necessarily require that humans are present, hence the first inconsistency evaporates: humans as well as non-humans may be the objects that produce, reproduce, or alter the powers of a piece of technology.

The second inconsistency was that, in Verbeek's theory, properties can only be properties of relations and not of things. This entailed that there are no things to which relations can relate, and we strangely had to say that what heats food is not the microwave but rather a relation between a human being and the artefact. For OOO, artefacts clearly do have their own properties. An artefact relates to other entities in terms of powers that, in themselves, *are*. This undoes the second inconsistency, as endowing entities with their own properties allows them to be causally efficacious participants in events. Heating food is a manifestation of the powers of the microwave, and cleaving skulls is a manifestation of the powers of the axe.

Thinking about artefacts as having powers that constitute their transcendental and essential aspect does not fall prey to Verbeek's worries about intrinsic properties. We saw how Verbeek thinks that positing essences implies a correspondence theory according to which humans would have direct access to "reality itself" (WTD, p. 143). Yet OOO denies that humans have unmediated access to the essences of things. Essences, whether conceived in terms of powers or real qualities, are "withdrawn" from such access (Harman, 2018, p. 7). We have seen why: no amount of manifestations, descriptions, and theoretical models of a power will ever *be* that power itself. To think that to describe a power amounts to making that power present to human awareness is to confuse ontology and epistemology.

Verbeek also worried that assigning intrinsic properties to artefacts gives rise to "a kind of realism", according to which such properties would be independent of other subjects and objects (WTD, p. 117). This, however, needlessly conflates two senses of "intrinsic". Essences as theorised by OOO are not intrinsic in the sense of *causa sui* Platonic abstractions that exist in a timeless and unchanging state. The powers of artefacts are produced, maintained, and altered in relations with other entities, just like a person needs to engage with all sorts of things to acquire the capacity to speak a language. Once acquired, powers are only "intrinsic" in the sense that they are irreducible to the sources that engendered them and the events that they help engender.

In sum, an OOO take on artefacts does not suffer from postphenomenology's inconsistencies. It gains in explanatory power by allowing for object-object relations between artefacts and by accounting for the "something" or "existences" that must exist beyond mere relations. We now move to the practical consequences of these metaphysical reflections.

Practical Consequences

Verbeek's theory leads him to two recommendations for the study and design of artefacts (WTD, p. 231).[6] The first is to design artefacts for "transparency" (WTD, p. 226). Their working parts are usually obscured — for example, by the hood of a car or the casing of a television. Verbeek proposes that such parts are instead exposed to users, giving the example of a printer whose parts are all clearly visible, with tags and colours indicating what each element does. Such transparency can help users grasp *how* things work instead of merely noticing *that* they work.

Verbeek also advocates that artefacts are designed to require active interaction (WTD, p. 230). A piano, for example, requires intimate human involvement to produce music, whereas a Walkman does not. Verbeek also gives the example of an ingeniously designed heater that stands in the middle of a room and that requires a series of manipulations to operate, as opposed to regular heaters that are simply tucked away under the windowsill. Such interactive design would increase our engagement with how artefacts mediate our existence.

Given its obvious interest in how the components of artefacts generate their powers, how such powers can be made to manifest, and how such manifestations affect other entities, OOO would not be opposed to such recommendations. It would, however, stress that there are relevant (design) aspects of technology that Verbeek's theory cannot properly account for. I here discuss five.

To start, there are relations of artefacts with beings *other* than humans. As discussed, postphenomenology has to "stand by helplessly" when it comes to these (WTD, p. 165). Yet arguably, the majority of artefacts have most of their relations with non-human entities. Obvious examples are that pistons must be constructed to function properly in relation to other mechanical parts, and solar panels must be designed in ways that maximise their capacity to capture sunlight.

Moreover, many artefacts engage in relations that, in terms of their spatial and temporal scale, are completely unlike those that humans have with, say, speed bumps and key chains. Just think of how the ecological impact of plastic waste, scrapyards, radioactive materials, industrial farms, and heavy industry unfolds over the course of decades or even centuries, as so aptly described by Timothy Morton (2013). Verbeek's human-centred philosophy of technology cannot account for such relations. The solution is obviously not to actively involve at least one human observer at every single point in the gigantic manifold of relations constituted by the combined force of all artefacts, so as to render a full postphenomenological analysis of the world possible (what would that even look like?). Instead, we simply ought to be less self-centred when it comes to our analyses of what technologies do.

Because it is agnostic about the kinds of entities that might feature in the (re)production of a technology's powers and their manifestations, as well as about the spatial or temporal scale at which that happens, OOO is better suited for such analyses. Its conceptual framework can in principle cover every possible relation that an artefact might have, whether it is an elaborate chocolate fountain designed to impress a crowd of aristocrats, or a humble sensor that allows an automated system to regulate the flow of water through a sewer pipe.

Second, a major feature of technology is the *effort* required to keep it running. No artefact naturally "fits" its environment or intended use. Other artefacts (or humans or animals or other things still) are always required to keep it functioning. Verbeek is of course well-aware of this, given his references to Heidegger's tool analysis throughout *What Things Do*. Nevertheless, Verbeek's theory does not adequately incorporate this insight. After all, if artefacts are what they are only in their use (WTD, p. 117), then no friction between an artefact and its usages could ever exist, except if several humans simultaneously lay competing claims to it. In all other cases, artefacts ought to always function seamlessly and effortlessly according to Verbeek's theory. After all, they would not have properties beyond our use-relation with them in which resistance or friction could be grounded.

OOO has the more plausible view here. The essence of an artefact always surpasses its use context, because a power need not manifest in order to exist. Nor does a power need to manifest in *this* or *that* specific way. Hence, there is always friction between an artefact and an environment that tries to get it to do a certain thing. Real effort is required, for example, to make a saxophone manifest sound, let alone make it manifest *this* specific sound rather than *that* one.

This can help deepen Verbeek's notion of how mediation is a matter of co-constitution. It is precisely because the powers and capacities of artefacts are not *a priori* attuned to our needs and capacities that, in order to make an artefact function, we often need to acquire new powers and capacities or change our environment in order for those to arise. As with artefact-artefact relations, this is a highly relevant design question. Designers worry, for example, about how senior citizens will acquire the capacities to operate tablets with touchscreens, how mobile phones might be charged in areas with few to no power sockets, or how social media affects the development of young children.

Third, part of understanding technology concerns the *non-relational features of artefacts*, meaning their private ontological aspect here defined in terms of powers. As Verbeek writes, good design anticipates "the future mediating roles" of products (WTD, p. 234). Yet here, too, Verbeek's conceptual framework cannot easily accommodate this insight. After all, his theory does not accord artefacts any properties beyond their use contexts.

As soon as we ask what a technology might do, however, we are already beyond artefacts conceived as being nothing but their actual relations with human beings in their current use contexts. Our imaginations, calculations, or models are then migrating the current artefact, and not the current relations of an artefact, into a hypothetical scenario. We are then asking how its powers might manifest to make a difference in such a scenario. Moreover, we are also asking how the powers and capacities of other entities might change if that were to occur. Given how OOO holds that each entity has a private essence that, by definition, surpasses its current relational engagements, OOO naturally guides us towards considerations of what things might do.

This is of course a highly relevant aspect of thinking about technology. Many technologies are things that we keep under lock and key, precisely because of what they will do when unleashed onto the world. Firearms, synthetic drugs, and nuclear weapons are obvious examples. We lock them away because they already have slumbering properties that might cause catastrophes, properties that they are currently not manifesting. These properties are not properties of human relations to these artefacts, but rather powers of the artefacts themselves. After all, a nuclear bomb rather than our comportment towards that bomb has the power to cause a nuclear explosion.

The fourth aspect concerns *symbiosis*. In the previous section, I started using this Harmanian concept in a modified sense. There is symbiosis when some entity causes significant change to the powers of a thing. I will now slightly expand this notion and add that symbiosis will often also involve a symbiont, meaning an entity without whom the relevant new or altered powers cannot be properly exercised.

In my view, this is an important notion for any philosophy that seeks to theorise artefacts. When considering how artefacts and (non-)humans co-constitute each other, we should be attentive to when such co-constitution results in relations of dependency. A concept of symbiosis and symbionts can help track such dependency, and distinguishing symbiotic from non-symbiotic mediations can help analyses of technology become more fine-grained.

For example, adding a new ringtone to a mobile phone is not a symbiotic event. Adding the internet to mobile phones, which eventually lead to their evolution into smartphones, definitely was one. In turn, the introduction of smartphones into many aspects of our lives has been a symbiotic event for countless people (the smartphone being the symbiont). The effects that smartphones and social media have had on dating, friendship, news dissemination, and political campaigning makes this abundantly clear. Other examples of symbiotic relations to technology range from macrophenomena, such as the history of how we came to depend on modern agriculture, to microphenomena, such as a single drug addict who cannot function without regularly taking synthetic drugs. There can be no doubt that the (potential) symbiotic effects of technologies are a crucial aspect of artefact design. The history of digital artefacts such as Facebook, Twitter, and Google clearly demonstrates this, as many now wish that these technologies would have been designed and implemented based on better information about how invasive they could be.

Note that attention to symbiosis also reintroduces a hint of what Verbeek rejected in the "transcendentalism" of Heidegger and others, only now it is not technology as a single force that can loom large over entire epochs and civilizations, but individual technologies instead. From modern agriculture to digital platforms, there are plenty of examples of technologies that succeed in becoming a nexus that countless humans and things need to attune themselves to in order to exercise their own capacities.

The fifth and final aspect is that Verbeek cannot account for *the perspective of artefacts themselves*. From a powers ontology, it follows that every entity can only ever encounter others in terms of the powers that it has. A human being, for example, can only experience reality insofar as they have the capacity to hear, see, think, smell, and so on. Given that all entities are defined by their powers, the same is true for artefacts. Just as Jakob von Uexküll's ethology imagines the life worlds of bees and ticks based on their specific capacities to register their surroundings, so too must we uncover the worlds of artefacts. Note that we already do this in some cases — for example, when programmers model how self-driving cars register the world.

This leads to what Bryant, following Ian Bogost, calls "alien phenomenology" (Bogost, 2012; Bryant, 2014). Every entity has its own perspective, even if most entities are not consciously aware of having it. This helps account for why artefacts, ranging from relatively compact ones like computers and printers to relatively dispersed ones like institutions or digital networks, often strike us as uncomfortably alien. The reason is that artefacts do not register the world on our terms.

Bryant gives the striking example of dealing with an insurance company (2014, p. 58). Submitting forms to an insurance company to get a medical procedure covered is often a frustrating experience. Part of the reason is that such a company is utterly incapable of discerning people, personalities, thoughts, and moods. What the company is capable of registering are *forms* and the data found on them, hence the frustration. Our intentions are clear to ourselves, but the thing that we are dealing with cannot recognise them and demands a mediator to translate our demands into a form that it can register. In the case of tax services, insurance companies, and other bureaucracies, forms are needed as mediators between us and them, precisely because a bureaucracy is literally blind to human beings (ibid.). Something similar is true for all other artefacts as well, as anyone who has ever shouted at a computer or printer can attest to.

Ethology or alien phenomenology is necessary to emphasise that our relations with artefacts are not reciprocal. How we register the thing is not how it registers us. This is highly relevant to the analysis of technology. Just think of the vast difference between how people experience social media and how those technologies register their users. People experience social media as a place to exchange photos and anecdotes with friends and strangers. The technologies themselves, however, register a completely different and even alien world of clicks, seconds lingered, the intensity of traffic between bits of content, pathways between websites, and so on. A theory that stresses how artefacts themselves register their world can foster a less naive and more realistic view of the technologies with which we populate the world.

Alien phenomenology would also facilitate moving the analysis of technology beyond the medium-sized material artefacts that Verbeek prefers. Many technologies are not as easily grasped in terms of their "materiality" as speed bumps and furniture. What is the materiality of a social media platform? Certainly not my smartphone. But through alien phenomenology, OOO opens doors to analyse even relatively disembodied artefacts and technologies.

Do note that ethology or alien phenomenology does not come down to writing arbitrary science-fiction pulp, as an ungenerous critic might object. Von Uëxkull was certainly using his imagination when modelling the life world of animals, but he was doing so based on the best information available to him. The same must be true for all alien phenomenologists. To determine how a new technology might register its surroundings; to gain understanding of what kinds of encounters will make it manifest its capacities; to envision how it might alter its environments in future scenarios; to keep track of the things it might cause as an irreducible force unleashed on the world; and to combine all of that information into models and narratives that are of use to designers and users alike: this is no easy feat. Generating a solid and useful ethological description requires as much patience, knowledge, and skill as any other aspect of the design process. The results of such speculative labour much like well-written fiction, can sometimes have the same or even more cognitive value than a scientific or philosophical theory.

Conclusion

If we really want to go to the artefacts themselves, we should accept that artefacts have private properties that make them ontologically irreducible to their use contexts. These properties can be understood in terms of powers. Much like humans, artefacts can only register their surroundings in terms of the powers that they have, even if they are not reflexively aware of this registering.

This OOO perspective does not suffer from the inconsistencies of Verbeek's postphenomenology. It can accommodate the full scope of phenomena that Verbeek seeks to capture with his concept of mutual co-constitution, including the richness of intentional experience that he fears is undervalued in ANT. After all, nothing in OOO speaks against human beings having the power or capacity to relate to how they experience the world.

In addition, we saw how OOO is the more promising theory if we want a philosophy of technology that can take into account (1) the relations between artefacts and non-human entities; (2) the friction between artefacts and their functioning or use; (3) the properties that technologies currently do not manifest but might manifest in a different setting; (4) the difference between two kinds of mediation: superficial engagements and symbiotic alterations; and (5) the ways in which artefacts register their own surroundings.

References

Bogost, Ian. *Alien Phenomenology, or What It's Like to Be a Thing.* Minneapolis: University of Minnesota Press, 2012.

Brassier, Ray. "Concepts and Objects". In *The Speculative Turn: Continental Materialism and Realism*, edited by Levi Bryant et al., pp. 47–65. Melbourne: re.press, 2011.

Bryant, Levi. *Onto-cartography: An Ontology of Machines and Media.* Edinburgh: Edinburgh University Press, 2014.

DeLanda, Manuel. *A New Philosophy of Society: Assemblage Theory and Social Complexity.* London: Bloomsbury, 2013.

DeLanda, Manuel & Graham Harman. *The Rise of Realism.* Cambridge: Polity Press, 2017.

Harman, Graham. *Object-Oriented Ontology: A New Theory of Everything.* London: Pelican Books, 2018.

Harman, Graham. *Immaterialism: Objects and Social Theory.* Cambridge: Polity Press, 2016.

Harman, Graham. *The Quadruple Object.* Winchester: Zer0 Books, 2011.

Heidegger, Martin. "The Question Concerning Technology". In Martin Heidegger, *The Question Concerning Technology and Other Essays,* translated by William Lovitt. New York: Harper & Row, 1977.

Ihde, Don. *Postphenomenology and Technoscience: The Peking University Lectures.* Albany; New York: SUNY Press, 2009.

Ihde, Don. *Postphenomenology: Essays in the Postmodern Context.* Evanston; Illinois: Northwestern University Press, 1995.

Kleinherenbrink, Arjen. "Metaphysical Primitives: Machines and Assemblages in Deleuze, DeLanda, & Bryant". *Open Philosophy* 3 (1) (2020), pp. 283–297.

Kleinherenbrink, Arjen. "The Two Times of Objects: A Solution to the Problem of Time in Object-Oriented Ontology". *Open Philosophy* 2 (1) (2019), pp. 539–551.

Kleinherenbrink, Arjen. *Alles is een machine.* Amsterdam: Boom, 2017.

Latour, Bruno. *Reassembling the Social: An Introduction to Actor-Network-Theory.* Oxford: Oxford University Press, 2005.

Latour, Bruno. *Pandora's Hope: Essays on the Reality of Science Studies.* Cambridge; Massachusetts: Harvard University Press, 1999.

Latour, Bruno. "On actor-network theory: a few clarifications". *Soziale Welt* 47 (4) (1996), pp. 369–381.

Latour, Bruno. *We Have Never Been Modern*, translated by Catherine Porter. Cambridge; Massachusetts: Harvard University Press, 1993.

Meillassoux, Quentin. *After Finitude: An Essay on the Necessity of Contingency.* New York: Continuum, 2011.

Morton, Timothy. *Hyperobjects: Philosophy and Ecology after the End of the World.* Minneapolis: University of Minnesota Press, 2013.

Ortega y Gasset, José. "Thoughts on Technology". In *Philosophy and Technology*, edited by Carl Mitcham & Robert Mackey, pp. 290–313. New York: Free Press, 1972.

Rosenberger, Robert & Peter-Paul Verbeek (eds). *Postphenomenological Investigations: Essays on Human-Technology Relations.* Lanham; Maryland: Lexington Books, 2015.

Verbeek, Peter-Paul. "Let's Make Things Better: A Reply to My Readers". *Human Studies* 32 (2009), pp. 251–261.

Verbeek, Peter-Paul. *What Things Do: Philosophical Reflections on Technology, Agency, and Design*, translated by Robert Crease. University Park; Pennsylvania: Pennsylvania State University Press, 2005.

Notes

1 This chapter is an expanded and reworked version of a paper presented at the "Objects, Technology, Existence: Engaging with Graham Harman's OOO" conference at the Free University of Brussels on 24 February 2021.

2 Verbeek is not the only postphenomenologist. The American philosopher Don Ihde is the founding father of postphenomenology (1995, 2009). For other scholars in the field, see the contributions to Rosenberger & Verbeek (2015).

3 Verbeek notes that Latour himself has little sympathy for phenomenology, but thinks Latour's worries are overstated (WTD, p. 163; Latour, 1993, pp. 57–8). Since postphenomenology abandons the notion of preformed objects and subjects, and holds that objects (including artefacts) and subjects are mutually co-constituted in networks of relations with artefacts, Verbeek thinks to have parried Latour's potential objections to splicing ANT with phenomenology. I think that Latour would still have serious reservations for reasons beyond the scope of this chapter, but we will let Verbeek have the benefit of the doubt here.

4 Verbeek is not entirely clear about which exact theories he considers to be "classical phenomenology".

5 This leads to interesting questions about powers and mereology (is it the axe or just its blade that has the power to cleave?), but those are beyond the scope of this chapter.

6 Verbeek once also mentions a third one, designing artefacts to show traces of their history of usage, in passing (WTD, p. 232).

MATHEMATICAL EXTRACTION: SET THEORY AND CATEGORY THEORY AS THE FORMS OF DUOMINING

Michael J. Ardoline

This paper argues that a realist but non-correlationist understanding of mathematical descriptions follows from central commitments of Object-Oriented Ontology. A realist, non-correlationist account of mathematics, I claim, requires showing three positions to be consistent and to be the case: (1) accurate or predictive mathematical descriptions count as knowledge; (2) there are limits of what can be known through mathematics that are inherent to mathematics itself (and so not merely attributable to human finitude); (3) thought and being must not be exhaustively correlated within these limits. I take (1) as uncontroversial. To support (2) and (3), I will look to Harman's account of duomining as knowledge that does not exhaust its object. I will argue that duomining's two moments, undermining and overmining, are structurally isomorphic with two major foundations of mathematical description, set theory and category theory, respectively.[1] Given Harman's account of duomining, this entails that mathematical models do in fact give us knowledge of objects, but this, like all knowledge, is not an exhaustive description of the object modelled. Thereby, mathematical description can count as knowledge, but does not act as an exhaustive correlation between thought and being. While not exhaustive, I will go so far as to claim that this isomorphism establishes mathematical description as a privileged form of knowledge within OOO, tempered only by the caveat that OOO privileges wisdom above knowledge.

Let us begin with an important debate between Harman and Meillassoux.[2] Meillassoux takes there to be a formal equivalence between mathematical knowledge of a thing and the thing itself. In other words, there is a common or identical form shared between a thing and a successful mathematical description of that thing. Meillassoux allies this position with Descartes and against Pythagoras. The Pythagorean claims reality is inherently mathematical; Meillassoux, in Cartesian fashion, instead claims that reality is material, but mathematics allows thought to extract an exact description of all essential properties from material reality (Meillassoux, 2008, p. 12). From the point of view of knowledge, reality can be split into form and "dead matter".

In response to this, Harman argues that the mathematical model differs from the thing modelled in important ways. For example, the thermodynamic equations that model the burning of a piece of paper will not themselves be hot, nor will they burn. The form/dead matter dichotomy is thus rejected by Harman for several reasons; one of which is that Harman rejects the idea of matter *tout court* (see Harman, 2010 and 2016), but I will not treat this here. More fruitful for our investigation is Harman's response that knowledge is always an undermining or an overmining of an object or objects. This is explicated in detail below, but the response begins with the realist commitment that to extract something always involves a change, whether we are extracting ore from the earth or mathematical forms from physical systems.

In entering this debate, I am arguing in a way that cuts off a move made by Meillassoux in "Iteration, Reiteration, and Repetition". Here, Meillassoux argues that mathematics should be understood as operating by way of "empty signs", that is, signs without any meaning or significance. This lack of significance of the mathematical sign assures the "singular ontological import of mathematical formalism as such". I will not critique Meillassoux's account of the nature of mathematics as following from a power of the mind to think through empty signs. Instead, I aim to show that mathematics does not have "singular ontological import".[3] By this claim, I take Meillassoux to mean that mathematical truths uniquely tell us about the structure of the world. I will argue that, by the structure of set theory and category theory, there are ontological claims that these mathematical formalisms cannot formulate, yet we have independent reasons for accepting these claims. If this is the case, then mathematics may remain a privileged form of knowledge, but would not have singular ontological import because other sources of knowledge provide extra-mathematical information. Since this extra-mathematical information is ontological, it would be applicable to all possible objects. This entails that translation into a purely mathematical description would always abstract away from something knowable about the object(s) described.

Duomining and Knowledge

Let us summarise Harman's account of duomining in order to later point to what mathematical translation abstracts away. This gap between knowledge, description, or, more generally, access to an object and the object itself is the fundamental commitment of Object-Oriented Ontology. For OOO, the term "object" "is used in a specific and technical sense to refer to anything that is ontologically irreducible, namely anything which cannot be reduced downward (or, in Harman's terms, 'undermined') into its constituent pieces, upward into its relations and effects on other entities ('overmining'), or both of these simultaneously ('duomining')" (Young, 2021). The *sine qua non* of an object is that it is something in excess of both its parts and its relations to other things. This excess is said to be that aspect of an object that "withdraws" (Harman, 2002). Put simply, withdrawal means "that any given object has its own interiority independently of its relations to other entities or its engagement with them in various contexts" (Young, 2021, p. 85). In one sense, the terms undermining, overmining, and duomining are used critically, though they also describe useful aspects of how objects relate. Critically, undermining refers to any attempt to understand or reduce an object to a mere aggregate or product of its parts. To undermine an object is to seek an explanation "deeper" than what is the case. Similarly, in its critical sense, overmining an object means reducing it to its relations, thereby treating the object as an empty node within a system of relations without real *relata*. In either case — or in the case of duomining, where both reductions are employed simultaneously — the mistake is that objects are not explained but rather explained *away*.

These criticisms do not reject wholesale the explaining of objects partially in terms of their parts and relations. In fact, these sorts of explanations are all that are available to us as sources of knowledge. As Harman puts it: "There are only two basic kinds of knowledge about things: we can explain what they are made of or explain what they do. The inevitable price of such knowledge is that we substitute a loose paraphrase for the thing itself" (Harman, 2016, p. 7). The access that constitutes knowledge is merely one type of relation between objects among others; the object equally withdraws from epistemic relations. There is, then, always something more to the object than can be known. Conversely, if something can be known exhaustively, or translated[4] without loss, then it is not an object in Harman's sense. We only fall into error if we confuse the explanation for the object itself, or if we forget that our "paraphrase" of an object is partially a result of our limited access to the object. More so than the question of matter, this difference between the view of knowledge as extracting an accurate and exhaustive form of a thing and as a loose paraphrase of the thing is the difference between Meillassoux and Harman. The question, then, is how are we to understand mathematical knowledge as a "loose paraphrase" while still maintaining its unique form of truth and its predictive power?

I intend to show below that set theory and category theory are structurally isomorphic with undermining and overmining, respectively. They are not simply two paraphrases of things, but rather the form of the two different ways of paraphrasing. If all knowledge is undermining, overmining, or both, and these foundations of mathematics are the forms of undermining and overmining themselves, then mathematical description is still a — perhaps *the* — privileged form of knowledge. Yet there will be, inherent to mathematisation itself, an excess not captured by such knowledge. The point here is that there is always a gap between knowledge of things and things themselves. This gap is not itself expressed by these mathematical formalisms. Therefore, if we have reasons to believe in such a gap — I am with Harman that we do — then, contra Meillassoux, there exist non-mathematical ontological truths. In other words, the privileged status of mathematised knowledge does not amount to a monopoly on ontological import.

Objects, on Harman's account, have a fourfold structure (Harman, 2011), but we will only be concerned with what he calls the Real Object, or more importantly, the fact that every object is something in excess of its relations. Not wanting to beg the question by abusing the word "real", I will refer to these simply as objects. It is also common to use the term "mathematical object" to refer to things like sets, categories, and so on. This raises the unfortunate possibility of equivocation because, as we will see below, sets and categories do not raise to the level of a Real Object (i.e., they do not withdraw from their relations).[5] When I use "mathematical object", I do not mean to import Harman's fourfold structure or an excess that withdraws from relations to sets, categories, numbers, and other mathematical objects.[6] The same is true for "formal object".

Mathematics and Knowledge

As said above, referring to set theory and category theory as forms of undermining and overmining respectively is not a criticism of the mathematics in any sense. Rather, let us take two relatively uncontroversial views on the nature of mathematics: (1) mathematical truths are necessary (and so hold in all possible cases); and (2) mathematical truths tell us about the structural constraints of relations between things (i.e., there will be non-mathematical relations, but they will not violate constraints described by pure mathematics). Then, we add (3) the OOO view of knowledge as a relation a certain epistemically capable object (e.g., a human) has to another object of any sort. We should then expect mathematics to express (1) necessary (2) constraints on that (2&3) knowledge relation. Following this, my argument is that analysing the formal structure of set theory and category theory shows that they place exactly the kinds of constraints on knowledge-relations as Harman's account of duomining claims. In doing so, they are structurally isomorphic with its two moments of duomining. The argument will proceed by looking at the ways in which set theory and category theory described their mathematical objects and what it means for mathematical objects to be shown to be identical in each formalism. It will be shown that these forms of mathematical identity are not equivalent to the ontological identity of the real object, and so there exist extra-mathematical statements with ontological import.

Set theory is the most well-known branch of mathematics among philosophers. It is a foundational theory in that it provides a unifying language within which to build and ground the other branches of mathematics. While there are different axiomatisations of set theory and continued controversy over whether to accept certain axioms, such as the Axiom of Choice, we here need only look to a non-controversial axiom common to all versions of set theory: the Axiom of Extensionality. Formally, the AoE is:

$$\forall A\, \forall B\, (\forall X\, (X \in A \leftrightarrow X \in B) \rightarrow A = B)$$

Informally, AoE states that any two sets have all and only the same members only if they are the same set. This asserts fundamental truths about the nature of sets. First, it establishes membership ("A ∈ B" is read "set A is a member of set B") as the fundamental relation between sets. That is, sets are defined by what they contain, and only by what they contain. This is established by the equality above; if two sets have all and only the same members, they are by definition the same set. If their membership differs, then they are two different sets. A set *qua* mathematical object is nothing more than the fact of a collection of what makes it up. We should not go so far as to say that a set is its parts, because it is one thing to be the null set and another to be that which contains only the null set (i.e., the numbers 0 and 1, respectively). A set, then, expresses something of its parts over and above them (the fact that they are collected together), but that excess over its parts has no character of its own outside its relations to other sets.

What, then, is it to translate something into set theoretical terms? Simply, it is to rigorously describe something in terms of its parts, or most precisely, formal surrogates for its parts. For a mathematical example, a geometric space is translated into a set of points. These points are ordered n-tuples where n is the number of dimensions the space has. Any shape within that space is then modelled as a function over various points. Such a function is itself a set made up of the ordered n-tuples. In other words, while we may normally think of spatial relations as continuous, when modelled set-theoretically, such relations are not expressed as relations but as collections of relata. There are enough relata to approximate any needed continuity, but "relation" is merely a euphemism for set membership. A set, then, is the exemplar of an undermined entity.

Set theory works by abstracting away what a thing may be over and above its parts beyond the mere fact of being a collection of those parts. Insofar as objects are emergent from their parts, not mere collections of those parts, a set-theoretical rendering will miss this dimension of the object. To describe something set-theoretically is to describe a thing in terms of what it contains, in terms of its parts, because all relations are actually relations of set membership, and a set is nothing more than the collection of its members. However, there is always more to a real object than this. A bag containing all the separated component parts of a human being is not itself a human being, despite containing the same parts, having some excess over those parts, and the fact that inspecting its contents would provide us some knowledge about human beings. Similarly, a real object is robust to the change of some of its parts; the loss or growth of a single skin cell does not change the body. Insofar as there is more to the excess of an object over its parts than the mere fact of this excess, it is the specific character of the excess that set theoretical translations lose in their paraphrase. Undermining, then, as the rendering of the object in terms of its parts, is structurally isomorphic with set-theoretical translation.

It is worth noting that, excepting the proof-theoretical tradition, formal logic makes use of set-theoretical resources to provide a formal surrogate of meaning for propositions. By doing so, a concept or a universal is reduced to a set containing those terms (names that stand in for the objects) of which the concept can be truly said. There are then two levels of translation that are obscured: the translation of objects and concepts into set-theoretical surrogates, and the translation of sets into propositions. Taking these as wholly accurate renderings rather than paraphrases produces a sort of transcendental illusion, which truthmaker theorists critique as the mistaken assumption of an isomorphism between logic and ontology.[7] The implicit acceptance of this isomorphism is perhaps the most prominent form of correlationism in the analytic tradition. Such a position is supported by many thinkers who would otherwise call themselves realists and laugh off continental anti-realisms and idealisms as unserious or confused. Yet, if one takes logic and ontology to have the same structure, one has posited the *a priori* correlation of thought and being insofar as logic is the structure of rational thought and ontology the structure of being. In practice, this means assuming the world comes pre-packaged as intelligible, or making inferences from logical structure to ontological structure without warrant. Like we said of mathematics above, this is not to reject logic's usefulness, even in the realm of metaphysics. It is merely to assert that world and thought do not come pre-correlated in some privileged, rationally accessible way. If we are going to infer from a logical result to the structure of the world, we must have an independent, non-correlational, metaphysical account of how and why such an inference is warranted, and what the limits to that warrant are.

Category Theory and Overmining

Whereas set theory is immediately familiar to many philosophers, category theory has received much less attention. There are a few excellent engagements — such as the collection *Categories for the Working Philosophy*, Landry's semantic account of Categories as the language of mathematics (Landry 1999, 2006); Badiou's *Logic of* Worlds; Zalamea's *Synthetic Philosophy of Contemporary Mathematics*; and Gangle's *Diagrammatical Immanence* — but so far, these are the exception. This is despite the rise of category theory being perhaps the major mathematical event of the latter half of the twentieth century. While set theory focuses on the construction of mathematical entities in terms of their parts, category theory takes a more holistic approach. Its fundamental components are points and arrows. The points stand in for mathematical objects, and arrows are mappings from one mathematical object to another. A category is a collection of points and arrows that describes a mathematical structure. For example, **Set** is the category that contains points that stand in for sets and arrows that preserve the relationships of set membership between sets.[8] Arrows may also map other arrows: collections of points and arrows can be "condensed" into points and mapped by a single arrow, or whole structures may be mapped by "bundles" of arrows. For example, say you wanted to describe a geometrical shape as a 3 × 3 collection of points. Category-theoretically, this can be done by taking a single point with nine arrows, each one mapping from the same point to a different point on the 3 × 3 grid. It can be shown that the space itself is mathematically equivalent to the map from a point into the space.

This machinery makes category theory particularly adept at translating or mapping from one branch of mathematics to another. The classical example of mapping that most people will be familiar with is how a Cartesian coordinate system allows for translating a geometric shape into an algebraic equation or vice versa (this of course predates category theory by a few centuries, but category theory provides a language for describing the movement from geometry to algebra and back). Because category theory can describe **Set**, and most of the rest of mathematics can be described in terms of sets, this makes category theory an alternative foundation of mathematics (though there are other reasons for this, and there are some things category theory can do that set theory cannot).

In category theory, identity is limited to identity up to isomorphism. Category theory has powerful and interesting ways to take about lesser degrees of identity, with isomorphism being the highest (hence the phrase "up to"). We will, however, only need this highest degree to make our argument here. Two mathematical objects are identical up to isomorphism if there exists a one-to-one mapping between their points and arrows. This can easily be thought of as a proof that two mathematical objects have the same structure. There is a joke that if a Catholic category theorist is asked whether they believe the Nicene Creed that "one God, the father almighty, maker of heaven and earth, of all things visible and invisible…", they could only respond "yes, up to isomorphism!"

The similarity between category theory and overmining is more obvious than between set theory and undermining. In only being able to assert identity up to isomorphism, category theory cannot say whether we are really talking about one or more objects. This is not even the classic distinction between the map and the territory; rather, it is the point that you and I might both have identical maps of the same city, and we can distinguish that there are, indeed, two maps. Yet, identity up to isomorphism can tell us that the maps both connect all the same streets to the same landmarks in the same way (i.e., the maps are structurally isomorphic), and so declare them identical, but this does not track the number of maps we are discussing. However, claims about the number of maps we have clearly have ontological import. Furthermore, a mathematical object is modelled by way of its relations to other mathematical objects. A point does not encode anything about the mathematical object itself; it only makes possible its description in terms of its relations. This is a straightforward isomorphism with overmining. In overmining and category theory, individual objects are only ever understood in terms of their role as nodes within a larger structure. The object's depth is hidden in order to highlight its relations to the extent that either relata are not characterised at all, or to the extent that we cannot even distinguish the number of objects we are talking about.

One might respond: "But surely set theory lets us easily talk about the number of objects, and the holism of category theory allows us to characterise the excess of the object over its parts that set theory could not? If we do not restrict ourselves to one branch at a time but take all the tools of mathematics together, is non-paraphrastic description then possible?" This amounts to asking whether mathematics as a whole can do what Meillassoux says it can, or if there is some ontological remainder that mathematics as a whole could only ever fruitfully duomine but not exhaust. The response here is straightforward: no amount of undermining and overmining together can ever present the object in itself. Set theory has only the resources to render things in terms of what they contain, and category theory in terms of to what they are related. Alternating between these two approaches will generate ever deeper understanding, but if an object is precisely its excess over its parts and external relations, it will not be exhausted by these procedures. Therefore, if we have independent reasons for accepting this account of objects, then we have at least one statement with ontological import that mathematics cannot give us. Mathematics, then, does not have Meillassoux's singular ontological import.

Here we can show why this raises a more general problem for Meillassoux. Both Harman and Meillassoux are thinkers of emergence, though in different ways. For Harman, emergence is a relatively common result of the interaction of objects. While it cannot be known in advance, emergence is still predictable enough that we can regularly expect it to take place in complex interactions. For Meillassoux, on the other hand, emergence is radically unpredictable based on the impossibility of totalising possibility itself (Meillassoux, 2010, pp. 103–5). Emergence is thinkable, but unexplainable on this account. We can show that this account of emergence is not mathematically assertable, and so Meillassoux himself is committed to a non-mathematisable statement with ontological import. While the claim about the untotalisability of the possible is mathematisable, the claim that this therefore licenses emergence is not.[9] What emerges cannot simply be a collection of already existing parts or a result of new relations of already existing things, or (for Meillassoux) even of thinkable parts and thinkable relations. Yet, these are the only things available to mathematical description. That is, the excess of the object over its parts and relations is precisely what emerges, and what cannot be thought by mathematics. Thereby, Meillassoux cannot maintain both the emergence of the new and the mathematisability of all knowledge.

Conclusion

Let us return to our criteria for a realist but non-correlationist philosophy of mathematics: (1) mathematical descriptions count as knowledge; (2) there are limits of what can be known through mathematics that are inherent to mathematics itself; (3) thought and being must not be exhaustively correlated within these limits. We have supported (2) and (3), and given a more rigorous understanding for (1).

With regard to (1), mathematical description is a privileged form of knowledge because its expressive powers are isomorphic with the procedures for generating knowledge in the first place: undermining and overmining. If rigorous and reliable mathematical models of a phenomenon of interest exist, then philosophers ought to acquaint themselves with those models before offering their wisdom on the topic. This is because such a description expresses something true about the relations between that thing, its parts, and other things. That said, this account shows the formal limits to knowledge, that every encounter with any object demands of us a certain degree of wisdom, and that there is more than truth when it comes to understanding the worlds of things around us.

As for (2) and (3), we have shown that set theory and category theory, as paradigm foundations of mathematics, are unable to express the excess of the object from its parts and external relations. This means that there is a limit to the ontological truths they can express. That mathematical description is a form of translation, and so is not done *a priori* and thus cannot express all possible ontological truths, means mathematical truth does not imply a necessary correlation between thought and being. This amounts to the claim that the world is neither inherently mathematical (or logical) nor exhaustively mathematisable, but that the ability to translate large swaths of the world into mathematical descriptions constitutes our best ways of knowing the world. There is no way to undertake this translation completely — *a priori* (e.g., mathematics is an *a priori* science; mathematical physics is not), nor to guarantee the universal generalisation of any particular translation. This is not to reject projects like the search for a Grand Unified Theory, it is only to reinforce what the working physicist already knows: it will be hard work to get there and success is not guaranteed. It is a simple point we should not lose sight of in our world where we have an embarrassment of mathematised riches: no amount of knowledge will annul the need for wisdom.

References

Ardoline, Michael J. "What Laws? Which Past?: Meillassoux's Hyper-Chaos and the Epistemological Limitations of Retro-Causation". *Open Philosophy, 1* (1) (2018), pp. 235–44.

Badiou, Alain. *Logics of Worlds*, translated by Alberto Toscano. London; New York: Continuum, 2008.

Cogburn, Jon & J. Heller. "Meillassoux's Dilemma". In *New Perspectives on Realism*, edited by Luca Taddio & Kevin William Molin. Mimesis Press, 2017.

Gangle, Rocco. *Diagrammatic Immanence: Category Theory and Philosophy.* Edinburgh: Edinburgh University Press, 2015.

Harman, Graham. *Tool-Being: Heidegger and the Metaphysics of Objects.* Chicago: Open Court, 2002.

Harman, Graham. "I Am Also of the Opinion That Materialism Must Be Destroyed". *Environment and Planning D: Society and Space, 28* (5) (2010), pp. 772–90.

Harman, Graham. *The Quadruple Object.* Winchester: Zer0 Books, 2011.

Harman, Graham. *Immaterialism: Objects and Social Theory.* Malden, MA: Polity, 2016.

Landry, Elaine. "Category theory: The language of mathematics". *Philosophy of Science, 66* (3) (1999), p. 27.

Landry, Elaine. "Category theory as a framework for an in re interpretation of mathematical structuralism". In *The Age of Alternative Logics*, edited by Johan van Benthem, Gerhard Heinzman, M. Rebushi, & H. Visser, pp. 163–179. Springer, 2006.

Landry, Elaine (ed). *Categories for the Working Philosopher.* Illustrated edition. Oxford, United Kingdom: Oxford University Press, 2018.

Meillassoux, Quentin. *After Finitude: An Essay on the Necessity of Contingency*, translated by Ray Brassier. London; New York: Continuum, 2010.

Meillassoux, Quentin. "Iteration, Reiteration, Repetition: A Speculative Materialist Analysis of the Sign Devoid of Meaning". In *Genealogies of Speculation: Materialism and Subjectivity since Structuralism*, edited by Armen Avanessian & Malik Suhail. London: Bloomsbury, 2016.

Morris, Michael. "Realism Beyond Correspondence". In *Truthmakers: The Contemporary Debate*, edited by Helen Beebee & Julian Dodd. London: Clarendon Press, 2005.

Young, Niki. "On Correlationism and the Philosophy of (Human) Access: Meillassoux and Harman". *Open Philosophy, 3* (1) (2020), pp. 42–52.

Young, Niki. "Object, Reduction, and Emergence: An Object-Oriented View". *Open Philosophy, 4* (1) (2021), pp. 83–93.

Zalamea, Fernando. *Synthetic Philosophy of Contemporary Mathematics*, translated by Z.L. Fraser. Illustrated edition. Falmouth, U.K.; New York: Urbanomic, 2012.

Notes

1 Treating the current rising star of mathematical foundations, Homotypic Type Theory, or HoTT, will be the topic of a future paper.

2 I will only focus on the issue of mathematisation. For a more general exploration of the contrast between Harman and Meillassoux on knowledge and access, see Young, 2020.

3 Modus Tollens — this will give reason to doubt Meillassoux's account of the empty sign, but I will not explore that here.

4 I take it we should read terms like "paraphrase" and "translation" as somewhat metaphorical in that they should not imply any inherent linguistic nature to objects.

5 This is not to say that nothing mathematical could count as a Real Object. Set theory, group theory, and other branches of mathematics, I would argue, are in fact Real Objects, but these are not usually called "mathematical objects".

6 I take it that mathematical formalisms and theories are objects in Harman's sense, in that set theory, for example, is never present in full to the set theorist, but that mathematical objects are more like placeholders in the structure of formalisms and theories. The argument here will not hinge on this claim.

7 For an example of the truth-maker critique, see Morris, 2005.

8 Because of the difference between a set and a category, the category of Sets does not raise the sorts of paradoxes that the set of all sets does.

9 In fact, it is directly related to a paradox in modal logic known as Kaplan's paradox. For more, see Cogburn and Heller, 2017; and Ardoline, 2018.

CHAPTER 2
SPECULATIVE NATURE

TRANSCENDENTAL MATERIALISM AND SCHELLING'S DYNAMICAL POWERS OF BECOMING: ON THE *NATURPHILOSOPHIE* OF IAIN HAMILTON GRANT

Leon Niemoczynski

1. Introduction: A Speculative, Realist, and Ordinal Phenomenological Account of Nature

Speculative philosophy in the early twenty-first century, if anything, has had its strongest hand of cards in unifying the ordinal metaphysical approach to a phenomenological account of nature.[1] This is to say that the ontological *realism* of ordinal metaphysics engages a type of ontological parity that, whilst allowing for specifically non-human (i.e., non-anthropocentric) qualitative immediacies or forms of consciousness to subsist as possible analytical points of departure, nevertheless refrains from succumbing to a "subjectalism" that dualistically posits a consciousnesses existing separately and "apart" from the natural world. Instead, being fully natural and as equally real as anything else, such forms of consciousness are part and parcel of the natural world and are indeed contiguous with it.[2] Of course, I borrow from one Quentin Meillassoux the term "subjectalism" to indicate the ontology of an idealism that is simply unable to maintain purchase upon the real being always and already indelibly correlated to an ontological *perspective.* Once taken, this correlationist coupling of world and consciousness becomes the cage within which one is locked and unable to escape. This is not to say that idealisms of the realist variety do not figure into an account of the natural world in any productive manner whatsoever. They can, and often do. Again taking cue from Meillassoux: "The most underrated thinkers in the history of philosophy are Reinhold, Jacobi, Maimon: the German thinkers who formed the junction between Kant and Fichte. With these philosophers, we draw close to the edge of what would soon become the volcano of German idealism. It is a volcano that would not have been able to erupt without them, even though Schelling and Hegel esteemed them lightly."[3]

It is this latter point that the *Naturphilosophie* of Iain Hamilton Grant develops in an effort to account for a certain form of transcendency within the natural world — a sort of transcendency that is not "beyond" the world or which is indeed somehow supernatural and "apart" from the world — but which is responsible *for* the world being, ultimately, part and parcel of it as its own immanent yet transcendental ground of *generation* and *production* (in a way that is possible to gain access, *phenomenologically*, without subjectalist trappings.) Further, and perhaps even more interesting, one discovers that this transcendency may be given through the qualitative immediacy of conscious intuition — albeit in the form of categorical analysis, logico-mathematical deduction, or onto-cosmological abduction. Thus Grant's "transcendental materialism" is a direct attempt to move past the sort of Kantian finitude that Husserl bolstered when he relegated the real to mere first-person conscious representation by embarking upon a new post-Kantian *Schellingean* understanding of nature, matter, and consciousness. Here Grant picks up German idealism's retrieval of an ancient Platonic conception of matter and consciousness to construe a relationship between the two in a way that understands nature as being both immanent and transcendent, ideal and real, and finite and infinite. While I have elsewhere discussed at length how philosophers such as C.S. Peirce, Alfred North Whitehead, or Gilles Deleuze offer radically different *Naturphilosophies* that are conducive to a realist phenomenological account of nature other than the sort of (Kantian) transcendental phenomenology that one finds in Husserl, I have not as of yet explored how Iain Hamilton Grant's own *Naturphilosophie* develops this same sort of ordinal phenomenological account of nature, which mediates ontological dipolarities traditionally thought to be at odds with each other.[4] In short, it is Schelling's dynamical powers of becoming, which Schelling himself interprets in light of Plato's *Timaeus*, that serves as the lynchpin of Grant's own transcendental materialism and *Naturphilosophie.*[5] It is the purpose of this essay, therefore, to briefly explain Grant's transcendental materialism and how it is indebted precisely to both Schelling and Plato.

As regards speculative philosophy's retrieval of a realist, materialist metaphysics that is capable *also* of accounting for conscious experience and the many dualities that often problematise the inclusion of conscious experience within the natural world — whether these dualities point toward ideality in the form of non-human intelligence or ontologically to the idealities of mathematical number or Platonic form — *the* pressing question is this: is the phenomenological reduction made by human consciousness (as an act intended for human consciousness) essential to the phenomenological method itself? And moreover, if consciousness is part of the natural world and is indeed contiguous with it — as the German idealists in fact took it to be — then must one must abandon a phenomenological account of nature altogether for fear of a human, subject-centred misconstrual of nature-as-ideal reality? It seems that, in Husserl's tireless attempt to define the phenomenological method throughout the course of his career, such a question could never have been legitimately asked, for its denial is the supposition upon which the whole of the method rests. This seems true if only because, as a method, phenomenology's very identity as a "description-of-appearances-to-consciousness" — the science of the experience of consciousness — begs the epoché's necessity as *a sheer act of the human intellect.* The epoché seems necessary for the sake of scientific objectivity in terms of what is described by consciousness, but not for the sake of what itself is being described. That is to say, Husserl seemed to be pointing toward objective appearances to consciousness, but not to objective realities apart from conscious appearances. As it turns out, ordinal metaphysics, when coupled with phenomenology as *ordinal phenomenology*, is able to account for consciousness in nature in such a way so as to relate it to a more objective and realist categorial determination of nature's ontological modes. In other words, it is through ordinal phenomenological analysis that we are able to see how the categories and modes of consciousness are isomorphic to the categories and modes of an onto-cosmological nature. Both are fully natural; neither is more nor less real than the other.

In terms of the content behind this approach, one may further press the question. For phenomenology, does the range of its method and "objective" correlate (the "what", so to speak, of its analysis) match "all of the way down"? Or, is it possible that whatever content is to be described exceeds the consciousness attempting to describe it? If phenomenology is properly made speculative (that is, mathematised, if we follow C.S. Peirce or Alain Badiou, or turned logically modal or categorical, as in C.S. Peirce, Justus Buchler, Alfred North Whitehead, or Charles Hartshorne), then current-day speculative philosophy's ontologically realist demonstrations are capable of becoming epistemological descriptions should speculative philosophy decide to follow the methodological tenets of the ordinal phenomenological approach. Moreover, if the qualitative aspect of modal-categorical revelation present in the ordinal approach is provided an adequate level of objective demonstration, we then need only ask how does such an approach regard the conditions for consciousness, which utilise it as a method? In other words, how are the categories of cosmos isomorphic to the consciousness that happens to be rendering those categories and employing them? Note that this does not work the other way around (moving from the categories of conscious *experience* or one's conscious *perspective* to cosmos, which was the Kantian-Husserlian transcendental mistake). In the ordinal approach, one moves to transcend beyond conscious "experience" through the categories of objective onto-cosmological determination, where any qualitative dimension presented is in a dimension excised of *relative* perspective being described "purely" in categorical-modal (e.g., "mathematical") terms. (This is why C.S. Peirce saw phenomenology as a branch of applied mathematics.)

Given that a speculative, realist phenomenology is possible if coupled with ordinal metaphysics, we are able to follow the above lines of thinking (that a properly "speculative" realism and phenomenological account of nature means ordinal phenomenology) to a conclusion. It is only possible for conscious appearance of the world and world to cohere by embracing strictly an ordinal metaphysics — that is, the metaphysics of ontological parity and ordinality in modal-categorial terms. The "experiential" component of phenomenological analysis, its "qualitative" dimension, is then able to rely upon self-disclosure of cosmos rather than description by observing consciousness. In other words, cosmos is preserved in its extra-human (inhuman) qualitative elements, despite the elimination of its first-person "present to consciousness" viewpoint. This is to say that the objective reality of sensation, quality, experiential feeling, need not be felt or experienced or "presented to" in order to be real as it is already a part of a reality that is itself independent of the human experiencing or perceiving it. Methodologically, this would not be the knowing-what of experience but rather the exhibition of the *becoming-how* of the real in all of its various dimensions (categorical, modal, qualitative, etc. etc.); it would be a demonstration and then description of reality's possible becoming independent of that becoming's appearance to a conscious being describing it.

2. Iain Hamilton Grant's Transcendental Materialism: Fichte, Plato, and a New Understanding of Matter

In a talk presented at the Memorial University of Newfoundland, Iain Hamilton Grant laid out a very interesting observation concerning how Fichte and Plato might actually be the philosophers we turn to in order to help us to grasp a much-needed revision of how matter functions in the natural world. In short, it is Plato and Fichte who, while pointing toward a self-grounding dynamic generative "ground" within nature that is nature's own self-sustaining transcendental ground, nevertheless articulate a sound conception of what *actualised* dynamic nature looks like — in its transcendental immediacy. Grant states, and I quote him at length to make the point:

> The most profound attempt to articulate linguistic sovereignty over a non-linguistic cosmos is Fichte's. It is profound because in his quest to do so he eliminates a priori any question of a cosmos which is not fundamentally logically constituted, by which I mean constituted from the position of the constitutor — from the Ich that posits. This is not as it were an absolute Ich, this is just an Ich that posits… All that he is ultimately interested in is that constitutive position as subjectivity, but linguistically or logically, in order to articulate whatever cosmos can be articulated at the cost of the elimination or reduction, as far as possible, of the actual cosmos. I thought that this was ingenious actually, and I spent some time working through how Fichte does this….

> Now, that same Fichtean moment, I think you find it in Deleuze. You find it expressly in Deleuze's relationship to Plato. There's an extraordinary series of passages in *Difference and Repetition* where he says the time to overcome Platonism has come, but the question of what Platonism is has elided us save only for a few caveats that Plato is not a Platonist — there were no Platonists after Plato. But the question is what is Deleuze doing with Plato? And we find this out in *Logic of Sense* where he situates Plato as the materialist wise enough to invert the order of the normative with respect to the ontological… So what Deleuze is is a Fichtean. You can back this up, I think, by looking at the reception of German idealism in France. France has been dominated by Fichte, there is a constant influence of Fichte there. So Deleuze is a Fichtean, that is my thesis…
>
> The real reason why I argue this is because in *Difference and Repetition* you'll find Deleuze saying the present inquiry must accommodate all the categories of nature and freedom. But why are there two sets of categories, why the split? Where are there a set of categories for nature and the other for freedom? And in what does Deleuze's materialism consist if he acknowledges this pre-categorical split as it were, between nature and freedom? […] Here you have precisely the recipe for the categories of nature without the need for Fichte at all. [But] Deleuze celebrates the tradition of German idealism for their discussion of the auto-positing concept [of the categories]. So I don't think it's too much of a reach actually to see the dominance of the ontological as being the precursor to the dominance of the ontological over the normative.[6]

Here Grant's Schellingean roots are directly revealed in how Grant retrieves the Platonic-Fichtean moment of transcendence in immanence, further developed in his "The Law of Insuperable Environment: What is Exhibited in the Exhibition of the Process of Nature?" There (and in the comments above) Grant addresses logical constitution as a "nature as container" problem. That is to say, in other words, he wishes to address "nature" as a problem of nominalisation and location through the following question: how does one refer to nature if nature is no-thing in particular yet nothing is non-natural? Even if nature is not any "thing", then nor could nature be a process nor multiple individuated processes, let alone an "object" constituted by a positing subject or Ich. Grant's solution to the nominalisation of nature is to say that, categorially, nature is process rather than processes, and while language often slips into the language of nominalisation, it is Schelling's articulation of the problem and its solution that works best, for Schelling addresses nature in generative terms, specifically generative terms which establish material conditions. This was precisely how Schelling read Plato's *Timaeus* in seeking to establish the "how" of nature as much as its "what". Essentially, Schelling reveals how a distinction might be made, at least in one reading of that Plato text, between visible and invisible matter; between nature actualised as *natura naturata* and nature's generative dynamic ground of potential, or *natura naturans*. To be more precise, only matter that has taken ideal form becomes ordered and thereby "visible". On the other hand, "matter" is distinct as an invisible (i.e., insensible) "element" that determines "matter as form". This dynamical nature of matter is indeed what positions it as generative and ecstatic, as self-transcending and self-sustaining.[7]

Grant's own transcendental materialism here sits close to *process-relational philosophy*, especially in the American philosophical tradition — for example, the thought of C.S. Peirce, Alfred North Whitehead, Charles Hartshorne, or the lesser-known figures of Justus Buchler, William Ernest Hocking, and John William Miller — in that, as much as there is an emphasis on *matter*, it is the *potential* or *powers* of matter that draw analysis towards ideality and the taking of ideal Platonic form. For process-relational philosophers working in the American tradition, this has generally been described as "naturalistic idealism" (John William

Miller, William Ernest Hocking), "ecstatic naturalism" (Robert S. Corrington, Robert Cummings Neville), or "ordinal naturalism" (Justus Buchler, C.S. Peirce). More recently, further infusions of German idealism — notably Friedrich Schelling and Schelling's impact on the likes of Whitehead, Hartshorne, and Corrington — have been incorporated into a "speculative naturalism" that seeks to reveal lines of connection between onto-cosmological insight and nature's own infinitely productive vibrant ground of *natura naturans*.[8]

At this point, Schelling articulates how the elements, "matter", or perhaps "materials", are invisible (insensible) because they have not yet acquired form by way of the divine understanding. Once engendered by the activity of the understanding (the Idea), they obtain form and then congeal into visible nature according to their "ultimate empirical constitution". It is through human understanding that the elements appear to the philosopher, though not through any empirical phenomenal appearance or representation, but rather through intellectual intuition alone — the "true organ of philosophy". Intellectual intuition is, for Schelling, the highest activity of any transcendental philosophy, exhibited, for example, in conducting a speculative physics of nature or by enacting mathematical and logical philosophy, particularly through abductive (not deductive) reasoning. This is contrary to Aristotle's thinking about the relationship between matter and form, which is both empirical and inductive. Against Aristotle's view of matter, Schelling instead, in agreement with Plato's *Timaeus*, invokes a Platonic physics of the Idea, writing that any object of nature begins "in invisible and shapeless form — all receptive — but partaking somehow of the intelligible". In this way, Plato's "invisible materialism" is responsible for material substances taking on the form that they do — rendered by, but not due to, the activity of intelligence: a "divine reasoning" available to the human within speculative philosophy. (Thus, in this sense, reasoning is "in-human" as much as it is "extra-human"). The power of insensible matter, the elemental at the base of visible material being, is therefore responsible for any determinate empirical and singular character filling out the activity of a respective form.

As Schelling tells us, this power is "base" in its being One, despite its infinite distribution throughout many. Thus a "power" ontology where, through decomposition (the literal self-decomposing of the Absolute), the Absolute's basal becomes fragments and multiplies, proliferating the real and the visible matter of it. Here it is important to note that, despite a plurality of materials in which this activity is found, there is still only one basal condition of activity, and so it may be better to speak of "ground" rather than "grounds"; "power" rather than "powers". Or, in the words of Plato, other than being One, Being *is* power. (Here I must note that, if we follow Plato in the *Sophist* fully and state that there is only power where there are things, then still, power must be of a general type — a category — that, despite its being in things, is not partitioned in its own universal integrity according to those things being its consequence. This is to say that, if we say there are as many powers as there are things, then what activity is common to these things despite their multiplicity?)

This is all fitting considering it is Schelling's goal to provide a reading of Plato as a "one-world theorist". Finding duplicity in the unity between real and ideal, there is only one "nature" for Schelling, and in the *Timaeus*, a transcendental materialism finds its development through the concept of insensible or invisible matter.

3. Grant Reading Plato as Transcendental Materialist: The Schellingean Dynamical Powers of Becoming

Grant lays out this Schellingean reading of Plato in detail in his *Philosophies of Nature After Schelling* (2006).[9] There we find that Grant advocates for a Platonic "physics of the All" — the absolute — where matter is the "in which" and "from which" all later developments evolve: "matter is the general seed of the universe". The new understanding of matter as it is outlined in the previous section of this essay is coupled with *transcendental* conditions of dynamical becoming. In other words, Grant wishes to analytically disclose the conditions "for the possibility" of nature qua nature; or in terms of being, both *what is* and what *can be*. The fact that the powers of becoming are both dynamical (*dunamis*) and ontologically as well as categorically modal (real potency, or *die Potenzen* in Schelling, and logical possibility) points to the sort of ontological parity conducive to ordinal phenomenological analysis. (It is not a secret that C.S. Peirce influenced Justus Buchler's own ordinal phenomenological approach in taking nature to be "whatever is in whatever way it is". This includes all of possibilities various concepts and modes, both in ontological reality and mere logical possibility.)

One may suspect Grant of succumbing to a sort of neo-Kantian re-privileging of the correlationist subject in attempting to transcendentally discern nature's conditions of possibility, which uncannily relate to the origination of consciousness. But Grant recommends Schelling's 1794 *Timaeus* commentary as offering a conceptual map for how one might "absorb" Kant's transcendental philosophy and its dipolarisations of nature into a supernatural "above" or "beyond" — the noumenal realm — and the phenomenal realm of conscious appearances, the natural world "below". Schelling, in the tradition of Fichte and Hegel, sees consciousness — indeed, *spirit* — as being contiguous with nature. Other naturalists close to the tradition of German idealism — for example, the American naturalist and pragmatist John Dewey — also saw "mind" or consciousness "stretching" to meet the possible boundaries of nature.

In short, for Grant as for Schelling, Platonism provides, through the Idea, a "theory of the universe" where the status of the absolute or nature is itself "according to itself". Just as a new understanding of matter is required in Grant's Schellingean ontology of dynamical becoming, a new understanding of the Idea is needed if one is to make sense of that which serves as the very ground of becoming — indeed, a true *lack* of ground (*Abgrunden*), in the sense that, being the unconditioned that conditions all else, it is no-thing in particular. Hence Grant's antipathy toward particular "objects" in favour of powers whose objects are a mere consequence — for if there are powers, these powers cannot be exhausted in any respective objects. Thus objects aren't coincident with Being/power, which nature qua nature is itself as *powering* (infinite production). If that were the case, there would be no need for a hypothesis of powers, since all would be objects — indeed, all would be an eternal domain of objects.

Grant follows Schelling's Platonic Idea as the "infinite concept", which is a concept of the "infinite universe". That is, he follows the Schellingean construal of ideality and materiality invoked as categorical modes of being — a construal not at all unlike C.S. Peirce's trichotomic categorical division of the universe into the three "universes of being": being's potential, actuality, and generality. As such, transcendental materialism means the Platonic Idea includes the physical universe, where "the physical universe is capable of ideation" in a naturalism that is both realist and idealist without sacrificing either the reality of matter or Idea taken as form. Schelling reiterates this in his "On the Relation of the Ideal and Real in Nature" (1806):

> The most obscure thing of all, yes obscurity itself according to some, is matter. However, it is precisely this unknown root out of which arises all the forms and living appearances of nature. Without knowledge of it, physics is without scientific basis and science itself loses the bond by means of which the idea is connected to reality.

Schelling's genetic philosophy of dynamical becoming uses the Platonic Idea as the means by which "we must think the emergence of the world". In other words, only through a Platonic theory of matter can consciousness, the mind, *spirit*, be properly understood, for only then does the problem of the materiality of the Idea come to the fore in that context.

4. Transcendental Materialism and Transcendental Naturalism: Ray Brassier and Iain Hamilton Grant Contra Object-Oriented Ontology

In explaining the dynamical powers of becoming, and having explained how powers cannot be reduced to their consequent objects, it becomes necessary to take a very brief detour through another speculative, realist, and naturalist philosopher — Ray Brassier, and in particular his critique of object-oriented ontology — so that we may gain a better perception of how dynamical ground is *self*-grounding and, thus being immanent, more deeply naturalises the transcendental philosophy under discussion here, while also allowing that transcendental philosophy to accommodate material and ideal modes of being.

Brassier's critique of so-called "object-oriented ontology" is devastating. His primary purpose is to re-level the function of generality within immanence and hence re-invigorate a naturalised form of transcendence, which is independent of perceiving transcendent consciousness and its horizon of apprehension. It is thus a form of scientific realism, pragmatism, and what I am currently referring to as "transcendental naturalism" in my own angle of vision, which follows this part of Brassier's thinking. One might think of this as a vector, an intersection, of Brassier's work with that of Iain Hamilton Grant, as transcendental naturalism is also simultaneously a transcendental materialism that admits the reality of the vital negative, among other organic yet immanent features of the Hegelian and Schellingean systems.

As Brassier correctly points out, the sort of "flat ontology" merely posited by object-oriented ontology fails not only because it is simply posited, but because it lacks what Justus Buchler has articulated as "ontological ordinality". In Buchler's famous *Metaphysics of Natural Complexes*, he identifies two necessary pillars required for any ontology that purports to be a naturalism as well. One is "ontological parity" — the idea that no object of nature is more real, nor any less real, than any other object of nature. (This idea sounds remarkably similar to the "ontological flatness" posited by the object-oriented ontologists, despite Buchler having articulated it 35 years earlier.) The other pillar is "ontological ordinality" — the idea that whatever is, is naturally complex, meaning there are no metaphysical "simples". And further, as such, ordinality means that no object can be entirely unrelated to anything else and still be considered a singular, simple individual (thus it follows that to be is to be related).

Buchler provides us with a picture of nature that is more capacious and robust than the "flatness" posited by the object-oriented ontologists. For Buchler, nature is "whatever is, in whatever way it is". Buchler does not reduce any items of nature to assumed grounds independent of the traits that relate them, nor does he reduce objects simply to the relations among and between objects themselves. This is important because Buchler's ordinal ontology contains parity, successfully, in a way that object-oriented ontology fails to do. And thus, Buchler's ordinal naturalism and its twin principles of ontological parity and ontological ordinality are immune to the sorts of criticisms levelled against object-oriented ontology and its failure to provide for an adequate rendering of nature.

There are four theses of object-oriented ontology that Brassier identifies that fail (quite miserably), specifically within the scope of ontology, and more generally within speculative and realist metaphysics. They are as follows:

1. There is no transcendence. No one sort of entity is the origin or ground of explanation of all others.
2. There is no generality (universality). No one sort of entity (or presumably method or discipline) accounts for (or explains) any possibility of unity or commonness to be had among all others.
3. There are no internal relations among entities. All relations are external and involve sensuous qualities only.
4. There is not ontological "dignity". No entity can be asserted to rank higher or lower within an ontological continuum and thus all entities are ontologically univocal. (All "is". Nothing is not.)

Aside from the fact that at least two of these are mutually contradictory, it is Brassier's calling out as fatal one of these theses alone that I find to be relevant here. For even though it is but one point of contention, Brassier demonstrates, quite clearly, why the failure of this thesis as posited fails on several fronts at once and collapses the whole project, in a future essay deathblow, to a quasi-naturalistic ontology as well as charlatan metaphysics that has no right to claim any kind of systematicity whatsoever (let alone rationalistic rigour).

There are four corollary claims that match with Brassier's theses:

1. Brassier points out that the denial of transcendence (at least as its denial is posited here) denies forms, species, and genera, natural kinds (and thus also natural difference; that is, an internal principle of differentiation), abstracta, and law.
2. He also points out that the second thesis denies the possibility of totality, whether universe or One-All. This would also deny the Absolute.
3. The third denies subjectivity. This thus denies not only epistemological relevance to any and all objects, but also any re-presentation (repetition) required for any meaningful notion of ontological difference.
4. And finally, the fourth thesis inadvertently denies ontological integrity as it denies ontological "dignity". The vital negative is lost, as is difference sui generis, also by theses one and three.

Following Brassier, I only wish to address one of these theses. It is the same thesis Brassier addresses and then identifies as being fatal for the very ontology operating within "object-oriented" ontology.

As the objects of nature are claimed to be immanent to themselves, the essential nature of (and relevant relations to) objects collapse upon themselves. Correlationism is still present, although it is merely shifted from subject-object relation to object-object relation. As an aside, this move accomplishes nothing other than illegitimately attempting to save essential natures ("quiddity") and internal relations without calling those relations as such.

As Brassier points out, fatal problems result. As transcendental naturalists believe (as do transcendental materialists), it is impossible to specify the ground or principle of object-individuation. Moreover, if we add the loss of generality (universality) to the loss of transcendence (or the "transcendental", the conditions for the possibility of *x*, to follow Kant), then we cannot precisely identify what objects are in general — they become vacuously empty — nor can we say what objects are in particular, for we have lost quiddity. Objects cannot enter into relations, for there is no internal nature to be related. If there are only sensuous qualities that could interact or be related, then those relations proliferate to the extent that they cannot refer (intend) any essence. Brassier writes: "the immediate consequence of adopting this full-blown object-oriented immanence is that we cannot say what anything really is".

The pluralism so fondly cherished by the object-oriented ontologists suddenly collapses as well. As it does, it finds itself ruthlessly subjected to its own second thesis. No internal principle of difference, no ground of differentiation, no internal relations, and suddenly All is One. Again, Brassier: "if we cannot specify the essential qualities that distinguish one real object from another, how can we be sure that the discrete multiplicity of sensual objects does not mask an underlying continuity…?" Object-oriented ontology has "undermined" (as compared to "over-mining") itself. Further, without real difference, we are left with nominalism — or better even, psychological nominalism; bundles of perceptions that cannot be explained without a correlational observer and philosopher of access to impart upon the perceptions a unity. As such, there is no rational way to determine the nature of identity, no logical way to render the supposed pluralism found within the univocal sense of being posited. Hegel's critique of Hume, using the sugar cube example in *The Phenomenology of Spirit*, is an excellent illustration of this fatal foundational flaw in the object-oriented ontologist's metaphysics.

As we have seen, any thorough-going naturalism, whether materialist or transcendental, cannot simply mimic the commitment to individuals. Yet, in throwing out any unitary ground of differential production, this denies the functional components required for any object to be an individual from the start. Thus, the ultimate failure of object-oriented ontology is not just a failure of transcendence, it is one of immanence as well. And it is immanence, and the sort of transcendency available within immanence of generativity or production, that secures both the materialism and naturalism of the *Naturphilosophie* that is at issue in this essay.

5. Conclusion: Schelling's Absolute as Infinite Production, or, Nature's Endless Beginning

To underscore the *transcendental* materialism of Grant's Platonic reading of the Schellingean dynamical powers of becoming, it may be helpful to close this essay by contrasting Schelling's notion of the Absolute as a plenum-in-process of *infinite production* against Hegel's own notion of "infinity" — which, according to Grant's view, is itself a "bad infinity". This will help determine what is meant by the sort of transcendency within the natural world, which is a power of transcendence not "beyond" the world, or indeed somehow supernatural and thus "apart" from it, but an ultimacy of potential that grounds the natural world's very own *generation* and *production.* Thus, *being* ultimate, the integrity of this ground is indeed "Absolute" — it is nature's infinite production and endless beginning in spontaneous creativity, freedom, and power. This notion of an Absolute, understood as infinitely productive ground, stands in contrast to Hegel's notion of "bad" infinity — a far cry from the sort of "true" infinity (sometimes rendered as "spurious" versus "genuine" infinity) that Schelling himself had posited in his *Naturphilosophie.*

We can begin by looking at the specific terms Hegel used to describe the infinite nature of his Absolute as either spurious and "bad" or "true" and "endless": *schlect Unendlichkeit* versus *wahrhaft Unendlichkeit.* Hegel's analysis of the Absolute's infinite nature centres mainly on his larger *Logic* and its section on infinity, which is part of chapter 2, "Determinate Being", section c, (a) through (c). While these sections are incredibly cumbersome in their precise description of the metaphysics of infinity, Hegel's larger goal of establishing how the Absolute is both productive and dynamical also serves to provide a response to Fichte, which was begun in the 1801 pre-*Phenomenology of Spirit* essay, "The Difference Between Fichte's and Schelling's Systems of Philosophy".

In a nutshell, a bad infinity, for Hegel, is one that is open-ended. For Hegel, true infinity — accessible by reason, but still beyond the understanding — is a totality. Intensive and extensive mathematical infinities, such as those infinitesimally available between any two numbers, or those which are sets of numbers to be aggregated indefinitely to any other set, fail before the sort of actual infinity that is an absolute total requiring nothing outside of itself. The interesting part isn't that Hegel's critique of the bad infinite is one that is a possible infinite; it is that Hegel states an infinity that "sets itself over and against" any other (such as the finite) is bad precisely because it lacks an infinite nature that is its own and is therefore delimited by negating something else so as to take on its own identity. So, the logic of contrasts that establishes an infinite — precisely because it is not finite, or "in-finite" — is one that necessarily fails, having no essential nature that is itself properly infinite or total.

For this reason, Hegel compares the "true" infinite to a circle. A circle does not "go on and on forever", but rather is "unending" in the sense that it is a closed actual total. This total encompasses the finite, or contains it, but is in no way limited by it. God, for Hegel, in traditional definitions, fails to capture the logical meaning of true infinity because God's nature and infinitude is always set over and against finite creation, and thus is always dependent upon it to be what it is. God, in that sense, is limited and finite, but not truly infinite.

Here it is appropriate to see how Schelling's take on infinity more adequately accounts for the dynamical becoming of the natural world, the Absolute, as both source and ground of potential. Schelling's description of a "bad infinity" more accurately serves as a model to understand Hegel's own division between true infinite and spurious infinite, as the question is not necessarily how or to what extent might the Absolute be understood as an infinite divine being, but rather how and to what extent does the dynamical nature of the Absolute as source or ground of generativity and potential allow for the continual becoming of nature. Further, it is Schelling's conception of the Absolute as infinite — that is, as endless and without beginning — that establishes the sort of *contingency* required for there to be freedom, creativity, and production understood as self-determination. To wit, then: might we be able to define the Absolute not necessarily as something unending, such as, on the one hand, in an unending series of numbers (a potential infinite) or, on the other hand, as something total as in a closed circle (an actual infinite). Perhaps, rather, might not the Absolute be something absolutely unconditioned, as Schelling ventured to maintain? That is, an unconditioned infinite? What might this mean?

It was Schelling's view that absolute being — "the Absolute" — must mean unconditioned being, and as unconditioned being, the Absolute must therefore be "endless", for any "beginning" or "end" of it would qualify some condition as being other to that absolute's identity. The result of this would be a non-absolute identity. Here we see that, for Hegel, the Absolute contains its own identity, as well as all else, and this is what makes it "genuine" or "true" (*wahrhaft Unendlichkeit*). In this way, we might say its infinite nature is of a pure metaphysical positivity of sorts. Schelling's absolute, on the other hand, is said to be "spurious", for it is absolutely indifferent to any particular identity in the sense that nothing can be other to it, save only for itself. Paradoxically, to be "itself", it must both be "itself" and "not itself" in different respects (so that there is no "other" conditioning it). Therefore, Schelling's absolute is "endless" but without closure as a totality, because there is nothing other that it could be other than its own identity, but also quite strangely, its "non-identity" — that is, it accommodates for "that which it is not". In this way, we might say that Schelling's absolute is "in-different". And so, with that said, why might Schelling's notion of the Absolute be preferable to Hegel's? And how does Schelling's understanding of the absolute-as-infinite help us to grasp Grant's own project of transcendental materialism?

Hegel's absolute is a *thing*. It is an identity; it is the Absolute, the All, which contains all things. But Schelling's main point was that the Absolute, unlike in Hegel's philosophy, could never be a totality or a thing. Schelling claimed instead that the Absolute was no-thing at all. Here, Hegel railed against Schelling for thinking that the Absolute had no identity sensu stricto, and raved that, as "nothing", Schelling's absolute could only be a blanket that simply absorbed all things in its cloak of night, in a "blank" identity, where those particular things would not be preserved within the circle of infinity. This is to say that Hegel was fearful that Schelling's absolute annulled particular things within an indifferent identity instead of raising them up and encircling things within the identity of an absolute that is itself complete and total. Thus, Hegel claimed that Schelling's absolute was an identity that was a "night in which all cows are black".

In short, then, it seems that Schelling's infinite or absolute is conditioned by no other indeed, but it is "absolutely unconditioned" as indifferent to identity in its being unconditioned. And this, therefore, can be said to be its positive. Schelling's unconditioned infinite is absolute indifference — that is, it is unconditioned ground in perpetuity, and as such, it nevertheless exhibits a sort of metaphysical positivity that Hegel claimed it was lacking. It is in this very deficiency, in this "spurious" nature, that there lies hidden a more adequate and "positive" conception of the Absolute and hence its virtue, whereby we can at the same time understand what precisely allows for the vibrancy and creative ground behind Grant's notion of nature-as-infinite-production.

References

Buchler, Justus. *The Metaphysics of Natural Complexes*, second expanded edition, edited by Corrington, Marsoobian, & Wallace. New York: SUNY, 1989.

Corrington, Robert S. *Nature and Spirit: An Essay in Ecstatic Naturalism*. New York: Fordham University Press, 1992.

Grant, Iain Hamilton. *Philosophies of Nature After Schelling*. New York: Bloomsbury-Continuum, 2006.

Meillassoux, Quentin. "Iteration, Reiteration, Repetition: A Speculative Analysis of the Sign Devoid of Meaning". In *Genealogies of Speculation: Materialism and Subjectivity Since Structuralism*, edited by Armen Avanessian & Suhail Malik. London and New York: Bloomsbury, 2016.

Niemoczynski, Leon. *Charles Sanders Peirce and a Metaphysics of Nature*. Lanham, MD: Lexington Books, 2011.

Niemoczynski, Leon. "21st Century Speculative Philosophy: Reflections on the 'New Metaphysics' and Its Realism and Materialism". *Cosmos and History: The Journal of Natural and Social Philosophy* 9, No. 2, pp. 13–31, 2013.

Niemoczynski, Leon. "Speculative Naturalism: A Bleak Theology in Light of the Tragic". *Journal for the Study of Religion, Nature and Culture* Vol. 8, No. 1, pp. 236–253, 2014.

Niemoczynski, Leon. *Speculative Realism: An Epitome*. Leeds: Kismet Press, 2017.

Schelling, Friedriech. "Timaeus", translated by Arola, Jolissant, & Warnek. *Epoché* Vol. 12, No. 2, pp. 205–248, 2008.

Notes

1 See Niemoczynski, 2013, pp. 13–31. Also, Niemoczynski, 2017.

2 The most famous statement of ordinal metaphysics is found in Buchler, 1989.

3 Meillassoux, 2016.

4 Niemoczynski, 2011.

5 See Schelling's 1794 commentary, *Timaeus*, in Schelling, 2008, pp. 205–248.

6 Iain Hamilton Grant in conversation with Sean J. McGrath at the Jockey Club, St. John's, Newfoundland, 6 June 2014.
7 "Ecstatic Naturalism" is developed in Corrington, 1992.
8 Niemoczynski, 2014.
9 Grant, 2006.

F.W.J. SCHELLING: RADICAL KANTIAN, HEGEL CRITIC, AND FOUNDER OF SPECULATIVE REALISM

Tyler Tritten

Despite[1] a sort of Schelling renaissance — spawned by Slavoj Žižek's brief fascination with the philosopher almost three decades ago (Žižek, 1996, 1997), and Iain Hamilton Grant's book on Schelling over one decade ago (Grant, 2006) — contemporary continental philosophy is still only beginning to come to terms with the debt it owes to him. A few years prior to Žižek's flirtation with Shelling, Andrew Bowie, in his *Schelling and Modern European Philosophy* (Bowie, 1993), first drew attention to a number of contemporary themes and authors influenced by him, including the possibility of post-Kantian metaphysics as well as *différance* in Jacques Derrida. The current reflection, however, will focus on Schelling's contributions to what is currently trendy in continental philosophy: speculative realism and new realism.

"Speculative realism" is a title that emerged from the event, "Speculative Realism: A One-Day Workshop", held on 27 April 2007, at Goldsmiths, University of London. This term is now most prominently attached to the names of the event's speakers: Ray Brassier, Iain Hamilton Grant, Graham Harman, and Quentin Meillassoux. Grant bears the closest affinities to Schelling, with much of his acclaim stemming from his aforementioned "Schelling book", *Philosophies of Nature after Schelling*. The term "new realism" was apparently coined by Maurizio Ferraris[2] in close collaboration with Markus Gabriel.[3]

Before presenting affinities and critical divergences between Schelling and contemporary realist trends, I will first rebuff the assumption that Schelling could not possibly have anything positive to offer realism because he was a German Idealist — which supposedly entails, of course, that he was an idealist. Section 1 will thus provide criteria for demarcating realism from non-realism — principally, the thesis that there is not being because there is thinking or intelligibility, but vice versa. In Section 2, I will show how Schelling's realism stemmed from his confrontation with Kant's transcendental idealism (although he also distances himself from Fichte's idealism, which Grant, pitting it in opposition to Schelling's *Naturphilosophie*,[4] aptly dubs "practicism" or "ethicism" [Grant, 2006, p. xi] — that is, an idealism without nature at its base, which implies action or will without a prior resistant). This is significant because those associated with the speculative and new realist movements normally share in common, if nothing else, the tendency to be critical of transcendentalism as a form of "correlationism" (a term coined by Meillassoux). In this instance transcendentalism ranges from Kant's transcendental idealism and Husserl's transcendental phenomenology to Heidegger's quasi-transcendental, neo-Kantian insistence, in *Being and Time* (Heidegger, 2010), that there is only being (*Sein*) because there is *Dasein* (Heidegger's term of the art for human existence, literally meaning "being-there") and its existentialia (which, as the conditions of "being-in-the-world", replace the structures and categories of transcendental consciousness in Kant).[5] Section 2 will also highlight how Grant's and Ferraris' criticisms of transcendental philosophy relate to Schelling's own critique. In Section 3, I will suggest an alternative — that is, non-German — lineage of robust realism in France, transmitted from Schelling through French spiritualism (Émile Boutroux, Maine de Biran, and Félix Ravaisson) and Henri Bergson to the speculative — which is to say "post-transcendental" — ontologies of the later Maurice Merleau-Ponty and Gilles Deleuze.[6] I will conclude in Section 4 by indicating why contemporary realism must be "speculative" or non-transcendental (at least in the traditional sense), which ensures that it cannot but be Schellingian in spirit.

Is Schelling an Idealist or a Realist?

What could a German Idealist contribute, apart from critique, to realism? This preemptive objection is precluded by the fact that Schelling — especially the later Schelling (from 1809 until his death) — is one of the greatest critics of idealism (a critic of Kantian transcendentalism throughout his oeuvre, of Fichtean practicism early in his career, and of Hegelian logicism later). Schelling was, in fact, a German realist.

To refer to Schelling as a German realist prior to 1809 likely only expresses a half-truth, as Schelling was then primarily concerned with the unity of realism and idealism, arguing that, in isolation, each is one-sided and incomplete. Nevertheless, one can find, in even the earliest works, assertions like the following: "Whoever does not feel and recognize anything real in oneself and outside oneself, whoever generally only lives from concepts and plays with concepts [...] how can this one speak about reality (how can a blind person speak about colours)?" (Schelling, 1797a, p. 353). This predilection for realism is likely what caused Schelling to claim that he was a Spinozist — in particular, identity philosophy or "the doctrine of identity in Spinoza" (Schelling, 1812, p. 27) — because the very identity of the subjective and objective must itself be thought objectively, which is to say that the identity of the real and ideal must itself be thought as real. However this identity is conceived in earlier works, it is fairly indisputable that, after the *Philosophical Investigations into the Essence of Human Freedom and Matters Connected Therewith* (i.e., the *Freedom Essay* of 1809), the weight of this unity lies with the real. In the last of three remaining drafts of *Ages of the World* (Schelling, 1811, 1813, 1815), Schelling, speaking of the necessity of a "higher realism", writes the following: "It will be seen in the greater age that realism is indubitably superior to idealism" (Schelling, 1815, p. 344). By 1827, in his lectures *On the History of Modern Philosophy*, he comes to relate his current position to his earlier thought, with his current thought clearly tending more toward realism. In 1832–1833, he is even able to assert that it

> is a necessary question: Why is there sense at all, why is there not nonsense instead of sense? [...] The whole world lies, as it were, ensnared in reason, but the question is how it came into this net (since there is manifestly still something other and something more in the world than mere reason, even something that strives beyond these borders). (Schelling, 1832–1833, p. 222)

Finally, in a lecture delivered in 1850, he asserts, "In this unity priority is not on the side of thinking; being is the first, thinking is first what is second or what follows" (Schelling, 1850, p. 557). Perhaps most incisive, however, is what he wrote in 1830: "It is not because there is thinking that there is being, but because there is being there is thinking" (Schelling, 1830, p. 161n1). It is not implausible, then, to view the progression of Schelling's thought as increasingly realist. This is not to neglect, however, that he was concerned with the unity of the real and the ideal his whole life, almost always according priority (if not superiority) to the real.[7] Many contemporary philosophers have turned to Schelling precisely on account of the possibilities he offers realism. Emilio Carlo Corriero describes Schelling as

> an author who right in the midst of the philosophical project of German Idealism, forcefully insinuated the *natural*-realistic objection [...] the renewed interest in Schelling's philosophy lies mainly in the reconsideration of the theories that, in an attempt to overcome Kantian transcendentalism within the philosophical project of German Idealism, later determined a "realistic" position. (Corriero & Dezi, 2013, p. vii)

Corriero also speaks of "the *overrealism* (or *speculative realism*) that links Heidegger and Schelling" (Corriero, 2013, p. 71).[8] Žižek surmises:

> The first to formulate this materialist problematic of "real genesis" as the obverse of transcendental genesis was Schelling: in his *Das Weltalter* [*The Ages of the World*] fragments from 1811 to 1815, he deploys the programme of deriving the emergence of the Word, *logos*, out of the abyss of the "real in God", of the vortex of drives [*Triebe*] that is God prior to the creation of the world. (Žižek, 2006, p. 176)[9]

Granting that Schelling has something to contribute to contemporary realism, why is realism important for contemporary philosophy? I am convinced that the principal reason why realism as a general movement is returning with a vengeance lies in its reactions against transcendentalism (see the following section) and postmodernism. Against postmodernism, broadly construed, contemporary realism offers grounds for rejecting that all theories are equally legitimate so long as they are politically desirable. In other words, the contemporary realist would be willing to affirm truth over beauty. Additionally, contemporary realists often reject, as Ferraris never tires of repeating, the Nietzschean view that there are no facts but only interpretations, which he argues has led to Bushism[10] and Trumpism — that is, to the post-truth world of "alternative facts". The linguistic turn of the twentieth century is also to be critiqued, which suggests that there is no experience of the real that is not already ideational or theory-laden (Feyerabend, 1993, p. 11), that "language is the house of being" (Heidegger, 1998, p. 239), that "there is no outside (of the) text [*Il n'y a pas de hors-texte*]" (Derrida, 1997, p. 158), or that we are like a fly trapped within the bottle of our language games (Wittgenstein, 2009, §309). A realist can push back by affirming that being is not exhausted by thinking or conceptual schemes and, perhaps, even by affirming that there is a brute experience of reality prior to its filtration through language. There is decidedly *more* than contexts, structures, language games, signs, or texts. At the risk of colonialism, a realist might even go so far as to affirm the existence of universal logical laws as laws of being instead of parallel formal systems each with their own arbitrary axioms and rules. However differently contemporary realists stand with respect to these issues, one can safely describe contemporary realism as a form of opposition to both transcendentalism (at least transcendental idealism)[11] and postmodern constructivism,[12] as both of these share the conviction that reality is conditioned/determined — either as such or for thought, depending on whether one's idealism is strong or weak — by something other than reality itself, be it by structures of subjectivity, language use, social practice, or something else.

Schelling is employed against these trends because he forcefully argues not just that the real has priority with respect to the ideal, but also that the two never had to co-belong; reason/thinking/ideality is an accident, an accessory, a surplus; the real or "unprethinkable being" — as he terms it in his latest thought — does not have to stand in correlation with intelligibility. If, as the following section argues, Schelling rejects transcendentalism, at least as an idealism, it is because he acknowledges the real apart from its correlation with the ideal. Put in contemporary jargon, Schelling, as a German realist, is no correlationist.

How to Move Beyond Kant: Some Contemporary Schellingian Realists

Schelling regards transcendental philosophy — that is, critical philosophy — to be negative rather than positive, where negative or purely rational philosophy only elucidates the conditions without which the world could not be thought or conceived, so that positive philosophy would be about the actuality and facticity of the world, genetic determinations of actuality rather than transcendental conditions of possibility. In this context, Ferraris always praises, and nowhere criticises, Schelling. For instance, he asserts the following: "From a historical perspective, new realism can be inserted into a long genealogy that goes back to Schelling's 'positive philosophy'" (Ferraris, 2015a, p. 9). Ferraris elsewhere remarks:

> "Ego cogito ergo sum", "intuitions without concepts are blind", "what is rational is real": all these expressions mean that certainty is to be sought in epistemology, in what we know and think, and not in ontology (what there is). For the later Schelling however, the opposite direction is the one to follow. Being is not something constructed by thought. (Ferraris, 2015c, p. 4)

Ferraris here criticises Descartes, Kant,[13] and Hegel, whose philosophies are all negative in the Schellingian sense insofar as they begin from thought in order to gain access to or, worse still, construct being. The opposite direction, however — the "inverted" direction taken by positive philosophy — itself a realist alternative, does not, as transcendental idealism does, subject being to thought. In this section, then, I begin with an abbreviated account of Schelling's late critique of Kant by means of the "inverted idea"[14] or an inverted transcendentalism, since this opens up the realist possibility of thinking being from itself rather than as an object for thought — that is, as determined and/or conditioned by thought.[15] As Merleau-Ponty states the matter in his late lectures on nature, where he is most explicitly Schellingian, "Kantian: Being is determinable only as Being-object; there is no access to ontogenesis" (Merleau-Ponty, 2003, p. 239). To move beyond Kant, one must show how being is not just an object — meaning an object of thought set before a subject — but how being generates both itself as well as its own thought and expression.[16]

Kant, the first to designate his own critical philosophy as negative rather than positive, sets the parameters of transcendentalism as follows:

> Such a thing would not be a doctrine, but must be called only a critique of pure reason, and its utility in regard to speculations would really be only negative, serving not for the amplification but only for the purification of our reason [...] I call cognition transcendental that is occupied not so much with objects but rather with our *a priori* concepts of objects in general. A system of such concepts would be called transcendental philosophy. (Kant, 1781/1787, A11–12/B25/p. 133)

Transcendental philosophy is not concerned with objects themselves — that is, their actuality or thatness (i.e., what, in scholastic Latin, was called their "*quoddity*") — but with the cognition of their essence, their conceptualisation or whatness (i.e., "*quiddity*"). As Žižek thus describes: "Schelling is the exact opposite of Kant: Reason is [...] outside itself; it never begins in itself; its activity is never founded in itself, but always triggered by some traumatic encounter [...] which provides the impulse to thought" (Žižek, 1996, p. 74). Kant, however, is "a good compulsive neurotic" who

> sets up the network of the conditions of possible experience in order to make sure that the actual experience of the real, the encounter with the thing, will never take place, so that everything the subject will effectively encounter will be the already gentrified-domesticated reality of representations. (Žižek, 1996, p. 75)

If the order of transcendental questioning is to be inverted, then rather than a question of epistemic access — how can thought transcend its own immanence in order to reach (minimally, conditioning to make possible the experience of or, maximally, constructing) the real? — the question concerns the ontological emergence, the real genesis, of the epistemic and transcendental domain itself. Being, the real, must become intelligible, must construct its own idea, the "idea of being", whereby the "of" is understood as both a subjective and objective genitive. The conditions of experience and knowledge are constructed by being; being is not constructed by thought. Is this a relapse into dogmatism? Does this not transgress the Kantian boundaries of finitude? Schelling is convinced that he has circumvented this problematic by beginning prior to the erection of the boundaries of finitude. In a startling passage, Schelling explains the matter as follows:

> Everything transcendent is actually something relative; it is [transcendent] only in relation to something which is transcended. If I conclude to the existence of the supreme being from its idea, then this is an act of transcendence. I have first posited the idea and will now, from this, reach over into existence; here is thus a transcendence. If, however, I proceed from that which comes before every concept, then I have committed no transgression here and rather, if one calls this being transcendent, if I continue in this toward the concept, then I have transgressed the transcendent and have, in this way, once again become immanent. The transcendence of the former metaphysics was a merely relative transcendence, i.e., a fainthearted, half-transcendence, whereby one wanted to remain standing with one foot in the concept. The transcendence of positive philosophy is absolute and just for this reason not a transcendence in the sense in which Kant forbids. If I have first made myself immanent, i.e., enclosed within pure thinking, then transcendence is hardly possible,

> but [not] if I begin from the transcendent (as does positive philosophy). (Schelling, 1842–1843a, p. 169)

The real cannot transcend thought, because thought, the transcendental and epistemic domain, is immanent to the real. As such, it is being's thought. The problem of transgression and transcendence — that is, of that relative transcendence that still wants to conceive in thought what is supposed to be outside of thought — only appears if one has first (neurotically), and without reason, enclosed oneself, for instance, within an inner subjective sphere (Descartes), within a system of categorical concepts (Kant), or within the absolute dynamics of reason (Hegel). These positions all begin with conditions that preclude cognition of the real as the real.

Schelling thus offers an earlier, and arguably better, conception of Meillassoux's "great outdoors" or "absolute outside" (Meillassoux, 2007, p. 7). Meillassoux wants to think radical immanence, which is what Schelling provides, even if Schelling rather terms it "absolute transcendence". This transcendence is transcendent to nothing; everything is, in fact, immanent to it. Things are not immanent in the sense of pre-containment, as Spinoza's attributes and modes are contained within infinite substance, in which case all truths are analytical. Quite the contrary, everything — thought and the transcendental included — is a novel consequent that synthetically relates to its real basis as absolute antecedent. Schelling thereby offers a "great outdoors" that is also not merely formal, as it is for Meillassoux, who is a self-proclaimed rationalist, and for his predecessor, Alain Badiou, who thinks the absolute on the basis of set theory or quantification. According to Schelling's account, however, one must not *abandon* the search for transcendental conditions of experience, but one must first account for how the transcendental has *really*, and not just ideally, been constructed as a novel consequent for and by the real.

Schelling's late positive philosophy begins anterior to reason (the ideal) and thus cannot be understood any other way than as a radical realism. Schelling's realism emerges from his critique of Kant's transcendentalism, but without abandoning transcendentalism *tout court*; he instead inverts it. Inverted transcendentalism thinks not towards but *from* the absolutely real, which is anterior to thinking. It does, however, think toward a *consequent* correlation between thinking and being. Schelling does not fall prey to correlationism in the beleaguered sense of the term because he endeavours to give an account of the real in advance of its correlation with thinking or the ideal. He progresses *towards* the correlation and not *from* it, as negative philosophy, transcendental idealism, and, in some sense, constructivisms do.

Grant, a co-presenter with Brassier, Harman, and Meillassoux at the Goldsmiths workshop, also utilises Schelling to attack transcendental philosophers for not being robustly realist (Kant was only an *empirical* realist), but always in the name of *Naturphilosophie*, thus primarily by appealing to the early and middle Schelling (see Grant, 2014b). Grant's project stems from the conviction that "Schellingianism is resurgent every time philosophy *reaches beyond the Kant-inspired critique of metaphysics, its subjectivist-epistemological transcendentalism*" (Grant, 2006, p. 5). Concerning what he takes to be the most significant link to contemporary philosophy, Grant remarks that "Deleuze and Guattari's repeated attempts to construct a philosophy capable equally of nature and the idea prompted the reengagement of *Naturphilosophie* alongside the return of Schelling" (Grant, 2006, p. x). Grant, then, employs Schelling to return to a *Naturphilosophie* or physics that, contra transcendentalism, provides a natural and realist account of the idea or ideality.

Grant's project denies any radical break between Schelling's pre- and post-1809 thought.[17] According to Grant, in the *Freedom Essay* and beyond, Schelling remains a *Naturphilosoph*. He proposes that

> it is equally a mistake to present Schellingianism in general as a "philosophy of freedom" in precisely the practicist vein responsible for the "aphysia" of so much contemporary

> Kantianism […] Nature does not, accordingly, depend on freedom, but rather the converse […] The naturephilosophy does not seek to give an idealistic explanation of nature, but rather a "physical explication of idealism" (IV [Schelling, 1800b], p. 76). (Grant, 2006, p. 61)

Notwithstanding the significant differences between Schelling's earlier and later thought, Grant is right to insist that, from beginning to end, nature is always thought as the ground of freedom rather than vice versa, although the disequilibrium between freedom and its ground becomes more rather than less pronounced in Schelling's middle and later philosophies.

If robust realism requires affirming the precedence of the real (nature) with respect to the ideal (freedom and/or the transcendental), then, according to Grant, Schellingianism is realist insofar as it provides a "physics of the idea". As Grant phrases it, in a manner that is faithful to Schelling's own language: "If there is a concept of being, it is not given, but emergent or *constructed*" (Grant, 2013, p. 8). The idea of being is being's own consequent construction; the ideal is not, contra idealism, antecedent. Grant elaborates:

> It follows from Schelling's argumentation that no ground may be posited as original if origination is to occur. *That consequents arise* is therefore the ground of antecedents *consequently*, not antecedently. If antecedence is operative at all, then it is itself emergent, not merely given. (Grant, 2013, p. 17)

This means that time cannot be a transcendental structure of consciousness, because the emergence of temporal determination, too, requires a realist explanation. Time requires an explanation of its genesis because it is not a given, neither a given of intuition nor a pure form of intuition, but a real consequence, being's own construction, rather than something imposed upon being by a transcendental consciousness. An antecedent is only an antecedent if it has a consequent; or, put differently, not to have a consequent is not to be. To be is thus either to be a consequent or the antecedent retroactively posited by the consequent. Being is never timeless or an eternal present; it is either antecedence or consequence. Being is never given *sub specie aeternitatis* but always only *sub specie durationis*. It is not just that there is no being apart from temporal determinations, but that there is not time apart from being, which is the absolutely antecedent, the absolute past, the absolute first or original (*prius*), or the "unprethinkable", namely, that which is precedent to thought or the ideal as such.[18]

Another contemporary Schellingian, Gabriel, finds himself at the centre of "new realism". Schelling thus plays a formative role for seminal authors in both the so-called "speculative realist" and "new realist" movements. Gabriel's realism, however, is more compromised or, at least, qualified than Grant's or Ferraris' Schelling-inspired realism. He considers himself a realist because he "rejects the idea that the meaning of 'existence' can be fully or relevantly captured by the language of quantification" (Gabriel 2015, p. 8). In spite of the fact that he is eager to avoid reducing being to mathematical cognisability, he nevertheless fails to grant any meaning to being prior to its conjunction or correlation with thinkability. "New realism is the idea that in order to be a realist there is no need to introduce the idea of mind-, or more generally, perspective-independent reality" (Gabriel, 2015, p. 10). Gabriel seems to repudiate Schelling's question: "Why is there sense at all, why is there not nonsense instead of sense?" (Schelling, 1832–1833, p. 222), instead proclaiming that "There are no objects without senses" (Gabriel, 2015, p. 340). Admitting that no specific objects exist without sense, this still fails to take Schelling's question seriously, which asks why there should be any objects at all rather than none whatsoever.[19] Gabriel's conviction "that domain-like field-structures are laid out independent of how we settle the criteria for identifying them" (Gabriel, 2015, p. 13), although denying that being and sense would necessarily be constructed *consciously*, does not necessarily affirm that being and sense would exist independently of sense-making practices and/or (unconscious) modes of thought. Gabriel decrees, as if by *fiat*, that "[t]here really are many domains of objects corresponding to the right division of scientific labour whether we have already reached it or not [...] Fields are generally unconstructed" (Gabriel, 2015, p. 157). Realist as this conviction may be, a question poses itself: wherein lies human beings' seemingly groundless ability to form disciplines of thought that correspond to the fields of sense that apparently carve reality at the joints? How is this not a bald assertion? To realise, as Schelling does, that the ideal cannot account for its own facticity and genesis, and so to affirm the real (by no means as object) in advance of the ideal (reason, mathematicisation, subjective transcendental conditions, etc.) — that is, as absolutely antecedent to thinkability — is one thing; to be convinced that the real rarely evades sense and thinkability, and so stands firm in the faith that scientific and (presumably) other sense-making practices correspond to *objective* reality, is another thing. The latter strikes me as an incredible fideism.

Furthermore, Gabriel, ontic thinker that he is — his ontology is more mundane or deflationary than Schelling's own insofar as there seems to be absolutely no sense to being apart from beings — trivialises the notion of reality or existence. To exist is just to appear (in a field of sense), hence why the objects that appear within fields — for instance, unicorns that appear within folklore, fiction, and poetry, as well as the localised fields of sense themselves, such as science, religion, democracy, and so on — exist, but the field of fields, the world, cannot appear, since to appear is to appear *within* a field. The world, the field of fields, thus does not and cannot exist. This notion of existence as nothing but appearance (in a field of sense) is trivial because unicorns and cyclops are then as real as atoms, ether and quarks as real as gods (despite Gabriel's apparent atheism), and mirages as real as the rock kicked by G.E. Moore. To appear (in a field of sense) is to exist; therefore, all these things exist. Apparently, then, almost all fields would get reality right, since "fields are generally unconstructed" (Gabriel, 2015, p. 157), or almost none of them would, at least not less so than any other — indeed, folklore no less than astrophysics. The apparent "ontic" democracy and egalitarianism of all fields trivialises reality by rendering the existence of the unicorn as real within its respective field(s) as the existence of my body in its field(s). If to exist is just to appear (in a field of sense), there is no basis for an appearance/reality distinction, at least not across fields. How are deception and illusion, then, possible? Does the word "fiction" not name unreality but simply a different *locus* of existence? Gabriel would seem to think so: "everything exists [...] everything is actual" (Gabriel, 2015, p. 264).

My own misgivings with Gabriel seem to be shared by his collaborator, Ferraris, who confesses: "My concern is that to make existence depend on sense is excessive. There can be existence without any sense, as our own lives can very well demonstrate" (Ferraris, 2017, p. 74). Although this, one must point out, conflates Schelling's notion of nonsense, the absolute absence of sense or of anything at all, with absurdity, Ferraris' reservation nevertheless remains well-founded. Gabriel's Schellingianism, while certainly not an idealism, shares too much with non-realism, since he does not see the need to posit a language-independent and/or theory-independent reality. As Gabriel remarks: "Schelling, Heidegger, and Wittgenstein argue that there is no ultimate meta-theory, no standpoint outside the limits of language" (Gabriel, 2009, p. 19). Humbly to refuse a meta-theory is one thing, but to repudiate the existence of and access to a reality outside of language need not follow from this humility. This unfounded move risks falling back into the possibly non-realist, even postmodern and constructivist, notion that there are only language games, that language is the house of being, or that "being that can be understood is language" (Gadamer, 1992, p. 474), even if it is only Richard Rorty's reading of this passage (Rorty, 2000) rather than Gadamer's own that is anti-realist.[20]

Whether one follows Grant's arguments for elevating *Naturphilosophie* over transcendental idealism and "practicism" of all varieties, or whether one follows Gabriel, who does not see the need to posit a mind-independent reality in order to be a realist, or whether one follows Ferraris, whose use of Schelling, like most of his writing, is fairly polemical with respect to postmodern anti-realism and constructivism, it is obvious that Schelling serves as a central and positive resource for contemporary realism. Additionally, it has also been argued that Schelling is even influential, albeit more indirectly, for process thinkers, who are certainly realists. As one commentator, who sees a lineage from Schelling to process thought, writes: "For Schelling, knowledge is not transcendental insofar as it determines nature for consciousness. Nature is transcendental as the producer of intelligence able to cognize nature. Nature must be seen as capable of organizing itself, generating life and the human consciousness capable of knowing nature" (Gare, 2011, p. 29). This invokes the notion of what I have termed "inverted transcendentalism". Inverted transcendentalism, however, like the "transcendental realism" or "critical realism" of Roy Bhaskar, or the "transcendental ontology" of Gabriel, is still thought in confrontation with transcendentalism — that is, in relation to Kant and the tradition that follows. To close, therefore, I provide hints for an alternative French lineage in philosophy, which does not take all its cues from Kant, perhaps only to pass through Schelling's critique, but a lineage that takes its lead more directly from Schelling himself.

The Transmission of Schellingian Realism Outside Germany

By means of French spiritualism (Boutroux, Biran, and Ravaisson), Schelling's realist influence was transmitted through Bergson (who may or may not have read Schelling himself)[21] to Merleau-Ponty's late *Naturphilosophie* and to Deleuze's genetic and speculative ontology. Concerning the lattermost heritage, Grant insisted, as I already cited earlier, that "Deleuze and Guattari's repeated attempts to construct a philosophy capable equally of nature and the idea prompted the reengagement of *Naturphilosophie* alongside the return of Schelling" (Grant, 2006, p. x). This remark occurs in the

Preface of Grant's *Philosophies of Nature after Schelling* and it is not hard to imagine that it is precisely Deleuze's philosophy of nature that he has in mind in the title. Žižek has called Deleuze "a great Schellingian" (Žižek, 1997, p. 61), and Deleuze himself has stated, with great approbation for Schelling, that

> The most important aspect of Schelling's philosophy is his consideration of powers. How unjust in this respect, is Hegel's critical remark about the black cows! Of these two philosophers, it is Schelling who brings difference out of the night of the Identical [...] testifying to the presence in Schelling's philosophy of a differential calculus adequate to the dialectic. (Deleuze, 1994, p. 190–191)

Merleau-Ponty, in his late lectures on nature, arguably draws from Schelling more than any of the aforementioned French thinkers, even if he confusingly cites from all periods of his thought at once. Merleau-Ponty surmises: "This excess of Being over the consciousness of Being is what Schelling wants to think in all its rigor" (Merleau-Ponty, 2003, p. 38) and "Schelling defines his philosophy as a 'real idealism,' deduced from a realism" (Merleau-Ponty, 2003, p. 42). Merleau-Ponty clearly understood Schelling as a realist and he regards this realism as a way out of "philosophies of reflection" (Merleau-Ponty, 2012, p. 64) or "philosophies of consciousness" (Merleau-Ponty, 2012, p. 171). Merleau-Ponty perspicaciously sees that Schelling did not abandon idealism so much as demonstrate that the ideal itself is not ephemeral but has a real basis that can never be entirely subdued or sublated. In Schelling's own words,

> The world as we now behold it, is all rule, order and form; but the unruly lies ever in the depths as though it might again breakthrough, and order and form nowhere appear as if they would be original, but it seems as though what had initially been unruly had been brought to order. (Schelling, 1809, p. 359)

Although space does not permit a detailed discussion, it could be argued that Boutroux and Ravaisson inherited from Schelling the idea that matter is not inert but possesses its own spontaneity and that freedom must have its basis in nature. From this, in combination with Aristotle and the science of the day, they develop an ontological account of habit. If David Hume utilises the habit of the mind as a psychological category in order to assuage an epistemic problem — namely, scepticism — then these French thinkers (as well as C.S. Peirce and A.N. Whitehead in America) spread habit across the whole of nature. The same tendency deemed "habit" in psychology, this same propensity to repeat or extend an action indefinitely, could be called "motor habit" at the level of biology and "inertia" at the level of physics. Consequently, contra Kant, laws of nature and causal relations are not transcendental structures of the mind, but relations stemming from habit as a real and vital force of nature itself. In other words, instead of following Kant, who transcendentalises Humean psychology, French spiritualism (and American pragmatism) ontologises habit, rendering it a real principle of nature, which allows them to be causal realists. This realism about causal relations and laws of nature opens a different and more positive avenue to science than the one by which Kant had proudly "saved science", an avenue by which Bergson rightly capitalises, for whom space and time are not transcendental structures imposed on nature, but real elements of nature itself. Finally, in Merleau-Ponty and Deleuze, this Schellingian-based realist lineage culminates in the repudiation of philosophies of consciousness and philosophies of representation respectively, which are both rejected because they fail to acknowledge anything recalcitrant to consciousness and because both only know how to think identity and difference on the basis of the concept. Note too how important the notion of habit is for Deleuze's own notion of repetition in Chapter 2, "Repetition for Itself", of *Difference and Repetition* (Deleuze, 1994, pp. 70–128). My contention (which cannot be fully justified here)[22] is that this entire historical trajectory can be traced back to Schelling's critique of Kant's transcendentalism,

Fichte's practicism/ethicism, and Hegel's purely rationalist logicism based on the primacy of the concept (*der Begriff*). This route, in any event, surely promises more robustly realist possibilities than the phenomenological tradition that originated in Germany and the ensuing post-phenomenological traditions of structuralism and post-structuralism.[23]

Post-Kantian Realism as Inherently Schellingian

Günter Zöller once published an article with the title "German Realism: The Self-Limitation of Idealist Thinking in Fichte, Schelling, and Schopenhauer", intentionally omitting Hegel. In this text, he observes: "Through Schelling's thinking there is a systematic concern with a reality outside of and prior to any thinking and willing, human or divine" (Zöller, 2000, p. 208). Schelling is a realist first and foremost because he is convinced that there is not being (the real) because there is thinking (the ideal), but vice versa. His task thus consists in explaining the fact of thinking and reason itself, providing the real ontology behind transcendental and epistemic conditions. To think or reason about the very emergence of thinking or reason from unreason, however, is a necessarily speculative enterprise. Like contemporary speculative realism, Schelling has long understood that any robustly realist position — since it wishes to speak of the real, prior to its correlation with the ideal, with the intelligible — must think otherwise than according to the necessary inferences of reason. Radically realist thinking is thus inherently speculative. As Schelling himself puts the matter:

> We are not in the domain of a necessary thinking, but in the domain of free thinking, i.e., of genuinely speculative thinking [...] To speculate means to look around for possibilities by means of which a certain aim in knowledge can be achieved. These are admittedly only possibilities at first, which must prove to be actualities in what ensues. (Schelling, 1839, pp. 344–345)

Schellingianism, perhaps, names contemporary philosophy's mode of ontological speculation, the means by which philosophy can finally move past Kant rather than merely confining itself to questions of formal analysis, epistemology, ethics, and social-political critique.

References

Bowie, Andrew. *Schelling and Modern European Philosophy: An Introduction.* London: Routledge, 1993.

Corriero, Emilio Carlo. "The Necessity of Contingency in the Late Philosophies of Schelling and Heidegger". In *Nature and Realism in Schelling's Philosophy,* edited by Emilio Carlo Corriero & Andrea Dezi, pp. 55–85. Torino: Accademia University Press, 2013.

Corriero, Emilio Carlo & Andrea Dezi. "Introduzione. From Nature to...". In *Nature and Realism in Schelling's Philosophy,* edited by Emilio Carlo Corriero & Andrea Dezi, pp. vii–xiv. Torino: Accademia University Press, 2013.

Deleuze, Gilles. *Difference and Repetition,* translated by Paul Patton. New York, NY: Columbia University Press, 1994.

Derrida, Jacques. *Of Grammatology,* translated by Gayatri Chakravorty Spivak. Baltimore, MD: John Hopkins University Press, 1997.

Ferraris, Maurizio. *Goodbye, Kant!: What Still Stands of the Critique of Pure Reason,* translated by Richard Davies. Albany, NY: State University of New York Press, 2013.

Ferraris, Maurizio. *Introduction to New Realism,* translated by Sarah de Sanctis. London: Bloomsbury, 2015a.

Ferraris, Maurizio. *Manifesto of New Realism,* translated by Sarah de Sanctis. New York, NY: State University of New York Press, 2015b.

Ferraris, Maurizio. *Positive Realism.* Winchester, UK: Zer0 Books, 2015c.

Ferraris, Maurizio. "A Brief History of New Realism". In *New Perspectives on Realism,* edited by Luco Taddio, pp. 59–81. Milano: Mimesis International, 2017.

Gabriel, Markus. *Der Mensch im Mythos: Untersuchungen über Ontotheologie, Anthropologie und Selbstbewußtseinsgeschichte in Schellings "Philosophie der Mythologie".* Berlin: De Gruyter, 2006.

Gabriel, Markus. "The Mythological Being of Reflection: An essay on Hegel, Schelling, and the Contingency of Necessity". In *Mythology, Madness and Laughter: Subjectivity in German Idealism,* edited by Markus Gabriel & Slavoj Žižek, pp. 15–94. London: Continuum, 2009.

Gabriel, Markus. *Transcendental Ontology: Essays in German Idealism.* London: Bloomsbury, 2011.

Gabriel, Markus. *Fields of Sense: A New Realist Ontology.* Edinburgh: Edinburgh University Press, 2015.

Gadamer, Hans-Georg. *Truth and Method,* translated by Joel Weinsheimer & Donald G. Marshall. Second revised edition. New York, NY: Crossroad, 1992.

Feyerabend, Paul K. *Against Method.* London, UK: Verso, 1993.

Gare, Arran. "From Kant to Schelling to Process Metaphysics: On the Way to Ecological Civilization". *Cosmos and History: The Journal of Natural and Social History* 7 (2) (2011), pp. 26–69.

Grant, Iain Hamilton. *Philosophies of Nature after Schelling.* London: Continuum, 2006.

Grant, Iain Hamilton. "What is an Action? Ground and Consequent in Schelling's Philosophy of Nature". In *Nature and Realism in Schelling's Philosophy,* edited by Emilio Carlo Corriero & Andrea Dezi, pp. 3–26. Torino: Accademia University Press, 2013.

Grant, Iain Hamilton. "'World' in Middle Schelling: Why Nature Transcendentalises". *Pli: The Warwick Journal of Philosophy* 26, pp. 82–108, 2014b.

Heidegger, Martin. "Letter on 'Humanism'", translated by Frank A. Capuzzi, in *Pathmarks,* edited by William McNeill, pp. 239–276. Cambridge, MA: Cambridge University Press, 1998.

Heidegger, Martin. *Being and Time: A Revised Edition of the Stambaugh Translation,* translated by Joan Stambaugh & Rev. Dennis J. Schmidt. Albany, NY: State University of New York Press, 2010.

Jaspers, Karl. *Schelling. Grösse und Verhängnis.* Munich: Piper, 1955.

Kant, Immanuel. *Kritik der reinen Vernunft.* (1781/1787) [Cited A/B according to original pagination of the first or second edition respectively.] Riga: Johann Friedrich Hartknoch. *Critique of Pure Reason,* translated by Paul Guyer & Allen W. Wood. Cambridge: Cambridge University Press, 1998.

MacKinnon, Catharine A. *Feminism Unmodified: Discourses on Life and Law.* Cambridge, MA: Harvard University Press, 1987.

McGrath, S.J. "Is the Late Schelling Still Doing Nature-Philosophy?". *Angelaki: Journal of the Theoretical Humanities* 21 (4) (2016b), pp. 121–142.

Meillassoux, Quentin. *After Finitude: An Essay on the Necessity of Contingency,* translated by Ray Brassier. London: Continuum, 2008.

Merleau-Ponty, Maurice. *Nature: Course Notes from the Collège de France,* translated by Robert Vallier, edited by Dominique Séglard. Evanston, IL: Northwestern University Press, 2003.

Merleau-Ponty, Maurice. *Phenomenology of Perception,* translated by Donald A. Landes. New York, NY: Routledge, 2012.

Rorty, Richard. "Being That Can be Understood is Language: Richard Rorty on H.G. Gadamer". *London Review of Books* 22 (6) (16 March 2000), pp. 23–25.

Shain, Ralph. "Temporality and the Dissolution of Underdetermination Skepticism". In *New Perspectives on Realism,* edited by Luco Taddio, pp. 269–94. Milano: Mimesis International, 2017.

Schelling, F.W.J. *Abhandlungen zur Erläuterung des Idealismus der Wissenschaftslehre.* SSW 1, pp. 343–452 (1797a). "Treatise Explicatory of the Idealism in the Science of Knowledge [*Wissenschaftslehre*]". In *Idealism and the Endgame of Theory: Three Essays by F.W.J. Schelling,* translated & edited by Thomas Pfau, pp. 62–138. Albany, NY: State University of New York Press, 1994.

Schelling, F.W.J. *Allgemeine Deduktion des dynamischen Processes.* SSW 4, pp. 1–78, 1800b.

Schelling, F.W.J. *Philosophie und Religion.* SSW 6, pp. 11–70 (1804b). *Philosophy and Religion,* translated by Klaus Ottmann. Putnam, CT: Spring Publications, 2010.

Schelling, F.W.J. *Philosophische Untersuchungen über das Wesen der menschlichen Freiheit und die damit zusammenhängenden Gegenstände* [the Freedom Essay]. SSW 7, pp. 331–416 (1809). *Philosophical Inquiries into the Essence of Human Freedom,* translated by Jeff Love & Johannes Schmidt. Albany, NY: State University of New York Press, 2006.

Schelling, F.W.J. *Die Weltalter. Fragmente. In den Urfassungen von 1811 und 1813* (1811), edited by Manfred Schröter. Munich: Biederstein, 1946. *The Ages of the World (1811),* translated by Joseph P. Lawrence. Albany, NY: State University of New York Press, 2019.

Schelling, F.W.J. *F.W.J. Schelling's Denkmal der Schrift von den göttlichen Dingen etc. des Herrn Friedrich Heinrich Jacobi und der ihm in derselben gemachten Beschuldigung eines absichtlichen täuschenden, Lüge redenden Atheisumus.* SSW 8, pp. 19–136, 1812.

Schelling, F.W.J. *Die Weltalter. Fragmente. In den Urfassungen von 1811 und 1813,* (1813), edited by Manfred Schröter. Munich: Biederstein, 1946. *The Ages of the World (1813),* translated by Judith Norman, in Slavoj Žižek & F.W.J. Schelling, *The Abyss of Freedom/Ages of the World,* pp. 113–182. Ann Arbor, MI: University of Michigan, 1997.

Schelling, F.W.J. *Die Weltalter. Erstes Buch.* SSW 8, pp. 195–344 (1815). *The Ages of the World,* translated by Jason M. Wirth. Albany, NY: State University of New York Press, 2000.

Schelling, F.W.J. *Zur Geschichte der neueren Philosophie.* SSW 10, pp. 1–200 (1827). *On the History of Modern Philosophy,* translated by Andrew Bowie. Cambridge: Cambridge University Press, 1994.

Schelling, F.W.J. *Grundlegung der positiven Philosophie.* Münchner Vorlesung WS (1832/33) und SW 183, edited by Horst Fuhrmans. Torino: Bottega d'Erasmo, 1972.

Schelling, F.W.J. *Einleitung in die Philosophi* (1830),edited by Walter E. Ehrhardt. Stuttgart: Frommann-Holzboog, 1989.

Schelling, F.W.J. "Andere Deduktion der Principien der positiven Philosophie". SSW 14, pp. 335–56, 1839.

Schelling, F.W.J. *Einleitung in die Philosophie der Offenbarung oder Begründung der positiven Philosophie.* SSW 13, pp. 1–174 (1842–1843a). *The Grounding of the Positive Philosophy: The Berlin Lectures,* translated by Bruce Matthews. Albany, NY: State University of New York Press, 2007.

Schelling, F.W.J. "Abhandlung über die Quelle der ewigen Wahrheiten". SSW 11, pp. 573–590 (1850). "On the Source of the Eternal Truths", translated by Edward A. Beach, in *The Owl of Minerva* 22.1, pp. 55–67, 1990.

Sparrow, Tom. *The End of Phenomenology: Metaphysics and the New Realism.* Edinburgh: Edinburgh University Press, 2014.

Suskind, Ron. "Faith, Certainty and the Presidency of George W. Bush". *The New York Times Magazine,* 17 October 2004.

Tritten, Tyler. "Against Kant: Toward an Inverted Transcendentalism or a Philosophy of the Doctrinal". *Angelaki: Journal of the Theoretical Humanities* 21 (4) (2016), pp. 143–156.

Tritten, Tyler. *The Contingency of Necessity: Reason and God as Matters of Fact.* Edinburgh: Edinburgh University Press, 2017.

Tuvel, Rebecca. "In Defense of Transracialism". *Hypatia: A Journal of Feminist Philosophy* 32 (2) (2017), pp. 263–278.

Whistler, Daniel. *Schelling's Theory of Symbolic Language: Forming the System of Identity.* Oxford: Oxford University Press, 2013.

Whistler, Daniel. "Naturalism and Symbolism". *Angelaki: Journal of the Theoretical Humanities* 21 (4) (2016), pp. 91–110.

Wittgenstein, Ludwig. *Philosophical Investigations,* translated by G.E.M. Anscombe, P.M.S Hacker, & Joachim Schultze, edited by P.M.S Hacker & Joachim Schultze. Revised fourth edition. Oxford: Wiley-Blackwell, 2009.

Zahavi, Dan. "The End of What? Phenomenology vs. Speculative Realism". *International Journal of Philosophical Studies* 24 (3) (2016), pp. 289–309.

Žižek, Slavoj. *The Indivisible Remainder: Essays on Schelling and Related Matters.* London: Verso, 1996.

Žižek, Slavoj. *The Abyss of Freedom in Slavoj Žižek & F.W.J. Schelling, The Abyss of Freedom/Ages of the World,* pp. 1–104. Ann Arbor, MI: University of Michigan, 1997.

Žižek, Slavoj. "Hegel, Lacan, Deleuze: Three Strange Bedfellows". In *Interrogating the Real,* edited by Rex Butler & Scott Stephens, pp. 155–75. London: Bloomsbury, 2006a.

Zöller, Günter. "German Realism: The Self-Limitation of Idealist Thinking in Fichte, Schelling, and Schopenhauer". In *The Cambridge Companion to German Idealism,* edited by Karl Ameriks, pp. 200–218. Cambridge: Cambridge University Press, 2000.

Notes

1 A version of this chapter was previously published as "Schelling and Speculative Realism" in *The Palgrave Schelling Handbook*. Kyla Bruff, Joseph Carew, and Sean J. McGrath (eds), Palgrave Macmillan.

2 See Ferraris (2015b, p. xiii) for his own recounting of when he suggested the term "new realism" to Markus Gabriel. For more on the relationship between contemporary realism and Schelling, see Corriero and Dezi (2013), a collected volume to which Ferraris and Grant both contributed.

3 Gabriel's dissertation was exclusively on the later Schelling (see Gabriel, 2006).

4 I am following Grant's gloss on this concept, *Naturphilosophie*, and why it differs from "philosophy of nature". The latter refers to philosophy's study of a certain region of being, the natural, in opposition to others, which would apparently be unnatural or "spiritual", as in the German term for the arts or humanities, *Geisteswissenschaften*, literally "sciences of spirit", [...] generally operates solely as an objective genitive — namely, philosophising on or about nature. According to Schelling, however, the concept is rather to be understood as a subjective genitive, meaning nature's philosophising or philosophy as nature, whereby nature is the subject instead of the object of inquiry, hence Grant's persistence to translate *Naturphilosophie* not as "philosophy of nature" but as "naturephilosophy".

5 For a prime example of this tendency, see Sparrow (2014). For a convincing reply to speculative realists' penchant to treat all phenomenologists as correlationists, see Zahavi (2016).

6 A more tenuous and indirect lineage might be traced in America from Schelling to the speculative cosmologies of C.S. Peirce and A.N. Whitehead. Also note that both Merleau-Ponty and particularly Deleuze retain the notion of the transcendental, even if only in a very qualified sense. Note, for example, Deleuze's notion of "transcendental empiricism".

7 Even if Schelling only explicitly acknowledges a tragic element, the real, that all existence must overcome, even and especially in God, first in the *Freedom Essay* (Schelling, 1809), one must not forget that he had already

explicitly affirmed in *Philosophy and Religion* (Schelling, 1804b) that the world is the result of a real fall from the Idea.

8 Corriero's own contribution to *Nature and Realism in Schelling's Philosophy* is entitled "The Necessity of Contingency in the Late Philosophies of Schelling and Heidegger" (Corriero, 2013). I have argued for the exact opposite in *The Contingency of Necessity: Reason and God as Matters of Fact* (Tritten, 2017). Similarly, Gabriel's contribution to *Mythology, Madness and Laughter: Subjectivity in German Idealism*, co-authored with Žižek, bears the sub-title "The Mythological Being of Reflection: An Essay on Hegel, Schelling, and the Contingency of Necessity" (Gabriel, 2009). Thus Gabriel, too, argues against Meillassoux — as I do — for the contingency of necessity. Gabriel's thesis, however, is much more metaphysically deflationary than Schelling's and my own.

9 Žižek adds: "The late Schelling of the 'philosophy of revelation' recoiled from this previous radicality by conceding that God possesses in advance his existence [...] This way, god is no longer involved in the process of 'genesis'" (Žižek, 2006, p. 177). Žižek, not terribly familiar with the late Schelling, is actually correct that God is there not involved as a part of the process of genesis, but that this renders Schelling's position less radical is mistaken. Although the creative process emerges "outside" God for the later Schelling, God is still constituted *as God*, just as I am only constituted as a boss or father by changes or events that take place outside of me. The existence that "God" possesses in advance is only naked or unprethinkable existence, "*without* which God could not be God" (Schelling, 1827, p. 70), but it is not the essential attribute "*through* which God is first actually God" (Schelling, 1827, p. 70).

10 Karl Rove, a presidential consultant during the Bush regime, once retorted: "We're an empire now, and when we act, we create our own reality. And while you're studying that reality — judiciously, as you will — we'll act again, creating other new realities, which you can study too" (Suskind, 2004).

11 Not all transcendentalisms exclude realism or commit one to idealism. There is, for example, Deleuze's transcendental empiricism and Roy Bhaskar's transcendental or critical realism, both of which are explicitly realist and anti-idealist.

12 Note that not all third-wave feminism (e.g., Judith Butler) is constructivist. The following remark (cited in Shain, 2017, pp. 291–292) by Catherine A. MacKinnon is robustly realist and anti-constructivist: "Take the problem of 'is there a reality and how do I know I'm right about it?' The 'is there a there there?' business [...] Women know the world is out there because it hits us in the face. Literally. We are raped, battered, pornographed, defined by force, by a world that begins, at least, entirely outside us. No matter what we think about it, how we try to think it out of existence or into a different shape for us to inhabit, the world remains real [...] This anxiety about whether the world is really there independent of our will or of our representations [...] comes from the luxury of a position of power that entails the possibility of making the world as one thinks or wants it to be" (MacKinnon, 1987, pp. 57–58). For an apparent abuse and excess of constructivism in contemporary social philosophy, note Rachel Dolezal (former Chair of the NAACP Chapter in Spokane, WA, who passed herself off as black although white by birth), and Tuvel (2017), a highly controversial article that argues that race, like gender, may be a social construction.

13 For Ferraris' most detailed critique of Kant, see Ferraris (2013).

14 In Schelling's gloss, the "inverted idea [...] [is] the idea in which reason is set outside itself" (Schelling, 1842–1843a, pp. 162).

15 For the full version of this argument, see Tritten (2016).

16 The leading Schelling scholar concerned with how thought and language are to be viewed as being's own auto-construction is Daniel Whistler. See Whistler (2013, 2016a).

17 For the contrary thesis, see McGrath (2016b), who argues that Schelling is no longer doing *Naturphilosophie* in his late philosophy, at least not in the same sense as he was prior to 1809.

18 Furthering Grant's Schellingian project of naturalising or providing a real basis for ideality, note Whistler (2016 & 2013). Employing Schelling's "geology of language", Whistler treats language itself as a real "physical" object to be studied. Language is not a condition of reality, but it is a reality itself.

19 The originality of this question is normally attributed to Leibniz, but Karl Jaspers notes: "While with Leibniz the issue is quickly processed

with a logical operation and only occurs incidentally, through Schelling the question has first become an actual question" (Jaspers, 1955, p. 124).

20 Gabriel does not fully appreciate Schelling's criticisms of transcendental idealism or, as Merleau-Ponty might say, of philosophies of consciousness, contesting that "the late Schellingian effort [the philosophy of mythology and revelation] can indeed be thought of as a continuation of his earlier project of a 'history of self-consciousness'" (Gabriel, 2011, p. 72).

21 Merleau-Ponty suggests that "Bergson, who probably did not know Schelling's work, but who had read Ravaisson, who was himself steeped in Schelling's thought" (Merleau-Ponty, 2003, p. 39).

22 For a full account of this history as well as a systematic account the empiricism it presupposes, please note my manuscript currently in progress: *Speculative Empiricism and a Post-Humean Ontology of the Fact.*

23 See Tyler Tritten, "How Modern Schelling's 'Pre-Modern' Thought Made Postmodern Žižek 'Post-Postmodern'" in *The Palgrave Handbook to Poststructuralism and German Idealism*, Tilottama Rajan & Daniel Whistler (eds) (London: Palgrave, 2023).

CHAPTER 3
SPECULATIVE CONTINGENCY

THE ANHYPOTHETICAL GROUND OF REASON: THE ROLE OF DEMONSTRATION IN HEGEL'S AND MEILLASSOUX'S SPECULATIVE SYSTEMS[1]

Ørjan Steiro Mortensen

Abstract

This article draws an interesting parallel between Hegel's and Meillassoux's speculative systems that has been largely overlooked in the debate around speculative realism. I explore Hegel's and Meillassoux's similar use of demonstration as method for grounding speculative reason. For Hegel, the exposition of the historical-dialectical development of rational consciousness, which culminates in the emergence of absolute knowledge, is itself the demonstration that grounds his speculative idealism. For Meillassoux, reason emerges contingently in a contingent universe, and it is the demonstration of contingency as an absolutely necessary principle that becomes the foundation for his speculative materialism. For both Hegel and Meillassoux, the anhypothetical demonstration serves to show that reason can indeed account for its own foundation, and therefore that the concept of absolute knowledge can legitimately be rehabilitated.

Introduction

Ever since being introduced to Meillassoux's *After Finitude* in the early 2010s, I have been grappling with the historical-philosophical significance of speculative materialism as a philosophical programme. Particularly interesting to me in this regard is how speculative realism relates to and transforms the legacy of the post-Kantian philosophical canon, from Kant, via Hegel, to Heidegger.

In this paper, my aim is to bring out and explore some deeper similarities between Meillassoux's and Hegel's speculative projects. The affinity between these two projects is hinted at here and there, but generally disguised in Meillassoux's writings behind a traditional and underdeveloped reading of Hegel. Meillassoux portrays Hegel ultimately as a philosopher of dogmatic, metaphysical idealism. This interpretation has been amply criticised in later years and a new, post-metaphysical Hegel appears in the writings of Markus Gabriel, Rebecca Comay and Frank Ruda, and Slavoj Žižek among others. While acknowledging how controversial this new interpretation is among Hegel scholars, I am interested in seeing how this new interpretation would look when contrasted with Meillassoux's position of speculative materialism; one would think that a post-metaphysical Hegel has more in common with Meillassoux than the Hegel that Meillassoux himself describes.

My strategy in dealing with the respective "speculative turns" of these philosophers is to look at them from the perspective of what they were trying to achieve in their own historical contexts.

My hypothesis is that a historical-philosophical treatment would not only make evident that there are several points of resemblance between Meillassoux's and Hegel's systems, but even that Hegel, in a certain sense, is doing the same thing in his context as Meillassoux does, namely to turn around what is considered the decisive argument against absolute knowing, and deriving from it a new absolute principle to ground speculative reason.

For Meillassoux, this reversal takes place by means of refutational argumentation, what he calls *anhypothetical demonstration*. The aim of the anhypothetical demonstration is to show how thinking that tries to limit the scope of its own activity, as it were from within, necessarily will end up in inconsistency. I will therefore begin by looking closer at Meillassoux's methodological concept of anhypothetical demonstration, and then turn to Hegel to see whether it also can be applied to describe what is going on in Hegel's text.

Anhypothetical Demonstration and Correlationism

Kant argues in the *Critique of Pure Reason* that the function of conceptual reason is to furnish the contingent content of sense perception with the necessary logical structure to allow for meaningful experience. His critical procedure grounds the intelligibility of the empirical world in the speculative structure of reason, while leaving reason itself without intelligible foundation. Rational subjectivity for Kant can thus only be posited *hypothetically* as a spontaneous emergence, the origin of which is unknowable in principle. He therefore thinks that questions concerning the ground of reason are outside the scope of transcendental philosophy, and considers them instead a matter of faith.

For the post-Kantian speculative philosophies of Hegel and Meillassoux, it is crucial to re-establish an intelligible foundation for speculative reason. While they agree with Kant that such a ground can neither be established by way of traditional proof or deduction, it can — and must — be demonstrated *anhypothetically*.

In *L'inexistence divine*, Meillassoux defines an anhypothetical principle as a principle grounded in rational thought that is not posited in a contingent manner. He elaborates: "This principle breaks with hypothetical rationality. This rupture consists in the principle […] *not being posited* but grounded in a primary demonstration. Primary demonstration means this: argument stamped by necessity *presupposing nothing*. It is demonstrated without being deduced from another statement" (Meillassoux, 2016, pp. 31–32).[2]

In *After Finitude*, Meillassoux distinguishes the Platonic conception of an anhypothetical principle from its Aristotelian interpretation. Whereas, for Plato, the anhypothetical principle is revealed in the form of the intuitively accessible principle of the Good, for Aristotle the status of an anhypothetical principle must be confirmed in the course of rational argumentation. Meillassoux describes the Aristotelian version as "a fundamental proposition that could not be deduced from any other, but which could be proven by argument". He goes on: "This proof, which could be called 'indirect' or 'refutational,' proceeds […] by pointing out the inevitable inconsistency into which anyone contesting the truth of the principle is bound to fall" (Meillassoux, 2006, pp. 60–61). By adopting the Aristotelian method of indirect or refutational proof, Meillassoux aims at demonstrating the necessity of an absolute fundamental principle of reason without having to rely on mystical or intuitional experience.

Meillassoux performs his refutational argumentation against what he calls the *strong correlationist* paradigm defining much of continental philosophy even to this day. Correlationism is defined as a kind of silent consensus among philosophers that knowledge is grounded in the correlation, or co-givenness, of thought and being in experience. Whatever there is beyond the limits of possible experience is therefore considered epistemologically inaccessible even to speculative reason. As he says, according to the correlationist position, "we only ever have access to the correlation of being and thinking, never to either term considered apart from the other" (Meillassoux, 2006, p. 5).

Meillassoux's term "strong correlationism" refers to the post-modern, radicalised version of the Kantian "weak correlationism", introduced in the first *Critique.* As he explains in *After Finitude*, with Kant we get an *a priori* concept of the thing-in-itself of which we can at least know two things: that it actually exists and that it is non-contradictory. The strong model of correlationism denies even this rudimentary thinkability of the in-itself, and thus denies the very concept of absolute knowing. Instead, thinkers like Heidegger maintain a radical notion of epistemic finitude that correlates to a concept of the radical *otherness* of being in relation to thinking (Meillassoux, 2006, p. 35).

The strong correlationism implicit in the prevalent disciplines of phenomenology, hermeneutics, deconstructionism, etc., thus banishes the very possibility of speculative thinking, defined by Meillassoux as "every type of thinking that claims to be able to access some form of the absolute" (Meillassoux, 2006, p. 34). This anti-speculative consensus is the context in which Meillassoux enacts his speculative-materialist turn.

The Principle of Factiality

Meillassoux's demonstration of his anhypothetical *principle of factiality* begins by pointing out the seeming futility of reason as a true and necessary discourse of being itself. In order for reason to live up to its mandate, it has to overcome the problem of reaching the non-contingent ground of the contingent beings we interact with in the world. But if everything in existence, including reason itself, is ultimately contingent, how can we ever get to that necessary principle? Meillassoux's solution is to propose that, while there can be no existing *being* that is not factial, i.e., contingent, this condition of contingency is not itself a mere fact. As he says, "it cannot be a fact that what is, is a fact" (Meillassoux, 2016, p. 23). The only strictly necessary property a contingent being can possess is the very contingency of its mode of being. Not being a contingent fact pertaining to beings, the principle of factiality is therefore itself the necessary ground from which reason can begin its universal discourse.

This means that the agnosticism on behalf of knowledge, put forward by the Kantian limitation of reason, which states that we cannot deny the possibility of the thing-in-itself to be other than its appearance, must be turned into an absolute standpoint; it is not only possible, but *necessary*, that the thing-in-itself could be otherwise. The contingency of the appearance of things is in this way no longer considered to be a product of our inability to know the absolute ground of things. Rather than pointing to a "possibility of ignorance", it now points to a real possibility of change as a positive property of the thing.

Contingency, as the potential "capacity-to-be-other", is thus turned around, as Meillassoux says, into an "index of knowledge, rather than ignorance" (Meillassoux, 2006, p. 56). The *necessity of contingency* can be demonstrated in this way: if we were to propose that the contingency of a thing were itself contingent (say, upon my ignorance), we imply that the contingency itself could be otherwise, i.e., that the existence of the thing could also be necessary. But this means that what we are saying is that the thing equally well could be necessary as contingent (which, of course, would mean that the thing's existence isn't necessary after all). As Meillassoux says, "to contest the principle of factiality is thus to refute oneself, it is to claim that contingency is not absolute because it is absolute" (Meillassoux, 2016, p. 33). The anhypothetical demonstration in this way tries to force thinking to accept the necessity of contingency on the basis of the "unthinkability" of other alternatives (Meillassoux, 2006, p. 44).

Meillassoux's conception of absolute contingency is meant to sustain the Heideggerian (strong correlationist) emphasis on the primacy of time over being, by grounding this relation in iron-clad rationalist necessity. As he says, the principle of factiality translates into the "*very concept of a temporality delivered to its pure immanence*". This results in a conception of a pure time without becoming, whereby "the present is never pregnant with the future"

(Meillassoux, 2007, pp. 72–73; 2013, p. 100). The discussion of the rather eccentric consequences that Meillassoux draws from this principle unfortunately falls outside the scope of the current article.[3] I will instead now turn to Hegel and look at how he grounds speculative reason in a concept of dialectical movement by way of a similar argumentative strategy.

The Demonstration of Dialectical Movement as the Ground of Reason

At the beginning of Book One of the *Science of Logic*, Hegel ironically states that, in order for philosophy to get off the ground in the first place, it must either begin with something *mediated* — that is, a readily defined, dogmatically adopted, conceptual principle — or with something *immediate* — that is, inner revelation, faith or intellectual intuition that suddenly appears "like a shot from a pistol" (from nowhere) and withdraws from further logical determination. Since, as he says, "it is easy to show" that both alternatives lead to contradiction, Hegel chooses the third alternative: to begin with the contradiction itself (Hegel, 2010, p. 45).

It was Kant, with his antinomies of reason, who first demonstrated that the full exertion of pure rationality would necessarily lead to contradiction. He had thereby taken one step in the right direction, but he stopped short of accepting that contradiction itself therefore *is* the necessary ground of speculative reason. Kant instead concluded his inquiry with the provision that reason, the faculty of unconditional, universal — that is, *absolute* — knowledge, had to restrict its inherent impulse to go to the end in explanation, in order to avoid the contradictions that necessarily would follow (Hegel, 2010, p. 158). For Hegel, this amounts to an absurd, inconsistent position.

Hegel instead contends that the *demonstration of the dialectical movement of opposites,* inherent to pure conceptual reflection, must take the place of hypothetical reason. In order for reason to become truly speculative, he argues, the "oppositional movement" inherent to pure propositions must be given expression, not as an internal impediment to thought, but as the inherent feature of the subject matter of thought itself. What this means is that "actual speculation" is the expression of the "self-engendering" contradictions at work in all conceptual determination. As he says: "once dialectic has been separated from proof, the concept of philosophical demonstration has been led astray" (Hegel, 2018, p. 40). Rather than disqualify absolute speculation, as Kant had concluded, contradiction itself must be *shown* to be the central aspect of speculative thought. But how are we to understand the meaning of this originary dialectic and its consequences for the interpretation of the Hegelian system as a whole?

The Anhypothetical Demonstration of Contradiction

Hegel's speculative turn amounts to a relocating of the principle of contradiction, from the Kantian sphere of the transcendental, onto being itself. One could say that, analogous to Meillassoux's approach, he thereby changes the discourse, from the epistemological to the ontological, and turns contradiction into an index of ontological knowledge, rather than ignorance.

Hegel does this by way of demonstrating the inherent contradiction in the concept of being itself. At the beginning of the *Science of Logic*, Hegel famously demonstrates that the concept of "Being, pure being — without further determination", must collapse into its "other", nothingness, on account of both terms' equal lack of any discernible qualities (Hegel, 2010, p. 59). Hegel's speculative conclusion is that being itself is inconsistent, and therefore necessarily initiates *becoming*, graspable by reason as dialectical movement. Hegel refers to this originary contradiction inherent to being as "pure difference", a principle he associates with the emergence of *time*.

From this viewpoint, there seem to be many similarities between Hegel's and Meillassoux's procedure: both polemically invert the (if I may) "finitizing" argument of their opponent and end up with an ontological, or absolute, principle that is then interpreted as the intelligible explanation of the existence of time. But can we legitimately call Hegel's demonstration a *primary demonstration*, defined by Meillassoux as an "argument, stamped by necessity, *presupposing nothing*?"

Onto-ego-theo-logical Metaphysics

Not according to Meillassoux. Meillassoux seems to subscribe to the conventional continental interpretation of Hegel. This interpretation associates the movement of necessary contradiction with the presupposition of the necessary existence of some determinate, absolute entity: "Spirit, Will or Life". Hegel's philosophy represents, for Meillassoux, "an idealist absolutization of the correlation" of thinking and being that ultimately must "lead back to a dogmatic thesis" (Meillassoux, 2006, p. 60). For Meillassoux, the absolute contradiction at the core of Hegel's speculative philosophy entails the necessary existence of the subject-object correlation, or *Spirit* (with a capital "S"), understood as the sublated, positive expression of this co-relation.

This way of reading Hegel harkens back to Heidegger. In Heidegger's reading, being, essentially determined as dynamically inconsistent, which generates time as an aspect of its own movement, is associated with a presupposed, dogmatic concept of life (Heidegger, 1988, p. 142). There is some justification for this view in Hegel's text. For example, in the *Science of Logic,* where Hegel refers to the "necessity of contradiction" in its "positive aspect" as the "inner negativity [...] which is [the] self-moving soul, the principle of all natural and spiritual life" (Hegel, 2010, p. 35). The dynamic principle of contradiction inherent to being itself translates, in this interpretation, into a metaphysical vitalism, which grounds the emergence of finitude, time, in the presupposed eternal self-movement of living Spirit. Beings passing in and out of being are thus subsumed under the constant presence of Spirit, understood as the necessary being.

Subjectivity, understood as the contradictory identity of the in-itself and the for-itself of consciousness, in this light amounts to a particular instantiation of the originary contradiction. Because of the finite epistemic horizon of each particular consciousness, becoming appears phenomenally in an alienated form as *objective time*, but is in reality subsumed by the infinity of the immanent movement of the originary contradiction, which ultimately translates to the *life of Spirit* itself.

In Heidegger's interpretation, the speculative-ontological principle of the contradictory identity of being-in-itself-and-being-other thus translates into the ego-logical dimension of the "I=I", the identity of the in-itself and the for-itself of consciousness (Hegel, 2018, p. 463). After the teleological development of the dialectic of consciousness has played itself out the way Hegel shows in the *Phenomenology of Spirit*, the principle of pure difference attains the *theological* dimension of *Spirit*, which, for Heidegger, equates to the traditional metaphysical understanding of *eidos* or (divine) essence. For Heidegger, therefore, Hegel's idealism takes the form of an *onto-ego-theo-logical* metaphysics, the principle of which is the dialectical movement inherent to this speculative concept of (divine, Spiritual) life itself (Heidegger, 1988, p. 142). In this metaphysical interpretation, Hegel presupposes all along the traditional metaphysical first principle that in the end appears on the scene to resolve all the contradictions, eliminate contingency and close the system into a completed whole.

Idealism of Matter

This interpretation has repeatedly come under fire in recent years by scholars who find in Hegel a more post-metaphysical and materialist ontology than the one Heidegger and Meillassoux describe. For example, Hegel scholars Frank Ruda and Rebecca Comay go quite far in emphasising the centrality of contingency in Hegel's thought. As they state in their book *The Dash — The other side of absolute knowing*, Meillassoux's interpretation of Hegel's idealism, as an absolutisation of correlationism, completely misses Hegel's point. According to them, there is in fact *no correlation* between the dialectically opposed terms of being and thinking. Rather, there is a strict "*nonrelation*" between the terms, wherein no "preassigned place for the subject" can be found in substance nor "for substance in the subject" (Comay and Ruda, 2018, p. 18). In their interpretation, the contradiction between the terms remains irreducible throughout the development of the *Phenomenology of Spirit*, and the result is that every actual, situated instantiation of the subject/substance relation necessarily will be marked by contingency and incompleteness.

The emergence of self-determining or "absolute" spirit in the *Phenomenology* can therefore not be interpreted as a necessary outcome, nor a stable endpoint. "Absolute", in this sense, means nothing else than that spirit, as the intersubjective framework of knowledge, has ceased to look elsewhere than its own historical becoming to account for its existence. This reconciliation with the ultimate contingency of its existence is what makes spirit absolute. By renouncing the Kantian, non-contradictory sphere of the in-itself, Hegel's absolute spirit accounts for itself only in light of its own strictly contingent, and *ongoing*, historical becoming, which remains forever "riddled by negativity" and contradiction (ibid.).

Contingent Necessity

According to philosopher Markus Gabriel, Hegel's argument in the *Science of Logic* revolves around the concept of *contingent necessity*, which implies that an irreducible moment of contingency is always involved in Hegel's notion of dialectical becoming (Gabriel, 2011, p. 121). This means, very roughly, that while you *can* retroactively determine the necessary preconditions for the coming-into-being of a given entity once it has actually come into being, there is no way to predict the outcome of the dialectical movement in advance. The necessity with which being produces becoming does not therefore imply that *what* was brought into being thereby also is necessary as such. There is always a fundamental openness, or incompleteness, in Hegel's theory that must be assumed in order to account for the possibility of ontogenesis (becoming) in the first place. In Žižek's words, this amounts to an "ontological incompleteness of reality", which Hegel accounts for by way of the demonstration of the originary contradiction. Being is itself simply incapable of remaining a non-contradictory unity, and becoming, or *time*, is therefore unavoidable (Žižek, 2012, p. 149). One could say that the difference between Hegel's and Meillassoux's speculative commitments in this interpretation translates into a difference between the concepts of *contingent necessity* and *necessary contingency* (Gabriel, 2009, p. 15). Although this is a crucial distinction in its own right, it is not the same as a difference between dogmatic-metaphysical idealism, on the one hand, and materialism on the other, as Meillassoux would have it.[4]

This is why Comay and Ruda calls Hegel's idealism an idealism of (inconsistent) matter. At the beginning of the *Science of Logic*, all there is is the pure contingency of an event brought about by being's demonstrable, inherent inability to remain a consistent whole equal to itself. Only the "incompleteness and inconsistency of materiality itself" is presupposed (Comay and Ruda, 2018, p. 18). We could maybe venture to call this interpretation, with Meillassoux in mind, an *idealism of factiality*, where the contingent, or *factial,* emergence of historical-dialectical spirit is all that has been explained. And in this light, Hegel's principle of necessary contradiction from the beginning of the *Science of Logic* does rather seem to fit Meillassoux's description of an Aristotelian anhypothetical principle, which, "*presupposing nothing*", can only be proven by way of primary demonstration (Meillassoux, 2006, pp. 60–61).

Speculation through Refutational Demonstration: Conclusion

In summary, we can say that both Hegel and Meillassoux seek to overcome what was perceived as the determinative obstacle of their day to the legitimacy of speculative thinking. The difference between the two speculative results is thus explainable *via negativa*, in terms of what they try to refute: Hegel's speculative idealism is a reaction against the transcendental idealism of Kant, which posited a non-contradictory sphere of the thing-in-itself, considered inaccessible to speculative reason, on account of reason's inherent dialectical nature. Meillassoux's speculative materialism, although he references Kant as the instigator of correlationism, is primarily provoked by the anti-metaphysical philosophy of Heidegger, whose privileging of time over being introduced a concept of radical contingency that disqualified any knowledge as properly ontological.

One can thus understand Meillassoux's speculative project as trying to do to the Heideggerian (strong correlationist) paradigm what Hegel tried to do to the Kantian (weak correlationist) paradigm. And if we accept a post-metaphysical interpretation of Hegel, we can say that in both cases an anhypothetical, primary demonstration serves to turn the main argument of their opponents on its head. This speculative turn establishes that what was considered the condition of impossibility for absolute knowing must itself be regarded as the very ground of absolute knowing. For Hegel, this is the necessity of contradiction; for Meillassoux, it is the necessity of contingency.

References:

Bryant, Levi, Nick Srnicek, & Graham Harman (eds). *The Speculative Turn.* Melbourne: re.press, 2011.

Comay, Rebecca & Frank Ruda. *The Dash — The Other Side of Absolute Knowing.* Cambridge Mass. and London: The MIT Press, 2018.

Gabriel, Markus & Slavoj Žižek. *Mythology, Madness and Laughter: Subjectivity in German Idealism.* New York: Continuum, 2009.

Gabriel, Markus. *Transcendental Ontology: Essays in German Idealism.* New York: Continuum, 2011.

Gironi, Fabio. "Meillassoux's Speculative Philosophy of Science: Contingency and Mathematics". *Pli: The Warwick Journal of Philosophy* 22. Warwick: Department of Philosophy, University of Warwick, 2011.

Hegel, Georg W.F. *The Science of Logic,* translated by George di Giovanni. Cambridge: Cambridge University Press, 2010.

Hegel, Georg W.F. *Phenomenology of Spirit,* translated by Terry Pinkard. Cambridge: Cambridge University Press, 2018.

Heidegger, Martin. *Hegel's Phenomenology of Spirit,* translated by Parvis Emad & Kenneth Maly. Bloomington and Indianapolis: Indiana University Press, 1988.

Kant, Immanuel. *Critique of Pure Reason,* translated by Paul Guyer & Allen W. Wood. Cambridge: Cambridge University Press, 2013.

Meillassoux, Quentin. *After Finitude: An Essay on the Necessity of Contingency,* translated by Ray Brassier. New York: Continuum, 2006.

Meillassoux, Quentin. "Potentiality and Virtuality". In *Collapse II,* edited by Robin McKay. Falmouth: Urbanomic, 2007.

Meillassoux, Quentin. "Time Without Becoming". *Spike* 35, Theories for the 21st Century, edited by Armen Avanessian. Vienna and Berlin: Rita Vittorelli, 2013.

Meillassoux, Quentin. *L'Inexistence Divine,* translated by (partial) Nathan Brown. *Parrhesia* 25. Dundee and Melburn: Open Humanities Press, 2016.

Žižek, Slavoj. *Less Than Nothing: Hegel and the Shadow of Dialectical Materialism.* London and New York: Verso Books, 2012.

Notes

1 A preliminary version of this paper was given at the Nordic Society of Phenomenology's online PhD workshop, 22 April 2021.

2 These quotes are from Nathan Brown's partial translation of Meillassoux's dissertation work, *L'inexistence divine*, published in 2016 in the journal *Parrhesia*.

3 Detailed discussions on the problematic aspects of Meillassoux's concept of pure temporality as "hyper-chaos" or "time without becoming" can be found in Peter Hallward's and Martin Hägglund's contributions to Bryant, L., N. Srnicek, and G. Harman (eds), 2011. Another interesting critique of these aspects in Meillassoux, from the point of view of empirical science, can be found in Gironi (2011).

4 In fact, it could be argued that such a post-metaphysical Hegelianism, which acknowledges contingently emerging necessity, has many advantages over Meillassoux's speculative materialism, in that it avoids having to rely on the principle of "creatio ex nihilo", which follows from the concept of absolute contingency as "time without becoming". See Note 3.

CORRELATION WITHOUT CORRELATIONISM: A PHENOMENOLOGY OF THE ONTOLOGICAL INDEPENDENCE OF ANCESTRAL STARDUST

Dustin Zielke

Phenomenology: Correlational but Not Correlationist

In September 1959, a 220-pound rock from outer space crashed into Australia. Taking the name of the town closest to its impact, it came to be known as the Murchison meteorite. Over 60 years later, in January 2020, scientists confirmed that it contains the oldest material on Earth. They have dated its silicon carbide particles to be as old as 8.5 billion years. These particles existed in "our parent interstellar cloud", otherwise called the solar nebula, between 3–4 billion years before the birth of the Sun, the solar system, and the Earth (Heck et al., 2020).

The presolar grains inside the Murchison meteorite would certainly qualify as what Quentin Meillassoux has called an *arche-fossil*. By this, he does not mean a fossil in the usual sense of the term — the fossilised remains of now-extinct lifeforms. Instead, he means "materials indicating the existence of an ancestral reality or event; one that is anterior to terrestrial life" (2011, p. 10). The ancestral, to which the arche-fossil points, is "any reality anterior to the emergence of the human species" (2011, p. 10). An arche-fossil is *a physical remainder* of the ancestral. And scientists use them to make discoveries about events that happened long before human life evolved. For instance, geologists might use a rock that contains isotopes "whose rate of decay we know" to date the origin of the Earth (Meillassoux, 2011, p. 10). Or, in the case of the Murchison meteorite, astronomers might use traces of radiation exposure to establish the lifetimes of this interstellar dust (Heck et al., 2020). Arche-fossils allow scientists to make statements about the ancestral, but Meillassoux argues that the kind of philosophy he calls correlationism cannot philosophically establish the realist sense of such ancestral statements.

According to Meillassoux and other speculative realists, phenomenology is a type of correlationism. When I first encountered speculative realism over a decade ago, this was the part that I found least convincing. Zahavi (2016) has recently pointed out some of the broad deficiencies of the speculative realist critique of phenomenology. I agree with Zahavi that this polemic is not grounded in primary or secondary phenomenological literature; it is largely misdirected, and overall, it is not a fair characterisation of phenomenology. In each case of the founding figures, whether we are talking about Husserl, Heidegger, Sartre, or Merleau-Ponty, a strong case can be made that they are not correlationists in the derogatory sense of the term. Each of them has a deep and sophisticated awareness about the difference between epistemic and ontological levels of analysis. But it is precisely a lack of sophistication about these different philosophical levels that defines the "correlationist circle" as originally formulated by Meillassoux (2011, p. 5). While this basic category mistake may have proliferated after the linguistic turn amongst misled graduate students and non-philosophical theorists, it was not the fault of the great phenomenologists. Another commentator put this quite simply: "it should be the cause of great astonishment if the philosophers referred to as correlationists by Meillassoux, such as Kant, Husserl, and Heidegger were not capable of understanding that the sun has existed before man" (Gabriel & Žižek, 2009, pp. 86–87). But, of course, Meillassoux and other speculative realists are not just talking about what phenomenologists could understand, but what *they could philosophically establish*.

I have always found *doing* phenomenology in response to issues more interesting than writing about phenomenologists doing phenomenology. And so, instead of trying to defend any of the mainstream phenomenologists from the critique of correlationism, I will instead address the substantive issue. How can a phenomenological position establish the naive realism that Meillassoux says underlies ancestral statements? I take naive realism here to be the minimal realist requirements that one must adopt to affirm the real anteriority of the ancestral. Namely, (1) that the ancestral really existed, and (2) that the ancestral's existence is mind-independent. Note that when something's mind-independence is affirmed, this means that its being or existence is not ontologically reduced to the epistemic sphere. In other words, what is intended is something that would exist regardless of whether or not a cognising subject recognises this. As we will see with regard to the presolar grains of the Murchison meteorite, the phenomenological analysis of the givenness of the ancestral to a subject does not negate either its existence or its mind-independence. When properly understood, intentional analysis of the realness of the ancestral establishes the material referent's real independence from the referrer. The subject of the correlation thereby recognises the correlation's own contingency with regard to the ancestral. This *practice of phenomenology* will show how a transcendental phenomenological approach can establish the naive realism underlying scientific statements about the ancestral — exactly what Meillassoux and other speculative realists claim it should not be able to do (Meillassoux, 2011, p. 5; Sparrow, 2014, p. *ix*).

Meillassoux and speculative realism more broadly do not succeed in framing phenomenology as an anti-realist correlationism. Phenomenology may be epistemically correlational, but it need not be ontologically correlationist. Still, speculative realism does offer a positive opportunity for contemporary phenomenology — beyond just allowing it to defend its realist credentials. It presents the phenomenological tradition with another road into the long history of encounters with naturalism. Meillassoux's ancestral presents the possibility of thinking the correlation within a broader material context that precedes but also subtends consciousness. The challenge for phenomenology in relation to naturalism has always been about how to reconcile a naturalist perspective without reducing phenomenology's transcendental project to a scientific naturalism, where causal analysis is the last explanatory factor. The critique of correlationism provides the opportunity to re-think the transcendental project of phenomenology, to substantially revise the materialism underlying the naturalist perspective, and thereby to make both compatible with metaphysical realism. The Murchison meteorite and its presolar particles thereby provide the opportunity to illustrate the requisite form of emergent materialism: *ecstatic materiality*. They also occasion the opportunity to develop a naturalist transcendentalism compatible with phenomenology and its correlational perspective that I will call *ecstatic cosmology*.

The Ancestral and Mind-Independence

The critique of correlationism, as initially laid out by Meillassoux, is well-known to those familiar with speculative realism. As he originally put it in *After Finitude*, correlationism is any philosophy (but especially transcendental philosophy, postmodernism, and phenomenology), "according to which we only ever have access to the correlation between thinking and being, and never either term considered apart from the other [...]" (2011, p. 5). In other words, a correlationist would say we cannot speak or think about something mind-independent. To do so would amount to a performative contradiction, since any speaking or thinking would already imply the presence of the speaker or thinker. This is why Meillassoux thinks that correlationists collapse reality "in itself" into its givenness for an intentional subject.

Meillassoux indeed admits that correlationists can affirm that there is a real world outside of thought, but he argues that the consistent correlationist cannot hold that this world exists independently from consciousness: "consciousness and language certainly transcend themselves towards the world, but there is a world only insofar as consciousness transcends itself towards it" (2011, p. 7). For Meillassoux, even though correlationists can affirm a transcendent reality, they cannot affirm the mind-independent nature of this reality. This is what I take him to mean when he writes that "consequently, it becomes possible to say that every philosophy which disavows naive realism has become a variant of correlationism" (2011, p. 5). Naive realism, or its philosophical establishment, here amounts to not just the affirmation of the existence of the ancestral *but more importantly to the establishment of its ontological independence.* This elucidates his substantive issue with correlationism as well. It apparently cannot ground the ontologically independent objects of geology, astronomy, cosmology, and other scientific theories[1] — that is, it cannot establish the mind-independent status of natural phenomena.

Because of this, Meillassoux compares correlationism to Berkeleyian idealism (2011, p. 18; 2008, p. 3). Recall that, in Berkeley's metaphysical idealism, the actual existence of things is not called into question. He famously wrote "*esse est percipi (aut percipere)*" — to be is to be perceived (or to perceive). What is perceived *exists*, it is just that its existence is put under a global qualification. Something exists if and only if it is perceived (or perceiving). Meillassoux notes that contemporary correlationism, such as phenomenology, tries to distinguish itself from the "crude idealism of the Berkeleyian variety". But he adds, "what I try to demonstrate in *After Finitude* is that every correlationism collapses into this crude idealism when it tries to think the significance of ancestrality" (2008, p. 3). For him, phenomenologists must apparently insist upon the *mind-dependent status* of the referents of ancestral statements.

According to Meillassoux and other speculative realists, as a phenomenologist, I should not be able to establish the ancestral reality of the presolar grains and the interstellar medium as entities anterior to their givenness or manifestation to human beings today. I should not be able to affirm their mind-independence without contradicting myself. I *can* (according to Meillassoux) affirm literally and matter-of-factly the existence of the solar nebula, that some of the meteorite's silicon carbide particles are 8.5 billion years old, and that they predate the formation of the solar system. But I *cannot*, without "self-contradiction" (Meillassoux, 2011, p. 14), affirm the ontological independence of these apart from their manifestation and givenness to human subjects in the present, for this would be postulating the "givenness of a being anterior to givenness", which is "absurd" (Meillassoux, 2011, p. 14). My phenomenological method, apparently, requires me to *ontologically reduce* all ancestral existence and its present-day arche-fossil remainders to the epistemic conditions of givenness between subject and object.

Add to this Tom Sparrow's recent addendum to Meillassoux's critique of phenomenology as correlationism. Sparrow argues that even if I, myself — the person who otherwise identifies as a phenomenologist — holds realist positions like the affirmation of the mind-independence of the ancestral, these are not strictly speaking the result of my phenomenological method (2014, p. *ix*). They are, in other words, extra-phenomenological commitments.[2] This is highly problematic. For one thing, as a philosophical discipline, phenomenology is in the business of making arguments for certain positions (including metaphysically realist positions). Because it *is* a method for argumentation, it can very much yield realist and metaphysical commitments. Even if one takes Husserl's idealism as the pinnacle of phenomenological method (as Sparrow does), Husserlian scholars have shown how this epistemically establishes metaphysical realism without assuming the latter from the beginning (Bernet, 2004; Carr, 1999; Crowell, 2001; Zahavi, 2004). In other words, the methodological bracketing of metaphysical realism in Husserl's philosophy is accomplished to argue against and overcome global scepticism *while not assuming what one wants to prove*; namely, these very same realist commitments. Even Husserl's idealist phenomenological method is compatible with realism. It is a hard-won realism because the former establishes the possibility of the latter.

Phenomenology as a Distinct Method

Nevertheless, speculative realists like Meillassoux and Sparrow might question whether what I am doing in this paper counts as phenomenology. If it did not, then I really would not have made any advances on their critique of that style of philosophy. Phenomenology is indeed a method or practice, and as a form of doing philosophy, it is distinct in the following ways.

Like other philosophical approaches, but unlike the positive sciences, phenomenology is not an empirical investigation. In the tradition, this disciplinary difference is methodologically established through something similar to what Husserl called the phenomenological reduction (Husserl, 1983, p. 131ff). This is a method of bracketing the implicit yet foundational world-belief — or existential affirmation — at the core of every perceptual experience of the world. By suspending the affirmation of the existence of the intended object, the Husserlian phenomenologist puts out of play the empirical question about whether the intention is true or its object real, for this would require empirical investigation to ascertain, and phenomenology is not an empirical discipline. Above, I said "something similar" to the phenomenological reduction because not all phenomenologists follow Husserl's formulation of this methodological point. For instance, Heidegger (1962) and hermeneutic phenomenology more broadly do not pose it in this ego-centric way. Instead, this branch prioritises the hermeneutic circle, which is never a fully accomplished, interpretive back and forth with the world. Empirical, scientific investigation is only one interpretive framework to project onto the world (Heidegger, 1977). It is the best at discovering objective facts about the universe, but it is not the only way of understanding existence.

Differentiating itself from much traditional philosophy, phenomenology privileges intuition over unfulfilled speculative claims. Husserl once called this to be the principle of all principles (1983, p. 44). Phenomenologists after him modified this claim and expanded it to include phenomena that are difficult to "picture" (e.g., Heidegger's *das Nichts*). But all phenomenologists seek to ground their claims on *some kind of intuitive basis.*[3] In my case, training in phenomenology taught me to think and write with images in my mind's eye — so to speak. Those who have not been trained in phenomenology often miss this. Phenomenological argumentation is thus unlike much non-phenomenological theory and philosophy, which puts words and concepts into non-contradictory logical order to make sense. For phenomenologists, argumentation isn't just logical order or coherence; it needs to occur through *phenomenological seeing*. The words and concepts must be intuitively grasped in the phenomenon under discussion. Phenomenologists consider arguments without this intuitive exhibition to be ungrounded logical constructions. In all the main branches of phenomenology (eidetic, hermeneutic, existential), there is always an intuition both the writer and reader are referring to.[4] As I write about materiality and the Murchison meteorite in the following section, I will have in mind both the formal or essential phenomenon of the real (Zielke, 2018) and the actual scientific practice that astronomers used to produce ancestral statements about presolar dust (Heck et al., 2020).

Givenness and Evidence

The asteroid that eventually fell to Earth near Murchison formed billions of years ago in the interstellar medium. Astronomers refer to part of this vast, primordial region of dust and gas clouds as the solar nebula, because it would eventually accrete into the Sun and solar system. When the asteroid formed around this time, it captured some silicon particles from the clouds around it. The vast majority of presolar particles like this were destroyed "after accretion in their parent bodies during thermal metamorphism and aqueous alteration" (Heck et al., 2020). But the Murchison asteroid is special because it preserved them until now. After taking samples from the meteorite, astronomers isolated the particles in a process that the lead author of the study, Philipp Heck, likened to "burning down the haystack to find the needle" (Weisberger, 2020).

Once they had the presolar grains on their own, Heck and company used a technique to estimate their age. By looking at how long the grains were exposed to high-energy radiation blasting through the interstellar medium, the astronomers could say how old the particles were. Weisberger likens the process to putting a bucket outside in a heavy rainstorm, "As long as the rain falls at a steady rate, you could calculate how long the bucket had been outside based on the amount of rain that it collects" (Weisberger, 2020). The astronomers knew the rate of the radiation hitting the grains, so they could estimate how old they were. And this resulted in what Meillassoux would call an ancestral statement; namely, that they were up to 8.5 billion years old.

Let us see how phenomenology can establish the realist and mind-independent sense of this statement. In other words, how can we say from a phenomenological perspective that these presolar grains existed 8.5 billion years ago, regardless of whether or not human beings eventually came to understand this?

Meillassoux claims that, for a correlationist, it is absurd to affirm a time before givenness (2011, p. 14). If we are talking about phenomenology, what he is pointing towards, and what he is correct in pointing towards, is *the formal necessity* of the correlation.

Phenomenology, in all its varieties, is always an analysis of an intentional correlation between the one who intends (a subject) and that which is intended (the object).[5] When one speaks of givenness to a subject or, more specifically, evidence or data given to a scientist, for a phenomenologist this *always* entails the subject or scientist to whom it is given. I am calling this a formal necessity because the very form of intentional analysis, by definition, requires this co-relation. As Meillassoux points out, to deny this is to wander into self-contradictions. However, what he and other speculative realists seem not to understand is that *the correlation's formal necessity does not also necessarily entail the ontological reduction of that which is given within the correlation*. The givenness of evidence of a presolar past available to scientists today is an *epistemological* condition for this understanding. But elaborating upon the epistemological conditions for givenness does not require one to deny the referent existed before the *de facto* conditions for this givenness emerged (with the birth of humanity and the historical development of science), nor does it require the phenomenologist deny the ontological independence of that which is given.

In the case of Heck and company's experiments, phenomenologically elaborating upon the epistemological conditions for the appearance of the ancestral grains would, very roughly, go something like this. The grains in the lab were in fact the present-day embodiment of the ancestral grains. The solar grains as they were prior to the emergence of the Sun and Earth are not here today, bodily present, ready to be seen directly. They are not directly given. They are anterior to direct givenness. Because the ancestral grains (as *they were* during the ancestral) are not directly given to intuition in the present, the scientists must synthesise present intuitions given in experiments with already established knowledge about the universe to make inferences about the grains in the past. How is this possible? Not all givenness is full givenness. There are shades of givenness. The presolar grains give themselves indirectly through other measurable effects. The phenomenology of science here speaks of "mediate evidence", and it seeks to show how and why this kind of indirect evidence is valid in scientific investigation (Harvey & Shelton, 1992).

So far, in one sense, Meillassoux is correct in pointing out that "being *is not* anterior to givenness, it *gives itself* as anterior to givenness" (2011, p. 14). The being of the presolar grains gives itself as being anterior to any direct givenness, but still, it nevertheless gives itself to a present-day subject through mediate evidence or indirect "givenness". In phenomenologically epistemic terms — that is, in terms that elaborate phenomenologically upon how we know what we know and the way in which we can know something — this all indeed requires a *de facto* subject. And when we are speaking epistemically of that which is given to a subject, and elaborating upon the conditions for this knowledge, we must — *necessarily* — correlate that which is given with the one to whom it is given. However, even within an epistemological frame, the reference to an ontologically independent object does not collapse the object's being into the referrer's act of knowledge. To claim this would be self-contradictory, for it would then no longer be an act of objective knowing of a mind-independent object, but the mere projection of a subject. It would not be knowledge about the mind-independent world. An act of knowledge (when it comes to an objective referent) affirms the being of that referent as being objective and mind-independent — if that is the kind of being it is. Givenness is the way this knowledge is established. It does not reduce the ontological being of the object into a mere epistemic projection of a subject. It establishes the possibility of affirming and connecting the subject to a more-than-subjective reality that would be there regardless of whether a *de facto* subject is there to know it.[6] Even still, givenness need not only be understood in an epistemological way in phenomenology.

From the vantage point of a phenomenological ontology, what is in fact currently given to a subject need not have been given to a subject in the larger scheme of things. Here, one would direct their phenomenological gaze not towards the epistemic conditions within the correlation to show how a relation of scientific knowledge is possible, but to the ontological conditions of the very possibility of the correlation itself.[7] How can the subject and that which is given to it come into any relation in the first place? In this sense, the correlation's necessary relation between subject and object, the correlation itself, now has a deeper-level modality. The *de facto* relation between a subject and object formally required in any act of intentionality is modalised into a contingent possibility. In other words, the relation is only possible in principle, given certain conditions. There is no commitment to whether or not it must have actually happened. This ontological modalisation *relativises* the correlation's formal necessity into one mere contingent possibility amongst others. So, phenomenologically, we can very easily affirm the following: *if* given, then necessarily given to a subject; yet, *when* given, *only given contingently so*. From this perspective, there is nothing necessary about the givenness itself, even from within the intentional relation, because we are speaking about the possibility of givenness itself. There is givenness, but it is bracketed, so to speak, to show how it is possible. And showing how it is possible relative to the reality of the ancestral is to show how the givenness in the correlation is a contingent event in the material universe. This is where a phenomenologist can establish the mind-independence of that which is given (i.e., the ancestral) as really existing before any *de facto* subject and therefore any *de facto* givenness — regardless of whether the latter emerges or not. There is a correlation here, but without correlationism.

The Realness of the Presolar Grains

When Heck and company were intending the presolar grains in their laboratory, they were intending them as traces of the ancestral past to which they belonged. The grains themselves had endured over this timespan, from their incorporation into the Murchison asteroid in the solar nebula up until the time they were uncovered in the lab. Although I cannot speak for Heck and his colleagues, or their philosophy of science, let us assume that they hold a realist position like the one that Meillassoux would attribute to scientific statements. Their scientific realism would then amount to two important senses about the realness of the grains during the presolar ancestral period (and this time period itself). First, this position would say the particles were real in the sense *that they existed*; Heck et al. concluded that the grains were up to 8.5 billion years old, and this means that these grains actually existed up to 8.5 billion years ago. Second, the sense of these statements would also imply that the grains' existence *was* ontologically independent from the existence of a terrestrial subject. The reasons are obvious. The Earth did not emerge until several billions of years after the time in question and human beings did not evolve for another several billion years after that. In short, the ontological independence of the ancestral grains entails that they existed *regardless of whether or not they would eventually come to be given to a human being in a laboratory*. This implies a third sense of realism that is decisive for the current argument. Not only does it suggest that this independence *was* the case, but also that it *continues to be the case today*. In other words, we need to be able to phenomenologically establish, and thereby affirm, that even though human being has *de facto* emerged and can now recognise the ancestral, this does not ontologically reduce the existence of this ancestral time to its givenness in the present.

Now that we have mapped out this realist position, we can show how a phenomenological approach can justify, establish, or ground it. It does this by establishing the sense of the realness of the real, which includes the reference to a referent (the ancestral) that is ontologically independent from the referrer and, thereby, the reference itself (i.e., the correlation). The correlation can understand its own contingency with regard to the real past, thereby establishing the ontological independence of the ancestral that it intends. And, while making room for contingency *per se*, it can establish the real in a transcendental position — one which founds the material conditions of possibility for the correlation itself.

The Real: Actuality, Materiality, and Temporality

When Heck and the other scientists were intending the presolar grains, they were intending them as both material and actual things. The grains were there, in the laboratory, under the microscope, in the flesh, so to speak. And the scientists could see them and how their experiments affected them. To say they were there is to say that they were *actually* there. In other words, the grains were in the *act of existing*. When I say this, I do not mean to suggest that the grains were performing an act like an intentional subject. In the phenomenological tradition, the term "act" usually refers to motivated, purposive, or at least intentional achievements of consciousness. This is not what I mean. Instead, I mean to say that the grains were actual, but *in an active sense*. Like others who come from a posthumanist background (Heidegger, 1971; Latour, 2012; Bennett, 2010), I think that the traditional, modern subject-object dichotomy is too reductive.[8] What the tradition often characterised as inert, static things actually have their own modes or forms of activity. The grains, for instance, were actually existing and responding "to being prodded" so that the scientists could perceive and engage with them throughout their experiment. This brings me to the next point.

The grains in Heck's lab were also intended as being *material*. To be a material thing is to be part of a larger causal context. With regard to any one individual, this amounts to being both a causal "agent" (again, not an intentional agent necessarily) *and* a causal patient of effects passed on from other material things. To be both effector and affected. The experimental method that seeks to tightly control variables and factors to isolate and test certain relationships presumes this causal field. When the astronomers looked for evidence of exposure to interstellar radiation, they also assumed this. The grains were affected by the radiation and so, because of this, there were traces from its interaction with them. Each grain registered the radiation, and when the scientists looked for it, the grains presented this evidence of interaction. They yielded it. The grains' act of existing includes this active participation within a larger causal field that, as we know from the experiment, dates back 8.5 billion years.

The grains' existence is an act not just in the sense that it is active and material, but also in the sense that *it is an ongoing activity over time*. The act of existing is durational no matter how long or short. Even subatomic particles, which physicists tell us pop in and out of existence almost instantly, endure for some amount of time — no matter how short. As real things, the presolar grains also have a temporal existence, one which the astronomers sought to measure. Heck and the other scientists tell us that the Murchison particles have endured for an astronomically long time. Their act of existence has been a durative act that has lasted for up to 8.5 billion years. I have already explained how they established this unimaginably long time. What is important to explain now is *how* a real thing's act of existence occurs over time. How does an act of existing *actualise itself through time*?

Heck et al.'s study tells us that most presolar particles did not survive the solar nebula. They were destroyed during incorporation into parent bodies through heat or water. Beyond the *terrestrial* contingencies that needed to unfold so that the meteorite could end up in a lab (the discovery of the Murchison meteorite, the gathering of samples, etc.), there were various *pre-terrestrial* contingencies that had to happen for the silicon particles to eventually make their way to Heck and his colleagues. More generally, this points to the role of potential and contingency in a real thing's temporal act of existing.

An act of existing *is an actualisation* that its destruction or death would preclude. It is an actualisation of the potential to exist over time. As Heck points out, for most of the silicon carbide particles in the early solar system, the potential for existence was retracted by material conditions like gravity, accretion, thermal dynamics, and erosion. When the material conditions were no longer conducive to these particle's potential to exist, their act of existence ended. This already indicates that, when we are speaking about real, material things, their acts of existence are limited and enabled by material or causal conditions. The solar nebula within which the particles existed before incorporation was conducive to their existence, while accretion into larger bodies tended to be less so. This reflects a more general insight about the real. The potential for an actualisation of real existence is (1) potentiated by material conditions and (2) possibly de-potentiated by material conditions as well. In other words, the material limits of the material field, to which a real thing belongs, *enable* and *constrain* its act of existence.

As a whole, so to speak, the grains' possibility for existence was mediated by material conditions. The environment was either conducive to them or not. But there is also another sense in which the grains actualised their capacity to exist. An act of existing is not just (on the whole) a contingent potential *over time*, but it is also an actualisation of contingent potentials *through time*. At any given moment, its act of existing consists in actualising from a wider selection of potentials or contingencies.

A real thing's act of existence is an actualisation of a potential to exist. When material conditions are met, this potential can be actualised. But, more specifically, within a material field that is conducive to a real thing's actualisation, there are also more minute contingencies that it plays a role in determining. At any given moment, a material field contains contingencies that amount to a set of potentials for a particular thing to actualise or not. This set of potentials allow for mutually exclusive future states both in the individual thing and the field itself.[9] In response to this, at any given time, a real thing actualises its potential for existing by selecting from a range of potentials available to it, most of which never come to pass.[10] The silicon carbide particles in the Murchison asteroid selected potentials that amounted to their incorporation into this asteroid, whereas the vast majority of similar particles selected available potentials that eventually led to their destruction.[11] This is what an act of existing consists in: an actualisation of the potential to exist by way of selecting from a range of available potentials, enabled and constrained by material conditions *over time*.[12]

So far, I have shown that the sense of realness itself includes the existence of real things and explained some of its basic features. To show the sense of the real's independence, I will attend to the way that this independence sets a transcendental condition upon the correlation itself.

The Contingency of the Correlation

The astronomers refer both to the present grains and to the way they were 8.5 billion years ago. In other words, they refer to the grains in two different temporal dimensions: as present and as past. This timespan between the past grains and the way they are today is a period of 8.5 billion years. Despite the unimaginably long timescale involved, the scientists intend the past grains and the present grains as the selfsame grains. They are not, strictly speaking, identical — in the sense that they have not changed at all. We have seen that, over time, their properties changed because of interactions with radiation. Nevertheless, the grains are intended as being the same through change. We already have a phenomenological basis for constituting the sense of their selfsameness over time: durative acts of existing in a material field.

The referents here, the presolar grains, are intended as real, actual, materially interacting things, both past and present. By way of mediate evidence established during their experiments, the scientists refer to the grains before they accrued the effects of all the radiation they measured — the way they were up to 8.5 billion years ago before, as Heck put it, it started raining. As we know, referring to the grains 8.5 billion years ago includes the understanding that this predates human being, so the grains in their distant past mode are ancestral grains. This deep time of the grains contains the possibility of co-existing with human beings in the distant future (namely, our present). But it also contains the possibility of not co-existing with human beings, if human beings do not emerge. In this respect, even though the human being *did* emerge, the reference to the presolar grains at the time of the ancestral presents the *de facto* eventual emergence of the human being as a contingent event. In other words, to refer to the grains as real in the ancestral past is to relativise the modality of the present referrer and the reference itself, but not the referent outside of this reference.

Prior to the emergence of human beings, the range of potentials through which the grains could actualise their existence contained the possibility of their givenness to human beings, but also the possibility of not being given to human beings, because the latter might not have emerged. Even if such a being does emerge, if this being refers to the referents (i.e., the ancestral grains) as real and ontologically independent from the reference itself, this need not be a self-contradiction, for the referent's givenness is only a potential givenness to a *de facto* subject, not a necessary givenness to a *de facto* subject. The conditions for the referent's givenness to this subject only emerge when this subject *de facto* emerges. And this is not a necessary event.

Toward a Transcendental Materialism: The (Inter-) Independence of the Transobjective

How then can we see the ancestral as a transcendental condition for the correlation itself? Here, the ontological independence of the ancestral grains provides a way into a transcendental materialism that can be shown to subtend the *de facto* subject and its correlation. In a past paper, I have nominated the logic of this with the concept of the *transobjective* (Zielke, 2018). With this term, we can see how the ontological independence of the grains made possible the reference to their ancestral state in the lab as being mind-independent.

The transobjective is a formal concept that designates a real, objective relation between independent entities. It is formal in the sense that we are talking about possibilities, limited by ideal and material constraints. Thus, the actuality of the objective relation under discussion (e.g., between the grains and the scientists) is taken to be one possibility amongst others. It is a special kind of possibility though, because it has come to pass or come to be actual. So, by designating the actual as merely possible, this *does not negate* the respective actualities or existences of the grains or scientists. It simply places asterisks beside them — so to speak. This indicates that this actuality is only the manifestation of one possible state of the universe amongst mutually exclusive others. In other words, *designating the actual as possible highlights its contingency*. The universe could have evolved in such a way that these objective acts of existing did not emerge and did not come into relation.

The strength of the concept of the transobjective is twofold. It can show how (1) independent real beings can be inherently relational by way of (2) unleashing the possibility of novel emergence that reframes their independence into a co-relation — one which does not negate their mutual independence, because this relationality is contingent. It shows that there is no inherent contradiction between ontological independence and ontological interdependence when levels of analysis and modal logic are kept clear and distinct. The transobjective can then serve as a transcendental concept that is non-reductive, but which also allows for temporal and material relations of dependence between independent or ontologically irreducible beings.

The transobjective underlies Heck and company's ability to intend the grains in their lab and use them as arche-fossils to produce scientific knowledge about the ancestral past. For this correlation of reference between the ancestral past and the scientist's present moment to happen, the grains themselves must be present to the scientists for experimentation. In other words, the ancestral statement (in this case) can only be yielded if the grains themselves have survived from the ancestral past into the present. As we have seen above, the ancestral grains contained within them the possibility of a universe both with and without human being. And to make their way into the laboratory, various pre-terrestrial and terrestrial contingencies needed to occur. Once they did, the scientists used characteristics that accrued to the grains over time to infer statements about the past.

The grains' independent, physical properties, such as their hardness, gave rise to their durability. This property of hardness preserved the grains and contributed to the rocky composite of the asteroid. Hardness would be there, in the grains, regardless of whether or not human beings eventually evolved to recognise it.[13] Furthermore, the grains' chemical structure, which recorded its interaction with radiation over time, was also a quality that the grains would have retained whether or not human being emerged to measure this. All of this is implied by referring to the grains as real, existing and ontologically independent. Yet this reference itself can only emerge (in this case) through the potentials that the grains unleash for human being.

If and once there is a being like the human being in the universe, then novel potentials emerge for the grains. The independent characteristics just mentioned persist, but they become the material potential for emergent possibilities that were not possible before the human being evolved. This unleashing of emergent possibilities goes two ways: from the grains *for* human beings, and from human beings *for* the grains.

In the first way, the particles' hardness and chemical composition no longer just materially constitute their durability or the rocky nature of their asteroid or meteorite. These properties now unleash the capacity for human scientists to experiment on them and make measurements. In other words, the grains' own material potentials come to be taken up into newly unleashed potentials that are distinctly human. Being taken up here does not negate or reduce the grains' original potentials because these set material limits upon the human potentials that piggy-back on them. The grains' independent potentials (apart from human being) set a material limit upon the results that the scientists' experiments will yield. The grains' thereby limit what the scientists will be able to say about them. Yet, by virtue of setting these limits, the grains also now participate in the potentials that human beings unleash into the universe, such as scientific discourse, discovery, knowledge, and language. The human being's words and ideas about the grains match the material characteristics yielded by the grains through experiment. When in a *de facto* relation with a human being, *the objective qualities of the grains, which at first only amount to material potentials for its environment, afterwards now provide the material grounds for ideational content* — in this case, ancestral statements about their pre-terrestrial existence.

Here, phenomenology arrives at the same point Meillassoux makes: it is the ontological independence of the grains that provides the possibility for them to be taken as arche-fossils in the first place. But, phenomenologically, we can go further. While the first way shows how the human being unleashes new potentials for the grains, the second shows how these new potentials are founded upon the ontological independence of the grains.

The scientists traced back the history of actualisation that these grains have taken for 8.5 billion years. The ideational retrojection of the ancestral past is the mental reflection of the real "forward" projection the grains' acts of existing have taken. Their direct givenness in the lab, their indirect givenness in the past, along with the human capacity to know and speak about both, is *a contingent potential that follows from the real, independent anteriority of the grain*. The ancestral grain's temporal potential to be grasped by a *de facto* subject 8.5 billion years in the future is the very same material potential that the scientists grasp through their ideations about it, based upon the results in their experiments. Like any idea, the idea of the ancestral is not located in the scientists' minds. Ideas are not real things, physically located in someone's head. They surely have a material basis in the brain, but the brain itself is the kind of thing that is open to grasping and participating in potentials that are physically located outside itself. An idea as an image or content, physically located in the mind, is a hypostatisation of what an idea actually is: the condensation of a grasped, temporally expanded potential that can be followed and unravelled. If an idea is truly about material things, then it is located as *the grasped side* of a material potential in the real. The scientists merely grasp or condense this potential into an "idea" that results in a scientific discovery. The relation between the grains and the scientists thereby opens up a sphere of ideational potentials that are grounded (as scientific discourse is) in the real material limits of the matter at hand. Another term for these ideational potentials is scientific knowledge or statements, and in this case, another term for these ideas that spring from material potentials is an ancestral statement — namely, that the grains are up to 8.5 billion years old. The ontological independence of the grains makes possible the correlation that refers to them and to its own contingency with regard to them. It is one potential amongst others that stems from the real independence of ancestral events.

Conclusion: Toward an Ecstatic Cosmology — Ecstatic Materialism

Against Meillassoux and the larger speculative realist claim that, in phenomenology, the givenness of the ancestral past reduces it to a correlate of consciousness, the phenomenologist could say rather that the ontological independence of the ancestral past is a condition of possibility for the correlation itself. Nevertheless, Meillassoux's thought of the ancestral does present contemporary phenomenology with a positive opportunity to once again address its troubled relationship with naturalism.

Throughout its history, phenomenology has had a strained relationship with naturalism. The real problem of compatibility between the two is that naturalism takes subjective consciousness as just one object amongst others in a causal nexus. But for phenomenology, when it comes to the constitution of the meaning of things, consciousness is not a passive object brought about by external forces. It is a transcendental condition for the appearance of the world and universe. After rising to the challenge of addressing Meillassoux's ancestral, I have achieved a vantage point from which I would like to address this larger issue. By transforming the sense of the materialism underlying naturalism, from a field of cause and effect into a field of emergent material potentials, it is possible to show the unity between the real and the non-reductive activities of a being such as the human being. The transcendental field will not be found solely in either nature (as a physical system of cause and effect) or subjective consciousness (as a non-physical plane of meaning), but in a revised materialism called *ecstatic materialism.*

Those familiar with the existential tradition should not understand "ecstatic" as implying a *Dasein*-like intentionality; I am not endorsing an existential pan-psychism, holding that all material things engage in meaning-making activity. Without intending to imply that material things are conscious or purposive, I use the descriptor "ecstatic" to point to the way that nonliving things are not simply static beings locked-in on themselves. This was, of course, the way that they were presented in *Being and Time*, where *Dasein*'s ecstatic nature was explicitly contrasted with a rock locked-in on itself. By using this contrast, Heidegger's point was not to circumscribe real things from material potentials, but to point to *Dasein*'s unique meaning-receptive activity. Without transferring that meaning-making sense onto materiality, I am trying to point to the way that matter is always already opened up to potentials, whether grasped or not.

Material things are opened up beyond themselves and transcend themselves *materially*. This material self-transcendence is not like that of *Dasein*, because it is not a self-grasping or self-understanding of being-in such potentials. From a strictly Heideggerian lexicon, ecstatic matter does not make sense, since nonliving material things are not in a disclosive relationship with the world (in terms of the kind of relationship that has traditionally gone under the heading of truth). But there is at work within matter a similar structure of being temporally opencd up to a larger field. Non-intentionally selecting between various potentials in this field — as does a material thing — does not amount to *human* freedom, but it does point to contingency at the heart of the material universe. In this sense, ecstatic materiality relinquishes any traditional determinative view of nature, showing how causal relationships are *nested* in material contingencies or potentialities. Specifically human freedom and its ecstasies are *founded upon* but also *emergent from — and beyond —*

this material contingency. From ecstatic materiality emerges the novelty of ecstatic human being. A being who is grounded in the material universe, but who can also, in terms of its intentional demeanour, transcend or pass beyond it into non-physical, ideal, or metaphysical potentials.

The presolar grains are ecstatic materials. Their ancestral embodiment was opened up to material potentials, and the grains that eventually ended up in Heck et al.'s lab selected from a vast array of material contingencies in order to end up there. This line of material potential from the ancestral to the present was a material condition of possibility not only for the physical relation between the present grains and the scientists, but also for the correlation between the scientists and the grains in their presolar form, for the same potential the grains followed to end up in the lab and yield scientific results was the same as the one the scientists traced back through these results *but now grasped as such*. The great achievement of the scientific method is that it can so closely match words, models, and thoughts to potentials, while discovering patterns and general regularities within them. The ideational and semantic meaning by which the scientists refer to the grains' ancestral potential, which leads into a possible encounter with human beings in the present, is simply the grasped side of this very same material potential.

As a transobjective condition (a non-reductive, transcendental condition) for the meaningfulness of any such ancestral potential (or any material potential at all), human beings unleash and transpose such potentials into a higher register that we call meaning or sense. Through discourse, language, and other means of expression, humans express such material potentials, placing them in a context of significance (which is broader than but also includes causal relations and the scientific method for discovering these). The brain is the kind of thing that is caught up in and rides such material potentials, but that is also so lucid about them that it can abstract away from them, level-up, and soon find itself intending nonmaterial potentials, which outstrip its current situation or any material conditions whatsoever. Human being can be so distracted by the multitude of potentials and possibilities it encounters that it forgets to concentrate on its own contingency in the real. Taken with a grain or two of interstellar dust, Quentin Meillassoux and speculative realism more broadly can help phenomenologists remember to ground the constituting activity of subjective life in the more primordial ecstasies of the material universe.

References

Bennett, Jane. *Vibrant Matter: A Political Ecology of Things*. Durham: Duke University Press, 2010.

Bernet, Rudolf. "Husserl's Transcendental Idealism Revisited". In *The New Yearbook for Phenomenology and Phenomenological Philosophy IV*, pp. 1–20. Seattle: Noesis, 2004.

Carr, David. *The Paradox of Subjectivity: The Self in the Transcendental Tradition*. Oxford: Oxford University Press, 1999, pp. 1–20.

Crowell, Steven Galt. *Husserl, Heidegger, and the Space of Meaning: Paths Toward Transcendental Phenomenology.* Evanston: Northwestern University Press, 2001.

Gabriel, Markus & Slavoj Žižek. *Mythology, Madness, and Laughter: Subjectivity in German Idealism*. New York: Bloomsbury Publishing, 2009.

Harman, Graham. *The Quadruple Object*. Washington: Zer0 Books, 2011.

Harvey, Charles W. & Jim D. Shelton. "Husserl's Phenomenology and the Ontology of the Natural Sciences". In *Phenomenology of Natural Science*, edited by Lee Hardy & Lester Embree, pp. 119–33. New York: Springer, 1992.

Heck, Philip R., J. Greer, L. Kööp, R. Trappitsch, F. Gyngard, H. Busemann, C. Maden, J.N. Ávila, A.M. Davis, & R. Wieler. "Lifetimes of Interstellar Dust From Cosmic Ray Exposure Ages of Presolar Silicon Carbide". *Proceedings of the National Academy of the Sciences* 117 (4) (2020), pp. 1884–89.

Heidegger, Martin. *Being and Time*. New York: Harper & Row, Publishers, Inc., 1962.

Heidegger, Martin. *Poetry, Language, Thought.* New York: Harper & Row, 1971.

Heidegger, Martin. *The Question Concerning Technology, and Other Essays.* New York:

Harper Perennial, 1977.

Heidegger, Martin. *History of the Concept of Time: Prolegomena.* Bloomington: Indiana University Press, 2009.

Husserl, Edmund. *Ideas Pertaining to a Pure Phenomenology and to a Phenomenological Philosophy: First Book: General Introduction to a Pure Phenomenology.* The Hague: Martinus Nijhoff Publishers, 1983.

Husserl, Edmund. *Psychological and Transcendental Phenomenology and the Confrontation With Heidegger (1927–1931): The Encyclopaedia Britannica Article, the Amsterdam Lectures, "Phenomenology and Anthropology" and Husserl's Marginal Notes in Being and Time and Kant and the Problem of Metaphysics.* New York: Springer, 1997.

Latour, Bruno. *We Have Never Been Modern.* Cambridge: Harvard University Press, 2012.

Meillassoux, Quentin. "Time Without Becoming". http:// speculativeheresy.files.wordpress.com/2008/07/3729-time_without_ becoming.pdf

Meillassoux, Quentin. *After Finitude: An Essay on the Necessity of Contingency.* New York: Continuum Books, 2011.

Sheehan, Thomas. *Making Sense of Heidegger: A Paradigm Shift.* New York: Rowman & Littlefield, 2014.

Sparrow, Tom. *End of Phenomenology: Metaphysics and the New Realism.* Edinburgh University Press, 2014.

Weisberger, Mindy. "7-Billion-Year-old Stardust is Oldest Material Found on Earth". https://www.livescience.com/oldest-material-on-earth.html, 2020.

Zahavi, Dan. "Husserl's Noema and the Internalism-externalism Debate". *Inquiry: An Interdisciplinary Journal of Philosophy* 47 (1) (2004), pp. 42–66.

Zahavi, Dan. "The End of What? Phenomenology Vs. Speculative Realism". *International Journal of Philosophical Studies* 24 (3) (2016), pp. 289–309.

Zielke, Dustin. "Excess and Withdrawal: Critical Phenomenology and Speculative Realism". *PhænEx* 12 (2) (2018), pp. 103–22.

Notes

1 As Zahavi (2016, p. 303) has noted, Meillassoux does not engage the vast literature of the philosophy of scientific realism, constructivism, critical realism, etc. Because of this omission, I will not address it either. For the purposes of my argument, I will assume that scientific statements need a realist sense to be true or coherent, as Meillassoux implies — even though, in order to provide a robust argument here, this assumption would have to be philosophically established.

2 I will put aside Sparrow's claim that only Husserl's phenomenology counts as phenomenology. While I think he is right to emphasise that phenomenology is a method, I think he is short-sighted here. Phenomenology not only names a method, it also names a tradition that comments upon, critiques, and transforms this method. Unlike natural science, neither philosophy in general, nor phenomenology in particular, are the kinds of intellectual activity that require methodological consensus in order to be valid.

3 Current issues in Heidegger scholarship draw attention to this *sine qua non* of phenomenology when scholars such as Thomas Sheehan (2014) argue that Heidegger was a phenomenologist both early and late because he always adhered to phenomenological seeing.

4 Phenomenology does not cut up intuition as did Kant: intuition need not be empirical. There can be intuitions of formal phenomena like logical axioms, mathematical equations, and essences. These have no real-world correlates as they are ideal objects, but they can be established in inner insight, like when one first grasps a mathematical equation. The point is that there must be an exhibition of the phenomenon according to its type, whatever type it is — however it shows itself. What counts as intuition cannot be determined in advance, because there are different ways that phenomena show themselves, and phenomenology takes its determination of its intuition from the phenomena itself. Words uncover and point towards this, and then there is *phenomenological* argumentation.

5 Keep in mind that there are various ways of understanding this correlation and its philosophical status. Husserl frames it through subjective idealism (though this is epistemic and not metaphysical in nature). Heidegger upends Husserl's subjectivism and addresses how

the correlation is established from the outside-in, through disclosure of being (which is not always human being) and the world. Yet in both cases, there are transcendental concerns on the line. Transcendental phenomenology is an attempt to show how the correlation itself is possible. There was a disagreement about how best to characterise this possibility. Heidegger wanted to depart from Husserl's epistemic transcendentalism into an ontological transcendentalism. This underlies the confrontations between Husserl and Heidegger over the edits and revisions of the *Encyclopaedia Britannica* article on phenomenology (Husserl, 1997).

6 This is the general outline of a defence of Husserlian idealism against Meillassoux's claim that it would collapse into Berkeleyian idealism. Within Husserl's thought, givenness only requires a possible *de facto* subject, implying the possibility of objective being (i.e., mind-independent objects) without givenness to a *de facto* subject. And knowledge is knowledge precisely because it does not reduce the being of the world to the being of consciousness.

7 As I pointed to in the last note, this move is one that had great impact on the history of the phenomenological tradition as Husserl and Heidegger parted ways in their understanding of its transcendental status, direction, and aims (Heidegger, 2009). For Heidegger, the being of intentionality was not most authentically grasped with Husserl's subjectivist and epistemological approach. Instead, the being of intentionality needed to be shown to be possible from out of the disclosure of being. He located the transcendental not in consciousness, nor even in the co-relation between *Dasein* and world, but in a transcendental source (e.g., nothing, the "it" that gives) that never fully disclosed itself to an apprehending subject, nor to any given historical co-relation between a self and world. For my purposes, what is illuminating here is the way that Heidegger relativises the correlation itself to a measure and standard that stands outside of it — namely, the conditions of possibility of the correlation itself, not in a first cause but in the unleashing of possibilities from a primal nothingness.

8 Yet this is not to say that things cannot be bearers of effects, as a materialist framework would require. But it does allow us to offer a more sophisticated version of activity-passivity.

9 To speak of exclusivity here does not mean that the future states are essentially or materially incompatible, but that they are *temporally* incompatible.

10 When I say that something selects from a range of potentials, I do not mean that it must intentionally do so. Of course, living beings can make conscious choices. Nonliving things do not. But they still select from ranges of possible outcomes by the way that they actualise themselves in response to being affected and in the larger feedback that these responses have upon the material environment to which they belong.

11 I am putting to the side the deeper analysis of a feedback loop between a single thing's activity and its environment.

12 As a brief tangent on this point, I would like to note the difference between the perspective I am elaborating upon and Graham Harman's object-oriented ontology, which I have written more about elsewhere (Zielke, 2018). Harman speaks of a realm of excess belonging to all objects, a realm unto which finite human knowledge and real interaction do not extend (2011). Harman treats this realm of excess as inaccessible to knowledge. While agreeing with him that there is such a realm of excess that preserves the irreducibility of objects to knower or context, I do not think that this realm is completely inaccessible. It is a realm of potentials that have ideal and material limits. Because of this, it is possible to know about the potentials in this realm of excess even if they do not come to pass, much like I can know that the glass on my desk has the potential to shatter if it hit the floor, even though I did not knock it down. Knowing this does not reduce the independence of the known to knower.

13 To designate a quality such as hardness as an objective property is not necessarily as problematic in phenomenology as it would be with much post-Cartesian analytic philosophy. Givenness in phenomenology is givenness to a potential, *de facto* subject. Hardness is this potential *de facto* subject's nomination for the kind of atomic and chemical structure in real things that this subject recognises as hard. The referent of hardness lies in the referent itself. It is that from which the sense of hardness stems.

CHAPTER 4:
SPECULATIVE NIHILISM

THE DEMANDS OF DISENCHANTMENT: FROM NORMATIVE CRISIS TO SPECULATIVE OPPORTUNITY

Daniel Sacilotto

Introduction

One of the most interesting suggestions advanced during the so-called "speculative realist" sequence concerns a revalorisation of nihilism as a philosophical concept. In particular, the "neo-rationalist" orientation, following from the work of Ray Brassier, proposes to affirm nihilism as a "speculative opportunity" for thinking to rise to the demands of disenchantment in the name of a realist philosophy that decries all forms of humanist piety, including those entrenched in different materialist philosophies. Nihilism becomes aligned to speculation precisely insofar as it enables thinking to access a non-subjective form of absolute in a non-dogmatic form of materialism that escapes not only the epistemic anti-realism associated with correlationism, but the metaphysical anti-realism associated with idealist and vitalist forms of absolutism.

In this paper, I draw a three-stage genealogy of modern nihilism, culminating in the revalorisation of nihilism for and within philosophy, within which the tensions between vitalism and dialectics, and normativism and materialism, becomes intensified. In the first section, I focus on the Nietzschean conception of nihilism as a historical process and predicament for Western culture, leading to a vitalist affirmationism that positions itself against the philosophical dialectic, following the interpretative lines formulated by Heidegger's critique of metaphysics and Deleuze's metaphysics of Life. In the second section, I examine Nick Land's attempt to subtract nihilism from vitalist teleology in the name of a materialist eschatology, inspired by Bataille's general economy. In the third and final section, I explore Brassier's "speculative" realignment of nihilism with the traditional philosophical aspirations toward truth and knowledge within the scope of a reconstituted naturalist programme inspired above all by the works of Wilfrid Sellars, Alain Badiou, and Francois Laruelle. I show how his realignment supposes a more nuanced articulation between the task of accounting for the sensory and normative dimensions of subjective mediation, and the tasks of describing a world without subjectivity altogether. Finally, I propose to raise some methodological questions concerning the possible future of nihilism as a "speculative opportunity" for philosophy.

I – First Stage: Nihilism as Historical Destiny

As is well known, Nietzsche diagnoses nihilism as part of a terminal crisis of "meaning" for European man, coincident with the modern derogation of Christian and Socratic values.[1] The critical impetus behind modernity ends up ironically devouring itself, casting the interrogative and sceptical impulse against the very foundations of Western religion and philosophy, and with them the prevailing teleological narratives that provided European societies with a meaning. This collapse of "meaning" is therefore at once a hermeneutic and vital predicament: existence appears meaningless as the "prevailing interpretation" of Western culture collapses.

> At that point, not that the displeasure at existence has become greater than before but because one has come to mistrust any "meaning" in suffering, indeed in existence. One interpretation has collapsed; but because it was considered the interpretation it now seems as if there were no meaning at all in existence, as if everything were in vain. (Nietzsche, 1968, p. 35)

But nihilism does not simply designate a *stage* within the historical development of Western culture, coincident with the progressive secularisation brought about by the modern period. More deeply, Nietzsche characterises nihilism as the very process orienting Western history since its inception, so that the "death of God" is not *an* event within European culture, but more profoundly, *the* event through which it draws its gradient. It does not only designate the disempowerment of Christianity understood as a normative system and narrative framework, but the logical consequence of the very process that gave rise to religious and philosophical narratives. Taking the equivalence between nihilism and Western culture to its extreme, Heidegger radicalises Nietzsche's diagnosis and claims that "nihilism" is the name for *the history of being itself*: the process whereby "the "dominance of the transcendent" becomes progressively voided.

Nihilism is that historical process whereby the dominance of the "transcendent" becomes null and void, so that all being loses its worth and meaning. Nihilism is the history of being itself, through which the death of the Christian God comes slowly but inexorably to light (Heidegger, 1982, p. 4).

And yet, nihilism points to the turning point beyond itself that orients human history beyond itself. Indeed, it points beyond humanity itself, requiring a power of thought sufficient to enact an unprecedented historical break. This is what Nietzsche conceives in terms of the "transvaluation of all values", coincident with a power of affirmation that sets itself against not only the transcendent values of Socratic philosophy and Christian religion, but also against all forms of *reaction* against them. This affirmative rupture belongs to nihilism as its ultimate point and definitive realisation, as the invention of new values.

> For why has the advent of nihilism become *necessary*? Because the values we have had hitherto thus draw their final consequence; because nihilism represents the ultimate logical conclusion of our great values and ideals — because we must experience nihilism before we can find out what value these "values" really had. We require, sometime, *new values*. (Nietzsche, 1968, p. 4)

But for Heidegger, the overcoming of nihilism implicit in this transition cannot be realised within Nietzsche's own strictures, for Nietzsche continues to conceive of nihilism within a subjective typology of values as the "will to nothingness", which reveals its tacit complicity within a metaphysics of the will. The purported overcoming of nihilism would in truth only have guaranteed its perpetuation and consummation, hostage to a "valuative thinking" from which the future of Western thought is supposed to be determined as the "transvaluation" of the negative will and its destructive effects to a preservative and empowering vector that Nietzsche names "active nihilism".

> Nietzsche conceives of the essence of nihilism solely on the basis of valuative thought, and in that form alone does it become an object of his critique and his attempt at an overcoming. But because the valuation has its principle in the will to power, overcoming nihilism by fulfilling it in its classical form develops into an interpretation of being as a whole as will to power. The new valuation is a metaphysics of will to power. (Deleuze, 1983, p. 52)
>
> [...] But because active nihilism already recognizes and acknowledges will to power as the fundamental trait of beings, nihilism in general is not merely "contemplation", is not the

> mere "no" of judgment. It is the "no" of deed [...] One does not simply regard something as null, he sets it aside, overturns it, and creates an open field. Hence classical nihilism is itself the "ideal of supreme powerfulness". (Deleuze, 1983, p. 56)

For Heidegger, this residual metaphysical impulse occludes the true essence of nihilism, which lies in the *forgetting of being* that orients Western history: "nihilism is not a worldview that occurs at some time and place or another; it is rather the basic character of what happens in Occidental history". (Heidegger, 1979, p. 26). Accordingly, short of being a "liberating" movement through which mankind frees itself from the shackles of divinity, the nihilist consequence of modernity is but a symptom of Western man's ontological amnesia, where the being of beings recedes into obscurity as the preponderance of "ontotheology" becomes eroded as transcendence sunders. In this sense, nihilism encapsulates the mystery of the *ontological difference* itself: being is not *a* being, corresponding to no empirical object nor transcendent entity; it is, as Hegel already showed, strictly speaking, *nothing*. But nothingness cannot be conceived as an abstract *lack* of determination, any more than the "nihil" in nihilism is merely privative, symptomatic of a will that intends abolition as it defiles all values; it is positively ontological, signalling the non-alienable kernel that metaphysics conceals but haunts it from within. Rather than overturning the will to nothingness, the true historical rupture must retrieve the ontological question from the abyss in which it becomes lost, so that Heidegger must ask: "Does the nothing ever let itself be found, or even searched for? Or is it the case that it does not need to be sought and found at all, because it 'is' that which we least — that is to say, never — lose?" (Heidegger, 1982, p. 19).

For Heidegger, active nihilism overturns teleological finality in the name of a perpetual preservation and self-transformation and empowerment of the human subject, a movement which is directed to nothing but itself in a cyclical fashion. It is *the eternal return* which, in the last instance, restores the teleological movement by subordinating becoming to the will to power,

> Because all being as will to power — that is, as incessant self-overpowering — must be a continual 'becoming,' and because such 'becoming' cannot move 'toward an end' outside its own 'farther and farther,' but is ceaselessly caught up in the cyclical increase of power to which it reverts, then being as a whole too, as this power-conforming becoming, must itself always recur again and bring back the same. (Heidegger, 1982, p. 7)

In clarifying its complexity and integrity as a process defining Western history as a whole while resisting the Heideggerian diagnosis that, for Nietzsche, transvaluation must imply the failed overcoming of nihilism, Gilles Deleuze proposes a four-stage periodisation of nihilism, in which contrast between immanence and transcendence, negation and affirmation, and finally between dialectics and vitalism becomes distilled. In the first instance, Deleuze argues, nihilism has a *chronologically* and *logically* primary sense as *negative nihilism*, coincident with the emergence and institution of the Judeo-Christian and Socratic foundations of Western thought. It is defined by the simultaneous avowal of a supersensible world, considered itself as *essence*, correlative to a depreciation or *negation of Life*, considered as *appearance*, i.e., the transcendent nature of God. The purity of the domain of the forms, is thereby contrasted with the immanent world of material bodies, their actions and passions, etc. The postulation of "higher values" belongs to the construction of a narrative *fiction* of transcendence, one whose valorisation coincides with and is the obverse of *the nullification of the value of life as such.*

> Depreciation always presupposes a fiction: it is by means of fiction that one falsifies and depreciates, it is by means of fiction that something is opposed to life [...] The whole of life then becomes unreal, it is represented as appearance, it takes on a value of nil in its entirety. The idea of another world, of a supersensible world in all its forms (God, essence, the good, truth), the idea of values superior to life, is not one example

> among many but the constitutive element of all fiction. Values superior to life are inseparable from their effect: the depreciation of life, the negation of this world. (Deleuze, 1983, p. 147)

The depreciation of life institutes "bad conscience", characteristic of Christianity, where suffering attests to the injustice of existence at the same time as it provides the foundation and promise for divine redemption. There is thus an ultimate complicity between religious teleology and philosophical dialectics: only the positivity of divine transcendence justifies depreciated life by guaranteeing the possibility of a final reconciliation that amends the shattered rapport between Man and the Divine, in a process of ascent beyond the immanence of life. Yet from this primary sense of a negative nihilism follows a second *reactive nihilism,* through which the higher values upheld in the first instance by negative nihilism become themselves depreciated, and with them the grip that their hegemonic narratives hold over Western man: truth, beauty, justice, etc. The fiction of an essential, supersensible world becomes in this way itself denied, swallowed by the powers of the negative, leaving only appearance as depreciated life.

> Previously life was depreciated from the height of higher values, it was denied in the name of these values. Here, on the contrary, only life remains, but it is still a depreciated life which now continues in a world without values, stripped of meaning and purpose, sliding ever further towards its nothingness. Previously essence was opposed to appearance, life was turned into an appearance. Now essence is denied but appearance is retained: everything is merely appearance, life which is left to us remains for itself an appearance. (Deleuze, 1983, p. 148)

The reactive will becomes the bearer of reactive forces: those forces that fulfil an essentially mechanistic, utilitarian, or conservative function, and that remain subordinated to dominant active forces. Deleuze identifies reactive forces as the source of all *consciousness*, and furthermore with the faculties of habit and memory, in contrast to the fundamentally *unconscious* character of active forces. In the modern period, the powers of critical rationality that would challenge dogmatism and liberate man become eventually directed against the humanist foundations of reason, raising the reactive will against any semblance of positivity. At its limit, this sundering of values thereby culminates in a "pessimism of weakness" that Nietzsche names "weary nihilism", precisely at the point when the reactive will loses even the gesture of defiance, and exhibits a "fatigue of spirit" ("the last man") in which it passively waits to perish.

> [T]he weary nihilism that no longer attacks; its most famous form, Buddhism; a passive nihilism, a sign of weakness. The strength of the spirit may be worn out, exhausted, so that previous goals and values have become incommensurate and no longer are believed. (Nietzsche, 1968, p. 18)

Weary nihilism thereby consummates the path of the reactive will, and yet prepares the point of transition, as the last man sets the conditions for the overcoming of man himself, leading to a fourth and final phase in the development of nihilism as a historical process. What Nietzsche names *active nihilism* is thus the "sign of increased power of spirit", equivalent to an *affirmation of Life* as the supreme value that abolishes the reactive will and conceptual negativity. But this does not mean that vital affirmation is prised free of negation; Nietzsche subtracts negation from its envelopment in conceptual opposition, so that a kind of *non-dialectical negativity* unleashes a "violent force of destruction", through which the "transmutation" or "transvaluation" of all values is achieved. Indeed, this radical power of negation becomes itself identified with and subordinated to a power of affirmation or creation, at once rekindling the vigour of spirit and the value of life "in the destruction of everything that was degenerating and parasitical" (EH III, "Birth of Tragedy", pp. 3–4).

> Negation is no longer the form under which life conserves all that is reactive in itself, but is, on the contrary, the act by which it sacrifices all its reactive forms. In the man who wants to perish, the man who wants to be overcome, negation changes sense, it becomes a power of affirming, a preliminary condition of the development of the affirmative, a premonitory sign and a zealous servant of affirmation as such. (Deleuze, 1983, p. 176)

It is not then, as it is often suggested, that Nietzsche opposes Dionysian affirmation to nihilism as a crisis of Western values: nihilism is itself the process that begins with the depreciation of life by way of its opposition to transcendence, but which eventually sets the stage for its own transvaluation, culminating in the subordination of conceptual negativity to affirmation, against all reactive values.[2]

Form	**Operation**	**Consciousness**	**Figure**
Negative Nihilism	Transcendent Assertion / Depreciation of Life	Judaic-Christian	God-Christ
Reactive Nihilism	Reactive Negation / Depreciation of Higher Values	European	Man
Weary Nihilism	Passive Destruction	Buddhist	The Last Man
Active Nihilism	Transvaluation / Destruction of Reactive will	Atheist	Overman

But what could such an affirmative act amount to, if not a matter of establishing the falsity or obsolescence of those higher values upheld in the name of transcendence, proposing a set of values that stand in opposition in turn? By the same token, what could "affirmation" designate if it is not reducible to a mere assertion or avowal of an alternative set of values to take the place of those "higher values" avowed by Christianity and philosophy? What arbiter is to decide on which values deserve affirmation and become life-enhancing, in contrast to those "higher values" that merely depreciate life by instituting the fiction of a transcendent beyond? What narrative or meta-narrative framework holds the prerogative here, and who is its privileged historical subject?

These questions ultimately point to the difference between active nihilism and the three forms of nihilism comprising the reactive will (negative, reactive, and weary nihilism), which corresponds methodologically to the difference between *vitalism* and *dialectics*, for dialectics is identified not only with the Socratic mode of philosophical questioning, but also with an *ideology* adequate to Christianity, which reaches its paradigmatic expression in the Hegelian system. It is, in this sense, not only a mode of *theoretical* reasoning, but also a practical and normative system that inculcates the spirit of ressentiment that predates on life. Above all, Deleuze argues, the dialectic confuses abstract symptoms for genuine interpretations, as it seeks to at once depreciate and "justify life and submit it to the labor of the negative" (p. 18). Subordinating vital affirmation to conceptual negativity, the force of real difference and becoming is sedated under abstract conceptual oppositions to be eventually sublated in a moment of reconciliation, and so reassimilated under the seal of representation. It is therefore not, as Hegel argues, that pure being and nothingness only begin as indeterminate abstractions before their progressive determination in the Idea; the very dialectical movement of determinate negation, the "life of spirit", is but a play of abstractions, a theatre of false movement.

> The dialectic is the natural ideology of ressentiment and bad conscience. It is thought in the perspective of nihilism and

> from the standpoint of reactive forces. It is a fundamentally Christian way of thinking, from one end to the other; powerless to create new ways of thinking and feeling. The death of God is a grand, noisy, dialectical event; but an event which happens in the din of reactive forces and the fumes of nihilism. (Deleuze, 1983, p. 159)

But if this affirmative act, from which vitalism weaves new values, is not yet another philosophical or religious doctrine, this is because the historical break with the reactive will that it brings about cannot be interpreted in terms of a *semantic* act of declaration in favour of the essential nature of life, nor to an *epistemic* declaration of belief in the intrinsic value of life. Affirmation is *not* fundamentally a linguistic or epistemic act, nor is it the matter for theoretical or religious practice; it has a primary, *ontological* meaning, as the "quality" of the will to power itself, which brings about a transformative and creative power that is also a historical break. Accordingly, "affirmation" is understood above all as the proper name of *becoming*, which has no object other than itself. It represents nothing. But this purity associated with the force of real becoming implies in turn a second affirmation on the side of man, which takes becoming as its proper object, and so affirms the *being* of *becoming*. Every affirmation is thus double, Deleuze argues: at once the name for *becoming-in-itself*, and the *very act* that brings the *being of becoming* into self-consciousness, which conditions the transvaluation of weary nihilism into active nihilism, and the historical passage from the last man into the overman.

> In itself and as primary affirmation, it is becoming. But it is being insofar as it is the object of another affirmation which raises becoming to being or which extracts the being of becoming. This is why affirmation in all its power is double: affirmation is affirmed. It is primary affirmation (becoming) which is being, but only as the object of the second affirmation. (p. 186)

Because life must be affirmed "in-itself", the event of transvaluation can only lead to the creation of new values by, at the same time, subtracting life itself from all evaluation, making it the last and only arbiter on whose basis any normative order or conceptual system can be assessed. As Nietzsche writes: *the value of life cannot be evaluated.* In the last instance, and despite the substantive divergences, Heidegger and Deleuze's interpretations coincide in the historical dimension of the act of transvaluation: nihilism provides Western history with its meta-teleological narrative framework and teleological kernel, grounded simultaneously in a Heraclitan ontology of pure becoming as what underlies representation, and the Dionysian affirmation of the being of becoming and the internalisation of life-in-itself as what requires no justification, but which in turn serves to evaluate the possibility of the creation of new values.

But despite this presumed non-dialectical character, the destructive force and historical rupture against the reactive will, mobilised by vital affirmation, is in turn only concretised by identifying a set of values that can be said to be life-affirming — namely, the trinity of values that form what Nietzsche names the "Communion": *dance, play, laughter.* The underlying suspicion against the vitalist rhetoric, encapsulated in Heidegger's diagnosis, is that a residual metaphysical risk lingers when identifying how the force of historical break rests on an act of "transvaluation", as the latter remains wed to the creative and destructive force on whose name the will to power institutes itself as the heroic subject of history, and which Nietzsche christens under the name of "the Overman". For Heidegger, the purported "overcoming" of nihilism in European culture would therefore require something more radical than any act of transvaluation could ever perform: to escape the metaphysical destiny borne in Greek thought, within which all normative systems and modes of evaluation take place, the better to prepare a "crossing" to a second *post-metaphysical* beginning that wrests *thinking* from the dark trinity of Socratic philosophy, Christian religion, and modern science. Such radical interruption would thereby escape the residual impulse latent in Nietzsche's own occlusion of the fundamental ontological question under a metaphysics of the will, and the latter's complicity with "ontotheological" narrativisation. Liberation from metaphysics in turn requires a patient, *hermeneutic* attunement, continuous with therapeutics of historical release (*Gelassenheit*). Against both the Dionysian affirmation of vitalism and the reactive will complicit with the false theatre of dialectical negativity, Heidegger argues, the metaphysical impetus that devolves in the growing wasteland of European nihilism must be itself definitively interrupted. But this interruption cannot proceed by an act of affirmation of new values any more than a derogation of old ones: *being-historical thinking amends the shattered rapport between Dasein and Being by escaping all systems of valuation and appeals to the powers of the will, beyond philosophy and the subject in both its dialectical and vitalist forms.*

With this said, the prescription of *Gelassenheit* that conditions the possibility of such a "historical-crossing" is bound to relapse to obscurity, bordering on mysticism, precisely at the point of articulating how to "leap" from the deconstruction of the West's ontotheological history to a post-metaphysical recommencement is to take place. For while attempting to radicalise Nietzsche's anti-theological and anti-teleological impetus, Heidegger voids the restoration of the ontological question from any normative or epistemic content. It can thus no longer be annexed to a subject any more than to a transformative act commensurate to a conception of the will or system of values. The dialectician is predictably bound at this juncture to find, in the vacuity of the prescription of historical "release" demanding "one hundred years of silence", nothing but a reification of the emptiest of abstractions, a glorification of the poverty of the indeterminate immediacy of pure being in its identity with nothingness. But then, the recommencement of Western thought becomes a stillborn promise, incapable of generating any movement, relapsing into helpless patheticism. By the same token, the vitalist is bound to find in the lack of affirmative zeal an ultimate complicity between the hermeneutics of release and the reactive will, and particularly with the weary nihilist for whom the will to nothingness can no longer identify for itself any higher values but must embrace the certainty of annihilation with lethargic passivity. Abstraction and fatalism become thereby confused for the liberation of thought from metaphysics, voiding thinking from the force of dialectical negativity as much as vital affirmation, leaving nothing in its place. There where conceptual negativity and vital affirmation sunder, only an infinitely prolonged hermeneutic exercise revealing the dereliction of modern technology in its complicity with the Greek metaphysical beginning remains. The will to perish without redemption is, in this way, reinscribed under the self-pitying predicament of *Dasein*, facing flight of the Gods under the conditions of the forgetting of being with mournful melancholy, where the will to nothingness lingers under the rhetoric of a therapeutic release from metaphysics.

At the same time, the Heideggerian critique remains indicative of the lingering aporia that divides vitalism from dialectics, for if the dialectic seeks to arrest and counterfeit the movement of real becoming under the sieve of conceptual negativity in the name of reconciliation, then vitalism must continue to uphold that the powers of affirmation can and must always rise as power against all becoming. If Hegel reconciles Man and God through the sublation of conceptual difference, confusing symptoms for interpretations, then Nietzsche's vitalism defiles the rapport between Man and God through the *affirmation* of a *non-conceptual negativity* that exerts its power over the real, where creative power always can and must resist what reacts against and diminishes Life.

> The real, understood as the object, aim and limit of affirmation; affirmation understood as acquiescence in or adhesion to the real: this is the meaning of braying […] The Dionysian yes, on the contrary, knows how to say no: it is pure affirmation, it has conquered nihilism and divested negation of all autonomous

> power. But it has done this because it has placed the negative at the service of the powers of affirming. (Deleuze, 1983, p. 185)

But what could the capacity to "say no" or indeed to creatively affirm and potentiate life mean when the force of becoming becomes equivalent to that of the nature in which life and thought itself emerges and perishes? Vitalism's ultimate conceit to humanism is to insist on the powers of resistance of an act capable of making a stand before the real, to conquer its burden, to transform itself against the opprobrium of a real that stands against it. It is a consummate refusal of surrender, in which Man rises not only against the idols it has erected, but against himself, and indeed even against the forces of materiality from whence it came and within which it is destined to perish. The suspicion of a metaphysical undercurrent resonates anew once it appears that to subordinate becoming to life is no less pious than to subordinate it to the concept; the affirmation of creative act and its concomitant negation can only overturn dialectics by in turn reifying the preponderance of Man before the real, if only to overcome itself in the name of Life. In the end, what binds vitalism, idealism, and the hermeneutics of crossing remains the subordination of becoming to history, where human activity can always subordinate nature to its own designs. Whether in the name of the Overman, Spirit, or *Dasein*, philosophy perpetrates teleological humanism insofar as it renders natural becoming subservient to historical becoming.[3]

To refuse at once historicist lethargy, affirmationist voluntarism, and the false theatre of dialectics, is to accept that the force of a non-dialectical negativity or real becoming cannot be subordinated to Being, Life, or the Concept. Neither the transvaluation of all values at the hands of man, the reconciliation of man and God as spirit by consciousness, nor the historical crossing by *Dasein* can arrest real becoming. Just as becoming is the genetic condition for all eing and for all production, it is also the promise of its irresistible cessation: that which destroys the reactive and affirmative will alike, as well as the restorative will that prescribes silent release.

II – The Second Phase: Nihilism as Becoming Against History

The voluntarist pathos that animates philosophical teleology can be nevertheless considered as an instance of a more ubiquitous phenomenon composing what Georges Bataille famously characterises as an extrapolation from a *local economy*: the idea that work can always be transformed into useful wealth, adapted to our purposes and ends. Such conceit is, Bataille argues, nothing but a symptom of "man's disregard for the material basis of life", underwriting not only the conceptual or epistemic dimensions of the dialectic, but the play of forces that animate life in its aesthetic, cognitive, and practical dimensions, including those of vital affirmation. To alleviate this pious compulsion, Bataille proposes to place all local "economic" orders within the purview of what he names a *general economy*, according to which all labour and production are embedded in an energetic vector, where the frenzy of creative evolution and morphogenesis are ultimately destined to waste, a luxuriant excess that cannot be transformed into wealth or assimilated to productive ends.

> Man's disregard for the material basis of his life still causes him to err in a serious way. Humanity exploits given material resources, but by restricting them as it does to a resolution of the immediate difficulties it encounters [...] it assigns to the forces it employs an end which they cannot have. Beyond our immediate ends, man's activity in fact pursues the useless and infinite fulfillment of the universe. (Bataille, 1991, p. 21)

Economic activity, considered as a whole, is conceived in terms of particular operations with limited ends. The mind generalises by composing the aggregate of these operations. Economic science merely generalises the isolated situation; it restricts its object to operations carried out with a view to a limited end, that of economic man. It does not take into consideration a play of energy that no particular end limits: the play of living matter in general, involved in the movement of light of which it is the result. (Bataille, 1991, p. 21)

This anti-teleological operation inverts the subordination of natural history to human history, and becomes the foundation for a reconstituted nihilism. In *The Thirst for Annihilation,* Nick Land accordingly proposes to free the Nietzschean assault against humanism from its residual vitalist impetus and teleological kernel, adapting the tenets of Bataille's thanatropism in the name of a "virulent nihilism" that scolds at once the affirmationist avowal of Life and the dialectical play of conceptual negativity. This requires a systematic demolition of the intentional stance and the folk-psychological categories that underwrite what Wilfrid Sellars names the "manifest image of Man in the world". It is programmatically summarised in four principles:

1. Thoroughgoing dehumanisation of nature, involving the uttermost impersonalism in the explanation of natural forces, and vigorously atheological cosmology. No residue of prayer. An instinctive fastidiousness in respect to all the traces of human personality, and the treatment of such as the excrement of matter; as its most ignoble part, its gutter…
2. Ruthless fatalism. No space for decisions, responsibilities, actions, intentions. Any appeal to notions of human freedom discredits a philosopher beyond amelioration.
3. Hence absence of all moralising, even the crispest, most Aristotelian. The penchant for correction, let alone vengefulness, pins one in the shallows.
4. Contempt for common evaluations; one should even take care to avoid straying accidentally into the right. Even to be an enemy is too comforting; one must be an alien, a beast. Nothing is more absurd than a philosopher seeking to be liked. (Land, 1992, p. xx)

To this programmatic agenda corresponds the attempt to ontologise Bataille's general economy into an "energetic materialism", instantiating a thanatropic inversion of Nietzsche's vitalist avowal of Lamarck in his account of active forces as a "power of transformation", and inspired above all by Ludwig Boltzmann's information-theoretic formalisation of thermodynamics. Extrapolating Freud's account of the death drive from its biocentric envelopment into a quasi-physicalist register, *death* is now identified as the cosmic subject of history: the true impersonal unconscious that subverts life from within. But this regressive movement is not only that of the return of the organic to the inorganic, but more radically designates the energetic vector orienting all natural becoming toward annihilation. It sets the grounds for a "libidinal economy" that achieves the very *transvaluation of teleology by eschatology*, summarised in four principles and central concepts approximating what Freud anticipated as a "'science' of the drives" (Land, 1992, p. 42):

1. *Chance* – Derogation of causal law in the name of probabilistic process, where natural becoming is oriented only by chance.
2. *Tendency* – Derogation of teleology in the name of tendential processes without purpose.
3. *Energy* – Derogation of qualitative vocabulary in the name of a purely quantitative vocabulary describing entropic differentiation.
4. *Information* – Derogation of all signification and intentionality in the name of energetic tendency. (Land, 1992, p. 42)

In this framework, the difference between pure becoming and being, unformed matter and its individuated forms, is reconceived in terms of the relation between entropy and negentropy, where order emerges as "a deviation from disorder" or chaos *qua* point of "zero-intensity". Following Boltzmann, Land translates the Kantian distinction between phenomena and noumena in a statistical and mechanistic register, in terms of the distinction between the observable "microstates" of a system and the unobservable "macrostates" expressing regularities deviating from thermal equilibrium. The apparent exorbitant improbability of negentropic disequilibrium ("high H-values") is thus rendered consistent with the Second Law by embedding observable events in vast temporal scales, where they become probable or even necessary. But since temporal intervals escape all means of measurement or observation, they can therefore never themselves be the objects of any empirical intuition; they are, like Kant's noumena, only inferentially known, though no longer understood as "objects of reason", but as natural events that resist representational access. Nevertheless, these events comprise the conditions of *real possibility* and the limits of all morphogenesis, destining all being and subjectivity to entropic annihilation.

> [Boltzmann] argues that the departure from troughs of thermal equilibrium occurs in periods of time so extended that they escape observational techniques and thus do not fulfill the epistemological conditions of being objects of possible experience [...] For Kant's timeless thing-in-itself Boltzmann substitutes vast stretches of time characterized by maximum entropy or thermal equilibrium, and thus by minimal H-values, whilst Kant's phenomenon is transformed by Boltzmann in order to rest upon an energetic foundation of negentropy, thermal disequilibrium, or high H-values. (p. 41)

All formed matters are in this manner reconceived as negentropic indexes of what, at the cosmic scale, remains destined to entropic dissipation, pulverising organic and inorganic matter. History itself, understood as the development of the subordination of work to human ends, becomes destroyed — not only the prevailing narratives or "interpretations" that Nietzsche associated with religious and philosophical narratives, but even the possibility of creative affirmation, which functions to resist the real and empower life, is irrevocably debased. Modernity no longer appears as the tipping point of human history, pointing to its creative sublimation at the hands of the Overman; it rather signals the terminal phase of human history, when the findings of science unleash a de-anthropomorphising potential for thought that reveals its fatal predicament.

> History is industrial history, and it only has one goal, which is God. Nihilism is the loss of this goal, the nullification of man's end, the reversion of all work to waste. It is in this sense that history is aborted by zero. There are those who in their eagerness for the continuation of effort take Nietzsche's overman to be a new goal, a restoration of teleology, a task commensurable with the nihilation of history. Perhaps Nietzsche himself succumbs to such a temptation at times, after all, German Protestantism had poisoned his blood. It must nevertheless be insisted that the world of work perishes with the One, and that zero is an engine of war. (Land, 1992, p. 147)

The irony is then that a more radical form of passive nihilism than that beholden to the reactive will is necessary to resist Nietzsche's metaphysics of the will, for annihilation cannot be subordinated to affirmation any more than to conceptual negativity; it designates a real power of becoming, which both conditions the emergence and cessation of life and thought, and indeed places a limit on all morphogenesis or material becoming. This involves a more radical anti-representationalism than that formulated by Nietzsche's assault against the dialectic, for energetic materialism not only purports to challenge the prevailing *doxas* of philosophy and religion; more radically, Land argues, it cannot itself be conceived as a physicalist *ontological* or even *scientific* theory at all, insofar as "the logical and mathematical concepts underlying any such theory are devastated by the radical interrogation of simple difference" (Land, 1992, p. 45). This "interrogation of simple difference" reveals that all forms of theorisation, including physicalism, remain implicitly theological, insofar as it postulates at once a transcendent "first cause" or event to explain the origins of the universe, with all inner events working within the framework of natural law, including the probabilistic framework of statistical mechanics.

> The physicalistic contention is that matter receives its impulsion or determination from without; through the combination of an essential lawfulness that transcends the particular entity and the influence of external bodies or forces. Any 'intrinsic' process (such as decay) results from the expression of natural laws, whilst all extrinsic process results from the passive communication of an original cosmic fatality (probabilistic physics makes no essential difference here, since the mathematical — hence formal and extrinsic — determination of probability is no less rigorous than that of causal necessity). (Land, 1992, p. 38)

It becomes therefore necessary, Land argues, to dissociate the representational object conceptually apprehended and real matter as the "irrecoverable other" of intellectual prehension in a more radical manner, one which presumably would resist any kind of avowal of natural lawfulness as much as any account of first causation. This *representational nihilism* leads Land thus not only to *deny* the possibility of epistemic access to cosmological temporal events or to *affirm* the necessity of annihilation for all matter; it leads him to deny that energetic materialism is a theory in the business of *explaining* or *describing* the world, making it a part of science or philosophical *discourse*.

At this juncture, however, the disavowal of its proper theoretical status leads energetic materialism to an internal incoherence. As Ray Brassier (2010) argues, having undercut the legitimacy of any appeals to the role of sensible intuition as much as the theoretical valences of conceptual representation in mediating the means of access to the world, the commensurability between thinking and becoming implicit in Land's writings becomes obscure. Indeed, its theoretical nihilism notwithstanding, it is clear that energetic materialism cannot but present itself as a set of principles, imperatives, generalisations, assertions, and theoretical explanations concerning the nature of materiality, as well as meta-theoretical evaluations and prescriptions about its own non-philosophical and non-scientific status.

> [Land] has supplanted representation, but he wants to supplant this kind of Bergsonian vitalist phenomenology for an unconscious thanatropism [...] The problem is that Land's materialist liquidation of representation, because it doesn't want to reaffirm, allegedly, the primacy of sub-representational experience, which Bergson and phenomenology do in various ways, he has to explain what it is he's talking about. He's doing a kind of materialist metaphysics, and there's an issue about what kind of traction this extraordinarily sophisticated conceptual apparatus can gain upon the process of primary production, the real as intensive difference, matter in itself, whatever you want to call it. (Brassier, 2010)

But the situation is more serious than this: energetic materialism faces analogous problems that eliminativist materialism also faces when accounting for its own theoretical function. This results in a variation of what John McDowell names "bald materialism", which proposes to obviate the pertinence of the intentional stance and of conceptual normativity wholesale by rendering the central concepts of description, explanation, and theorisation — upon which any materialism (indeed, any discourse whatsoever) rests — plainly unintelligible while remaining nevertheless presupposed. It is not only that, as Brassier argues, such a reductionist framework must ultimately lead to a *practical* impotence or pragmatic contradiction when staging a stand against all forms of religious, philosophical, and scientific discourse; moreover, it leads to a kind of *theoretical* impotence and incoherence, where the distinction between a theory and its object becomes voided, and with it the very epistemic grounds to adjudicate between different accounts of nature and subjectivity all the same. As a result, the most uncompromising of anti-philosophies unwittingly becomes indiscernible from garden-variety dogmatic metaphysics.[4] It is therefore not only that energetic materialism becomes the accomplice of a "reactive" will that cannot but passively await the fate of annihilation; more deeply, it is plagued by a methodological confusion when claiming to have done with the epistemic role of conceptual representation and experiential mediation while tacitly depending on them to formulate an alternative to philosophical and scientific discourse.

The methodological call for an epistemological delimitation of ontology is thus not some humanist conceit tantamount to a regression to idealism or a dialectics that occludes real becoming, nor is it a relapse into the "reactive will" that seeks to subordinate matter to the gauntlet of judgement and dialectics. The call is made to avoid allowing the critique of anthropomorphism to unwittingly relapse into pre-critical metaphysics, and to insist on the need to explain how it is that thinking may represent a world indifferent to human interests. To insist on explaining how any materialism "gains traction" on materiality itself is just to interrogate the epistemic conditions under which it can be evaluated that any such *theory* represents its world, including how it represents *the limits of representation itself.* Without such an *epistemological* propaedeutic, the most virulent assault against the normativity of reason becomes indiscernible from arbitrary affirmation.

It is precisely in order to reconcile the anti-vitalist and anti-humanist impetus behind energetic materialism with the demands of the problematic of conceptual representation and experiential mediation that Brassier proposes a "transvaluation" of Land's solar thanatropism, which reconceives nihilism as the epistemic condition for a realist philosophy that avoids the perils of eliminativist materialism, as much as the shortcomings of all forms of correlationism and idealism.

III – The Third Stage: Nihilism as Speculative Opportunity

In laying out the methodological stakes of the realignment of philosophy with nihilism, in *Nihil Unbound* Brassier famously affirms that "nihilism is not an existential quandary but a speculative opportunity". (Brassier, 2007, p. xi) Against both its vitalist, affirmationist and thanatropic iterations, nihilism acquires an *epistemic* function and *speculative* role in the precise Hegelian sense that Quentin Meillassoux (2016) characterises as encompassing all forms of *absolutism*, i.e., a mode of thinking that claims to access some form of absolute or another, whether of a subjective or asubjective kind. For Meillassoux, speculative *materialism* comprises the form of absolutist thought that claims to access a *non-subjective form of absolute*, in contrast to *subjectalism*, for which the absolute is identified with subjectivity as a whole or partially, e.g., with the sensible (vitalism), the conceptual (idealism), the pragmatic (practicalism), etc. The speculative opportunity that nihilism presents for philosophy is that of thinking a *materialist absolute* that not only affirms the "meaninglessness of existence", but which thinks of the discursive semantic powers of sapient thought as capable of representing a world indifferent to and ontologically independent from subjectivity in all of its dimensions through the resources of scientific theorisation. In an interview with Marcis Rychter (2010), Brassier clarifies that it is precisely the insistence in the valences of truth, which define philosophy, that implies the endorsement of nihilism, facing the disenchantment of the world first advanced by Nietzsche while resisting nevertheless the latter's vitalist and anti-philosophical solution.

Like Nietzsche, I think nihilism is a consequence of the "will to truth". But unlike Nietzsche, I do not think nihilism culminates in the claim that there is no truth. Nietzsche conflated truth with meaning, and concluded that, since the latter is always a result of human artifice, the former is nothing but a matter of convention. However, once truth is dismissed, all that remains is the difference between empowering and disempowering fictions, where "life" is the fundamental source of empowerment and the ultimate arbiter of the difference between life-enhancing and life-depreciating fictions…

> I consider myself a nihilist precisely to the extent that I refuse this Nietzschean solution and continue to believe in the difference between truth and falsity, reality and appearance. In other words, I am a nihilist precisely because I still believe

> in truth, unlike those whose triumph over nihilism is won at the cost of sacrificing truth. I think that it is possible to understand the meaninglessness of existence, and that this capacity to understand meaning as a regional or bounded phenomenon marks a fundamental progress in cognition. (Brassier, 2010)

Nihilism is in this way reconceived as the methodological condition adequate to a *philosophical realism* and *naturalist materialism* freed from humanist teleology as much as eschatological anti-representationalism, affirming the possibility of cognitive access to a non-subjective absolute. As Brassier puts it, declaring this distinctive epistemic role is tantamount to claiming that "thinking has interests that do not coincide with those of living; indeed, they can and have been pitted against the latter". (Brassier, 2007, p. xi) It follows that the subject of thought is irreducible to the preservative functions of the organism that supports it, or the historical ends that Man collectively sets out for itself as a social being. Thinking belongs to no one, and its theoretical functioning cannot be assimilated to the purposes that the human, or indeed its alleged overcoming, would claim for itself under what Bataille would name a "local economy". But unlike the Landian solution, for which an anti-vitalist materialism implies the wholesale destitution of both vital affirmation and conceptual negativity, Brassier's insistence on the speculative function of thought in accessing an asubjective absolute resists the eliminativist solution that does away with the normativity of thought.

In order to understand how the rehabilitation of conceptual rationality in its representational-theoretical functions can be prosecuted, and with it the classical aims of philosophical discourse, it becomes necessary to ask how can we insist on a principled distinction between thought and being/becoming without reproducing a pious separation between the transcendental and the empirical, i.e., between the "irreducible" normativity and intentionality constitutive of the human subject in its separation from the natural domain of mechanistic causation. By the same token, it must resist the eliminativist solution of simply doing away with the intentional stance, since, as we have seen, this leads to the logical incoherence characteristic of "bald materialisms", and which extend to Land's own energetic materialism. In short, we must ask how to avoid the Charybdis of a humanism that continues to separate man from nature, and the Scylla of a materialism that eliminates intentionality at the price of rendering the descriptive and explanatory basis upon which all ontology rests inexplicable.

Brassier's strategy follows Sellars' dialectic between the manifest and scientific images of man in the world, so as to show that the separation between reasons and causes is to be understood in an epistemic and methodological rather than ontological sense. First, against eliminativist materialism, and taking Paul Churchland's neurosemantic programme as a proximate target, Brassier argues that the purported reduction of the intentional stance not only leads to a methodological impasse when explaining the representational function of thinking. Moreover, it tacitly relies on what it overtly disavows, appealing to a series of "superempirical" virtues that cannot be explained causally at the neurophysiological level, but which must be *meta-theoretically* postulated, and dubiously tethered to an evolutionary explanatory register, i.e., simplicity, unity, and coherence. These would all be not only methodological assumptions guiding the working scientist or theorist, but inherent to the evolutionary adaptation of the human species to its distinct problem-solving tasks. And while this strategy might seem apposite to the strictures of a methodological naturalism that places the emergence of thought within the purview of natural history, Brassier argues that these superempirical virtues remain resolutely *normative* in character, depending as they do on pragmatic considerations whose explanatory rationale remains couched within the intentional stance. As such, they cannot be straightforwardly explained away within a neurophysiological register by plying them to an evolutionary narrative, unless one preemptively transposes the normativity of the intentional stance and its "folk psychological" categories into nature writ large. Short of securing the epistemic credentials of the eliminativist materialist stance, such a move would thus unwittingly relapse to a subjectalist metaphysics of normativity that extrapolates and reifies aspects of sapient experience to the natural world.

> It remains deeply unclear in precisely what way the extent of an organism's adaptational efficiency, as revealed by the degree to which its representation of the world exhibits the superempirical virtues of simplicity, unity, and coherence, could ever be 'read off' its brain's neurocomputational microstructure. In what sense precisely are theoretical virtues such as simplicity, unity, and coherence necessarily concomitant at the neurological level with an organism's reproductively advantageous behaviour? (Brassier, 2007, p. 20)

The latent incoherence in the eliminativist stance becomes acutely visible in the tension between its prescriptive and descriptive contents: if the choice between theoretical frameworks, vocabularies, or stances ultimately depends on evolutionary causal mechanisms of selection that obviate the affordances of deliberative cognition in "the space of reasons", then the survival or death of the manifest image cannot be adjudicated by appeals to norms of explanatory or theoretical superiority enjoyed by given naturalist approaches in relation to competing research programmes.

> [W]ere Churchland correct in maintaining that the superempirical virtues of ontological simplicity, conceptual coherence, and explanatory power are, as he puts it, 'among the brain's most basic criteria for recognizing information, for distinguishing information from noise', then a conceptual framework as baroque, as obfuscatory, and as allegedly incoherent as FP would have been eliminated as a matter of evolutionary routine, and Churchland would have been spared the trouble of militating so brilliantly for its displacement.

> If superempirical virtues were already endogenously specified and intrinsic to the brain's neurocomputational microstructure, then it would appear to be a matter of neurophysiological impossibility for an organism to embody any theory wholly lacking in these virtues. (Brassier, 2007, p. 23)

The same rejoinder applies, as we have shown, to all forms of "materialism" that purport to reduce or trivialise the manifest image of man in the world, and which lead to both a pragmatic and theoretical contradiction, rendering their own descriptive-explanatory functioning unintelligible, and their practical imperatives (including theoretical ones) impracticable. Making our earlier characterisation more precise, we can therefore say that the reconciliation of nihilism with the speculative tasks of a realist philosophy cannot proceed by simply eliding the intentional stance, either in the name of a theoretical reduction or announcing the certain destruction of the human and life in the horizon of natural history. But neither can it simply reify this framework of thought as a supernatural order. It must attest to the possibility of knowing a disenchanted nature and subjectivity, resisting at once:

(a) The piety of a *humanist teleology* that continues to separate man from the natural order and reifies the "folk psychology of intentions", thereby re-enchanting the world.
(b) The incoherence of an *eliminativist materialism* than undermines its conditions of intelligibility as a discourse or theory, relapsing to dogmatic postulation.

To describe how the irreducibility of the normative can be explained without relapsing into a metaphysical dualism or humanism, Brassier follows Wilfrid Sellars in pursuing a *methodological* rather than *ontological* dualism of reasons and causes. More precisely, he insists on the complementarity rather than incompatibility between (i) the *methodological* irreducibility of the normativity of thought, and (ii) the *speculative* task to think of the conditions of a realist ontology that thinks world without thought or without subjectivity. In this regard, the "left Sellarsian" assertion of a "second nature" proposed by McDowell and others, which reintroduces the Aristotelian framework of final causation to our naturalist world-story, simply won't do, for it again proceeds by reifying the normativity of thought in implicitly disavowed metaphysical terms. What an eliminativist materialism reintroduces in its appeals to superempirical virtues, the normativist inflation of naturalism reintroduces in the supplementary force associated with the ethical life of man; both eliminativist materialism and naturalised normativism thus peddle a *naturalised teleology* that delivers them right back to a humanist piety. The proposed alternative involves the reconciliation of the claim for the *epistemological dependency* of being-becoming on conceptual thought with the claim for the *ontological independence* of being with regard to thought and subjectivity more generally. This reconciliation is inherent to the critical function of thought that Kant imposes as a bulwark against dogmatic metaphysics, and is identified by Brassier as the "fundamental problem of philosophy".

> That the articulation of thought and being is necessarily conceptual follows from the Critical injunction which rules out any recourse to the doctrine of a pre-established harmony between reality and ideality. Thought is not guaranteed access to being; being is not inherently thinkable. There is no cognitive ingress to the real save through the concept. Yet the real itself is not to be confused with the concepts through which we know it. The fundamental problem of philosophy is to understand how to reconcile these two claims. (Brassier, 2011, p. 47)

This allows us to formulate two complimentary results from the reconceptualisation of nihilism as a speculative opportunity for philosophy:

1. *The articulation of thinking and being is no longer to be understood in methodological rather than metaphysical terms*: the irreducibility of thought concerns not their causal dimension but rather their normative functioning, which is not metaphysical in scope. Just like it is possible to "abstract" the functional role that a pawn plays in the game of chess across all material instantiations, so must concepts be understood as part of a functional structure binding perception, inference, and action, through which discursive beings represent their environments and themselves within it. Concepts are, in this regard, as Kant argued, functions of judgement that operate on the data of the senses, or indeed of any empirical measurement medium through which cognitive systems coordinate themselves to their environments. And this representational functional role is the explanatory condition to explain the very possibility of a world without thought. To affirm the possibility of an *epistemic correspondence* between thinking and being therefore does not imply asserting their *metaphysical identity*; while the conditions of sense determine the conditions of reference to anything whatsoever, these conditions cannot be identified with the referents of thought in pains of idealism. Accordingly, Brassier insists on the distinction between the (trivial) epistemological or *sense dependence* of being on thought, while nevertheless affirming their ontological or *reference independence*.

> Even were [the idealist] to demonstrate that the conditions of sense determine the conditions of reference, this would still not be enough to show that the existence of the referent depends upon the conditions of reference. To do that, one would have to show that 'to be' means 'to be referred to'; an equation tantamount to Berkeley's equation of 'to be' with 'to be perceived'; yet it would require more than another Gem to dissolve such a fundamentally normative distinction in meaning. (Brassier 2011, p. 62)

This is the speculative import that the concept of *extinction* brings for materialist philosophy; it reveals a temporal horizon that cannot be subordinated or relativised to the time of thought, but which appears as the very medium upon which thought itself emerges and perishes. It therefore designates the force not of a non-dialectical negativity — for extinction is not negation — but a destructive power and temporal order that cannot be reassimilated to the articulation between affirmation and negation, either in its idealist or vitalist iterations; nor can it be assimilated to a generalised "libidinal economy" that perpetuates subjectalism by extrapolating the logic of the drives and of the death drive into a "cosmic unconscious".

> Extinction turns thinking inside out, objectifying it as a perishable thing in the world like any other (and no longer the imperishable condition of perishing). This is an externalization that cannot be appropriated by thought — not because it harbors some sort of transcendence that defies rational comprehension, but, on the contrary, because it indexes the autonomy of the object in its capacity to transform thought itself into a thing. (Brassier, 2007, p. 141)

By the same token, following Sellars once more, while the referents of our perceptual takings might be said to be epistemically dependent on our capacity to have sensory episodes, it does not follow from this that the referents of such perceptual takings must be metaphysically identified with sensory episodes as such.

> [W]hile the referent of the most cautious perceptual taking can be construed as a sensation we need not conclude that the referent of all perceptual takings is a sensation. For while it could be argued that the ultimate referent is always a sensation, by construing our original complex demonstrative phrase along the lines of phenomenological reduction as 'This somehow (a cube of pink facing me edgewise) which is a cube

of pink facing me edgewise [...]' the initial stages of reference saving can proceed without interpreting the referent as a sensation. (Sellars, 1977, pp. 169–185)

2. *That thinking does not have guaranteed access to being provides a critical bulwark against all forms of dogmatic metaphysics*, even in their materialist and anti-humanist guises. It is not sufficient to uphold the rights of science to the real, hypostasising a specific theoretical paradigm or formal vocabulary, as with Land's quasi-physicalist ontologisation of information-theoretic thermodynamics, or Churchland's articulation of neurosemantics and evolutionary naturalism. The ontologisation of specific theories upheld by different forms of Platonism and naturalism alike advance a reduction or derogation of the conceptual determinations of sense and the qualities of sensing at the price of rendering unintelligible how it is that mathematicised *theories* play a descriptive and explanatory role by being coordinated to a *semantic* and *perceptual* basis. Nihilism must secularise the human and defy vitalism not by prophesising its demise or by eliding the rational or aesthetic bases of experience; the project of disenchantment must be extended to the latter to render experiential mediation intelligible as different modalities through which it is possible to know of a world indifferent to thought and life.

Nevertheless, the articulation between sensing, thinking, and being to think of a non-dogmatic, materialist absolute remains only programmatic in Brassier's work. In *Nihil Unbound*, Brassier draws from the positional realism of Francois Laruelle's non-philosophy and the mathematical Platonism of Alain Badiou's mathematical ontology, to find resources to think of a Real unbound from any correlation to thought or subjectivity more generally, while also avoiding the shortcomings of traditional substance metaphysics. The disenchantment of the world would thus coincide with the *formalisation* of nature and of the subject that extends the ideal of *mathesis universalis* to conceive of the relation between thinking and being within the scope of a *structural realism*. In this regard, Brassier follows Badiou in avowing nihilism as part of the process of "universal unbinding", by virtue of which being becomes subtracted from the realm of presentation, the better to hand over the tasks of ontology to science in a vector of mathematical formalisation.

> In order to be equal to the desecrating abstractions of modernity, philosophy must abjure any attempt to sanctify being in the figure of the bond. Thus it is not enough to denounce the hypostatization of being in the myth of presence; it is the phenomenological myth of presencing itself which must be deposed. The discourse of ontology must be disenchanted by being handed over to mathematical science. (Brassier, 2007, p. 98)

At the same time, Brassier draws from Sellars' methodological dualism of norms and causes to conceive of rationality as a self-correcting protocol coeval with the development of theorisation in empirical science, and not only pure mathematics (Badiou) or a "pure" transcendental science (Laruelle). This leads to a naturalised historicising of the transcendental that at once approximates Hegel's *conceptual realism*, according to which thinking progressively excavates the structure of the world to which it belongs, as well as a Peircean *convergent realism*, according to which reason follows an asymptotic "Archimedean" trajectory of approximation to the real. The coordination of nihilism and materialism remains in this way suspended between an ontic *structural realism* that subtracts thinking from the vagaries of aesthetic-semantic valences and affirms the ontological purchase of formalised scientific theories, and a *conceptual realism* that attests to the normative kernel of discursive rationality and scientific theorisation in its representational functions.

And yet, this polarity in Brassier's programme generates an unresolved methodological tension; for while conceptual realism affirms a relation of correspondence between concepts and objects, between the concepts and inferences of scientific theories and nature as such, structural realism postulates the incommensurability of successive theories at the qualitative and conceptual level, affirming instead a correspondence between the mathematical kernel of scientific theories and the world structurally understood. But in establishing a criterion of correspondence between concepts/formal structures and nature, both strategies risk a relapse to metaphysical idealism, endangering the articulation of nihilism with speculative materialism. On the one hand, conceptual realism postulates not only an isomorphy between the *alethic modal determinations* that furnish the discourse of scientific languages to describe causal relations in the objective mode and deontic modal determinations that describe proprieties of descriptive-explanatory practices in the discursive mode; furthermore, these alethic modal determinations are themselves identified with objective modal determinations in the world. But this is simultaneously to ontologise the conceptual and to idealise nature. On the other hand, structural realism postulates an isomorphy between the modality associated with mathematised theories in the "formal mode" and the "objective modal structure of the world". But this is to ontologise mathematical idealities while obscuring the criterion of the relation between the material and the discursive. This dual conflation between the discursive and the material is clearly reflected in the inferentialist articulation of Hegel's conceptual realism and objective idealism, and in the ontic structural realist conflation of the distinction between physical and mathematical structure.

> Conceptual realism says that when the understanding consciousness looks out at what to it is the in-itself, it sees something already in conceptual shape, a world that is conceptually contentful just as its own thinking is. Consciousness's own thinkings confront a thinkable world

> [...] There is no gulf of intelligibility separating intrinsically intelligible thinkings from intrinsically unintelligible (or at least not intrinsically intelligible) things thought about. Consciousness is conceptually structured, and the world it knows about is conceptually structured. (Brandom, 2019, p. 257)

> Physical structure exists, but what is it? If it is just a description of the properties and relations of some underlying entities this leads us back to epistemic structural realism. What makes the structure physical and not mathematical? That is a question that we refuse to answer [...] The world-structure just is and exists independently of us and we represent it mathematico-physically via our theories. (Ladyman et al., 2007, p. 158)

To insist on the problematic of access and the critical function of discursive rationality as necessarily propaedeutic to any materialist ontology is also to avoid preemptively conflating the conceptual or mathematical with the world. To conclude, I briefly indicate in a likewise programmatic fashion some methodological guidelines on whose basis the demands of disenchantment imposed by nihilism can realise the conditions of a speculative materialism that articulates both conceptual and structural realism, while avoiding the danger of idealism that haunts both projects.

A structural realism that does not relapse to a dogmatic metaphysical Platonism must explain how the formal-mathematical core of theories acquires a descriptive and explanatory role in relation to the conceptual and sensory dimensions of sapient experience, and the self-correcting enterprise of empirical science. Extending on Brandom's reading of Sellars, while resisting the anti-naturalist deflationary consequences of such "left Sellarsian" alternatives, we must explain how *semantic inferentialism* not only to understands concepts and languages as organised in relations of material incompatibility and consequence; moreover, we must explain how the formal structures of mathematicised languages acquire a *theoretical* role insofar as they are correlated to concepts with material *consequences of application* and observational *circumstances of application.*

Following Lorenz Puntel, to explain different dimensions of theorisation requires that we explain in a meta-theoretical register how sensory, conceptual, and theoretical consciousness enables cognitive systems to represent their environments and themselves within it. As we understand how representation achieves this task by formal theorisation, we not only theorise nature and subjectivity, but the very relation between sensing, thinking and being. This involves constructing a more capacious concept of structure, while making explicit the relation between formal structures, semantic structures, and ontological structures in relation to the observational roles ("language-entry transitions") through which representational systems coordinate themselves to their worlds.

To understand this map-making role theoretically, we must understand how representational functioning integrates the sensory, conceptual, and theoretical-formal capacities associated with sapient cognition. This involves providing an account of how representational systems instantiate *localisation* functions, through which they instantiate the function of what Sellars calls "map-making": generating model-structures that extract information from their environment on the basis of ostensive indexing-measuring capabilities, and how these models are embedded into higher-order structural models through the resources of conceptual and theoretical capabilities.

To understand how discursive modalities in both their conceptual and formal components can represent something like the "objective modal structure of the world", and so to understand how reason realises itself as a self-correcting protocol coeval with the historical development of modern science, we must reconstruct the generic logic of conceptual-theoretical revision and formalisation within a historicised epistemological framework. This involves extending the Peircean kernel of Sellars' naturalism to render intelligible the notion of epistemic progress, formalising how the evolution of scientific theories in succession can be themselves evaluated meta-theoretically as approximating the ideal of *absolute representational correctness*, i.e., following Seibt's definition, the point of enquiry in which "all of our predictions come out right and nothing is left unexplained". Following Jay Rosenberg, this constitutes the basis of a *convergent realism* that explains how theories can be organised diachronically as approximating an ideal-limit point, naturalising the Kantian notion of "noumenal" reality as a regulative ideal for rational enquiry, as opposed to a transcendent domain of entities or "things" understood substantively.

Against the Platonist compulsion to see evental ruptures incommensurate to the order of natural law or knowledge, as well as the structural realist compulsion to see theories as exhibiting radical discontinuities at the level of conceptual content, or a radical continuity at the level of mathematical form, the inferentialist semantic account of meaning in terms of conceptual use can enable us to track semantic preservation across theoretical changes. This is to explain how there is preservation of semantic structure, both of the circumstances of application that organise the concepts of divergent languages-theories, and of the observational circumstances of application in terms of which such concepts remain bound to representational-localisation dynamics. It becomes therefore possible to show that radical, "evental" discontinuities in the order of being are underwritten by semantic and formal continuities. This way, we refuse romanticising creation and theoretical invention by pitting them against representation; we explain how representation is a creative enterprise through which systems progressively and theoretically map the structure of the world to which they belong, so as to enable means of intervention into this world and themselves.

Finally, such semantic-structural continuity must allow us to understand the way in which the construction of *philosophical categories* is constrained and related to the labour of empirical science, i.e., to show how philosophical theorisation itself projects categories that don't only respond to the findings of current science, but which anticipate future science in sight of both the problems incumbent in the latter as well as its own proper questions and concerns. In other words, the very relation between ontology and science must be made explicit as part of a meta-theoretical natural consciousness that coordinates the diachronic and historical evolution of scientific theories to philosophical ones, realising the demands of a realist and naturalist view.

Notes

1 The term nihilism (*Neinismus*) was first coined in 1733 by Friedrich Lebrecht Götze within a literary register, but was subsequently developed into a philosophical term by the mystic philosopher and physician Jacob Hermann Obereit in 1787, referring to a kind of epistemic anti-realism, according to which the true nature of the world must remain unknowable, leading to a vacuity of consciousness. It was then used by Friedrich Heinrich Jacobi in a letter to Johann Gottlieb Fichte written in 1799, where it refers to the inevitable fatalism that results in rationalist and scientistic philosophical systems that uphold the "law of reason" at the price of abolishing freedom and God.

2 In *Difference and Repetition*, Deleuze argues that the eternal return is the return of difference, not of the same: the third Zarathustra.

3 It is no wonder, then, that, even when it purports to align itself to naturalism or materialism against dialectics, vitalism reveals a simultaneous avowal of biocentrism and voluntarism, as with Deleuze's claim in *Difference and Repetition* that entropy is a transcendental illusion.

4 In what follows, I adhere to Alain Badiou's broad use of the term "anti-philosophy" to describe that mode of thinking that proposes to challenge the aspiration toward truth distinctive of philosophical discourse in the name of an act that will in fact destroy philosophy. Land's machinic practicism can be thereby understood as a paradigmatic instance of a contemporary anti-philosophical narrative, where the force of the act is subtracted from the human and leveraged to an inhuman form of intelligence and capitalist production.

References

Bataille, Georges. *The Accursed Share, an Essay on General Economy: Volume 1: Consumption*, translated by Robert Hurley. Zone Books, 1991.

Brandom, Robert. *The Spirit of Trust: A Reading of Hegel's Phenomenology*. Harvard University Press, 2019.

Brandom, Robert. *A Pragmatist Semantic Reading of Hegel's Phenomenology: Lectures from A Spirit of Trust*, for the Forschungskolleg Analytic German Idealism (FAGI). University of Leipzig, 2019.

Brassier, Ray. *Nihil Unbound: Enlightenment and Extinction*. New York: Palgrave Macmillan, 2007.

Brassier, Ray. "Concepts and Objects". In *The Speculative Turn: Continental Materialism and Realism*, edited by Levi Bryant, Graham Harman, & Nick Srnicek. Melbourne: re.press, 2011.

Brassier, Ray. *Accelerationism: Ray Brassier*, transcribed from the Backdoor Broadcasting Company recording https://moskvax.wordpress.com/2010/09/30/accelerationism-ray-brassier/, 2010.

Brassier, Ray. "Interview with Marcin Rychter: 'I am a Nihilist Because I still Believe in Truth'". *KRONOS*, (2011). https://cengizerdem.wordpress.com/2011/03/05/ray-brassier-interviewed-by-marcin-rychte-r-i-am-a-nihilist-because-i-still-believe-in-truth/

Brown, Nathan. *Rationalist Empiricism: A Theory of Speculative Critique*. New York: Fordham University Press, 2021.

Deleuze, Gilles. *Difference and Repetition*, translated by Paul Patton. New York: Columbia University Press, 1995.

Deleuze, Gilles. *Nietzsche and Philosophy*, translated by Hugh Tomlinson. New York: Columbia University Press, 1983.

Heidegger, Martin. *Nietzsche: Volumes III and IV: The Will to Power as Knowledge and as Metaphysics*, translated by Joan Stambaugh, David Farrell Krell, Frank A. Capuzzi, San Francisco: Harper, 1982.

Ladyman, James, Don Ross, David Spurrett, & John Collier. *Everything Must Go: Metaphysics Naturalized*. Oxford University Press, 2007.

Land, Nick. *The Thirst for Annihilation: Georges Bataille and Virulent Nihilism*. London: Routledge, 1992.

Meillassoux, Quentin. "Iteration, Reiteration, Repetition: A Speculative Analysis of the Sign Devoid of Meaning", translated by Robin Mackay

& Moritz Gansen, in *Genealogies of Speculation: Materialism and Subjectivity Since Structuralism*, edited by Armen Avanessian & Suhail Malik. London: Bloomsbury, 2016.

Nietzsche, Friedrich. *The Will to Power*, translated by Walter Kaufman & R.J. Hollingdale, edited by Walter Kauffman. Vintage Books, 1968.

Puntel, Lorenz B. *Structure and Being: A Theoretical Framework for a Systematic Philosophy*, translated by Alan White. USA: The Pennsylvania State University, 2008.

Sellars, Wilfrid. "Some Reflections on Perceptual Consciousness". In *Selected Studies in Phenomenology and Existential Philosophy*, edited by R. Bruzina & B. Wilshire, pp. 169–185. The Hague, 1977.

SPECULATIVE OPTIMISM

Evrim Bayındır

There is something admirable in the becoming-reactive of forces, admirable and dangerous.
— Gilles Deleuze, *Nietzsche and Philosophy*

Introduction

Whether there is a speculative realism in Deleuze or not has been a matter of debate.[1] However, the very form of the question produces a deadlock, since to accept it merely rediscovers the philosopher in question as already saying what has later been said, and to deny it unavoidably reduces Deleuze to the dogmatism of a single idea ("correlation", in the case of speculative realists). Hence the possibility of a genuine problematisation and a creative encounter is precluded in advance. What I would like to suggest, instead, is to bypass the question itself and perceive speculative realism as effectuating the *future* of Deleuze. Precisely, this is the effectuation of Deleuze's completely overlooked but crucial Nietzschean foresight: the prospect of the self-annihilation of nihilism.[2]

Deleuze carves out from Nietzsche the idea that the collapse of nihilism is going to be an autonomous event — that is to say, it is going to happen *no matter what*, regardless of whether the free spirits and the associated active forces manage to destroy it or fail to do so. In this paper, not only do I fully embrace Deleuze's claim but also attempt to radicalise it. However, this radicalisation requires a long detour through a series of speculative realist and negativist objections to Deleuze's affirmationism.

To that end, I follow Ashley Woodward's claim that the very affirmationism that allows Deleuze to "posit" the overcoming of nihilism restricts him from thinking and experiencing this event.[3] Furthermore, as Ray Brassier, Benjamin Noys, and Andrew Culp have argued from different perspectives, what is primarily lacking in Deleuze is a negation that is powerful enough to disturb metaphysics, the functioning of capital and the long-lasting complicity of the philosopher with the state — all of which constitutes the once-expected outcomes of overcoming nihilism.[4]

There is thus a frustrating discrepancy between the *project* of overcoming nihilism and its *result*, in a similar manner to the kind of failure Deleuze finds in Kant.[5] Unlike these thinkers, however, I argue that the project needs to be embraced, provided that we venture into a result that Deleuze would not expect; a result in the face of which Deleuze himself "repented" in the same way as he criticised Plato.[6] While the project is necessarily affirmationist, the result is of a fundamentally different kind that demands recourse to the speculative realist literature as a negativist, post-continental, and post-Deleuzian current. Speculative realism is the very site to observe the unfolding of the self-annihilation of nihilism.

"Self-annihilation" implies that nihilism will be defeated by the very reactive forces that created it. I propose that the failure of Deleuze's project arises from its lack of sufficiently developed or autonomous reactive forces that can effectuate this event. To show how Brassier's work represents the self-annihilation of nihilism, I will interpret his work as an open-ended production of post-continental reactive forces that possess the power of negation required to destroy nihilism.

First, I explain the role of nihilism in Deleuze and in what sense his project fails. The second part of this essay focuses on the post-Deleuzian reactive forces in Brassier and various other members of post-continental thought. Finally, I claim that there is a radically optimistic lesson to be learned from these recent philosophical developments, such that the self-annihilation of nihilism becomes the new site of autonomy and a purely *non-traumatic* event.

1. Deleuze's Proof

1.1 Anticipating Speculative Realism

The essence of Deleuze's affirmationism is to *prove* that nihilism, understood as the degeneration of life through its subordination to an autonomous negation, will *necessarily* be overcome. No less ambitious than medieval philosophy's struggle to prove the existence of God on ontological grounds — the transcendental project of setting criteria to ground the sciences and the phenomenological endeavour to raise philosophy to the level of a rigorous science — Deleuzian ontology is a testimony to the superiority of life, which announces the fated defeat of forces that opposed and degenerated life by means of their collaboration with negation. Deleuze's anti-nihilism in this way subverts the philosophical passion for objectivity in order to overthrow the philosopher's complicity with nihilism and power. Although the primacy Deleuze gives to life rejects the historical polarisations between idealism and realism,[7] or the conceptual prioritisation of the distinction between subject and object,[8] the urge to demonstrate the inevitable ending of nihilism marks his project with an idiosyncratic objectivity that, as I will show, anticipates speculative realism.

1.2 The Concept of Force

"Force" is the most basic ontological unit through which Deleuze's proof operates.[9] The origin of existence is constituted by the irreducible hierarchy between active (affirmative, transgressive) and reactive (negative, limiting) forces.[10] Through these means, forces enable Deleuze to account for the genesis of all that exists from the point of view of its differential origin. Since forces are alterable, they also enable a change in that which is and is thought of: a different (non-nihilistic) world is not only "possible" but also a *necessity*, precisely because forces necessarily differ. Force is thus the concept whereby the unification of thinking and changing or philosophising and living is established.

However, the approximation of thinking and life is not a peaceful and egalitarian harmony of forces. Thinking cannot affirm, change, act, and merge with life without dominating or *acting* the reactions whose split and refusal to obey cause the separation of thinking and life and the cancellation of action. It is therefore not surprising that there is no single philosophical theme in *Nietzsche and Philosophy* that does not connect to the exigency of subjugating reactive forces to active forces. The crucial import of Deleuze's concept of force is to show how, throughout the history of philosophy and politics, we have had only a reactive image of domination or a nihilistic notion of violence, and so we have never understood its affirmative sense.[11] This comes down to saying that the totality of power relations and state violence that we have encountered so far are the symptoms of the degeneration of life and therefore nothing but illusory dominations. The stark optimism of Deleuze's proof hence arises from the realisation that power is impotent. The violence we know is the product of an inability to dominate on the part of active forces. A philosophy of affirmation is therefore impossible without learning how to perform a non-nihilistic domination.

1.3 The Fascination with Reactive Forces

Despite the superiority of active forces, Deleuze's theory of domination becomes particularly compelling and gains its full force when he asserts that the aggression towards reactive forces simultaneously provokes a "fascination" with their existence.[12] What makes forces more or less fascinating is the degree to which they pursue the ultimate consequences of their affirmations or negations. For this reason, while an active force can subside because of its inability to sustain affirmation, there are reactive forces that can endow us with "dangerous" and "interesting" powers. In this way, a reactive force can even become "grandiose" if it dares to navigate the ultimate horizons of negation.[13] They open us up to "new feelings" and "new ways of being affected" that are at times more arresting than those provided by active forces. But even more crucially, as he later suggests in *What is Philosophy?*, reactive forces, with their "remarkable" or "interesting" properties, are the very initiators of philosophy.[14] Deleuze thus brings the Platonic wonder a new orientation: what primarily diverges thought from common sense to philosophical sense is precisely the wonder or fascination that is felt in the face of reactive forces.

However, reactive forces are not only "admirable" but also "dangerous", precisely because of the same tendency for autonomisation. What causes *ressentiment* is their separation from the dominance of active forces, which later leads active forces to interiorise the resentful accusation, develop bad conscience,[15] and become reactive. Finally, a mixture of *ressentiment* and bad conscience is projected onto the totality of existence so that all forces are rendered reactive.[16] In this universe of reactive becomings, the task of the philosopher is to be susceptible to the different "nuances" of these reactive forces.[17] Fascination is our primary tool in navigating the dangers of this reactive universe and in gaining the capacity to dominate. One of the most remarkable outcomes of Deleuze's analysis is that *that which fascinates us also incites us to dominate it*. Overcoming nihilism requires that we also overcome common sense by realising the inseparability of fascination and domination.

But if we concede to the negativist objection that Deleuze cannot negate, we should also accept that active forces fail to be fascinated by and dominate reactive forces. In fact, Deleuze recognises this problem by claiming that the "greatest danger" that a philosophy of affirmation faces is that of becoming indistinguishable from the "beautiful soul" that can affirm only the federative differences and cannot perform a negation.[18] The beautiful soul thus has the bizarre status of an active force that affirms without dominating. This suggests that, like an inner enemy, there is something in affirmation that is harder to defeat than the actual targets.[19]

1.4 The Objectivity of the Eternal Return

Nevertheless, Deleuze finds the antidote to the beautiful soul in affirmation again: the "aggression" required to negate is *automatically* — that is to say, irrespective of whether *we* can — released when differences are raised to a "proper degree" of "positivity". This proper degree is reached through the "apodictic" and "absolute" test of the eternal return.[20] Any force that is subjected to an eternal repetition will *differ* by testifying to an objectivity that is immune to the possibility of a subjective error or the "wishes" of the beautiful soul. Although this experiment is primarily an *idea* — as it can be effectuated only by a thinker's eternal willing of that which is willed or of forces — it is also indeed a *test*, precisely because it triggers an *objective* process that simultaneously distinguishes between and transforms forces.[21]

However, as Brassier points out, Deleuze confronts a grave dilemma when he claims that the eternal return arrives at a final moment when all reactive forces are destroyed and nothing remains of negation: the eternal return cannot be performed without retroactively obliterating its condition as the original imbrication of active and reactive.[22] What Brassier cannot see, however, is that Deleuze's violation of the original imbrication takes place not only from the active but also from the reactive side.

1.5 Breaking the Correlation

The greatest difficulty in holding hierarchy and imbrication together is that the attempt to account for the irreducible superiority of active forces encounters the no-less-arduous task of thinking the irreducible inferiority of reactive forces. This makes reactive forces increasingly elusive to the point of breaking the imbrication. In his timely reading of Deleuze as the hidden progenitor of speculative realism, Arjen Kleinherenbrink realises this break in Deleuze's claim that *reactive forces prevail without a single struggle with active forces.*[23] Kleinherenbrink accurately interprets the truth of this perplexing *victory without struggle* as the utter lack of relation between active and reactive. This absence of relation allows him to see Deleuze as introducing into the history of philosophy, for the first time, the purely non-relational "objects"[24] whose realities are outside of all sorts of living, thinking, being, feeling, or perceiving that would be in the service of the "correlation". Kleinherenbrink's mistake, however, is to assume that the non-relational designates active forces and the relational expresses reactive forces. Although this might be much more faithful to Deleuze's text, Kleinherenbrink herewith misses, like Deleuze himself, the chance to follow the minor and implicit but ultimately determinant tendency to grasp this non-relational asymmetry in terms of the paradoxical triumph of the weak and submissive. The lesson to draw from Kleinherenbrink's juxtaposition of Deleuze and speculative realism is that *the speculative realist rupture with correlationism fully coincides with and is implied in the hierarchy between active and reactive.*[25] What is incomprehensible from a Deleuzian framework, however, is that the rupture takes place primarily on the reactive side.

The disintegration of the original imbrication is not merely a sign of inconsistency, as Brassier thinks; more importantly, the most optimistic aspect of *Nietzsche and Philosophy* can be discerned in its two "glad tidings": one is expressed in the autonomisation of active forces, the other in the autonomisation of reactive forces.

1.6 Two Glad Tidings

The first, *active* glad tidings declares that *it is possible to experience a joyful affirmation without fighting against nihilism.*[26] Active forces need not dominate reactive forces to prove their superiority. Deleuze imagines a purely isolated and sterile space for active forces, where they can play their game free from the limitations imposed by reactive forces and without being contaminated by them. Although Deleuze insists on the necessity of two violent negations — one prior to affirmation, the other subsequent to it — for the overcoming of nihilism,[27] they ultimately serve as a means to postulate the superior necessity of a *play without violence*, which characterises the innocence of the child as the apex of active forces.[28]

The autonomisation of reactive forces, by contrast, is stated through another glad tiding, namely that *nihilism will be defeated by itself*.[29] This statement appears towards the end of the text, where Deleuze has already set out why active is superior to reactive and why the collapse of nihilism is inescapable. However, one final step is needed to secure victory. The whole point of this step is that it is not going to be taken by active forces and affirmation, but by reactive forces and negation. Nihilism will collapse precisely because of its irreducible weakness.

But Deleuze retreats from this argument the very moment he proposes it, and sacrifices nihilism's self-defeat to the agency of the human who defeats him/herself.[30] Presumably to solve the unwanted entanglement of self-defeat's autonomy and agency's self-defeat, Deleuze argues that this *pusher* is neither an internal tendency in reactive forces nor an active agent, but *negation* as it is separated from reactive forces.[31] However, even this final move will not save Deleuze from betraying the autonomy implied in his initial statement, since negation destroys reactive forces only by "inspiring" in the human the will for self-destruction. In any case, there is an invaluable lesson to be drawn from the very fact that *an unprecedented inspiration is produced*: if the *idea* of overcoming nihilism appears to human beings, this is only because they encounter the violence of an autonomous necessity, which arises solely from the internal logic of the history of nihilism.

1.7 The Emergence, the Three Stages, and the (Un) Ending of Nihilism

Deleuze demonstrates that the emergence of nihilism depends on purely "material" relations between pre-nihilistic reactive forces. These forces are the "raw contents" of the subsequent fiction of a world beyond being or the real, through which nihilism gains power over life.[32] But where do these primitive reactive forces come from in the first place? Deleuze finds the answer in Freud's "topical hypothesis", which refers to the original traumatic event that enabled the distinction between inside and outside — by means of which we distinguish between thinking and the real.[33] The burst of excitation released in this original scission forces the organism to react, first through a consciousness that receives the excitations and then through a memory that records the transformations. However, Deleuze does not follow the conclusions that Freud derived from the topical hypothesis, which he deems incapable of giving an account of what a true activity is and how these reactions can be acted or dominated.[34]

The ensuing history of nihilism witnesses a brutal civil war, which determines its three-staged development and inevitable self-destruction. The first stage is "negative nihilism", which designates the mystification of a world beyond, made by using the "matter" of reactive forces that previously escaped active forces.[35] Here, reactive forces wilfully come under the reign of their own creation — God or being as the negation of life — in order to repress active forces. In "reactive nihilism", however, the complicity between reactive forces and negation is revealed to be provisional and strategic: human beings kill God and ascend to his throne. At this moment, the human represents the juncture where all forces become reactive.[36] Crucially, reactive forces soon become aware of *the radical impossibility of both invading and escaping the abyss of existence that is opened up after the death of God.* As I will discuss later, this signifies the discovery of the traumatic horror of existence, which plays a pivotal role in the encounter between Deleuze and Brassier. In the last form, which is "passive nihilism", reactive forces, having been exposed to the horror, get stuck in a somewhat purgatory state wherein they cannot but surrender to a peaceful "extinction".[37]

The crucial upshot of this final stage is that the passive extinction leaves behind a negation — the traumatic abyss — that neither rules over reactive forces nor becomes possessed by them.[38] Having lost its contact with life, which used to be established through reactive forces, there remains nothing for this autonomous negation to negate other than reactive forces. If reactive forces did not kill God, realise the impossibility of either invading or escaping the abyss, and retreat to the obscure state of a passive extinction, negation would never be directed towards the human. This is what Deleuze calls the self-defeat of nihilism, which is proven to be an autonomous event, arising necessarily from the logic of the history of nihilism, and which owes nothing to active forces and affirmation.

Nevertheless, negation has to be attached to an already reactive agent, which risks leaving the self-defeat to the vagaries of the agent's free will. Deleuze's solution lies in a shift from negation to affirmation that hopes to bypass this indeterminacy. This shift irreversibly abolishes the autonomy of negation by subordinating it to the superior autonomy of affirmation or by making it a "power of affirmation".[39] However, it is important to realise that such a sharp transition is possible only if we presuppose that all reactive forces can be reduced to the human and all active forces to the overman/child. The death of the human entails that human beings are not in a privileged position with respect to life and thinking. But one wonders why they would be in a privileged position with respect to reactive forces and how such a strict overlapping of the human and *all* reactive forces would not reproduce the same anthropocentrism, albeit in a negative form. We might thus ask if there are reactive forces that are not human and if they can bring us the non-nihilistic negation that does not need to be attached to an agent. Before moving to Brassier, it is important to see that these reactive forces can best be understood within the broader context of the "post-continental" turn.

2. Brassier's Reaction

2.1 Enlarging Upon the Outlines of the Post-Continental

The root of both the "speculative turn" and the self-annihilation of nihilism as an ensuing event can be found in what John Ó Maoilearca calls, as early as 2006, the "post-continental" turn.[40] According to Maoilearca, with the publication of four crucial texts by Deleuze, Michel Henry, Alain Badiou, and François Laruelle, a properly philosophical *event* occurred in 1988, an irreversible shift from what has been known as "continental philosophy".[41] Two essential features of this incipient turn are: 1) the renouncement of all forms of transcendence through the radicalisation of immanence; and 2) the abandoning of the prioritisation of philosophy over the sciences.[42]

It might be inferred from Maoilearca's analysis that what causes the emergence of these two tendencies is the discovery of autonomies that are deeper than those found in continental thought. In each of the four philosophers that Maoilearca examines, different forms of advanced autonomies are expressed through various new conceptions of immanence. For Maoilearca, the post-continental turn is post-Deleuzian because it was Deleuze who prefigured the rupture from the continental with his absolutisation of immanence. The outer edge of this turn, however, is expressed in Laruelle's real as radical immanence that is fully foreclosed to thinking, in contrast to the Deleuzian immanence that remains dependent on thinking. Furthermore, the connection between the first and second features of the post-continental turn becomes particularly explicit in Laruelle because his radical immanence relativises philosophy in such a way that no hierarchy remains between a primary ontology and regional ontologies.[43] This means that not only immanence but also the sciences in general become fully autonomous from thinking.

The subsequent growth of interest in a radically autonomous conception of reality can be regarded as an outcome of the post-continental turn — a clear justification of Maoilearca's foresight. In particular, the appearance of "speculative realism", which occurred only a year after the publication of Maoilearca's book, is evidently an immediate after-effect of this event.

For Maoilearca, the eventality of the post-continental turn is Deleuzian in character: it is not infinite, as the philosopher's long-standing "being" is said to be, but indefinite, which explains the "spiralling generation of different kinds of finitude".[44] Rather than considering being as the highest purpose of thinking, the philosopher should engage in the unfolding and the futurity of the event, which unavoidably takes the form of a prophetic discourse: thinking the event is a "prescription for what could be".[45] Crucially, what distinguishes the declaration of an event from a prophetic statement about how the state of things will be in the future is the attentiveness towards precisely this spiralling of a multiplicity of finite entities. In this sense, we might conceive the various strands of speculative realism as disparate post-continental entities that express different forms of autonomy.[46]

However, what is missing both in Maoilearca's prescription for the future of the post-continental and in the growing body of work in speculative realism is precisely the post-affirmationist and negativist dimension that follows from the attempt to bestow the real with full autonomy.[47] Negation should be added as the third feature of the post-continental. To do this, we need to see that the post-continental turn and the ensuing speculative turn evolve parallel to a negativist orientation in both Deleuzian and non-Deleuzian thought. Just as in the case of Brassier, in the works of thinkers such as Nick Land, Reza Negarestani, Benjamin Noys, Eleanor Kaufman, Andrew Culp, Daniel Colucciello Barber, and Jacob Vangeest, we can explore the manufacturing of post-Deleuzian/post-continental negations and reactive forces that are designed specifically as a challenge to Deleuzian affirmationism.

2.2 Post-Continental Reactive Forces

I would suggest that this post-continental orientation has brought about two new groups of reactive forces that demand a transfiguration of the Deleuzian schema of forces: the relatively autonomous "detached acted force", whose diverse examples are found in the aforementioned thinkers, and the fully autonomous "non-correlational reactive force", which is expressed in Brassier's speculative realism. The first group has an indispensable but ultimately transitional role, which leads to the completely developed reactive forces of the second group. (An elaboration of how this intermediary force is expressed by its individual members would exceed the limits of this paper, and as such I will have to confine myself to offering brief explanations in the notes.[48])

While differing significantly from each other, these negativist rivalries are nevertheless united on two key points: the explicit identification of the problem and the implicit logic of the various solutions offered. The openly declared problem is that Deleuzian philosophy cannot negate on account of its abiding affirmationism. The solutions offered are the diverse negativities that claim to accomplish what Deleuze cannot. The logic behind the construction of these negativities is the almost collectively unconscious attempt to *transfer affirmation's anti-nihilistic quality of non-resentfulness or aggression onto an autonomous negation that asserts itself as superior to affirmation*.

Considering that, for Deleuze, the reason for nihilism is the autonomisation of negation from affirmation,[49] the turn towards a new negativity designates the emergence of atypical negativities that are *non-nihilistic, despite being independent of affirmation*. If Deleuze is the ultimate target for the enaction of these negativities, this is only because, in a similar way to Maoilearca's suggestion, they are unmistakably post-Deleuzian, in that they cannot but account for the new standards set by the project of overcoming nihilism.

The first category of new reactive forces is a modification of what Deleuze calls the "acted" force, which is a largely overlooked but compulsory annex to his distinction between active and reactive.[50] "Acted" denotes an advanced reactive force that is dominated, trained, "precipitated",[51] and strengthened by an active force. The violence an active force exerts over a reactive force eliminates its nihilistic attributes and puts its ability to react into the service of acting. The difference between acted and non-acted versions of the same reactive force is that, while the former playfully destroys non-acted reactive forces, the latter resentfully reacts to active forces.[52] More importantly, the *ressentiment* of non-acted forces is an illusory movement while the *aggressive* movement of acted forces is real.[53] Contrary to affirmationism's satisfaction with its superior activity, each member of the first negativist group begins with the troubling realisation that the acted cannot be developed and strengthened by the active — *hence the contention that Deleuze cannot negate.* Consequently, they find it necessary to detach acted forces from active forces, allowing them to proceed alone, if they are going to continue their development. *A detached acted force is thus an all-the-more-advanced reactive force, which achieves the real and aggressive movement that can no longer be pursued under the dominance of active forces.*[54] In the detachment of acted forces, it is, therefore, possible to discern an exacerbation of the tension between active and reactive, which indicates the malfunctioning of affirmation.

Nevertheless, the detachment of acted forces puts them in an indeterminate and anxious situation of relative autonomy. They can neither remain attached to active forces nor pursue the consequences of a fully separated reaction, which leads to an irreversible destruction.[55] Incapable of perceiving such a radical termination as a component of their non-nihilistic development, they are obliged to transfer to active forces the peculiar strength they gained by separating.[56]

If the malfunctioning of affirmationism prefigures detached acted forces, the malfunctioning of this detachment itself signals the presence of a more decisive autonomy. This is revealed in Brassier's self-avowed nihilism. Although Brassier's identification of the problem and proposed solution are no different than the other post-Deleuzian negativities, his uniqueness lies in representing the radical moment when the *anti-nihilistic qualities of affirmation are transferred not only to negation but also to nihilism itself.* This puts him in a more antagonistic relationship with Deleuze than the first group, and for this very reason makes him much more significant, in a positive manner, for Deleuze's project.

2.3 Correlationism, Vitalism, and the Death of Thinking

In *Nihil Unbound*, Brassier conceives nihilism as the inevitable consequence of the speculative realist attempt to overcome "correlationism", understood as the belief that we only have access to the correlation between thinking and the real; we do not have access to either one independent of the other.[57] Nihilism is the only way to think the real in its full autonomy. In his equation of nihilism with a search for a real that cannot be subsumed by the correlation, we observe Brassier relying on three irreversible turns. The first is the inauguration of the correlation in the form of Kant's transcendental *a priori*, which serves as the condition on which all experience is grounded, and which invalidates all attempts to attribute substantiality to either thinking or the real. The whole of classical metaphysics then becomes common sensical or "naive" for leaving unthought that which is presupposed in experience. The second is Deleuze's affirmationist turn, which completes the post-Kantian progress by exalting life to the level of correlation. A view that not only Brassier but also the totality of post-Deleuzian negativities implicitly holds is that this signifies the moment after which no philosophy can be resentful — that is to say, its movement should be real. As I mentioned before, Deleuze in this way determines the affirmation of life and the overcoming of nihilism as the inseparable components of the post-Kantian rupture from classical naivety. The final turn is found in speculative realism, which arises as a logical consequence of the vitalist culmination of the correlation. If anti-nihilism is how correlationism culminates, then only by transforming nihilism into a "speculative opportunity" can the reality that is autonomous from life be thought.[58] From the perspective of the non-correlational real, what now becomes naive is the totality of transcendental and affirmationist turns.[59]

But Brassier does not stop at the critique of vitalism, since for him the exaltation of life and active forces bring about an even deeper process: the immortalisation of thinking that is characteristic of not just correlationism but the whole history of philosophy. The non-correlational real can be grasped only as thinking's death. The function of Brassier's new reactive force is to effectuate the aggressive movement that irreversibly terminates thought's all-pervasive perpetuity. As such, it provides the means to think the full autonomisation that cannot be provided by the detached acted forces.

2.4 Alien Theory

Brassier's speculative nihilism — and, as we will see, his later "neo-rationalism" — can be traced back to *Alien Theory* from 2001, which introduces Laruelle's non-philosophy as a polemic against Deleuze.[60] The three interconnected aims of this confrontation are: (1) the discovery of a radically autonomous reality that cannot be made an object of affirmation; (2) the full autonomisation of science from philosophy; (3) the liberation of the *act* of the real from the performance of a philosophical *agency*.

The Deleuzian association of thinking and life is expressed through the absolutisation of immanence, which exposes all transcendent identities as metaphysical fictions. However, Deleuze cannot but envisage this immanence as a fusion of thinking and matter in the form of a self-affirming and self-differentiating intensive materiality.[61] Consequently, far from overthrowing transcendence, he ends up creating — albeit in a differential manner — a new "mixture" of immanence and transcendence. The principle concern of non-philosophy is precisely to question the authority of the mixture itself, which constitutes the essence of the philosophical decision. Against Deleuze's absolute immanence or intensive matter, non-philosophy proposes a radical immanence or a radical hyle, which functions outside the logic of the decisional production of mixtures. What radical hyle does is unilaterally determine the mixture of thinking and matter, such that all forms of absolute, and hence philosophical thinking per se, become relative with respect to the real. In the face of this autonomous reality, philosophy loses its supposed priority over the sciences. Furthermore, since the real does not need a thinking mind to unilateralise thinking, unilateralisation does not have to pass through an agent. Unilateralisation thus occurs by equalising philosophy with the sciences and by liberating the autonomy of the real from the decisional vagaries of a thinking agent.

From these three aspects of unilateralisation derives the provocative and rather abrupt conclusion that the philosophical decision and capital are identical to one another.[62] For Brassier, there is nothing inherently anti-capitalist or anti-statist about the philosophical sense that diverges from the pre-philosophical common sense. On the contrary, this original philosophical divergence itself has to be conceived as a result of capital. While Deleuze continues to embrace the ancient critique of *doxa* by supplementing it with radical politics, non-philosophy renounces the very distinction between common sense and philosophical sense. Non-philosophy is not a new exit route from *doxa*. It rather claims that capital has always been at work in the production of the totality of *reconciliatory* common sense and *revolutionary* philosophical sense.

The non-philosophical operation of unilateralisation thus becomes the real's autonomous acting upon the identity of philosophy and capital, or upon "world-capital".[63] Such an act unleashes a completely new mode of knowing, a "cognitive activity" that is more destructive to world-capitalism than "revolutionary intellectual agency".[64] Notwithstanding, just as non-philosophy is not merely against philosophy, and the real is not a resentful transcendence beyond life, this "gnosis" neither opposes militant subjectivity nor aims to substitute it. Instead, this novel cognitive activity should be understood as a "prosthetic" upon the body of a militant subjectivity, which is a "transcendental supplement" allowing the revolutionary practice to *know* how the philosopher's "phenomenological experience" is regulated by world-capital and eventually becomes undecipherable by it.[65] This prosthetic is neither an agency nor an empirical instantiation that might be a better candidate for redeeming humanity. Instead, it allows us to gain a new perspective of ourselves, in which we are "already-redeemed" by the full autonomisation of the real.[66]

However, *Alien Theory* is indeterminate regarding the status of negation. On the one hand, it suggests that there is a more advanced form of negativity in non-philosophy,[67] and on the other hand, it warns against misunderstanding non-philosophical operations as expressions of a new negation.[68] Moreover, in contradistinction with the sheer anti-Deleuzian development of his argumentation, when confronted with the problem of negativity, Brassier is even in need of confirming Nietzsche: "[…] like Zarathustra's No, Laruelle's 'non-' is ultimately a No that performs the Yes".[69]

2.5 Nihil Unbound

It was not until *Nihil Unbound* that Brassier resolved *Alien Theory*'s indeterminacy and defined the true merit of non-philosophical unilateralisation as the discovery of a superior form of *philosophical* negativity. Arguably the most important difference between *Alien Theory* and *Nihil Unbound* is to reconstruct the confrontation between Deleuze and Laruelle entirely on the axis of the duality between affirmation and negation. This leads Brassier not only to leave behind non-philosophy as a "bootless exercise in extravagant sterility",[70] but also to reclaim philosophy as an essentially nihilistic activity.

The function of foregrounding this negativist dimension is to find in unilateralisation the capacity to conceptualise the traumatic extinction of the material universe and the concomitant death of thinking.[71] The scientific statement concerning the heat-death of the universe harbours a surprising fundamental equivocality because it overturns the distinction between origin and end.[72] That the universe will irreversibly be annihilated suggests that it has always-already been annihilated, that we are always-already dead, or our death has the form of a paradoxical "anterior posteriority". Indeed, one could say that there is still a difference between the "now" in which thinking is always-already dead and the "future" in which it is going to be terminally destroyed, but the whole point of extinction is to have always-already cancelled the distinction between now and future, rendering the now of my being always-already dead, identical with its future actualisation.[73]

To think of extinction or the death of thinking as the identity of origin and end, Brassier makes use of Laruelle's concept of real as non-dialectical identity.[74] "Non-dialectical" implies that the real cannot be created by thought, as in the case of Hegel's dialectical logic of identity. But neither can it be perceived as a symptom of the degeneration of life, as in the case of Deleuze's affirmative logic of difference. The real is a radical given, meaning that there is no dialectical negation or differential affirmation that gives.[75] We might thus say that the act of unilateralisation is neither *in* identity (Hegel's contradiction) nor *outside* identity (Deleuze's difference),[76] but *of* identity. It is the identity itself that unilateralises or *negates*. Non-dialectical identity is concurrently a non-dialectical negation.

Brassier conceives the ultimate function of decisional mixtures as the establishment of an immortal image of thought that resists being determined and terminated by such a negative identity. These philosophical decisions are exposed as attempts to avoid the possibility that thinking can be transformed into an object. The unilateral and irreversible negation of the real brings an end to this philosophical "hubris" by "turning thought itself into a thing".[77] The non-dialectical negativity is thought's tool to comprehend itself as a finite object and suspend its self-immortalising operations.

2.6 Reconsidering Death Drive

Brassier's realism becomes particularly intriguing when he argues that extinction is a reiteration of Freud's original trauma,[78] which was Deleuze's concern in his discussion of the pre-nihilistic and "material" state of reactive forces. For Brassier, this reiteration is a cosmological re-inscription of the death drive, which Freud determined as the tendency of organic life to dissolve into primordial inorganic matter. In this desire to identify with inert matter, the Freudian subject strives to bind the overabundant excitation released in the traumatic fracture. However, this attempt is deemed to be unsuccessful — and hence leads to neurosis — because of the very traumatic nature of the event, which entails that it has never been experienced. Trauma is not a function of experience; it can only be detected as malfunctioning.[79] The very fact that experience can be interrupted only by trauma — and not by experience itself —

proves that trauma is real. But what is deeper is that the real can be conceived only as trauma. Brassier radicalises this traumatic conception of reality by claiming that the traumatic real is discerned not only in the interruption but also in the full annihilation of experience. This brings an advancement in the concept of binding: while neurotic binding is structurally unsuccessful and relates to the past, the binding of extinction is *successful* and relates to the future. Nihilism is no longer the dominance of reactive forces that oppose life, but an attempt to bind the extinction, or to be the organon of extinction in order to successfully think the trauma and overthrow the so-called immortality of thinking.

In this context, Brassier conceives Deleuze's subordination of Freud's material model of death to the intensive death of the eternal return as the final version of thought's immemorial acts of self-immortalisation.[80] Brassier understands the eternal return as an eternity that is reflected into itself in the form of the self-affirmation of affirmation and wonders if this is anything other than a repeating of the Hegelian thesis that "being is coextensive with the act of its own reflexive self-positing".[81] The ultimate difference Deleuze makes here is to propose a vitalistic "inversion" of Hegel where difference-in-itself is converted into difference-for-itself. Deleuze's equation of a self-affirming or self-differentiating difference with the in-itself is only a manner of cancelling the in-itself altogether.[82] Consequently, Deleuzian life and thought are incapable of dying.

Although Brassier's positive resurrection of nihilism is operative completely within a post-Deleuzian register, he erroneously ignores the historicity of nihilism and assumes that his nihilism can overcome affirmationism without being related to this history. The superimposition of Brassier's nihilism over Deleuze's historical scheme changes the whole picture for both sides.

2.7 Speculative Realism as the Fourth Stage of Nihilism

For both Deleuze and Brassier, nihilism testifies to a series of extreme separations. In Deleuze, this begins with the separation of reactive forces from active forces. Furthermore, the end of nihilism comes with a second separation, namely the separation of negation from reactive forces. While, for Deleuze, this separated negation has nowhere to go and is destined to be subordinated to affirmation, for Brassier it has to go far beyond that, to the point at which it becomes separated not merely from the resentful reactive forces but, more importantly, from the human, life, and thinking. While Deleuze's autonomous negation is primarily a mystification created by reactive forces, which is then transformed into a power of affirmation, Brassier's negation is directly related to the original trauma, which is prior to the pre-nihilistic state of reactive forces. Rather than following what comes after the historical struggles and complicities between reactive forces and negation, Brassier thus goes back to the materiality *prior to* reactive forces and connects it to the ultimate annihilation of matter as such.[83] Brassier's extinction is thus a sneaky one: it is not added to the history of nihilism as a successive stage, but *transpierces it from its pre-history to an apocalyptic future by endowing nihilism with a non-dialectical logic of negation*. The speculative, fourth form of nihilism must function not merely by cumulatively advancing and expanding this history, but as a de-forming element that invites us to recast the relations of forces.

2.8 The Binding of Extinction as a Non-Correlational Reactive Force

What is the force that intervenes in life and thinking while carrying the trace of extinction? This is nothing other than the binding of extinction as an intellectual capacity, but Brassier would indeed refuse to conceive of it as a force since, for him, forces are essentially correlational. However, this prompts a refusal of the distinction between dominant (active) and submissive (reactive), thereby making his nihilism indeterminate about the problem of violence. Brassier in this way follows Laruelle's negative image of violence, which represents perhaps the most radical attempt to detach wonder from domination.[84] This image assumes that domination belongs to a human subject and is exerted over an innocent reality. It accuses the Platonic wonder that inaugurated philosophy of dominating the object of wonder. Yet, what is crucially missed in this perspective is the *neutralisation* of the object of wonder on which the same Platonism rests.[85]

As Deleuze shows, Freud's binding is a reactive force that belongs to a human subject.[86] It is a force of preservation that knows only how to resentfully oppress the burst of vital excitation. Besides, as he later shows in *Difference and Repetition*, binding's reaction is an integration of scattered differences of excitation to form an ego.[87] Brassier's binding, by contrast, is unmistakably post-Deleuzian and immune to the challenges posed by the critique of nihilism. Rather than being produced by a separation from active forces, it is introduced to thought by the real as such. It does not react to an original activity to integrate differences into an ego; on the contrary, it reacts to a negation unforeseen by the history of nihilism and effectuates a disintegration of thought. The movement in which it participates is not an illusion created by *ressentiment* but the real aggression of unilateralisation. Contrary to the reactive forces of the reactive and negative stages, it does not escape or invade, but — as I will soon show — arises from the *successful knowing of the traumatic impossibility of escaping and invading*. Finally, unlike the reactive forces of passive nihilism, its image of extinction is not that of a docile fading away, but rather that of an opportunity for a courageous attempt to turn thinking into an object.

The binding of extinction is unknown to Deleuze because it is a reactive force that is non-resentful, despite being autonomous from active forces — and hence more fascinating or "grandiose" than the previous reactive forces, as it follows the consequences of a negation whose aggressiveness cannot be subordinated to affirmation. *The binding of extinction is the non-correlational reactive force that corresponds to the non-dialectical negation.* While active forces prove the necessity of overcoming nihilism by liberating thought from the hegemony of God and the human, only by way of the intervention of extinction does force become non-correlational and capable of liberating the real from the hegemony of thinking. *The death of thinking, therefore, should be conceived as an inevitable continuation of the deaths of God and the human.*

For Brassier, the gains of this final death are the destruction of the pre-ontological understanding of being along with the resolution of the mystery and the horror of existence.[88] Let us first see how Deleuze discovers the same merits of nihilism in his own way.

2.9 Deleuze on Common Sense and Trauma

The essence of the idea of the affirmation of life in even its most disastrous aspects is that, in the reactive forces that caused those disasters, there is something necessary to learn and to utilise for the empowering of active forces. That is why there is a historical gain. There is thus a difference between the pre-historical/pre-nihilistic and the post-historical/post-nihilistic, which is produced solely by reactive forces.[89]

For Deleuze, the naivety of philosophical nihilism lies in the belief that thinking has an original affinity with being, whose ultimate formulation is in Heidegger's linking of the pre-ontological to the ontological.[90] In Heidegger, the "unfamiliar" ontological being is attained through a radicalisation of the "familiarity" or the "self-evidency" of the pre-ontological being. Unlike Heidegger, however, once familiarity is grasped as a product of reactive forces, we can conceive of it not as an effect of an authentic being, but as "a way of feeling" that can radically be altered. This occurs by following the further development of reactive forces, which breaks the supposed connection between pre-ontological and ontological and carries us towards the fascinating dimension of pathologies and traumas. The object of wonder that inaugurates philosophy is not neutral, and not even an action in the initial stage, but a reaction. Deleuze moves from common sense to philosophical sense first by pursuing the development of reactive forces.

Although Deleuze prioritises the epistemological function of reactive forces, the complex relationships between reactive forces and negation reveal, as we have seen, a properly ontological dilemma concerning the simultaneous impossibility of being and not-being, as if the atrocities of state violence were blindly carrying out an existential questioning and secretly collaborating with the philosopher.

Reactive forces are pathological not because they have sicknesses that cause them to suffer more and die sooner than active/healthy forces. The deeper sense of pathology lies in being susceptible to nothing but traumas. But there is a distinction between two traumas that Deleuze misses. The first trauma is the original/neurotic trauma where primitive reactive forces react to the vital excitation, which later leads to the invention of *ressentiment*. The second trauma appears to the subsequent forms of reactive forces, which make use of the weapons of *ressentiment* in order to kill God. This is the moment when reactive forces realise the deepest existential dilemma — the horror of existence — as the simultaneous impossibility of both inhabiting (being) and escaping (not-being). Once reactive forces realise this second trauma, they can't utilise it to advance themselves towards a further stage, as they did in the case of the original trauma.[91] Instead, the traumatic abyss irreversibly repels reactive forces to such an extent that they are constrained to renounce power and retreat into passive nihilism. That the abyss cannot be exploited and definitively rejects reactive forces allows Deleuze to find in it an objectivity that evidences the self-annihilation of nihilism.

From a Deleuzian point of view, active forces can dominate the knowledge of neurotic trauma and obtain an active psychology and physiology.[92] However, one thing is forbidden in Deleuze: we cannot make the second trauma or the horror of existence an object of knowledge. The power of knowing of reactive forces halts in the face of horror. Instead, as Woodward points out, horror is conceived of in and through art.[93] Horror, therefore, appears in Deleuze's persistent references to "dark" artists and authors such as Artaud, Bacon, Kafka, and Sacher-Masoch. The ultimate Deleuzian strategy is to subordinate horror — which is a purely reactive discovery — to the joyful affirmation of active forces.[94]

2.10 The Intelligibility of Horror

What Woodward misses, however, is that Brassier does not belong to the category of dark figures from whom Deleuze benefited as sources for the "heightening of the feeling of life". He neither dips into horror nor tries to dominate it with active forces, but instead declares that we finally *know* why there has been something like the pre-ontological understanding of being, why existence has been conceived of as inherently mysterious, and why horror established the affective limits of our venture into this mystery. The crucial achievement of the binding of extinction is the overcoming of horror — not its subordination — precisely by making it "intelligible". While Deleuze's artistic subordination of the traumatic horror is content with transforming it, and hence implicitly conforms to its mystery,[95] the intelligibility of horror objectifies and abandons it once and for all. Once we effectuate the binding of extinction, the simultaneous impossibility of being (invasion or habitation) and not-being (escape) can be *known* as the non-dialectical identity of being and not-being.[96] Brassier in this way radicalises Deleuze's equation of reactive forces with epistemology: while Deleuze's "human" reactive forces react to the original trauma and constitute the knowable aspect of life, Brassier's "inhuman" non-correlational reactive force reacts to the future trauma and knows that which is not *for* life.

Brassier's unspoken proposal is that *the objectification of thinking and the objectification of horror are the same operations.* Horror is not merely what a thinking subject *feels* when thought approaches the traumatic paradox of being, but rather announces the intersection of thinking and feeling when both are carried to their ultimate consequences. Indeed, all this begins with the questioning of familiarity as the feeling that corresponds to the self-evidency of being. Wonder is the minimum of affective divergence from familiarity, which is accompanied by the theoretical exposition of how the world is far from being self-evident. Wonder brings joy, but it is restless, and, as Maoilearca states, it is ultimately the same as horror.[97] Horror is wonder carried to its ultimate consequences. We have seen that the thought that corresponds to horror is the simultaneous impossibility of invasion and escape, being and not-being. But we cannot anymore speak of a correspondence as if thought and affect are distinct faculties.[98] If the diverse paths of conceptual abstraction each time arrive at the same horrific destination, this is because thinking, from the very beginning, is made of the same texture with horror (as well as with familiarity and wonder). Once thinking successfully thinks its death, we can contemplate thinking and horror as the same single *thing*. However, these implicit suggestions remain unexplored in Brassier's later work.

2.11 The Disappearance of Nihilism in Brassier

Since it is impossible, within the scope of a paper, to give a deservedly comprehensive account of Brassier's later writings which are generally regarded as a turn towards "neo-rationalism", I will restrict myself to very briefly pointing out that: 1) neo-rationalism is a way of pursuing the previous exploration of reactive forces; 2) this exploration ultimately fails to respond to the problems of trauma and horror; and 3) Brassier cannot distinguish between domination and repression, leading to a failure in interrupting the logic of state domination.

Brassier's writings after *Nihil Unbound* are a "work in progress" in the strictest sense of the word. In part lacking systematic unity, they present an experimental mapping of the scattered parts of the vast dimensions of the "great outdoors" that is indicated in the speculative turn. The connections between the discussions Brassier carries out on Kant, Hegel, the Frankfurt School, Marx, Sellars, Deleuze, Laruelle, analytic philosophy, the cognitive sciences, and information theory are, to an extent, loosely connected and often remain inconclusive. While the open-ended character of Brassier's work is the positive effect of the indefinite character of the "post-continental" — and hence a merit, inspiring the reader for further experimentality — it nevertheless contains the sign of a weakness that can be tackled by giving it a special kind of unity.

Perhaps the most important reason for the absence of a cement that can hold together Brassier's relatively disseminated debates, and that can point towards clearer horizons for his project, is the abrupt and rather frustratingly unexplained disappearance of nihilism after *Nihil Unbound*, since it was precisely nihilism that allowed Brassier to problematise, give coherence, and respond to the dogmas of continental philosophy.[99] Among the thirty-plus papers that have appeared so far, the term "nihilism" and the related issues of extinction, the death of thinking, and the horror of existence scarcely show up, leaving the reader to figure out their own connections. Does this mean that nihilism has stopped being a tool for Brassier? Did it lose its importance as a philosophical problem? If so, in what sense and to what degree? These questions have no answer in the later writings. I would like to claim that the problem of nihilism continues to dominate Brassier's work, albeit on a more subterranean level. Besides, this pullback is the sign of an inability to sustain a self-proclaimed nihilism, and hence a structural failure on the part of Brassier. But more importantly, it is an indication of the self-annihilation of nihilism, the outlines of which I draw towards the conclusion.

2.12 Neo-Rational Reactive Forces

The silent persistence of nihilism in Brassier's later work can be discerned in the way in which he maintains the philosophical experimentation with the post-continental reactive forces. Brassier's turn away from nihilism is parallel to his early refusal of speculative realism. The reason for this disclaimer is the regression to the pre-Kantian realism or to a "speculative dogmatism" that he detects in speculative realism; hence, his ensuing "neo-rationalism" can be conceived as a reworking of his previous realism through the critical lens of Kant.[100] The anti-Deleuzian and anti-Kantian last sentence of *Nihil Unbound* says that philosophy should not be affirmationist or justificatory, but be "an organon of extinction".[101] In the later papers, however, we observe Brassier being almost completely silent about the theme of extinction and fully embracing the justificatory or rational apparatus of Kant: neo-rationalism is an investigation into the enlargement of "our conception of what is revolutionary about rationality".[102]

For Brassier, the mistake of the whole post-Kantian tradition up until Deleuze is to *ontologise* or *substantialise* Kant's distinction between the transcendental and the empirical. This amounts to the confusion of causation with justification or reason, whose ultimate expression is Deleuze's genealogical reading of Kant.[103] Deleuze ontologises Kant by interpreting the transcendental faculties as symptoms of reactive forces. Deleuze's subordination of rational/reactive forces to irrational/active forces results in the production of a "belief toward an ultimately theological 'other' of reason".[104]

An adequate account of how rationality is enlarged falls outside the scope of this paper. For now, it is sufficient to note that neo-rationalism follows the logic of post-continental reactive forces, by *going back to the forces that Deleuze deemed as reactive and "rehabilitating" them.*[105] Previously, these were the "realist" reactive forces that expressed the superiority of the real, death, and binding; now they become "rational" and take the form of "representation", "consciousness", and "justification". Moreover, Brassier's ultimate aim is again to propose a negativity more suitable than affirmation in interrupting the functioning of power and violence. Neo-rationalism can thus be seen as an *enlargement of what is revolutionary about reactive forces* — a process that already began with speculative realism.

Two complementary figures, Wilfrid Sellars and Marx, play the most important role in neo-rationalism. While Sellars' naturalisation of the transcendental helps Brassier to question the correlation between subject and object without falling into affirmationist irrationalism, the function of Marx is to advance the critique of correlationism to the domains of theory and practice.

Contrary to correlationism, which depends on a confusion of mind-independence with concept-independence, Sellars helps us to understand that there might be mind-independent realities that can well be *known* by the transcendental or conceptual structures that we gained from that reality.[106] Marx's role, on the other hand, is to advance Sellars' naturalised transcendental into the socio-historical domain.[107] Marxism thus becomes Sellarsianism in practice, so to speak. In this connection, Marx is seen as discovering a new form of "consciousness", which is capable of making the "unconscious cognitively and practically tractable".[108] Against the Deleuzian "theologization" of Marx, which rests upon the construction of a revolutionary desire that transcends knowledge, the "rehabilitated" Marxist consciousness allows Brassier to reinstate the union of knowledge and revolution.[109] In opposition to the affirmationist unification of theory and practice, bringing to Marxist radical politics a transcendental power is an attempt to propose a *knowledge as negation* that disintegrates the correlation between theory and practice.[110]

We cannot but see in neo-rationalism a reformulation of the concerns of *Alien Theory* and *Nihil Unbound.* In these previous works, the aim was to obtain an autonomous mode of knowing through the transcendental prosthesis, which suspends world-capital, and the binding of extinction, which effectuates the death and the objectification of thinking. In both cases, *once knowledge becomes autonomous from affirmation, it becomes indistinguishable from a practice of revolutionary negation.* However, we might doubt if the neo-rationalist formulation of the same problem can be more successful than the previous non-philosophical and speculative realist options as long as it does not acquire a positive image of domination and leave behind its attachment to trauma.

2.13 Reconsidering Domination

It is deeply meaningful that Brassier's neo-rationalist attack on the correlation between subject and object, as well as theory and practice, comes along with a reconsideration of the problem of domination. The new negation that is acquired through the union of knowledge and revolution not only breaks these correlationist structures but also interrupts the logic of state domination. Brassier expresses the malfunctioning of this logic by recourse to Hegel. The

Spirit, which unites subject and object, and theory and practice, is expressed through the fundamental paradox of domination: nature continues to dominate us through the domination that we exert against nature.[111] Nevertheless, the circularity through which the Spirit perpetuates domination is inevitably interrupted by domination itself. There is a "self-interruption of domination", which arises from "the impossibility of absolute domination".[112] The idea here is that the concept of domination is essentially paradoxical and leads towards self-destruction through an entirely autonomous process.

However, Brassier's discussion remains ultimately unresolved and he seems unable to conceptualise the concrete mode of negation or self-destruction that might interrupt the circularity of domination. The reason Brassier's latest discussion on repression remains unresolved is that he cannot think of a *positive* domination that is exerted over reactive forces. Domination is therefore erroneously equated with repression, which merely expresses the resentful violence of reactive forces over active forces. As such, Brassier stays within a traumatic conception of domination whereby the status of the negation that is supposed to end domination gets stuck within the domain of compulsions and remains indeterminate.[113] How can domination interrupt its own logic and forbid itself the absolute if it is nothing other than repression? How could the *autonomous* — and not *us* — produce such a radical rupture from repression if it did not already have tendency for something other than trauma, negation and reactive forces? Can it be because the self-interruption of repression is only a part of the larger event of the self-interruption of nihilism?

The reason why Brassier cannot conceive of autonomy as the self-annihilation of nihilism is that he remains solely within the reactive side, albeit having made it non-correlational. Indeed, this problem is not peculiar to Brassier but marks the entirety of post-continental negativities. It is therefore necessary to take a fresh look at the project through the new perspective provided by these currents.

3. *Consequences for the Actualisation of the Glad Tidings*

3.1 The Reactive Aspect of the Glad Tidings

The reactive aspect of the glad tidings suggests that it is not us humans that will annihilate nihilism, but nihilism that will annihilate itself. What *we* do in *projecting* is deliver a fatal blow to state philosophy by exposing its complicity with power, detecting nihilism at the origin of existential questioning. Just as the discovery of the transcendental represents a "turn" to which no thought can remain indifferent, the proof-giving character of affirmationist ontology sets an objective standard for the emergence of a new idea, such that thereafter no novelty can appear without carrying the features of anti-nihilism and squarely taking a position against power. Establishing a bond between philosophy and radical politics is no longer a choice but an obligation. Regardless of the arbitrariness of the political inclinations of the philosopher, we are in an unprecedented and extraordinarily blissful moment in which no novelty with an explicit or implicit affinity with right-wing ideologies can emerge. The philosopher's longstanding complicity with the state, from Plato to Kant to Hegel to Heidegger, has finally come to an irreversible end.[114] This is the purely optimistic moment in which *even the autonomous reactive forces do not — and cannot — serve nihilism.*

Nevertheless, the bare fact remains that the overcoming of nihilism has long since lost the status of an ambitious and *aggressive* project. Once faith in its possibility is lost, the revolutionary power of its objectivity is reduced to a standard for political correctness or a democratic criterion to be inclusive of the inhuman.[115] At the level of radical politics, it at best becomes a strategy for breathing some unconscious vitality into leftist orthodoxy; and from the perspective of personal experience, the horror of existence turns out to be nothing more than a stimulant for the intensification of one's private enjoyment.[116]

Perhaps the greatest mistake that the project's proponents have made so far is to have never tried to acquire an image of what the self-annihilation of nihilism might look like and question whether we are capable of detecting when nihilism *actually began to collapse*. Philosophy after Nietzsche directs Kant's critical apparatus to the presuppositions that privilege the human and that establish the familiarity of experience or the pre-ontological understanding of being. However, we too easily presuppose that this is enough to automatically obtain privilege to a non-nihilistic event, that we are by nature suited to comprehend it, and that it would be familiar to *us*. In confusing the *actions* of the projection with the actual happening of the *aim*, we have failed to reckon with the necessity that the collapse of nihilism must bear an unfamiliarity that is far greater than the mystery and horror of the copula *is*.[117] If the self-evidency, mystery, and horror of being are fictions created by nihilism, then the self-annihilation of nihilism should be an event that has more fundamental determinations than self-evidency, mystery, and horror.

Indeed, Brassier is far from his mainstream image as "bleak"[118] or "pessimistic".[119] Nihilism accomplishes affirmation's *aim* — the aim of the liberation of negation from the negation *of* life and the liberation of the abyss from being a trauma *to* life — better than affirmation itself. The self-annihilation of nihilism does not start when negation destroys reactive forces by inciting in the human the desire for self-destruction, but when reactive forces become inhuman and begin to react to extinction. But how long can we continue to embrace nihilism if all it does is to take on the tasks of the project of its overcoming?

In Deleuze, the problem with nihilism was the autonomisation of a mystifying negation. In Brassier, autonomous negation becomes identical with the real as already-happening demystification.[120] Reading the two together allows us to approach the moment when *the new locus of autonomy is neither life nor the real but the self-annihilation of nihilism*. Once its true direction is revealed, the search for the non-correlational real — along with nihilism's redefinition as a speculative opportunity — is left behind as a transitional stage.

Perhaps everything lies in the extraordinary ease with which things are happening. If the real, with its already-happening redemption, solves the problem of being, can there be anything more exhilarating for life than finally being free from the cumbersome mystery of *is*? Can there be anything *lighter* than the fact that this happened *effortlessly*? Can there be anything better suited to the playful anti-labourism and the spirit of frivolity implied in Nietzsche's glad tidings? The true challenge, then, lies not in deciding whether there will be redemption in the future or not, but to reorganise ourselves in accordance with the *easy* reality that *redemption is already happening without needing to pass through an agent.* Brassier's compulsory defence *and* renouncement of nihilism, along with the other post-continental negativities, expresses the initial symptoms of the downfall of nihilism, whose scope, time, and outcomes are yet to be discovered.[121]

3.2 The Active Aspect of the Glad Tidings

We should then ask how the realisation of the self-annihilation of nihilism, the reactive aspect of glad tidings, effects its active aspect. This second glad tiding concerns *our* activity in the face of the autonomous self-defeat. Deleuze is right that we need to affirm without fighting against *ressentiment*, but his mistake is to presuppose a moment of the complete absence of reactive forces, and to never envisage the alternative of having non-nihilistic reactive forces for the realisation of Nietzsche's prophecy. I would like to conclude by sketching five features of this new *activity*.

1. Active forces can express a speculative optimism, which takes on the critique of correlationism but leaves behind both realism and rationalism, since the correlation is primarily between thinking and trauma, and not between thinking and the real or subject and object.[122] The experimentation with

the non-traumatic is the key to breaking the correlation and producing a revolutionary interruption.

2. One reason Brassier's search for "gain in intelligibility" cannot shift towards a revolutionary practice is that, along the way, it remains unresponsive to the problem of affect. The very capacity to know the trauma remains attached to the traumatic feeling: horror moves from being an artistic fuel for life (Deleuze) to an epistemological fuel for intelligence. But how can we continue to be horrified once horror becomes an object? The intelligibility and the demystification of horror should entail that horror stops being something felt, but what feeling follows from this is left unquestioned. It is no wonder that Brassier retreats to the brute positivism of passive nihilism when, faced with the problem of affect, his only proposal is the ending of suffering through the enhancement of our cognitive capacities.

The *different way of feeling* that comes *after* horror is possible only by changing our direction from the traumatic real to the self-annihilation of nihilism as a non-traumatic autonomy. This new affect is something to be produced along the way of experimenting with, acting upon, and even dominating the non-traumatic.

3. Fortunately, we are now in a position to speak of a domination without fighting nihilism, because the object of domination is already non-nihilistic. The object of wonder as the stimulant of domination changes beyond recognition, and hence alters the sense of domination as well. We saw that a non-nihilistic reactive force is non-correlational, meaning that it is not a limitation *for* an active force. In extending to a limit that is not its own, an active force is now in a position to approximate to a fundamentally indifferent reaction. This would then be a violence exerted over a reaction *to* extinction. To dominate a non-correlational limitation is neither an attempt to enhance life nor a preventive measure against prospective nihilism.

Moreover, the no-matter-what of the collapse of nihilism entails that we cannot make any changes to it. Like Laruelle's real, it causes an irrevocable alteration in thinking without being affected by thought's actions. The innocence of this violence arises not from the autonomous play of the child or the absence of a transcendent, religious, and accusatory imperative,[123] but from the *invulnerability of the object of violence.* It offers the possibility to overthrow all the nihilistic and inherently pathological images of violence from religious evils to human perversion to inhuman sociopathic indifference. Furthermore, it does this without reproducing the much-vaunted cruelty of the dark artist who, albeit in a subversive manner, remains tied to the same traumatic origin as their rivals. It expresses the cruelty that Deleuze sought, since guilt, *ressentiment*, and hence pity, are finally eradicated, along with the traumatic horror that served as their condition.

4. The pessimism concerning the possibility that power will always find ways of appropriating active forces comes to an end for two reasons. First, while the previous reactive forces could always appropriate active forces and present them as the "legitimate property" of the state,[124] they cannot appropriate the non-traumatic unfolding of the self-annihilation of nihilism. Second, the death of thinking and the appearance of non-nihilistic reactive forces prove that there is no infinite reservoir of active forces, just as there is no infinite "power of appropriation". This is not the old optimism that arises from the hope for a future redemption, but rather expresses the attentiveness towards the redemption that is happening now.
5. This new activity is an opportunity to reorient the task of the destruction of the state toward a series of experimentations that seek to confront power with non-trauma. Active forces can now compel the state to *see* the objective fact that it has lost reactive forces, nihilism, and trauma as its last resorts, just as it once saw the impossibility of invading God's absence. These experimentations abandon the negativisms that continue to nourish horror and that strive *to be a trauma for power.* The interruption that is expected to break the correlationist

structures and the logic of state domination does not have to remain within the regime of trauma. Concordantly, the non-traumatic does not have to remain as the guarantee for the continuity of experience, the indestructible play of the eternal return or the perpetuation of an immortal cosmic power (as in yogic traditions). The self-annihilation of nihilism forces us to think of an *interruption in experience that is non-traumatic*. Unlike the previous forms of traumatic interruptions that are ultimately determined by pathologies, we might try to think of this interruption as a new form of *healing*. The encounter with a non-traumatic event is an occasion to heal and to be healed outside the old habits of unification and immortalisation.

In recognising themselves as being always-already dead, and in contemplating, for the first time, the horror of existence as a finite and external object, active forces step out of horror and put behind their traumatic attachment to the quandary of being — a full *recovery* from the trauma of being, a courage to awaken from the nightmare, a growth into a new maturity, and the acquisition of a new capacity to heal the world's traumatised forces

References

Barber, Daniel Colucciello. "The Creation of Non-Being". *Rhizomes*, 29 (2016).

Brassier, Ray. *Alien Theory*. Unpublished PhD thesis, 2001.

Brassier, Ray. *Nihil Unbound: Enlightenment and Extinction*. New York: Palgrave Macmillan, 2007.

Brassier, Ray. "Concepts and Objects". In *The Speculative Turn: Continental Materialism and Realism*, edited by Levi Bryant, Graham Harman, & Nick Srnicek. Melbourne: re.press, 2010.

Brassier, Ray. "That Which Is Not". *Stasis*, Vol. 1, No. 1 (2013), pp. 174–188.

Brassier, Ray. "Deleveling: Against Flat Ontologies". In *Onder invloed: Wijsgerig festival Drift*, pp. 64–80, 2014.

Brassier, Ray. "Prometheanism and Its Critics". In *#Accelerate: The Accelerationist Reader*, edited by Robin Mackay and Armen Avanessian. Falmouth: Urbanomic, 2014.

Brassier, Ray. "Wandering Abstraction: Acceleration, Communization, and Real Movement". *Mute Magazine* (13 February 2014), pp. 64–80. http://www.metamute.org/editorial/articles/wandering-abstraction.

Brassier, Ray. "Postscript: Speculative Autopsy". In Peter Wolfendale, *Object-Oriented Philosophy.* Falmouth: Urbanomic, 2014.

Brassier, Ray. "The Metaphysics of Sensation: Psychological Nominalism and the Reality of Consciousness". In *Wilfrid Sellars, Idealism, and Realism: Understanding Psychological Nominalism,* edited by Patrick J. Reider, pp. 98–113, 2017.

Brassier, Ray. "Dialectics Between Suspicion and Trust". *Stasis,* Vol. 4, No. 2 (2017), pp. 111–129.

Brassier, Ray. "Concrete-in-Thought, Concrete-in-Act: Marx, Materialism and the Exchange Abstraction". *Crisis and Critique,* Vol. 5, No.1 (2018), pp. 111–129.

Brassier, Ray. "Concrete Rules and Abstract Machines: Form and Function in *A Thousand Plateaus*". In *A Thousand Plateaus and Philosophy,* edited by Henry Somers-Hall, Jeffrey A. Bell & James Williams, 2018.

Brassier, Ray. "After Too Late: The Endgame of Analysis" (with Nadia Bou Ali), in *Problemi International,* No. 4, pp. 11–30, 2020.

Brassier, Ray. "The Human". Unpublished manuscript.

Brassier, Ray. "Final Repression: Adorno and Marcuse on the Antinomy of Progress". Unpublished manuscript.

Culp, Andrew. *Dark Deleuze.* Minneapolis: University of Minnesota Press, 2016.

Deleuze, Gilles. *Nietzsche and Philosophy,* translated by Hugh Tomlinson. London: Athlone Press, 1983.

Deleuze, Gilles. *Difference and Repetition,* translated by Paul Patton. New York: Columbia University Press, 1994.

Deleuze, Gilles & Félix Guattari. *What is Philosophy?,* translated by Hugh Tomlinson & Graham Burchell. New York: Columbia University Press, 1994.

Kaufman, Eleanor. *Deleuze, The Dark Precursor.* Baltimore: Johns Hopkins University Press, 2012.

Kleinherenbrink, Arjen. *Against Continuity.* Edinburgh: Edinburgh University Press, 2019.

Kolozova, Katerina. *Cut of the Real.* New York: Columbia University Press, 2014.

Malabou, Catherine. *The New Wounded: From Neurosis to Brain Damage,* translated by Steven Miller. New York: Fordham University Press, 2012.

Land, Nick. *The Thirst for Annihilation.* London: Routledge, 1992.

Land, Nick. *The Dark Enlightenment.* http://www.thedarkenlightenment.com/the-dark-enlightenment-by-nick-land. Accessed 22 November 2022.

Land, Nick & Sadie Plant. "Cyberpositive". In *#Accelerate: The Accelerationist Reader,* edited by Robin Mackay and Armen Avanessian. Falmouth: Urbanomic, 2014.

Negarestani, Reza. "Differential Cruelty". *Angelaki,* 13.3 (2009), pp. 69–84.

Noys, Benjamin. *The Persistence of the Negative.* Edinburgh: Edinburgh University Press, 2010.

Parsa, Mehdi. "Speculative vs. Transcendental: a Deleuzian Response to Meillassoux". *La Deleuziana* 11 (2020), pp. 171–185.

Reszitnyk, Andrew. "Wonder without Domination". *Chiasma* 1.1 (2014), pp. 24–53.

van Tuinen, Sjoerd. "Deleuze: Speculative and Practical Philosophy". In *Genealogies of Speculation,* edited by Armen Avanessian & Suhail Malik. London & New York: Bloomsbury, 2016.

Vangeest, Jacob. "Deleuzian Pessimism". *TripleAmpersand Journal (&&&),* 2020. https://tripleampersand.org/deleuzian-pessimism. Accessed 22 November 2022.

Williams, James. "Matter and Sense in Gilles Deleuze's Logic of Sense: Against the 'Ism' in Speculative Realism". *Deleuze & Guattari Studies* 15.4 (2021), pp. 477–496.

Woodward, Ashley. "Deleuze, Nietzsche, and the Overcoming of Nihilism". *Continental Philosophy Review* 46 (2013).

Woodward, Ashley. "Nonhuman Life". In *Deleuze and the Non/Human,* edited by Jon Roffe & Hannah Stark. New York: Palgrave Macmillan, 2015.

Notes

1 Sjoerd van Tuinen, "Deleuze: Speculative and Practical Philosophy", in *Genealogies of Speculation*, eds. Armen Avanessian and Suhail Malik (London and New York: Bloomsbury, 2016); Arjen Kleinherenbrink, *Against Continuity* (Edinburgh: Edinburgh University Press, 2019); Mehdi Parsa, "Speculative vs. Transcendental: a Deleuzian Response to Meillassoux", *La Deleuziana*, 11 (2020), pp. 171–185; James Williams, "Matter and Sense in Gilles Deleuze's *Logic of Sense*: Against the 'Ism' in Speculative Realism", *Deleuze and Guattari Studies*, 15.4 (2021), pp. 447–496.

2 Gilles Deleuze, *Nietzsche and Philosophy*, trans. Hugh Tomlinson (London: Athlone Press, 1983), p. 172.

3 Ashley Woodward, "Deleuze, Nietzsche, and the Overcoming of Nihilism", *Continental Philosophy Review*, 46 (2013), pp. 143–4.

4 Ray Brassier, *Nihil Unbound* (New York: Palgrave Macmillan, 2007); Benjamin Noys, *The Persistence of the Negative* (Edinburgh: Edinburgh University Press, 2010); Andrew Culp, *Dark Deleuze* (Minneapolis: University of Minnesota Press, 2016).

5 Deleuze's anti-nihilism depends on the conviction that Nietzsche's "most general project" is a "resumption" of Kant's failed critical project. Kant's failure can be discerned in the opposition between the vastness of the project and the scantness of the results, which pose no threat to dogmatic conceptions of God, soul, freedom, and immortality (Deleuze, *Nietzsche and Philosophy*, pp. 1, 52, 89).

6 Gilles Deleuze, *Difference and Repetition*, trans. Paul Patton (New York: Columbia University Press, 1994), pp. 142, 166.

7 Deleuze's prioritisation of life entails that all variants of idealism and realism are modes of making life oppose itself (Deleuze, *Nietzsche and Philosophy*, pp. 181–185).

8 Similarly, the distinction between subject and object arises from the subordination of affirmation to negation (Deleuze, *Difference and Repetition*, pp. 131).

9 Deleuze, Nietzsche and Philosophy, pp. 39–44.

10 Ibid., p. 8.

11 Ibid., pp. 55–58.

12 Ibid., pp. 65–68, 172.

13 Deleuze states that domination is a "violent training", which both sorts out active forces and "reinforces" reactive forces so that they can be "acted". Reactive forces that are "sharpened" and "concentrated" in this fashion will not be the same as reactive forces that did not undergo such a training. If this training fails, reactive forces can invert the procedures of these trainings in order to put themselves into the service of a "domestication" that sorts out the reactive instead of the active. This is how the violence of active forces is presented as "the legitimate property" of the state (ibid., pp. 134–138).

14 Here, Deleuze doesn't speak directly of the "reactive", but celebrates Nietzsche's concept of "force" by referring to *ressentiment,* bad conscience, and the point of view of nihilism, all which, as we know from *Nietzsche and Philosophy*, are products of reactive forces. See Gilles Deleuze and Félix Guattari, *What is Philosophy?*, trans. Hugh Tomlinson and Graham Burchell (New York: Columbia University Press, 1994), pp. 65, 82, 83.

15 Bad conscience or guilt is the illusory inward movement as a continuation of the illusory outward movement of *ressentiment.*

16 Deleuze, *Nietzsche and Philosophy*, p. 168.

17 Ibid., p. 67.

18 Deleuze, *Difference and Repetition*, p. xx.

19 These targets are nothing but the products of negation and reactive forces: identity, opposition, resemblance, and analogy (ibid., p. 262).

20 Deleuze, *Nietzsche and Philosophy*, p. 193.

21 Objectivity is released through change and vice versa. Once forces are thrown into the machinery of the test, it will not be us but the test itself that will *decide* the transformation or annihilation of such docile differences. Without doubt, its decision will be in favor of affirmation and aggression, since what makes the principle genuinely objective is the return of that which differs and the destruction of that which stays the same (ibid., p. 55).

22 Deleuze, *Nihil Unbound*, p. 221.

23 Arjen Kleinherenbrink, *Against Continuity* (Edinburgh: Edinburgh University Press, 2019), p. 223.

24 In Kleinherenbrink's terminology, "object" is a synonym for "force".

25 Kleinherenbrink follows the speculative realist "fascination" with objects and departs from the prevalent idea that objects or individuals are internally connected through an overarching difference as intensity or a pre-individual field. His speculative realist and object-oriented Deleuze conceives of the world as consisting of non-relational objects that are more than the totality of relations that make up the world, such that there is *an* intensity/difference or *a* pre-individual field *inside* each single object (ibid., p. 41). Objects are thus fascinating and make the world fascinating because even the tiniest object is irreducible to and more than the rest of the world. However, this fascination operates through the same neutralisation of the object of wonder by exalting the very concept of "object" — allegedly the most devalued concept in the history of philosophy — to the status of the most wondrous and thought-provoking. Indeed, we find active forces being inscribed into the objects, but these are only the active forces of the beautiful soul. Object-oriented ontology is too quick to reconcile not only Deleuze with speculative realism, but also active forces with reactive forces, hence the problem of violence and the overcoming of nihilism remains unexplored.

26 Deleuze, *Nietzsche and Philosophy*, pp. 35–36, 198.

27 Ibid., p. 177.

28 Therefore, the question concerning the exact nature of the "cruelty" that belongs solely to the child, and how exactly it differs from the nihilistic modes of violence, goes unanswered. The best we are offered is that the child's "play of difference" is "war-like" (ibid., p. 191) or that negation "shoots out" from affirmation "like lightning" (ibid., p. 176). It is meaningful that Deleuze writes in the same sentence that this lightning as violent negation is immediately absorbed into the affirmation from which it emanated. In this way, he precludes the possible autonomisation of negation. However, it remains completely uncertain how this same negation might "shoot out" again. Perhaps aware of his insufficiency in accounting for an advanced form of negation, in various other works Deleuze intensively reworks the tension between affirmation and violence. Daniel Colucciello Barber is right in noting that this

tension ultimately remains "indeterminate" in Deleuze, as exemplified in the antagonism between "escape" and "weaponization" in *A Thousand Plateaus*. See Daniel Colucciello Barber, "The Creation of Non-Being", *Rhizomes*, 29 (2016), p 14.

29 Deleuze, *Nietzsche and Philosophy*, pp. 172, 175, 179.

30 Ibid., p. 174. This should not come as a surprise if we observe that the only reference he makes to Nietzsche in support of this statement contains nothing to imply that the collapse of nihilism bears such a radical autonomy. Nietzsche's claim is that the overcoming of nihilism coincides with the self-overcoming of the "man who wants to perish". The self-defeat of nihilism occurs *through* the self-defeat of the human.

31 Ibid., p. 174.

32 Ibid., p. 124.

33 Ibid., p, 112.

34 Ibid., p. 211.

35 The world beyond is not an instance that negates life, as if negation were an external verb that it takes on; rather, it is already nothing but negation or nihilism as such.

36 Deleuze, *Nietzsche and Philosophy*, p. 169.

37 Ibid., p. 149.

38 Ibid., p. 174.

39 Ibid., p. 71. However, here we find again the passage from the becoming-reactive of all forces to the becoming-active of all forces, which betrays the original imbrication of forces and tends to reproduce the beautiful soul.

40 John Ó Maoilearca, *Post-Continental Philosophy: An Outline* (London and New York: Continuum, 2006).

41 Ibid., pp. 10–11. These four texts are Deleuze's *Le Pli*, Badiou's *L'Être et l'événement*, Henry's *Voir l'invisible*, and Laruelle's discussion with Jacques Derrida in *La Décision Philosophique No 5.*

42 Ibid., p. 22.

43 Ibid., p. 138.

44 Ibid., p. 34.

45 Ibid., p. 1.

46 As we can particularly discern in the works of Iain Hamilton Grant, Graham Harman, and Quentin Meillassoux, what becomes more

important than the struggles between immanence and transcendence, on the one hand, and philosophy and the sciences on the other, is the revival of the historical polarisation of idealism and realism, whereby the real is radicalised by granting it full autonomy. As is well known, in Grant, this occurs through a reanimation of *naturphilosophie*; in Harman, through the ontological prioritisation of objects; in Meillassoux, through the absolutisation of contingency.

47 Maoilearca conceives the event through an asymmetrical but ultimately harmonious dialogue between Deleuze and Laruelle (along with Henry and Badiou), where Laruelle's critique of Deleuze dissolves into a higher form of diagrammatical thinking. It is no wonder that, for Maoilearca, negation never becomes a determinant element of the post-continental, since an event can best be understood as a (diagrammatical) relationship *between* its proponents (ibid., pp. 9, 10).

48 Nick Land, *The Thirst for Annihilation* (London: Routledge, 1992); Reza Negarestani, "Differential Cruelty", *Angelaki*, 13.3 (2009), pp. 69–84; Benjamin Noys, *The Persistence of the Negative* (Edinburgh: Edinburgh University Press, 2010); Eleanor Kaufman, *Deleuze, The Dark Precursor* (Baltimore: Johns Hopkins University Press, 2012); Andrew Culp, *Dark Deleuze* (Minneapolis: University of Minnesota Press, 2016); Barber, "The Creation of Non-Being"; Jacob Vangeest, "Deleuzian Pessimism", *Triple Ampersand*, accessed November 22, 2022, https://tripleampersand.org/deleuzian-pessimism

49 Deleuze, *Nietzsche and Philosophy*, p. 178.

50 Ibid., p. x.

51 Ibid., p. 111.

52 Ibid., pp. 134–6.

53 Ibid., p. 10.

54 Land can be seen as the pioneer of the post-continental negativities with his radicalisation of Nietzschean anti-anthropocentricism. While, for Deleuze, the death of the human is part of a deeper affirmation of life, Land conceives of the rupture from the human as a series of experiments with non-vitalistic and inhuman reactive forces. Land's accelerationism should thus be understood as a *supplementary* acceleration, since it accelerates that which is already "acted" or "precipitated" by active forces (Land, *The Thirst for Annihilation*).

In his unorthodox reading of *Difference and Repetition*, Negarestani applies the same Landian logic by arguing that the deeper issue at stake in Deleuze is not the liberation of (active) difference from (reactive) representation, but the discovery of a new mode of cruelty that has no trace of active forces. To that end, Negarestani rethinks the distinction between intensity and extensity in terms of what he calls the "two systems of cruelty", where intensity is understood as a dead void that belongs to nothing, while extensity is the dead material body to which nothing can belong (Negarestani, "Differential Cruelty", pp. 73–75).

Noys is distinguished by his post-continental reactive forces being completely anti-Deleuzian. However, the superior negativity he develops is inseparable from a traversing of affirmationism (Noys, *The Persistence of the Negative*, p. 48). He attempts to make use of the "energising political effect" of affirmationist concepts in order to obtain a reinforced Marxist negativity that is capable of thinking and interrupting the logic of capital (ibid., p. 173). These negations express the precision and determinacy that are absent from affirmation. Crucially, they take place "in the margins of Deleuze" (ibid., p. 4). The attack on capital thus coincides with the attack on affirmationism. Noys' transmission of the features of affirmation to negation reaches its ultimate end when he surprisingly embraces the resentful "lamb" in order to counter the dysfunctional nobility of the "bird of prey" (ibid., p. 128).

Eleanor Kaufman follows the same logic, but this time by taking a squarely Deleuzian position. She uncovers the "diabolical underside" of Deleuze in order to develop a "dark" Deleuzian ontology. This leads her to embrace reactive conceptions such as sadism, inertia, dialectics, being, and structure outside the dominance of affirmationism (Kaufman, *Deleuze, The Dark Precursor*, pp. 4–11).

Culp radicalises Kaufman's strategy by developing a self-destructive Deleuzianism. He makes use of the reactive forces of the Deleuzian toolbox in order to turn them against the vitalism of Deleuze himself (Culp, *Dark Deleuze*, p. 21). This transforms Deleuzian politics into a "hatred for the world", which exposes the pact between affirmationism and global capitalism (ibid., p. 8). The death of the World is a necessary consequence of the death of God and the human, and the only way to overcome *ressentiment*.

Barber turns Deleuze "against affirmation" in an attempt to show the complicity of "habits of affirmation" with the "anti-black grammar" of the world (Barber, "The Creation of Non-Being"). This requires a break with the association of creation and affirmation and a redefinition of the negative as the new locus of creativity. To that end, he offers a rereading of Deleuze's concept of "non-being" as a better expression of "difference-in-itself".

In accordance with Barber's afro-pessimist reading of Deleuze, Vangeest argues that Deleuze's idea of the eternal return fails to negate and transgress precisely because it remains within the confines of "white possibility" (Vangeest, "Deleuzian Pessimism"). It thereby conceives of a negation extending beyond affirmation — an absolute deterritorialisation — as a threat to the safe space of stratification, which is reserved only for the white. The aggression of afro-pessimism thus proceeds from the moment at which Deleuzian deterritorialisation or active forces has the privilege of being "cautious" — a possibility foreclosed to blackness.

55 It could be said that Land's accelerationism is an example of such an irreversible rupture from active forces, but his later regression to the resentful reactive forces of fascism is a testimony to the fact that no such radical destruction happens with acted forces. Therefore, the acted should return to the active not only to transfer back the excess of energy it gained from the act of separation, but also to avoid regressing to a non-acted state that is necessarily associated with a right-wing ideology of some sort. See Nick Land, *The Dark Enlightenment*, accessed 22 November 2022, http://www.thedarkenlightenment.com/the-dark-enlightenment-by-nick-land.

56 Kaufman expresses this position clearer than the other members of the first group when she says that the "dark" side of Deleuze that she explores ultimately serves another kind of positivity (Kaufman, *Deleuze, The Dark Precursor*, pp. 6–7).

57 Brassier, *Nihil Unbound*, p. 51.

58 Ibid., p. xi.

59 Ibid., p. 129.

60 Ray Brassier, *Alien Theory* (unpublished PhD thesis, 2001).

61 Ibid., p. 207.

62 Ibid., p. 438.
63 Ibid., p. 430.
64 Ibid., p. 435.
65 Ibid., p. 436.
66 Ibid., p. 44.
67 Ibid., pp. 351–52.
68 Ibid., pp. 218, 259, 321–22.
69 Ibid., p. 260. Indeed, the suggestion here is that unilateralisation accomplishes the task of Zarathustra better than himself. This is a clear expression of the logic of post-continental negations that I mentioned before: unilateralisation is more suitable for effectuating a real negation, which is originally an affirmationist discovery.
70 Brassier, *Nihil Unbound*, pp. 119.
71 Ibid., pp. 229, 56–9.
72 Ibid., pp. 230–31.
73 This peculiar identity cannot be thought through either pre-Kantian realisms or post-Kantian correlationisms because extinction overturns not only the origin-end distinction but also the difference between transcendental and empirical or the givenness and the given. The pre-Kantian realisms cannot account for the *a priori* conditions or the genesis of the scientific statement; hence, they remain commonsensical for not being able to think the presuppositions hidden in thought's confrontation with the real. As for the Kantian turn, it tends towards completely ignoring the reality that is indicated in the scientific statement; hence, it risks being indistinguishable from superstition, which is uncannily a more dangerous version of the pre-Kantian naivety.
74 Brassier, *Nihil Unbound*, p. 229.
75 Ibid., pp. 137–38. We might see how this position is fundamentally opposed to Deleuze, who constructs his theory of forces on the assumption that the totality of experience is produced by forces (Deleuze, *Nietzsche and Philosophy*, p. 3). This idea is later deepened in terms of the intensive procedures that *gives* the extensive magnitudes, which is apparently a reworking of the active-reactive distinction (Deleuze, *Difference and Repetition*, pp. 222–23).
76 Deleuze, *Nietzsche and Philosophy*, p. 288.

77 Brassier, *Nihil Unbound*, pp. 131, 141.
78 Ibid., p. 234.
79 Ibid., p. 236.
80 Ibid., pp. 218, 185–56.
81 Ibid., p. 221.
82 Ibid., p. 200. Brassier's claim is not, however, that indifference is superior to difference, or that difference is cancellable by a state of statis, but rather that the real as material death is the identity of difference and indifference, which produces an irreversible cut within the fabric of the correlation between thinking and the real (ibid., pp. 148, 203, 223).
83 Such an antecedent materiality is not possible for Deleuze, since pure or extensive matter is already a reactive idea in the service of the cancellation of differences. It either serves as the raw material for the metaphysical imposition of forms (God, being) or remains as the unthought presupposition of positivism. We therefore see religion, metaphysics, and science serving the same nihilism. Deleuze later finds the solution in subordinating this extensive materiality to the intensive matter. For Brassier, what makes possible a materiality prior to the distinction between — and the mixture of — extensive matter and intensive matter is Laruelle's concept of radical hyle. The radical hyle is not the "pure matter" that is fabricated or retrojected after the separation of reactive forces, but an unproduced given. In this way, it provides the means to escape both metaphysics and positivism.
84 For an account of the rigorous way in which Laruelle opposes wonder to domination, see Andrew Reszitnyk, "Wonder without Domination", *Chiasma*, 1.1 (2014), pp. 24–53.
85 Neutralisation is precisely how reactive forces triumph over active forces and create the mystification of an "in-itself" (Deleuze, *Nietzsche and Philosophy*, p. 123). Deleuze's analysis shows that, once we are incapable of being fascinated with reactive forces, we remain in-between the alternatives of the illusory violence of negative and reactive nihilisms, the non-violence of passive nihilism, or, at best, the reconciliatory affirmations of the beautiful soul.
86 Deleuze, *Nietzsche and Philosophy*, pp. 112, 115.
87 Deleuze, *Difference and Repetition*, p. 97.

88 Brassier, *Nihil Unbound*, pp. 137, 73, 238.

89 Deleuze, *Nietzsche and Philosophy*, pp. 133–141.

90 Deleuze, *Difference and Repetition*, pp. 129–131.

91 Land provides one of the most striking typological analyses of this horror when he defines Kant's transcendental philosophy as "the most elaborate fit of panic in the history of the Earth" and interprets the following period as a series of desperate reactionary attempts to prevent the horror leaking into thought (Land, *The Thirst for Annihilation*, p. 2). Like Deleuze, Land assumes a subversive Kantianism but only to exacerbate the "fit of panic" witnessed by the reactive forces. Land's contention is that it is possible for reactive forces to leave behind *ressentiment*, pursue the further consequences of their traumatic discovery and effectuate an irreversible rupture from the human.

92 Deleuze, *Nietzsche and Philosophy*, pp. 116, x.

93 Ashley Woodward, "Nonhuman Life", in *Deleuze and the Non/Human*, eds. Jon Roffe and Hannah Stark (New York: Palgrave Macmillan), p. 34.

94 Ibid., pp. 38–9.

95 Brassier, *Nihil Unbound*, pp. 40, 68, 73, 91.

96 Brassier conceives the traumatic discovery of reactive forces through Levinas' analysis of the horror of *there is*, which designates the simultaneous impossibility of being and not-being. However, just as Deleuze subordinates this horror to active forces, the Levinasian subject subordinates it to the "good beyond being", and is hence incapable of understanding why there is such a paradoxical impossibility in the first place (ibid., pp. 232–34).

97 John Ó Maoilearca, *All Thoughts Are Equal: Laruelle and Non-Human Philosophy* (Minneapolis: University of Minnesota Press, 2015), p. 42.

98 Catherine Malabou expresses the identity of thought and affect through what she calls "cerebrality" as the new domain of the autonomous. However, this identification is ultimately a *subordination* of affect to thought or enjoyment to the death drive, which occurs under the regime of trauma. See Catherine Malabou, *The New Wounded: From Neurosis to Brain Damage*, trans. Steven Miller (New York: Fordham University Press, 2012).

99 One rare example for making a connection between nihilism and neo-rationalism is from Brassier's "That Which Is Not", in *Stasis* (Vol. 1, No. 1, 2013, pp. 174–188), p. 185.

100 Ray Brassier, "Postscript: Speculative Autopsy", in Peter Wolfendale, *Object-Oriented Philosophy* (Falmouth: Urbanomic, 2014), pp. 412, 420.

101 Brassier, *Nihil Unbound*, p. 239.

102 Ray Brassier, "Dialectics Between Suspicion and Trust", in *Stasis* (Vol. 4, No. 2, 2017, pp. 98–113), p. 112.

103 For Brassier's further discussions on the problem of substantialisation, see ibid. pp. 98, 103, 104, 106; "The Metaphysics of Sensation: Psychological Nominalism and the Reality of Consciousness" in *Wilfrid Sellars, Idealism, and Realism*: *Understanding Psychological Nominalism*, ed. Patrick J. Reider, (London and New York: Bloomsbury Academic, 2017), p. 67; "Deleveling: Against Flat Ontologies" in *Onder invloed: Wijsgerig festival Drift* (2014, pp. 64–80), p. 77; "The Human" (unpublished manuscript, 2020), p. 5.

104 Ray Brassier, "Dialectics Between Suspicion and Trust", p. 98.

105 Brassier, "Postscript: Speculative Autopsy", p. 417.

106 Ray Brassier, "Concepts and Objects" in *The Speculative Turn: Continental Materialism and Realism*, eds. L. Bryant, G. Harman, and N. Srnicek (Melbourne: re.press, 2010), p. 58.

107 Ray Brassier, "Prometheanism and Its Critics", in *Accelerate: The Accelerationist Reader*, eds. A. Avanessian and R. Mackay (Falmouth and Berlin: Urbanomic/Merve Verlag, 2014), p. 487.

108 Brassier, "Dialectics Between Suspicion and Trust", p. 106. In Nietzsche, however, the unconscious remains something that resists conceptual justification and therefore can only be affirmed. This shows that affirmation necessarily conforms to the mystery of that which is affirmed.

109 For further discussion on the relationship between Marxism and representation, see Ray Brassier, "Concrete-in-Thought, Concrete-in-Act: Marx, Materialism and the Exchange Abstraction" in *Crisis and Critique* (Vol. 5, No.1, 2018, pp. 111–129), p. 121.

110 This negation is oriented directly against the "affirmationist consensus" (Brassier, "That Which is Not: Philosophy as Entwinement of Truth and Negativity", p. 175).

111 Ray Brassier, "After Too Late: The Endgame of Analysis" (with Nadia Bou Ali), *Problemi International* (No. 4, 2020, pp. 11–30), p. 26.

112 Ray Brassier, "Final Repression: Adorno and Marcuse on the Antinomy of Progress" (unpublished manuscript), p. 7.

113 Ibid., p. 8; Ray Brassier, "Wandering Abstraction: Acceleration, Communization, and Real Movement" in *Mute Magazine* (13 February 2014) [http://www.metamute.org/editorial/articles/wandering-abstraction], p. 53.

114 Land and Sadie Plant present perhaps the most solid expression of this irreversible moment when metaphysics is indistinguishable from the state violence as a "xenocidal neurosis": "Heidegger completed the degeneration of authenticity into xenocidal neurosis. Being died in the fuhrer-bunker, and purity belongs entirely to the cops" ("Cyberpositive", in *#Accelerate*, eds. Robin Mackay and Armen Avanessian (Falmouth: Urbanomic, 2014), pp. 306).

115 Indeed, there are reasons to gain the impression that Deleuze's project is motivated by teleological presumptions, and Woodward presents a comprehensive account of why this is the case (Woodward, "Deleuze, Nietzsche, and the Overcoming of Nihilism", pp. 140, 144). For Woodward, Deleuze's reliance on the definitive overcoming of nihilism arises from a longing for "existential guarantee" and a "desire for security", which are themselves reactions to life, as we know from Nietzsche. Furthermore, he writes that Deleuze's strict determinism "unwittingly repeats the metaphysical view which gives rise to it" and, even worse, reinstates "religious nihilism" (ibid., pp. 134, 135). Woodward thus finds in Deleuze an expression of old teleological ideas disguised as vitalism. However, these claims would be true only if we remained within the ambit of the project alone and conceived the result as a mere failure. In contrast, if we perceive Deleuze's project from the perspective of a result that is entirely different than the project, Deleuze's strict determinism — the absolute necessity of the overcoming of nihilism — can become an opportunity to think of a

new form of autonomy and a new event outside teleological constraints and a reactionary will for security.

116 As in the case of what Culp rightly criticised as the exploitation of the powers of the outside by the Deleuzian "aesthete" (Culp, *Dark Deleuze*, p. 29).

117 It is precisely this unfamiliarity that the dogmatic exaltation of thinking and life, which is our correlationist naivety, cannot notice. As long as the power of non-nihilistic autonomy that terminally breaks the complicity between philosopher and state is unthought, philosophy will remain stuck in the self-enclosed world of its project and the reconciliations of the beautiful soul, whose source lies, as Brassier's nihilist adaptation of Laruelle shows, in thought's self-immortalising hubris.

118 Kleinherenbrink, *Against Continuity*, p. 10.

119 Woodward, "Nonhuman Life", p. 34.

120 The most important discovery of the speculative realist and neo-rationalist venture into the great outdoors is the intersection of autonomy and nihilism. But it should be noted that this intersection is at the apex of a multiplicity of unorthodox meetings that bring together the Frankfurt School, phenomenology, post-structuralism, pragmatism, scientific realism, psychoanalysis, and speculative realism. Yet without doubt, Brassier's overarching perspective on twentieth-century philosophy operates against the backdrop of a whole history of philosophy seen through the lens of anti-nihilism. Perhaps the foremost attempt to synthesise the disparate continental and analytic intellectual currents of the twentieth century occurs through *first embracing and then transmitting the features of affirmationism to nihilism.*

121 This is not to say, as Heidegger did of Nietzsche, that they represent the culmination of nihilism and not its overcoming, but rather that they represent the beginning — and only the beginning — of *the process of the self-annihilation of nihilism.* Nietzsche, Heidegger, and Deleuze all imagine nihilism as something that they have overcome on a philosophical level, but which has not been actualised yet. The matter is not whether they have overcome nihilism; rather, the very image of nihilism as something that can be overcome by *us* is wrong.

122 Katerina Kolozova is right, to a certain extent, in her insight that "trauma has a multitude of instantiations, forms, and qualities of experience", and that the thinking of the autonomy should begin with an investigation of trauma's "experiential diversity" (Katerina Kolozova, *Cut of the Real* (New York: Columbia University Press, 2014), pp. 9–10). However, this is ultimately a transitional period and once the autonomous is grasped not as the real per se but as the self-annihilation of nihilism, the investigation should accordingly be directed towards the non-traumatic — and perhaps, towards a "non-traumatic diversity" to come.

123 Deleuze, *Nietzsche and Philosophy*, pp. 22–25.

124 Ibid., p. 138.

CHAPTER 5:
ANALYSIS AND IMPACT

"OBJECT AS COMRADE": THE ROLE OF THE SUBJECT IN OBJECT-ORIENTED POLITICS

Slavoj Žižek

In times of the proliferation of realism in philosophy and the threat of post-humanism, it is the function of subjectivity in its old-fashioned Cartesian, Kantian, Hegelian, Freudian, and Lacanian tradition which proves to be strangely ineradicable, almost tenacious in both contemporary philosophy and the artefacts of popular culture of the twenty-first century. Why does it seem that we cannot do without the purely logical entity of the subject? And what is the conceptual frame in which to account for this great "undead" of Western, and increasingly global, thought? A case should be made for the emergence of the subject at the interstice of an irreducibly idealist element taking shape within the ontological priority of reality: subject is not an entity "which is", it rather arises as the name for "what is not" in a given situation, hence as a form of nothingness. It is the survival of the subject in the era of post-humanity that perhaps testifies to the need to rehabilitate idealism — a stance which never fully recovered after the death of Hegel. The implications of this stance affect even today's popular culture: can we really presume to explain the success of, say, Todd Phillips' film *Joker* without recourse to the logical operations immanent to the form of subjectivity?

Revolutionary Self-Destitution...

Far from being constrained to the clinical experience, what Lacan called subjective destitution, the concluding moment of the psychoanalytic process, also has a political dimension described by Brecht. In his *Beggar's Opera*, Brecht condenses four basic existential stances (the longing for everyday joys, brutal reality, religious feeling, cynical wisdom) into two, with joyful cynicism as the last word. However, this was not Brecht's own last word: with a breathtaking consequence, Brecht added in his learning plays (*Jasager, Die Massnahme*) another subjective position, that of a purely formal gesture of self-sacrifice grounded in no deeper meaning or goal. The implicit logic is here that one cannot overcome cynical wisdom with some positive ethical ideal: cynicism can undermine them all; it is only a totally meaningless self-sacrificial act that undermines the cynical distance itself. The Freudian name for such an act is, of course, death drive, and its Hegelian name self-relating negativity. However, we should be very careful here: Brecht makes it clear that this act is not a kind of pure excessive suicidal gesture of stepping out of the symbolic space (something that belongs more to the theory of Bataille). In yet another case of "infinite judgment", death drive coincides with its opposite, with radical alienation in the symbolic order. Along these same lines, Saroj Giri described "revolutionary self-destitution, self-objectification" as a specific form of subjectivity:

> A specific, individual life, a unique human being, is now an object, a mere object who can be taken down any time:

> The "comrade as object" is a continuation of de-classing and de-personification, now taken to the point of revolutionary destitution, involving the courage to die, death. To the extent that the comrade is a living human being, his or her objectification will and must involve the openness to death. Life is hanging in a balance, and the vulnerability to death is a constant presence. You are never safe and the willingness to sacrifice life is best embraced graciously. [1] (Giri, 2021, p. 11)

Giri establishes here a double link with the past, recent and more ancient. Recent: the idea of objectification and destitution is close to the idea of Fanon's idea of declivity: "an utterly naked declivity is where an authentic upheaval is born". Or when he says, "the Negro is a zone of non-being, an extraordinarily sterile and arid region, an utterly declining declivity" (Giri, 2021, p. 22). Ancient past: Buddhist revolutionary self.[2] The void (of destitution) "as the 'path,' the rupture/opening to a 'new world' can be found in the Buddha's nibbana. Nibbana is often known as Awakening or Enlightenment, but actually nibbana is, in the first instance, extinction, the blowing out, the vanishing". (p. 14)

What Giri calls subjective destitution is therefore not just a new form of political subjectivity but simultaneously something that concerns our basic existential level, "a different way of being, involving a different modality of life and death" (Giri, 2021, p. 15). In his afterword to Peter Hallward's collection *Think Again,* Badiou approvingly quotes Lin Biao: "The essence of revisionism is the fear of death."[3] This existential radicalisation of the political opposition between orthodoxy and revisionism throws new light on the old '68 motto "the personal is political": here, the political becomes personal, the ultimate root of political revisionism is located in the intimate experience of the fear of death. Badiou's version of it would be that, since "revisionism" is, at its most basic, the failure to subjectivise oneself, to assume fidelity to a Truth-Event, being a revisionist means remaining within the survivalist horizon of the "human animal".

There is, however, an ambiguity that clings to Lin Biao's statement: it can be read as saying that the root of political revisionism lies in human nature which makes us fear death; but it can also be read as saying that, since there is no unchangeable human nature, our very intimate fear of death is already politically overdetermined, for it arises in an individualist and egotistical society with little sense of communal solidarity; which is why, in a communist society, people would no longer fear death.

"Comrade as object" does not imply that we should observe and manipulate ourselves from a cold "objective" distance. It is to be supplemented by its inversion, "object as comrade": "Instead of going over to the fetishistic powers of the commodity, one had to go towards the 'hidden' engineering/artistic powers of things, objects and materials — this would, as it were, allow the object to commune and speak, providing us the first contours of the 'object as comrade'" (Giri, 2021, p. 6). This "object as comrade" displays what Giri calls idealism in the (material) thing itself, of what we may call spiritual corporeality as opposed to the fetishist idealism which imposes on a thing from outside a social dimension as its reified property: to treat an object as "comrade" means to open oneself up to virtual potentials of an object in an intense interaction with it. Maybe, a surprising link can help us understand what is meant by "object as comrade" which supplements "comrade as object": today's object-oriented ontology — here is Graham Harman's concise description of OOO's basic stance:

> The arena of the world is packed with diverse objects, their forces unleashed and mostly unloved. Red billiard ball smacks green billiard ball. Snowflakes glitter in the light that cruelly annihilates them, while damaged submarines rust along the ocean floor. As flour emerges from mills and blocks of limestone are compressed by earthquakes, gigantic mushrooms spread in the Michigan forest. While human philosophers bludgeon each other over the very possibility of 'access' to the world, sharks bludgeon tuna fish and icebergs smash into coastlines.[4]

Such a way of treating object as a "comrade" also opens up a new way of being ecological: to accept our environment in all its complex mixture that includes what we perceive as trash or pollution, as well as what we cannot directly perceive since it is too large or too minuscule (Timothy Morton's "hyperobjects"). Along these lines, for Morton, being ecological

> is not about spending time in a pristine nature preserve but about appreciating the weed working its way through a crack in the concrete, and then appreciating the concrete. It's also part of the world, and part of us. Reality is populated with 'strange strangers' — things that are 'knowable yet uncanny.'

This strange strangeness, Morton writes, is an irreducible part of every rock, tree, terrarium, plastic Statue of Liberty, quasar, black hole, or marmoset one might encounter; by acknowledging it, we shift away from trying to master objects and toward learning to respect them in their elusiveness. Whereas the Romantic poets rhapsodised about nature's beauty and sublimity, Morton responds to its all-pervading weirdness; they include in the category of the natural everything that is scary, ugly, artificial, harmful, and disturbing.[5]

Is not a perfect example of such a mixture the fate of rats in Manhattan during the pandemic? Manhattan is a living system of humans, cockroaches… and millions of rats. Lockdown at the peak of the pandemic meant that, since all restaurants were closed, rats who lived off the trash from restaurants were deprived of the source of their food. This caused mass starvation: many rats were found eating their offspring. A closure of restaurants which changed the eating habits of humans but posed no threat to them was a catastrophe for rats, rats as comrades. Another similar accident from recent history could be called "sparrow as comrade". In 1958, at the beginning of the Great Leap Forward, the Chinese government declared that "birds are public animals of capitalism" and set in motion a large campaign to eliminate sparrows who were suspected of consuming approximately four pounds of grain per sparrow per year. Sparrow nests were destroyed, eggs were broken, and chicks were killed; millions of people organised into groups, and hit noisy pots and pans to prevent sparrows from resting in their nests, with the goal of causing them to drop dead from exhaustion. These mass attacks depleted the sparrow population, pushing it to near extinction. However, by April 1960, Chinese leaders were forced to realise that sparrows also ate a large number of insects in the fields, so that, rather than being increased, rice yields after the campaign were substantially decreased: the extermination of sparrows upset the ecological balance, and insects destroyed crops as a result of the absence of natural predators. By this time, however, it was too late: with no sparrows to eat them, locust populations ballooned, swarming the country and compounding the ecological problems already caused by the Great Leap Forward, including widespread deforestation and misuse of poisons and pesticides. Ecological imbalance is credited with exacerbating the Great Chinese Famine, in which 15–45 million people died of starvation. The Chinese government eventually resorted to importing 250,000 sparrows from the Soviet Union to replenish their population.[6]

Three examples from the cinema of Joris Ivens perfectly exemplify this dimension of object as comrade. Is his documentary *Regen* (Rain, 1929), a portrayal of Amsterdam during a rainfall, not a portrait of rain as comrade? One should mention here Hanns Eisler's *Fourteen Ways of Describing the Rain*, a 12 minute exercise in dodecaphony for flute, clarinet, string trio, and piano, written as a musical accompaniment to Ivens' *Regen*. Then, there is Ivens' "Pour le Mistral"(1966): wind as a comrade — scenes of life and landscape in Provence where a chilly wind called the Mistral blows down the valley of the Rhône to the Mediterranean. Plus there is another portrayal of wind as a comrade: "A Tale of the Wind" (1988), shot in China, old and ill Ivens' attempt to depict the insight that "the secret of breathing lies in the rhythm of the autumn wind".

However, we have to bear in mind something that OOO ignores which Giri is fully aware of: while subjective destitution (a term

Giri took from Lacan), reduction to an object, does not mean de-subjectivisation it *does* mean de-humanisation — after subjective destitution, a subject is no longer "human" (in the sense of the depth of personality, of "rich inner life" as opposed to external reality and similar psychic baggage). Only in and through destitution a subject in its purity (a capitalised Subject) emerges:

> The activist-comrade as object is still a Subject—a subject who perhaps speaks in the name of History and invokes the "metanarrative" of the "stages of History", but whose self-destitution and self-objectification open up a revolutionary possibility by creating a null point, a void in History itself. (Giri, 2021, p. 13)

Through subjective destitution, we do not enter a happy interaction of "object as comrade" and "comrade as object" in which a destitute subject deals with objects that surround him as his equal interlocutors, renouncing to act as their master who exploits them. In subjective destitution, the subject is not simply immersed into the flux of reality, he is rather reduced to a void, a null point, a gap in reality. It is only through this reduction to a void, from the subjective position of that void, that a subject can perceive and experience the interaction of comrade as object and object as comrade. In other words, through subjective destitution, the subject is radically divided: into a pure void and the object that he is. In this way, we overcome mortality and enter undeadness: not life after death but death in life, not dis-alienation but extreme self-abolishing alienation — we leave behind the very standard by means of which we measure alienation, the notion of a normal warm daily life, of our full immersion into a safe and stable world of customs. The way to overcome a topsy-turvy world is not to return to normality but to embrace turvy without topsy.

Already from this brief description it is clear that the phenomenon of subjective destitution assumes many forms which cannot be reduced to the same inner experience. There is the Buddhist nirvana, a disconnection from external reality which enables us to acquire a distance towards our cravings and desires — I assume a kind of impersonal stance, my thoughts are thoughts without thinker. Then there are so-called mystical experiences which should not be confused with nirvana: although they also involve a kind of subjective destitution, this destitution takes the form of a direct identity between me and a higher Absolute (typical formula: the eyes through which I see god are the eyes through which god sees himself) — my innermost desire gets depersonalised, it overlaps with the will of god himself, so that the big Other lives through me. In short, while in nirvana one steps out of the "wheel of desire", the mystical experience enacts the overlapping of our enjoyment with the enjoyment of the big Other. Then there is the subjective stance described by Giri: the destitution of a revolutionary agent who reduces itself to an instrument-object of the process of radical social change — he obliterates his personality, inclusive of the fear of death, so that revolution lives through him. Then there is the explosion of self-destructive social nihilism — think of *Joker*, but also of a scene in Eisenstein's *October* in which a revolutionary mob penetrates the wine cellar of the Winter Palace and engages in an orgy of massive destruction of hundreds of bottles of expensive champagne. And, last but not least, subjective destitution in its psychoanalytic (Lacanian) sense of traversing the fantasy, which is a much more radical gesture than it may appear: for Lacan, fantasy is not opposed to reality but provides the coordinates of what we experience as reality plus the coordinates of what we desire — the two coordinates are not the same, but they are intertwined (when our fundamental fantasy dissolves, we experience the loss of reality which also impedes our ability to desire). (We should also recall that traversing the fantasy is not Lacan's final word: in the last years of his teaching, he proposed as the final moment of the analytic process identification with the symptom, a gesture that enables us a moderately acceptable form of life.)

How are these versions related? They seem to form a kind of Greimasian semiotic square since there are two axes along which they are disposed: active engagement (self-destructive social explosion; revolutionary destitution described by Giri) versus disengagement (nirvana, mystical experience); self-contraction (destructive explosion against external reality; nirvana) versus reliance on a big Other (God in mystical experience, History in revolutionary destitution). In a destructive explosion, we contract into ourselves by way of destroying our environment; in nirvana, we just withdraw into ourselves leaving reality the way it is. In mystical experience, we disengage from reality by immersing ourselves into divinity; in revolutionary destitution, we renounce our Self by engaging in the historical process of revolutionary change. (From the Lacanian standpoint, these last two stances court the danger of falling into a perverse position of conceiving oneself as an object-instrument of the big Other.)

What Lacan calls subjective destitution is the zero level, the neutral abyss in the centre of this square. Here one should be very precise: what we reach in subjective destitution is not the absolute Void out of which everything springs but the very disturbance of this Void, not the inner peace of withdrawal but the imbalance of the Void — not the fall of the Void into finite material reality but the antagonism/tension in the very heart of the Void which causes the emergence of material reality out of the Void. The other four versions of subjective destitution structurally come second; they are attempts to pacify the antagonism ("self-contradiction") of the Void.

The question that arises here is: how should destitution in its politically engaged form avoid the fall into perversity? The answer is clear: it should suspend its reliance of the big Other (of historical necessity, etc.). Hegel constrained philosophy to grasping "what is", but for Hegel "what is" is not just a stable state of things, it is an open historical situation full of tensions and potentials — one should therefore link Hegel's insight with Saint-Just's claim: "*Ceux qui font des révolutions ressemblent au premier navigateur instruit par son audace* (Revolutionaries are akin to a first navigator guided by his audacity alone)." Isn't this the implication of Hegel's confinement of the conceptual grasp to the past? As engaged subjects, we have to act with a view to the future, but for a priori reasons we cannot base our decisions on a rational pattern of historical progress (as Marx thought), so we have to improvise and take risks. Was this also the lesson Lenin learned from reading Hegel in 1915? The paradox is that what Lenin took from Hegel — who is usually decried as the philosopher of historical teleology, of inexorable and regular progress towards freedom — was the utter contingency of the historical process.

The common-sense counterargument that arises here is: subjective destitution is such a radical gesture that it is limited to an enlightened elite, and remains an impossible ethical ideal for the masses, except in rare episodes of revolutionary enthusiasm. But I think that this reproach misses the point: Giri emphasises that subjective destitution is not an elitist stance of Leaders, but, on the contrary, a stance displayed by numerous ordinary combatants, like thousands who risk their life in the struggle against Covid.

...versus Destructive Nihilism

It is crucial to note here that subjective destitution as the emergence of a radical gap in the continuity of History is here not an explosion of destructive violence which can only in a later stage be transformed into a pragmatic and realist construction of a new order: Giri describes subjective destitution as a stance which enables us to engage in a construction of a new social order. As such, revolutionary subjective destitution should be strictly separated from the outbursts of radical negativity which appear as self-destructive political nihilism. There is no better example of this topic in art than Todd Phillips' *Joker* — one cannot but express admiration for a Hollywood in which it is possible to make a film like *Joker*, and for the public which turned it into a mega blockbuster.

However, the reason for the film's popularity resides in its meta-fictional dimension: it provides the dark genesis of the Batman story, a genesis that has to remain invisible for the Batman myth to function. Let's try to imagine *Joker* without this reference to the Batman myth, just as the story of a victimised kid who adopts the mask of a clown to survive his predicament — it simply wouldn't work; it would have been just another realist drama. *Time Out* characterised *Joker* as "a truly nightmarish vision of late-era capitalism" and categorised it as a "social horror film" — something unimaginable till recently, a combination of two genres which are perceived as totally disparate, the realist depiction of social misery and fantasised horror, a combination which, of course, only works when social reality acquires dimensions of horror fiction.

The three main stances towards the film in our media perfectly mirror the tripartite division of our political space: conservatives worry that it may incite viewers to acts of violence; Politically Correct liberals discerned in it racist and other clichés (already in the opening scene, a group of boys who beat Arthur appear black) plus also an ambiguous fascination with blind violence; Leftists celebrate it for faithfully rendering the conditions of the rise of violence in our societies. But does *Joker* really incite spectators to imitate Arthur's acts in real life? Emphatically *no* — for the simple reason that Arthur-Joker is not presented as a figure of identification — the whole film works on the premise that it is impossible for us, viewers, to identify with him.[7] He remains a stranger up to the end.

Before *Joker* was released, the media already warned the public that it may incite violence; the FBI itself specifically warned that the film may inspire violence from Clowncels, an Incel subgroup obsessed with clowns such as Pennywise from *It* and Joker. (There were no reports of violence inspired by the film.) After the film was released, critics were not sure how to categorise it: is *Joker* just a piece entertainment (as is the entire Batman series), an in-depth study of the genesis of pathological violence, or an exercise in social criticism?

Since *Joker* depicts radical rebellion against the existing order as a self-destructive orgy of violence with no positive vision underlying it, it can also be read as anti-Leftist — for Tyler Cowen, the film "quite explicitly portrays the egalitarian instinct as a kind of barbaric violent atavism, and it is pointedly critical of Antifa and related movements, showing them as representing a literal end of civilization. Only the wealthy are genteel and urbane and proper."[8] The lesson of the film is thus: no radical steps; we can only count on the benevolent charity of the rich to gradually improve things. The Leftist answer to this reading is that the self-destructive rebellion portrayed in *Joker* is that such a nihilist explosion of brutal rage precisely signals that we remain within the coordinates of the existing order, and that a more radical shift of political imagination is needed. From his radical Leftist standpoint, Michael Moore found *Joker* to be "a timely piece of social criticism and a perfect illustration of the consequences of America's current social ills": when it explores how Arthur Fleck became Joker, it brings out the role of bankers, the collapse of healthcare, and the divide between rich and poor. Moore is therefore right to mock those who feared the film's release:

> Our country is in deep despair, our constitution is in shreds, a rogue maniac from Queens has access to the nuclear codes — but for some reason, it's a movie we should be afraid of [...]. The greater danger to society may be if you DON'T go see this movie [...]. This movie is not about Trump. It's about the America that gave us Trump — the America which feels no need to help the outcast, the destitute.

Consequently, "the fear and outcry over *Joker* is a ruse. It's a distraction so that we don't look at the real violence tearing up our fellow human beings — 30 million Americans who don't have health insurance is an act of violence. Millions of abused women and children living in fear is an act of violence."

However, *Joker* does not only depict this America, it also raises a "discomfiting question": "What if one day the dispossessed decide to fight back? And I don't mean with a clipboard registering people to vote. People are worried this movie may be too violent for them. Really? Considering everything we're living through in real life?" In short, the film tries to "understand why innocent people turn into Jokers after they can no longer keep it together": rather than feel incited to violence, a spectator "will thank this movie for connecting you to a new desire — not to run to the nearest exit to save your own ass but rather to stand and fight and focus your attention on the nonviolent power you hold in your hands every single day".[9]

But does it really work like that? The "new desire" Moore mentions is not Joker's desire — to see this, one has to introduce here the psychoanalytic distinction between drive and desire. Drive is compulsively repetitive, in it, we are caught in the loop of turning again and again around the same point, while desire enacts a cut, it opens up a new dimension. Joker remains a being of drive: at the film's end, he is powerless, and his violent outbursts are just impotent explosions of rage, actings-out of his basic powerlessness. In order for the desire described by Moore to arise, one step further is needed: an additional change of subjective stance is to be accomplished if we are to pass from Joker's outbursts to becoming the one able to "stand and fight and focus your attention on the nonviolent power you hold in your hands every single day" — when you become aware of this power you can renounce brutal bodily violence. The paradox is that you become truly violent (in the sense of posing a threat to the existing system) only when you renounce physical violence.

This does not mean that Joker's act is a dead-end to be avoided — it is rather a kind of Malevich moment, reduction to zero point of minimal frame of protest. Malevich's famous black square on white surface is not some kind of self-destructive abyss we should beware of not being swallowed by it but a point through which we should pass to gain a new beginning. It is the moment of death drive which opens up the space for sublimation. And in the same way that, in his minimalist paintings like Black Square, Malevich reduced a painting to its minimal opposition of frame and background, *Joker* reduced protest to its minimal content-less self-destructive form. An additional twist is needed to pass from drive to desire, to leave behind the nihilist point of self-destruction, to make this zero-point function as a new beginning. However, the lesson of *Joker* is that we have to go through this zero-point to get rid of the illusions that pertain to the existing order.

This zero-point is today's version of what was once called a proletarian position, the experience of those who have nothing to lose — or, to quote Arthur from the film: "I've got nothing left to lose. Nothing can hurt me anymore. My life is nothing but a comedy." This is where the idea that Trump is a kind of Joker in power finds its limit: Trump definitely did not go through this zero-point. He may be an obscene clown in his own way, but he is not a Joker figure — it's an insult to Joker to compare him with Trump. In the film, Wayne the father is a "joker" in the simple sense of the agent who displays the obscenity of power.

Now we can see where M.L. Clark goes ridiculously wrong when he reads my own philosophy as a version of Joker's nihilist stance: "Žižek's Hegelian-philosophy-meets-flimsy-pop-science relentlessly insists that the only objective reality is not the Nothingness from which Something was created, but rather the tension between the true nothing-burger underpinning existence, and the moral depravity of our every, inevitable attempt to impose meaning upon it." In short, for me, the basic ontological fact is the tension between the ultimate meaningless void/crack and our (humanity's) attempts to impose some universal meaning onto this chaotic crack — such a position is nothing special, it simply reproduces a certain existential humanism which perceives humans as beings who heroically endeavour to impose some meaning onto the chaos of the world into which we are thrown. However, according to Clark, I make here a step further in the Joker direction: since all attempts to impose meaning onto the primordial chaotic Void obfuscate this void and are thus hypocritical, i.e., since they escape from the basic nonsense of existence, they are acts of moral depravity — or, to bring this point to extreme, morality itself (attempts to impose a universal meaning onto reality) is a form of moral depravity. The only consequent moral stance is thus the one of full nihilism, of joyfully endorsing the violent destruction of every attempt to impose a moral order onto our chaotic life, of renouncing every universal humanist project that would enable us to surmount our discords:

> no matter how much we might want to insist that our shared humanity is stronger than our momentary discords and our abiding individual differences [...] the Jokers and Žižeks are never quite going to be persuaded. Their respective ideological frameworks require them to keep pointing to the social tensions that remain: the chaos that will always be a part of our collective press towards a better-synthesized societal whole.[10]

I, of course, consider this stance of radical nihilism not only totally at odds with my clear political engagements but also self-contradictory: it needs its fake-moral opponent to assert itself in its nihilistic destruction and in the unmasking of its hypocrisy. Therein resides the limit of all the desperate attempts to reverse tragedy into triumphant comedy practiced by Incels, Clowncels and Joker himself who, just before shooting Murray, his TV host, tells him: "Have you seen what it's like out there, Murray? Do you ever actually leave the studio? Everybody just yells and screams at each other. Nobody's civil anymore! Nobody thinks what it's like to be the other guy. You think men like Thomas Wayne ever think what it's like to be someone like me? To be somebody but themselves? They don't. They think that we'll just sit down and take it like good little boys! That we won't werewolf and go wild!" The assertion of joyful destruction remains parasitic on this complaint. Joker doesn't go "too far" in the destruction of the existing order, he remains stuck in what Hegel called "abstract negativity", unable as he is to propose its concrete negation.

Insofar as the Freudian name for this negativity is death drive, we should thus be careful not to categorise Donald Trump's self-destructive defence against the attempts to impeach him as manifestations of death drive.[11] Yes, while Trump rejects the accusations against him, he simultaneously confirms (and even boasts with) the very crimes he is accused of and breaks the law in his very defence — but does he not thereby just enact (more openly than usual, true) the paradox that is constitutive of the rule of the law, i.e., the fact that the very agency that regulates the application of the law has to exempt itself from its reign? So yes, Trump is obscene in acting the way he acts, but in this way he merely brings out the obscenity that is the obverse of the law itself; the "negativity" of his acts is totally subordinated to (his perception of) his ambitions and well-being, he is far from the self-destruction of the existing order enacted by Joker. There is nothing suicidal about Trump's boasting about his breaking the rules, it is simply part of his message that he is a tough guy president beset by corrupt elites and boosting the US abroad, and that his transgressions are necessary because only a rule breaker can crush the power of the Washington swamp. To read this well-planned and very rational strategy in terms of death drive is yet another example of how it is the Left liberals who are really on a suicidal mission, giving rise to the impression that they are engaged in bureaucratic-legal nagging while the President is doing a good job for the country.

In Christopher Nolan's *The Dark Knight*, Joker is the only figure of truth — the goal of his terrorist attacks on Gotham City is made clear: they will only stop if Batman takes off his mask and reveals his true identity. What, then, is Joker who wants to disclose the truth beneath the Mask, convinced that this disclosure will destroy the social order? He is not a man without mask, but, on the contrary, a man fully identified with his mask, a man who IS his mask — there is nothing, no "ordinary guy", beneath his mask. This is why Joker has no backstory and lacks any clear motivation: he tells different people different stories about his scars, mocking the idea that he should have some deep-rooted trauma that drives him. It may appear that *Joker* aims precisely at providing a kind of socio-psychological genesis of Joker, depicting the traumatic events which made him the figure he is.[12] The problem is that thousands of young boys who grew up in ruined families and were bullied by their peers suffered the same fate, but only one "synthesized" these circumstances into the unique figure of Joker. In other words, yes, Joker is the result of a set of pathogenic circumstances, but these circumstances can be described as the causes of this unique figure only retroactively, once Joker is already here. In one of the early novels about Hannibal Lecter, the claim that Hannibal's monstrosity is the result of unfortunate circumstances is rejected: "Nothing happened to him. He happened."

However, one can (and should) read *Joker* also in the opposite sense and claim that the act that constitutes the main figure as "Joker" is an autonomous act by means of which he surpasses the objective circumstances of his situation. He identifies himself with his fate, but this identification is a free act: in it, he posits himself as a unique figure of subjectivity...[13] We can locate this reversal at a precise moment in the film when the hero says: "You know what really makes me laugh? I used to think that my life was a tragedy. But now I realise, it's a fucking comedy." One should take note of the exact moment when Arthur says this: while, standing by the side of his mother's bed, he takes her pillow and uses it to smother her to death. Who, then, is his mother? Here is how Arthur describes her presence: "She always tells me to smile and put on a happy face. She says I was put here to spread joy and laughter." Is this not maternal superego at its purest? No wonder she calls him Happy, not Arthur. He gets rid of his mother's hold on him (by killing her) through fully identifying with her command to laugh.

This, however, does not mean that Joker lives in a maternal world: his mother is a half-dead impassive victim of paternal violence, obsessed with the ultra-rich Wayne as the father of her child, hoping to the end that he will help her and Arthur.[14] (The film elegantly leaves it open if Wayne effectively is Arthur's father or not.) Arthur's sad fate is thus not the result of a too strong maternal presence — far from being guilty, his mother is herself the victim of extreme male brutality. Apart from Wayne, there is another paternal figure in the film: Murray, the comedian who invites Arthur to his popular TV show and thus gives him a chance of social integration and public recognition. One is almost tempted to say that this duality of Wayne and Murray enacts the opposition between "bad" and "good" father (in this case, the father who ignores Arthur and the father who recognises him), but the integration fails, Arthur sees through Murray's hypocrisy and shoots him in the midst of the TV show, and it is only at this, after repeating the murder of his mother in the public murder of a paternal figure that he fully becomes Joker. (In yet another elegant move, Arthur does not kill Wayne, his putative father, himself — this act is left to an anonymous man wearing a clown mask, a member of Joker's new tribe. Both Oedipal enigmas, the question of who is Arthurs' father and the question of who enacts the parricide, are thus left in dark.)

Because of his act, Joker may not be moral, but he definitely is ethical. Morality regulates how we relate to others with regard to our shared common Good, while ethics concerns our fidelity to the Cause which defines our desire, a fidelity which reaches beyond the pleasure-principle. Morality in its basic sense is not opposed to social customs, it is an affair of what in ancient Greece was called *eumonia*, the harmonious well-being of the community. One should recall here how, at the beginning of Antigone, the chorus reacts to the news that someone (at this point one doesn't yet know who) violated Creon's prohibition and performed funeral rites on Polynices' body — it is Antigone herself who is implicitly castigated as the "cityless outcast" engaged in excessive demonic acts which disturb the eumonia of the state, fully reasserted in the last lines of the play:

> The most important part of happiness / is therefore wisdom — not to act impiously / towards the gods, for boasts of arrogant men / bring on great blows of punishment / so in old age men can discover wisdom.

From the standpoint of eumonia, Antigone is definitely demonic/uncanny: her defying act expresses a stance of de-measured excessive insistence which disturbs the "beautiful order" of the city; her unconditional ethics violates the harmony of the polis and is as such "beyond human boundary". The irony is that, while Antigone presents herself as the guardian of the immemorial laws which sustain human order, she acts as a freakish and ruthless abomination — there definitely is something cold and monstrous about her, as is rendered by the contrast between her and her warmly human sister Ismene. And it is in this same sense that Joker is ethical but not moral.

One should also take note of Arthur's family name, Fleck, which in German means stain/spot — Arthur is a disharmonious stain in the social edifice, something with no proper place in it. But what makes him a stain is not just his miserable marginal existence but primarily a feature of his subjectivity, his propensity to compulsive and uncontrollable outbursts of laughter. The status of this laughter is paradoxical: it is quite literally ex-timate (to use Lacan's neologism), intimate and external. Arthur insists that it forms the very core of his subjectivity: "Remember you used to tell me that my laugh was a condition, that there was something wrong with me? It isn't. That's the real me." But precisely as such, it is external to him, to his personality, experienced by him as an autonomised partial object that he cannot control and that he ends up fully identifying with — a clear case of what Lacan called "identification with a symptom" (or, rather, "sinthome": not a bearer of meaning, of a coded message from the unconscious but a cypher of enjoyment, the elementary formula of subject's enjoyment. The paradox here is that in the standard Oedipal scenario, it is the Name-of-the-Father which enables an individual to escape the clutches of maternal desire; with Joker, paternal function is nowhere to be seen, so that the subject can outdo mother only by over-identifying with her superego command.

The film provides not only the socio-psychological genesis of Joker but also implies the condemnation of the society in which a protest can only assume the form of a new tribe led by Joker. There is a subjective act in this Joker's move, but no new political subjectivity arises through it: at the film's end, we get Joker as a new tribal leader, but with no political programme, just an explosion of negativity — in his conversation with Murray, Arthur insists twice that his act is not political. Referring to his clown makeup, Murray asks him: "What's with the face? I mean, are you part of the protest?" Arthur's reply: "No, I don't believe any of that. I don't believe in anything. I just thought it'd be good for my act." And, again, later: "I'm not political. I'm just trying to make people laugh."

A.O. Scott (in the *New York Times*) therefore misses the point when he dismissed *Joker* as "a story about nothing": "The look and the sound [...] connote gravity and depth, but the movie is weightless and shallow." There effectively is no "gravity and depth" in *Joker*'s final stance — his revolt is "weightless and shallow", and that's the utterly desperate point of the film. There is no militant Left in the film's universe; it's just a flat world of globalised violence and corruption. Charity events are depicted as what they are: if a Mother Theresa figure were to be there, she would for sure participate in the charity event organised by Wayne, a humanitarian amusement of the privileged rich. However, it's difficult to imagine a more stupid critique of *Joker* than the reproach that it doesn't portray a positive alternative to the Joker revolt. Just imagine a film shot along these lines: an edifying story about how the poor, unemployed, with no healthcare coverage, the victims of street gangs and police brutality, etc., organise non-violent protests and strikes to mobilise the public opinion — a new non-racial version of Martin Luther King... and an extremely boring film, lacking the crazy excesses of *Joker* which makes the film so attractive for viewers.

Here we touch the crux of the matter: since it seems obvious to a Leftist that such non-violent protests and strikes are the only way to proceed, i.e., to exert an efficient pressure onto those in power, are we dealing here with a simple gap between political logic and narrative efficiency (to put it bluntly, brutal outbursts like those of Joker are politically a deadlock, but they make a story interesting), or is there also an immanent political necessity in the self-destructive stance embodied by Joker? My hypothesis is that one has to go through the self-destructive zero-level for which Joker stands — not actually, but one has to experience it as a threat, as a possibility. Only in this way can one break out of the coordinates of the existing system and envisage something really new. Joker's stance is a blind alley, a total deadlock, superfluous and non-productive, but the paradox is that one has to go through it to perceive its superfluous character — there is no direct way from the existing misery to its constructive overcoming. Or, insofar as Joker obviously is a kind of madman, one should recall here Hegel for whom madness is not an accidental lapse, distortion, "illness" of human spirit, but something which is inscribed into individual spirit's basic ontological constitution: to be a human means to be potentially mad.

> This interpretation of insanity as a necessarily occurring form or stage in the development of the soul is naturally not to be understood as if we were asserting that every mind, every soul, must go through this stage of extreme derangement. Such an assertion would be as absurd as to assume that because in the Philosophy of Right crime is considered as a necessary manifestation of the human will, therefore to commit crime is an inevitable necessity for every individual. Crime and insanity are extremes which the human mind in general has to overcome in the course of its development.[15]

Although not a factual necessity, madness is a formal possibility constitutive of human mind: it is something whose threat has to be overcome if we are to emerge as "normal" subjects, which means that "normality" can only arise as the overcoming of this threat. This is why, as Hegel put it a couple of pages later, "insanity must be discussed before the healthy, intellectual consciousness, although it has that consciousness for its presupposition".[16] In short, we do not all have to be mad in reality, but madness is the real of our psychic lives, a point to which our psychic lives necessarily refer in order to assert themselves as "normal". And it is the same with Joker: we are not all Jokers in reality, but the position of Joker is something the human mind in general has to overcome in the course of its development. The elegance of *Joker* is that, in order to articulate a new positive political vision, we don't have actually to become Jokers — the film does it for us. The film stages the madness, confronts us with it, and thereby enables us to overcome it.

In his interpretation of the fall of East European Communism, Habermas proved to be the ultimate Left Fukuyamaist, silently accepting that the existing liberal-democratic is the best possible, and that, while we should strive to make it more just, etc., we should not challenge its basic premises. This is why he welcomed precisely what many Leftists saw as the big deficiency of the anti-Communist protests in Eastern Europe: the fact that these protests were not motivated by any new visions of the post-Communist future — as he put it, the central and eastern European revolutions were just what he called "rectifying" or "catch-up" revolutions: their aim was to enable central and eastern European societies to gain what the western Europeans already possessed, i.e., to rejoin the West European normality. However, although the Hong Kong protests may appear to fit this frame, the ongoing wave of protests in different parts of the world tends to question this very frame — and this is why figures like "jokers" accompany them. When a movement questions the fundamentals of the existing order, its basic normative foundations, it is almost impossible to get just peaceful protests without violent excesses.

The elegance of *Joker* resides in how the crucial move from self-destructive drive to what Moore called a "new desire" for an emancipatory political project is absent from the film's storyline: we, the spectators, are solicited to fill in this absence… Are we? Will *Joker* not turn out to be just another proof that today's sphere of culture and entertainment can easily integrate even the most "subversive" anti-capitalist messages and practices? Just imagine a biennale whose programme does not question Eurocentrism or the all-pervasive reign of financial capital or our destruction of environment? Why should *Joker* be different from paintings which destroy themselves, from galleries which "make us think" by displaying rotten animal corpses or sacred images soaked in urine? Maybe, it's not as simple as that. Maybe, what makes *Joker* so unsettling is that it does not engage itself in calling for a political action — it leaves the decision to us. Visiting an "anti-capitalist" art performance or engaging in social charity makes us feel good — seeing *Joker* definitely does not do that, and that's our hope. Joker practices what Giorgio Agamben called courage of hopelessness — in short, he enacts a version of subjective destitution.

Notes

1 Saroj Giri, "Introduction", in K. Murali, *Of Concepts and Methods*, Keralam: Kanal Publishing Center 2021.

2 Saroj Giri, "The Buddhist Ineffable Self and a Possible Indian Political Subject", *Political Theology*, 19:8 (2018), p. 734–750.

3 Peter Hallward, ed., *Think Again: Alain Badiou and the Future of Philosophy*, London: Continuum 2004, p. 257.

4 Quoted from Timothy Morton's "Hyper-Pandemic", *The New Yorker*.

5 Quoted from op. cit.

6 See https://en.wikipedia.org/wiki/Four_Pests_campaig.

7 The most one can argue is that the film incites us, the viewers, to act through Joker: Joker acts for us, he actualises our brutal rage against the social order, thus enabling us to go on living as usual since we vented out our frustration through him.

8 Quoted from https://marginalrevolution.com/marginalrevolution/2019/10/the-joker.html.

9 Quoted from https://www.good.is/the-five-most-powerful-lines-from-michael-moores-masterful-joker-review.

10 https://www.patheos.com/blogs/anotherwhiteatheistincolombia/2019/10/tribelessness-secular-zizek-joker/.

11 See https://www.lrb.co.uk/v41/n20/judith-butler/genius-or-suicide.

12 Before seeing the movie and knowing just critical reactions to it, I thought it provided the social genesis of the figure of Joker; now, after seeing it, I must admit, in the spirit of Communist self-criticism, that I was wrong: the passage from passive victimhood to a new form of subjectivity is the pivotal moment of the film.

13 Clowncels are also not just determined by their circumstances: even more than Incels in general, they enact a symbolic gesture of turning their suffering into a form of enjoyment — they obviously enjoy their predicament, parading it proudly, and are therefore responsible for it, not just victims of unfortunate circumstances.

14 I rely here on Matthew Flisfeder (private exchange).

15 Hegel, Encyclopaedia, Par. 408, Addition. Quoted from The Subjective Spirit (marxists.org).

16 Ibid.

MEDIATION, GLOBAL THEATRE, AND ART'S REALISM AFTER TRUTH

Amanda Boetzkes

The Blue Marble — the 1972 colour photograph of Earth taken from outer space by a human — is considered iconic of the rise of ecology. It could also be considered a key image in the history of speculative realism. Taken by NASA astronauts of the Apollo 17 mission on their way to the moon, *The Blue Marble* was neither the first image of the Earth from outer space, nor was it an exceptional technological accomplishment. It was preceded by images of the Earth taken from several perspectives in the 1940s: by suborbital satellites, and later, by orbiting satellites and satellites that landed on the moon. In 1957, Sputnik, the artificial satellite launched by the Soviet Union, rotated the Earth every 96 minutes for 3 months, transmitting radio signals as it orbited. Sputnik's orbit registered as a delimitation of territory, activating the Space Race and a flurry of photographs from NASA that punctuated the politics of the Cold War. Nevertheless, *The Blue Marble*'s perspective — its specific coordination of the Earth as an object in a seemingly infinite expanse of space and time — expressed a new mediation of reality.

In an interview with *Der Spiegel* in 1966, Martin Heidegger described seeing some NASA photographs produced that year, saying of them:

> Everything functions. That is exactly what is uncanny. Everything functions and the functioning drives us further and further to more functioning, and technology tears people away and uproots them from the earth more and more. I don't know if you are scared; I was certainly scared when I recently saw the photographs of the earth taken from the moon. We don't need an atom bomb at all; the uprooting of human beings is already taking place. (Augstein, 1966, p. 203)

With this statement, Heidegger reiterates his argument that Being disappears into equipment, and in this instance, into a new technological totality.

The media theorist Marshall McLuhan, however, saw this genre of representation somewhat differently. In a fascinating essay written in 1974, he observes, "Ecological thinking became inevitable as soon as the planet moved up into the status of a work of art" (McLuhan, 1974, p. 49). In part, McLuhan was referring to how the mediations of space exploration produced a widespread sense of the beauty and intricacy of planetary life. But beyond the ecological truism that "everything is connected", McLuhan suggests a more attenuated reflection that corroborates his famous dictum, "the medium is the message". The dawn of the ecological perspective, he suggests, was effected by a media system that interpreted the planet in a specific way: *the medium interpreted the planet as a work of art.*

Whereas, for Heidegger, the planet had been absorbed into a new horizon of technological Enframement (*Gestell*), a world picture *par excellence*, for McLuhan, the more relevant shift in perspective took place as Sputnik's radio signalling created an environment for the planet through resonance. This mediated environment changed our understanding of what the planet was. The delimitation of the satellite's orbit activated the planet as art, a prime site of the revealing of ontological being (though not exclusively human being, necessarily). The origin of ecological thinking, I argue here, falls at the axis and contradiction of such media systems: though the technological medium is human made, its rendering of the planet as art suggests a deprivileging of the autonomous human subject as the exclusive site of ontological being. More importantly, it suggests that the rise of ecology destined art to the challenge of mediating realism after the "truth" of a singular human perspective.

To position the varied mediations of the planet at the origin of ecological thinking, in and as art, is also to infer a shift in the understanding of realist aesthetics in the post-truth era, for not only was Earth-imaging steeped in the politics of the Cold War, itself characterised by feints of political spectacle and spy-craft it inaugurated a grass-roots scepticism regarding the legitimacy of space exploration and other kinds of technological development such as big agriculture, toxic chemicals like DDT, and nuclear power. While it seems as ridiculous to dismiss the veracity of the moon-landing as it is to dispute the reality of an ethnic genocide, such contestations of historical facts were nevertheless also born of the same era. It is thus with an insistence that ecology be accompanied by an extended form of democratic deliberation (the negotiation of concerns and actions across beings and epistemes) that Bruno Latour developed the imperatives of political ecology in tandem with his actor-network theory (ANT).

In what follows, I will consider art as a "real object" in the OOO sense, and its role in navigating the ecology of mediated experience in the post-truth era, following McLuhan's statement that it is not only the lens with which we see that informs the subject matter of mediated appearances — it is not just that we interpret perceptions, but that our mediations are integral to the appearance of reality. Art is therefore a crucial concept by which to experience the real, even in its withdrawal. McLuhan's triangulation of media, art, and ecology is not just a matter of the recursion between the image and its "message", but of the disjoining of subject matter and object matter, and the active perception of this rupture as integral to both the production and interpretation of art. I therefore suggest that McLuhan's media ecology is an implicit site of politics precisely because of art (and not in spite of it). Art was refounded through ecology and politics in a "global theatre", as per the wordy title of McLuhan's essay, "At the moment of Sputnik the planet became a global theatre in which there are no spectators but only actors" (McLuhan).

Contemporary art has maintained, rather than jettisoned, its connection to theatricality in the post-truth era. But its media ecology is best thought in terms of a *viewership without authority*, a concept I define by way of Hannah Arendt's account of collective understanding of the incomprehensible. Viewership without authority characterises the way in which art *withdraws into appearance*, and in so doing, convenes viewers to a site of deliberative interpretation regarding its realism by way of its theatricality. I discuss three works of art in relation to the post-truth media ecology: the first is by Forensic Architecture, *77sqm_9:26min* (2017), which I examine for the way it uses a media simulation to expose the false testimony of a German State Officer under investigation for the murder of a Muslim youth, and for how it invites deliberation over the realism of the simulation. The second is Courbet's famous *L'Origine du monde* (1866), which I discuss in terms of Michael Fried's dialectic between absorption and theatricality, and Graham Harman's repositioning of theatricality as an appearance fundamental to all objects (and not just art). I suggest further that art's theatricality also invokes a viewership to deliberate over its realism, and not just a singular beholder. Thus, the theatricality of *L'Origine du monde* (and its overcoming as realism) is contiguous with McLuhan's statement about the origin of ecological thinking — an implicitly collective form — as an effect of the planet being elevated to the status of a work of art. Finally, I position Julian Charrière's *Blue Fossil Entropic Stories* (2013) as an artistic practice that articulates the media ecology of realism as a matter of viewership without authority by bringing the invisibility of glacier melt into view against the politics of climate change. Heidegger's world picture of the planet might be reconsidered now as a global theatre of actors.

Art's Realism as a Mediatised Appearance

The artist collective Forensic Architecture is exemplary of contemporary art's post-truth realism. Formed in 2010 under the leadership of the architect Eyal Weizman, Forensic Architecture is notable for its incisive mediatic approach to the analysis of contested political situations. The collective is hired by human rights organisations to expose forms of systemic negligence and violence (one might even say negligence *as* a form of violence). It reconstructs events based on factual evidence and then stages the deliberation over these facts. Forensic Architecture does not merely "stay with the trouble" of reality, as in Donna Haraway's formulation of response-ability, but gives that troubled reality an appearance of due process, a quasi-justice in the absence of real justice. But it is precisely because it assumes that reality can be simulated and visualised even in its disappearance — that reality is always withdrawn into an appearance that can be replicated — that it enables the possibility of responsibility for that reality.

Forensic Architecture's work *77sqm_9:26min* was presented at Documenta 14 in Kassel, Germany, in 2017 as a video installation and as part of a broader public programme entitled *The Parliament of Bodies*. The programme included a series of public discussions about the artwork's content: the race-based murder of a young Muslim man named Halit Yozgat when he was working at his family-run internet café in Kassel in 2006. The fatal shooting was the ninth in a series of murders of immigrants in Germany by a Neo-Nazi organisation called the National Socialist Underground. It was determined by the police investigation that the gun that killed Halit Yozgat was the same as the one used in the eight previous murders. Yet nobody was charged with the crime. A group called the Society of the Friends of Halit was formed under the auspices of Documenta to conduct their own investigation, 11 years after the murder. The Society investigated and presented their findings to the public in a series of lectures called "Unravelling the NSU Complex". They also enlisted Forensic Architecture to analyse the evidence and testimony in the murder.

Of particular significance in Forensic Architecture's post-trial art-investigation was the fact that a state intelligence officer named Andreas Temme, who worked for the State Office for Constitutional Protection in Kassel, was at the internet café at the time of the murder. He did not disclose this to police but was later identified from his internet records. He was a frequent customer at the internet café, but his records indicated reason for suspicion. Where he usually spent 1 or 2 hours online, on the day of the murder he only spent 15 minutes. However, he claimed to have logged off his computer, moved to the front of the café, and seeing nobody at the front desk, placed a coin on the desk and the left the shop within seconds of the murder. He was the only person among the three other (Muslim) witnesses who claimed not to have seen, heard, or smelled the three gunshots. In its investigation, the court accepted his testimony, which included a re-enactment of his movement through the café at the time of the murder. Subsequently, in 2015, this evidence was leaked to the public from a website called NSU LEAKS. Forensic Architecture used the leaked testimonial video to conduct its own investigation.

Keeping in mind that, while Forensic Architecture assembles experts, the most precise technological tools, and facts established through scientific method to produce its artwork, it was Temme's testimony that was the object of investigation. Forensic Architecture analysed the testimonial video by re-enacting it; in other words, their analysis was a re-enactment of a re-enactment. What is important, however, was not to positively prove that Temme was guilty, but that his testimony was fabricated. From this simulation, they generated a report that concludes: "These results establish that Temme's testimony was untruthful". But it is only by way of

Forensic Architecture's mediation of the evidence *as art* that it can come to this statement.

The group reconstructed three possible scenarios: either Halit Yozgat had left the shop with four customers inside (though there were no witnesses to this), come back in after Temme had left the coin on the desk, and then been shot (a sequence of events that would have to happen in perfect sequence in a matter of 39 seconds); or Temme had simply not been aware of the murder taking place while he was at the back of the café, nor seen the body behind the desk when he left the coin; or that Temme was covering up what really happened. Forensic Architecture's report reveals that Temme was obstructing the truth to the point of criminal negligence: either covering up for the gunman (perjuring himself) or that he was the gunman himself (a murderer). The only other possibility would be that Temme was at the scene of a murder but did not notice it in any way — a level of impossible dissociation and denial. The video *77sqm_9:26min* thus reveals Temme's incoherence and conspicuous lack of detail regarding what he sensed as he moved through the limits of space and the timeframe at stake in his testimony.

Forensic Architecture's realism is a post-truth art form: it does not require the witnessing, description, or other articulations of truth to prove criminal violence. In their drive to prove guilt rather than prove reality, they locate a key site of concealment by the factual evidence and, by contrast, show that a sensorial occlusion had taken place. They made this occlusion stand out against the abundant data of possible set of relations and actions in the situation. Paradoxically, it is the disappearance of the murderer that reveals who is lying, and only by deduction, who is culpable. The obstruction becomes apparent against the fullness of the media ecology.

Forensic Architecture's mediation, which combines data analysis and re-enactment, invites viewers to deliberate over reality, and in so doing, it introduces an implicit political dimension. This, I would say, is key to the periodisation of art's realism in the post-truth era, for it is also important to acknowledge that the other testimonies carry weight as an integral part of what constitutes the reality of the murder *as a murder*, and not as a spontaneous event that only coincidentally effected the disappearance of a life. The witness statements are taken as overlapping experiences of the sensual appearance of the murder *as a real object*. As art, the murder is revealed in the otherwise unseen political equipment that obscures it. The work turns its common media ecology inside out, so that reality is revealed by subtraction.

Forensic Architecture's realism therefore accomplishes something that the justice system could not (and perhaps does not even strive to): it affirms the reality of the murder in the absence of truth. Moreover, it does so by way of *art*. By convening a viewership to deliberate over a withdrawn reality, Forensic Architecture weighs the reported actions and sensations within the surrounding media ecology of the event. What ratifies the realism of the murder is the viewing situation in its presentation as art. Indeed, Forensic Architecture's theatricality puts art to work in its capacity to reveal the withdrawal of reality. Its re-enactments, yielded to a public viewership, draw a fine but nonetheless definitive line. It is not the line between truth and fiction, but rather between reality and appearance.

Art's Theatricality After Truth

My example of Forensic Architecture's oeuvre suggests that art's realism is intertwined with a political imperative in the post-truth era, and that this imperative comes to the fore in and through its implicit theatricality. Concealment is not necessarily the outcome of a totalising surrounding of neutral equipment. The enframement against which art defines itself happens in the midst of ideologically charged forms of thoughtlessness that are particular to our time in history: forms such as denial, negligence, and insensibility; all variations of what Hannah Arendt called "the banality of evil". In this respect, art decentres the human, as in the case of satellite images of the Earth. But it recuperates ontological being by way of its political ecology in Latour's sense, including and especially its media appearance. It provides an important counterweight to the derealisation of today's mediasphere, interspersed as it is with fake news, "alternative facts", the use of social media platforms as sites of political parlay, deep fakes and artificial intelligence, a digitised stock market, and climate change data.

To situate art's realism in the context of the post-truth era acknowledges that reality recedes from art's mediated appearance of it. In this regard, I keep with Heidegger's statement that the technological perspective that comprises the "world picture" is a fundamental concealment of ontological being, and thus the very antithesis of thinking (Heidegger, 1938). At the same time, I am insisting on an attentiveness to the terms of art's theatrical expression in and through its media ecology. Art's mediation of reality's expression of itself *as* what it is. In this regard, I want to address Graham Harman's redistribution of Michael Fried's concept of theatricality with respect to the expression and viewership of reality. Further, the two terms that art conjoins — theatricality and the post-truth era — are crucial for understanding the historicity of realism (and hence an account of speculative realism *today*). Harman's development of OOO, through Michael Fried's distinction between art's absorption and its theatricality, points the way to rethinking art's ecology in terms of the viewership it convenes. My formulation of theatricality in relation to a viewership invites a further consideration of the common origin of aesthetics and politics in art's realism.

Over the course of his career, the art historian and critic Michael Fried elaborates art's emergence in and through the overcoming of its theatricality. The terms of this overcoming vary depending on the artist and critical discourse of the time period that animates it. Among his many formulations is his account of Courbet's realism in the nineteenth century (Fried, 1992). Fried argues that Courbet's oeuvre was underpinned by the critical project of absorption. Absorption is the antithesis of the painting's theatricality and central to Courbet's realist project. Through absorption, the painting defeats its own tendency to call the viewer's attention to its status as an object; its way of saying "I am a painting". Courbet's realism takes place in capturing this fine line between the painting's implicit theatricality and its absorption. At length, Fried parses this interplay through Courbet's thematics, materials, figures, compositions, and even the artist's own signature. Courbet's realism overcomes its theatrical tendencies by "absorbing" the viewer: drawing the viewer to the interior world of the painting through themes of introspection (reading, sleeping, contemplating, dying), as well as suggesting a bodily continuity between the "painter-beholder" and the painting's subject matter. Absorption is undertaken as an "eclipsing of vision" concomitant with the bodily absorption of the painter-beholder into the painting (Fried, 1992, p. 153).

Courbet's *Origin of the World* — a painting notorious for its confrontational rendering of a reclining woman's splayed thighs and genitalia, which the psychoanalyst Jacques Lacan purchased and mobilised as a thought-image for his conceptualisation of "the gaze" — achieves its realism not merely through its naturalistic rendering, but as an elaboration of absorption overcoming theatricality specifically. In Fried's view, there is more to this painting than a spectacle of female nudity — or worse, a *regressum ad uterum*. The absorption of the viewer is at stake, but is contingent on the co-implication with the viewer that it infers. The painting thematises this engagement as a post-coital moment of figure and beholder *falling back from their entangled position.* Art's realism is achieved as an *ex-nihilo* emergence, inferred as shared embodiment, after co-enfleshment has taken place.[1]

The chiasmic tie between artwork and viewer mediated by the painting is an experience of art *as an act of creation itself.* Creation — the origin of art — in Fried's terms, is a setting aside of the literal real and the coming into appearance of art as a real object in and of itself. Realism is the appearance of art through the undoing and remaking of its perceptibility in the wake of communion with it, which it infers by its very original (and originary) appearance. Or, to put this in ontological terms that echo Graham Harman's, it is to understand that, as an integral part of the creation of art, *perception is taken up in its sensual appearance as a real object.*

Fried argues that the absorption is essential to the overcoming of art's theatricality, and its way of asserting itself only literally as an object among other objects. By contrast, Harman argues that an account of art's realism via OOO would understand absorption as an infinite depth, that the real object withdraws into inaccessibility, to the point that "no literal description or perception could ever hope to reach it" (Harman, 2018, p. 17). However, the union of the real object with its sensual qualities is activated through the "performance" of the beholder. Otherwise put, beholding is a performance as such, an activity by which the viewer plays out the sensual qualities of the artwork. When a beholder views a painting, they spring forward to perform its sensual qualities. The artwork as real object originates through the beholder's performance of its sensual appearance. Indeed, art object and beholder found one another as such.

The beholder is an *a priori* real that performs, cognises, and experiences the painting *as* art. One's perception from the position of a viewer (as such) originates the artwork in gathering and providing a support for its sensual qualities. In this respect, Harman recomposes Fried's anti-theatrical realism to come to the thought that the beholder must be theatrically engaged with the artwork if it is to be an artwork as such. The beholder's performance of the sensual qualities of the real object — art as such — emerges and is conferred aesthetically in a sensual nexus with that art object. In this vein, Harman suggests that there is an implicit theatricality to all aesthetic experience: "theatre is everywhere" (Harman, 2018, p. 18).

It is in virtue of its inherent theatricality that an artwork must always try so hard to overcome itself in the manner of Courbet's realism (as absorption in that case), or by Fried's account, why the modernist project at large requires the overcoming of the theatricality of objecthood to become art. Realism relies on the performance of beholding — on theatricality as the registering of reality in perception, through the mediation of its appearance by the viewer's experience of it. Thus, McLuhan can arrive at the statement that Sputnik's mediation renders the planet as a work of art; indeed, it "elevates it" to that status. With this statement, McLuhan captures the way the Earth is registered as both newly real and newly meaningful to the perceivers it convenes. Ecology appeared as a realism.

Note, however, that I am suggesting an additional shift from a scenario in which a singular beholder is co-founded with the art object (a painting), to one in which a collective experience of mediated perception founds the planet as an artwork. Art's mediated appearances (or rather its appearances by way of mediation) must be taken as integral to the deliberative process, the experience by which something real is understood as such. The performance of the artwork in the perceiver's experience is implicitly a re-enactment of the infinitely withdrawn real object of art. But since it is one that is fundamentally theatrical, it is reliant on an open and undetermined — but no less real — viewership to (re)constitute it by performing its sensual qualities. That is to say, real objects may all be theatrical, but for them to appear as the specific real object that art is — which is to say, for its emergence to possess a historicity that identifies it in a given era *as art* — its appearance must also be performed by a plural totality. Theatre requires an audience, after all, and not merely an individual perceiver.

Though it is true that the viewing situation of modernist art was imagined, under the sway of neo-Kantian aesthetic theory, as one in which a singular beholder engages the artwork in a controlled situation, this scenario is historically specific. One might even say that the autonomous subject of modern art is mythic, and thus occupied our sense of experienced by way of a plural world (a *sensus communis*), like so many mortals in a temple. The historicity of the artwork therefore requires a different understanding of the performance of beholding (the "who" or "what" is registering art's appearance), hence my insistence on thinking art in the post-truth era by way of a complex media ecology rather than a singular and hypothetical beholder who stands vertically in a modern museum, or lies horizontally on an analyst's couch.

Global Theatre and the Performance of Viewership

I am arguing that the post-truth problematic redefines the relationship between art's theatricality and its realism. Art assumes a disjunction between reality and its appearance in order to preserve and corroborate its ontological existence. But against the backdrop of post-truth, art's theatricality achieves a new level of self-expression regarding the viewership of its contents, in a way that overcomes the division of subject matter and object matter. I connect this self-expression to what McLuhan aptly calls "global theatre" in the title of his essay. Such a viewership of art is both the forum and the occasion of a deliberative experience as I have suggested with the example of Forensic Architecture. Art's realism after truth exhibits a politico-aesthetic distribution of the sensible that defines the viewing situation as a collective endeavour — a dimension of *to-whom* and *for-whom* that is essential to the experience of art in the first place.

McLuhan's diagnosis of the emergence of global theatre does not simply respond to the appearance of the Earth as a spherical globe captured by a satellite's orbit. It is the unprecedented appearance of that globe as a work of art that corroborates the emergence of a global theatre *in which there are no spectators, only actors* (McLuhan, 1974, p.48). McLuhan's global theatre is an object experienced not by way of a generalised spectatorship, but rather by the gestures of its actors, whose performance brings its existence into perceptibility. Paradoxically, then, the viewership of the planet as art is not so much viewed as a purely optical experience but perceived as a political action of reifying an appearance. Otherwise put, the actors of this global theatre might also be seen to be originating the planet as art by way of their deliberation over its realism, for it is not so much that scientists did not know that the planet was real until they saw satellite images, but rather that their mediations of it rendered the planet as a real object, as art, performed by a newly self-conscious set of global actors. This self-consciousness is nothing short of the ecological paradigm, of which McLuhan was a cornerstone theorist.

I want to consider this McLuhanist theatricality at play in the work of the Swiss artist Julian Charrière, whose practice inherits from ecological aesthetics a form of post-truth viewership. Charrière captures a realist approach to climate change, a phenomenon that has been a site of public scepticism (for which the validity of the sciences has paid a serious political price), but also for the philosophy of speculative realism. (I am thinking here of Timothy Morton's account of climate change as a "hyperobject" (Morton, 2013.) Charrière's agonistic performances with icebergs are especially revealing of the kind of viewership his realist art convenes. Icebergs are contradictory entities: they are symptoms of glacier melt but are nevertheless entirely self-possessed and powerful objects, capable of creating tsunamis on Arctic beaches. Their realism requires mediation to understand, needless to say. His imagery performs its own mediation of icebergs as a strife between the real object and its appearance to viewers.

In *The Blue Fossil Entropic Stories* (2013), Charrière boarded an iceberg in the Arctic Ocean near the coast of Iceland and spent 8 hours submitting it to the heat and light of a blowtorch. The resulting photographs position him as a solitary figure that vainly tries to penetrate its exterior. For all his dramatised labour he is refuted by its immense scale, its solidity, its slippery but nevertheless porous surface, and the purity of its blue colour, which remains preserved beneath a surrounding sheath of dirty sediment. The exertion of the blowtorch merely magnifies the iceberg's inaccessibility. For even though the iceberg is a symptom of the extinction of glaciers worldwide, the temporality of its own disappearance remains invisible to the viewer, seemingly untouched by the fire and heat. The performance does nothing to hasten or impact it because the melting of the iceberg — of glaciers overall — takes place on a scale of time and space that exceeds the human field. The work points to a condition in which the appearance of the Earth's ice is sensuously immediate, while at the same time it remains unyielding to any fundamental transformation as an object as such.

Viewers experience both the immediacy of the iceberg and its escape from view. Through his photographs and installations, the artist draws us into a reflection about the performance of our own viewership, an endeavour that is undertaken precisely in his dramatised mediation of the image. Charrière journeys into oceans and fjords; he follows icebergs, scales them, melts their surfaces, illuminates them, hovers over them with a drone and photographs them. Through all his gesturing toward the icebergs — from close and intimate proximity to a distant, hovering vantage point, from the physical to the virtual, in the darkness and under the casting of light — their presence becomes real only insofar as it thwarts being encompassed by the play of actions. The mediation of the icebergs' appearances and the withdrawal of their reality appear in concert with the viewers' play of perceivable actions.

Further, Charrière's work sets the question of reality in motion rather than either presupposing the applicability of facts about glacier melt toward a representation of the phenomenon, or by simulating the outcome (a succession of images of receding ice, charts, maps, or other environmental measures). The realism of the work does not rest in a display of knowledge; rather, Charrière's practice directs a questioning of reality's recession into an appearance as art. It is this questioning that is at stake in the performance of viewership.

I link the hermeneutic work in the performance of viewership, as I have addressed it here, to the interplay between the faculty of understanding and the reality that infinitely defers it. Hannah Arendt elaborates such terms in her famous essay "Understanding and Politics (The Difficulties of Understanding)", in which she addresses, among many other considerations, the Eichmann trial. Importantly, the titular difficulties of understanding are the sites of incomprehensibility at the origin of political thinking. In this regard, Arendt manoeuvres Kantian judgement towards an account of its emergence as a collective endeavour of struggle with what cannot be understood (in this case, totalitarianism). Arendt argues that banal evil need not be understood to be thought, and this enables her insights on judgement (indeed, justice itself) as a speculative form.

The shift from understanding to thinking, by which the incomprehensible requires collective judgement to be thought, is a struggle that can only be tackled by gleaning freedom from an imagined futural form that is distinctly collective. Otherwise, judgement would remain nothing short of punitive causal consequences for subjective intentions. Here, Arendt repudiates social-scientific approaches to human behaviour, which are completely inadequate in their address of the "banality of evil". Her generously defined form of collective judgement draws from the concept of the *Sensus Communis*, but unfolds as a combined political and aesthetic form. Understanding cannot be socialised nor governed by the authority of the social; instead, understanding and its implicit politics are discovered from preserving the freedom of reflective judgement in the face of senselessness. Arendt's analysis shifts freedom from a concern for the social to a way of freely thinking, reflecting, and understanding through the adjacency of knowledge to existence. We must judge without knowing, understand in the absence of knowledge.

Here is where a common origin of political deliberation coincides with realist viewership. I am suggesting that the performance of viewership, as opposed to the performance of beholding (as a singular subject-viewer), acknowledges the implicit collectivity and heterogeneity at stake in the gesturing appearances at play in art. The paradigm of the "beholder of art" presumes a singularity and potentially scopophilic scenario that risks betraying a Kantian reliance on autonomous subjectivity to make statements about objectivity (singular perspectivism as avenue to realism). But if there is a performance of beholding at play in art, a realist art in the post-truth era, its mediated condition assumes that such a performance is as much a collective performance as it is a singular one. Indeed, by what manoeuvres can one ensure that they are alone in their acts of viewership of a work of art, once one has conceded that theatre is everywhere?

To make the determination that the performance of viewership is what makes art what it is, the scenario of viewership must be collectively defined if it is to define itself against a history of transforming appearances, a history of art that is continually shifting the terms of what defines it. As I have argued, the realism of art after truth lies in the continuous movement of deliberation over its terms by way of its mediation. Which is to say, art's realism rests in its condition of being constituted by the viewership that performs it in a media ecology. Art's realism is always, therefore, anterior and posterior to that process: experienced as unknowable but appearing in the very struggle from which it withdraws. As per McLuhan, art is born of actors in a global theatre; and such signalling between actors is both what mediates it, and what makes art what it is.

References

Arendt, Hannah. "Understanding and Politics (The Difficulties of Understanding)". In *Essays in Understanding, 1930–1954, Formation, Exile and Totalitarianism.* Berlin: Schoken Press, 2005.

Augstein Rudolf & G. Wolff. "Interview with Martin Heidegger", 23 September 1966. "Nur noch ein Gott kann uns retten". *Der Spiegel* (31 May 1976), pp. 193–219.

Fried, Michael. *Courbet's Realism.* Chicago: University of Chicago Press, 1992.

Harman, Graham. "Aesthetics and the Tension in Objects". In *[Met]afourisms: Art Practice & Documentation*, pp. 11–19. Malta: Midsea Books Ltd., 2018.

Harman, Graham. *Art and Objects.* Medford, MA: Polity Press, 2020.

Heidegger, Martin. "The Age of the World Picture" (1938), in *The Question of Technology and Other Essays.* New York: Harper & Row, 1977.

McLuhan, Marshall. "At the moment of Sputnik the planet became a global theatre in which there are no spectators only actors". *Journal of Communication* 24.1 (1974), pp. 48–58.

Morton, Timothy. *Hyperobjects: Philosophy and Ecology After the End of the World*. Minneapolis: University of Minnesota Press, 2013.

Robbins, Christa Noel. "The Sensibility of Michael Fried". *Criticism* 60.4 (2018), pp. 429–454.

Note

1 Having said this, however, I would suggest somewhat provocatively that Fried is precisely "literal" in his understanding of this mutual embodiment, for he sets aside the manifold possibilities afforded to the painting's viewership in this scene of the origin of the world in order to give a (presumably) historically specific and phallocentric reading of the absorption at stake in the painting. Is he not presuming to identify with Courbet's sexual proclivities and call that historicism, at the expense of an account of the historicity of the painting's realism, however? It is worth noting Christa Noel Robbins' reading of the homophobia at work in Fried's critique of theatricality in her recent article on the subject (Robbins, 2018). If we are to consider visuality and sensibility in terms of the performance of the beholder at play in viewership, we must also embrace the queer affordances of real objects, including art itself. Here queerness might be read in terms of the withdrawnness of the real object; its capacity to be irreducible to the (hetero)normative visual field and to gather within itself the capacity for the many possible sensible appearances of its viewers. This is art, after all.

WHAT IS JUSTICE FOR SPECULATIVE REALISM?

Micah Tewers

The purpose of this article is to retrieve answers to that original philosophical question, "*what is justice?*" from the initial four theorists who appeared under the name *speculative realism*. In preparation for this, the now-famous problem of correlationism — that reality can only be treated as a correlate to human thought — is first formulated in terms of its perceived injustice, namely as a critically informed alibi for all sorts of *self-justification*. Following from this reformulation, each of the original speculative realists' work is summarised as an account for the reality of justice beyond the self, justification, or both. This paper concludes with closing remarks anticipating the future of philosophies that may attempt to synthesise these answers — namely, Ray Brassier's trust in universal reason, Iain Hamilton Grant's defence of the general autonomy of nature, Graham Harman's fair hearing for all particulars, and Quentin Meillassoux's singular fidelity to the yet possible becoming of cosmic justice, as well as a brief survey of some other emergent *speculative realist* philosophies just beginning to broach the theme of justice.

From Cosmic Justice to Correlationism

It may appear odd to look *here* for answers to the question of Justice. Speculative Realism (SR), the name given to a famously fruitful workshop in 2007, brought together four distinct thinkers — Ray Brassier, Iain Hamilton Grant, Graham Harman, and Quentin Meillassoux — around one common concern: *the abandonment of reality apart from its correlation to human access in contemporary philosophy.* From this brief description, the reader may begin to glean the most pervasive *ethico-political* critique of speculative realism: that it coldly and narrowly focuses on epistemological-ontological arguments "while Rome burns". Conversely, from the standpoint of a speculative realist, what could be more baldly manmade, socially constructed, and anthropocentric than notions of justice?

The reason for pursuing this question anyway — *what is justice for speculative realism?* — is to address a problem SR implicitly poses in defining the subject matter of philosophy. Strictly on the basis of concrete records of evidence, the theme of *justice* is certainly the predominant and original subject matter of philosophy. Even excluding the entire canon of proto-philosophical holy texts, which nearly always double as divine *laws* (as is certainly the case with Judaism, Confucianism, Buddhism, Hinduism, and Islam), the history of philosophy has looked at the world through the prime lens of justice. From the first fragments of Anaximander's cosmic courtroom drama of injustices (ἄδικος) within the ordinance of Time, to the Ionian idea of the *laws* of Nature (that standard metaphor underlying science and mathematics even today), to Parmenides' visionary dialogue with Lady Justice herself, *Díkē*; from Heraclitus' paradoxical concept of *justice-strife*, to Socrates' dialectical demand for *higher justice* from Sophist-lawyers, Plato's following Ideal unity of *truth-justice*, and those golden scales undergirding the whole of Aristotle's philosophy of the *mean*. The theme continues up to and through modernity with Hobbes' grand notion of *sovereignty*, Rousseau's primitive *innocence*, Kant's *tribunal* of reason, as well as Nietzsche's revaluations after the death of the Highest *Judge*, and those innumerable post-Kantian philosophies, which take *freedom, equality*, and *rights* as the keys to a supra-modern epoch of *Justice* — including Fichte, Hegel, Marx, Du Bois, de Beauvoir, the doctrine of *beneficence* built into Pragmatism, plus even Derrida's insistence that *justice* itself cannot be deconstructed. It is therefore imperative we ask: *does the main theme of philosophy come to an end with speculative realism?*

A corollary reason for pursuing this issue now is that I am convinced the best way to evaluate the legacy of this speculative movement is by finally driving a confrontation between the mountain-face of Philosophy's clear protagonist and SR's apparent blind-spot. Accordingly, this essay will offer a provisional address to the key problem stated above by reading the efforts of the original four speculative realists *as* Justice-philosophies through a reformulation of their common enemy in terms of its perceived *injustices* — namely, the injustices of *correlationism:* the disturbingly persuasive argument that we cannot think reality independent of its correlation to human thought. Put positively, we will explore here each philosophy as an attempt to *do justice to reality itself.*

Ray Brassier's Trust in the Tribunal of Reason

In the burrows of the Nightmare
Where Justice naked is,
Time watches from the shadow
And coughs when you would kiss.
— W.H. Auden[1]

In Ray Brassier's first and thus far only published book, *Nihil Unbound,* we find a theorist defending "transcendental nihilism". Hardly anything would seem more acidic to the idea of justice than the notion that existence is meaningless. But in the dense pages of this book, we find that nothing is more essential for Brassier than the *tribunal of reason* itself. For him, nihilism is not merely the opinion that "existence is worthless" (Brassier, 2007, p. x), but rather the proper name for the *cutting edge* of reason, which alone pierces through the vibrant fog of delusion, appearance, and false testimony, obstructing an honest view of reality in-itself. Indeed, even Plato famously stated that the worst injustice was *false justice*. Thus, the line of humankind's intellectual progress — on Brassier's account — is a series of *disenchanting negations*, which place an irreversible stranglehold on what can be justifiably posited as the case. The clear heroes of such progress have been the great critics, scientists, and materialists, like Copernicus, Kant, Darwin, Marx, Nietzsche, and Freud, who irrevocably uncovered that we are not in fact the centre of the solar system (let alone the cosmos), that the beginning was not a *Word* but a *bang*, that humans are equally animals, that the socio-moral order was not set by a God but by conflicts of class and power, and that even our own conscious intellects are ruled by unconscious forces. Rather than being "bewailed as a debilitating impoverishment", Brassier thinks this "disenchantment of the world deserves to be celebrated as an achievement of intellectual maturity" (ibid., p. xi) — *humanity is growing up*. Nihilism here is no longer "an existential quandary but a speculative opportunity" (ibid., p. xi).

While the stale justifications of myths and dogmas are certainly a target on which to unleash the forces of critical thought, they are far from being the most sophisticated and insidious enemy of our time. Since the advent of Kant's epoch-defining *Critiques*, there has emerged many *sheep in wolves' clothing* — and it is correlationism that provides ample cloth. We will see that we have yet to do justice to the disrobing power of reason.

On the Correlationist's Defence-Strategy – To state this modern sheep-wolf problem in a technical fashion, we might say that *pre-critical belief* has been surpassed by *post-critical suspicion*. While a critically informed scepticism may seem like a natural ally to this *nihilating* project, Brassier wisely points out how such surface-level similarity is precisely the strength of this modern enemy of truth, for while Kant's grand achievement over metaphysical dogmatism was in revealing a "fundamental difference between rational justification and causal explanation" (Brassier, 2016, p. 102) — thus breaking the calcified dogmatic fusion of thought and being — this move inadvertently rendered a new status quo of agnosticism about being itself, as it is simply presumed wholly cut off from our thoughts about it from the start. Therefore, the real danger with correlationist scepticism is that no two claims, no two testimonies, can any longer be weighed against one another, as both will *equally* be presumed false — serving an elaborate excuse from standing trial in the tribunal of reason, exonerating all frauds.

But against such fraud, Brassier shows that even a declared materialist constitution — like Nietzsche's reduction of all stated justifications to the globalised explanation of "will to power" — ultimately backfires, and gives in to the myth-loving enemy it first rose to strike. For example, the Judeo-Christian culture Nietzsche set out to destroy is given a new lease on life by this constitution, so long as this religiosity *feels will to power* in its mythic belief. For Brassier, whether caught in outspoken religiosity or materialist atheism, the "notion of unintelligible justice, of a rightness that refuses discursive justification is ultimately theological" (ibid., p. 107). He finds fault with all globalised genealogical reductions[2] — regardless of Idealist, Materialist, or even Nihilist title — as all will have this fraud-friendly theological residue, and so must be overcome with an "always local" method of critique more resembling the natural sciences. This begins to explain the "transcendental" aspect of his nihilism, which he even calls a "non-materialist materialism" (i.e., a materialism without any one final material explanation at bottom), as he prefers an on-going intellectual commitment to mind-independent truth following the nihilist's insight that *the work of disillusionment is never complete.*

More insidious perpetrators of this "post-metaphysical theology" have mutated into the contemporary philosophies of phenomenology, vitalism, and process, which go to extreme measures to offer a "reactionary philosophical protectionism" (Brassier, 2011, p. 21) of consciousness, life, and creativity. Like Freud once noted about the neurotic who protects their illness like a lioness her cubs,[3] each one is "determined to stave off this putative 'disenchantment' of phenomena by science by delimiting a dimension of radically unobjectifiable transcendence" (ibid., p. 24). Brassier uncovers one of the most glaring artefacts of this lingering theological residue, this distortion of reason that makes these philosophies incapable of *realism*, which is evident in their treatment of *time* — what Brassier calls "the correlationist privileging of transcendental temporality" (Brassier, 2007, p. 149). For the phenomenologist, time can only pass once an *observer* is present (Husserl, Heidegger, et al.); for the vitalist, time passes only between the pulses of living beings (Bergson, et al.); for the philosopher of process or "difference", time is a vague mixture of the preceding two under the guise of primal "givenness" or "creativity" (Whitehead, Deleuze, et al.). They each "deny the ontological autonomy of 'time itself' and [...] reduce it to our temporality" (ibid., p. 156). Having woven ourselves into the fabric of time, we've come to believe that it runs on anthropic illusion itself. For Brassier, this is the great modern injustice to reality, dulling the blade of critique and providing a new shield for people-pleasing enchantments. Far too long, we have lived on the false-time of correlationism. In order to do justice to reality in itself, we must first take our grubby human fingers off the scale, always tipping it in our favour. It is at this point that Brassier proposes a speculative test for philosophical realism: *to think the ordinance of time beyond our jurisdiction* by contemplating an age where *we do not exist and will not return.*

Judgement Day as Extinction Event – As the laws of thermodynamics foretell a final state of asymptopia — i.e., the inevitable exhaustion of all physical matter in the universe — Brassier asks: "*How does thought think a world without thought?* More urgently: *How does thought think the death of thinking?*" (ibid., p. 223).[4] The thought of our inevitable personal deaths, let alone the extinction of our entire species, is usually ignored, repressed, and denied. What greater injustice is there than our complete erasure, with not even a soul to remember our having been? Nothing will have happened (ibid., p. 205), and in light of this future state, "[n]either knowing nor feeling, neither living nor dying, amounts to a difference that makes a difference" (ibid., p. 205). But it is precisely within this horrific injustice of extinction that Brassier discovers a pinhole into the deepest depths of time — a temporal horizon cleared of all human, conscious, and living existence. Here we find that "there is an absolute disjunction between correlational time and the time of extinction" (ibid., p. 230), because "[e]xtinction turns thinking inside out, objectifying it as a perishable thing in the world like any other" (ibid., p. 229). Taking our fingers off the scales and stepping back to view the larger picture of real time, we glimpse our lives as a finite detour from infinite nothing to infinite nothing, and discover that, in this grander scheme, we are "already dead".

Clearly, phenomenology and vitalism fail to think through this event to its fullest, instead "placing its faith in creative evolution, and by insisting that solar extinction is merely a local and temporary setback, which life will overcome by transforming its conditions" (ibid. p. 228). For example, in the opening pages of Nietzsche's *The Gay Science*, he expresses a relevant idealistic prejudice around the topic of extinction, stating faith that our deepest instincts for life render it *literally impossible* for the species to destroy itself;[5] an invisible hand — a God — protects us. This is a faith that will likely strike even a pedestrian thinker today as recklessly optimistic. Indeed, we are already rapidly waking up to reality's indifference to our living or dying — though, of course, many still deny this reality, even in the face of global viruses, atom bombs, and abundant scientific evidence that the Earth is not an "inexhaustible reservoir of becoming" (ibid., p. 227).

But Brassier's project does not end by simply forcing young philosophers to meditate like dark, new sorts of monks, who wake up and are enlightened by this one, unnerving far-off future — although he *does* recognise the contemplation of extinction is a sublime "naturalization of eschatology and a theologization of cosmology" (ibid., pp. 231–2). But this merely serves as a litmus test to judge which of us are not hiding, but rather are willing to face the full truth of things — to get closer to "what matter is" rather than "what matters for us" — no matter how dark and meaningless this reality turns out to be. For Brassier, this allows us to obtain a new lease on *realism* and finally cut through the seductive correlationist's veil. Once we open up to the possibility of this *ultimate injustice* to humanity, and the cold indifference of the laws of nature to stop it, we even begin to notice things about the *lifeless, mindless, indifferent reality* within life, the mind, and judgement — insights previously repressed with wishful myths. Brassier spends a large portion of the final part of his masterwork on such insights, like the hitherto ignored evidence that life itself runs exclusively on death,[6] that consciousness is an information processor ultimately reducible to its neurological states — in no material way distinct from the thoughtless bladder, weather system, or computer, and that it is actually trauma and the death drive — not love, pleasure, or pure creativity — which sparks the mind into minding. In later work, he even proposes that the first-person experience of Selfhood may too be an enchantment to overcome.[7]

The reader might be wondering at this point, *why even do philosophy?* Or, as is particularly relevant here, *what does this really have to do with justice?* The thought of extinction may well get us beyond the clear injustice that correlationism has done to space-time, but is this really all that philosophy has to offer on this theme? Luckily, there remains a sliver (or more accurately, an infinitesimal) ray of something *akin* to hope, for Brassier believes that a philosophy which allows itself to be fully traumatised "strives to become equal to the trauma of the in-itself whose trace it bears" (ibid., p. 239).

Revolutionary Reason and Promethean Communism – We allow myths and ghosts to legislate the present world and, as Brassier warns, "This is what renders philosophy an apologia for the status quo at best, or a rationalization of oppression at worst"

(Brassier, 2016, p. 103). Again, for him, the worst injustice must be a false justice, for which he offers a "materialist dialectic of theory and practice that challenges the Platonic entwining of truth, justice, and justification" (ibid., p. 103). So let us briefly imagine, *what would become of our world if we let go of these illusions?* What would be made possible if we were — as the title of his chief work suggests — *unbound* by nihilism from the false testaments that have reigned over us so far? Much to his credit, Brassier takes this thought seriously. He speculates that breaking the chains of common delusion could unlock a new Promethean politics, capable "of re-engineering ourselves and our world on a more rational basis" (Brassier, 2014, p. 487), where humanity is no longer constrained by artificial limits on what is possible for it to achieve. He explains: "Prometheanism is simply the claim that there is no reason to assume a predetermined limit to what we can achieve or to the ways in which we can transform ourselves and our world" (ibid., p. 470), even if nature is indifferent to it all. Recall, for example, the strange proposition just mentioned — that our very experience of Selfhood may be illusory. A world free of such an illusion, he notes, would certainly lend itself to wholly new notions of agency and property. What he has in mind here is a Communist project constituted by rationally *selfless subjects*. Indeed, within the grand scope of extinction, all are made equal under the universality of death.[8] Such a revolutionary Promethean-Communist state would certainly need to be freed from the lies of old royalty, divinity, sentimentality, and global capitalism, which are sustained by fantastical desires. And against the neoliberal lie that there can be a peaceful end to the world's oppressions, he gives us a dose of political realism, that "[t]here is no escape from the slaughterbench of history" (Brassier, 2016, p. 112). And in this grand scheme of real-time, what are all our petty squabbles and power games anyway?

But how realistic is this *nearly* positive side of Brassier's thought? Will the truth set us free, pure and simple? He readily admits that globalised materialist theories and pretensions to complete disillusion are themselves daydreams. So, we are left to wonder, by what means could a global Revolution of reason ever take place? His own prescriptions toward achieving this aim come at the end of his thesis, *Alien Theory*: to make a lot of *meaningless noise*, which would — supposedly — break up the machinery of World Capital.[9] But even if this dark political noise *were* to finally liberate us from authoritarian myths, and even unjustifiable feelings of desire or selfish thirsts for power, it is unclear what we'd be living *toward*. Put another way, it is in no way self-evident, with the discursive criteria Brassier has laid out for us, that a nihilist is capable of *positively justifying one mode of life over any other.* We may finally be capable of comparing justifications between truth claims about reality *apart from ourselves*, but when it comes to comparing human values, we are left with only *empty normative noise*. Why ought we strive toward a communist universalism where all material needs are met over a World Capitalist slave-trade that leaves most to rot?

It appears to this reader that Brassier backtracks the progress made toward a functional tribunal of judgement — not dissimilar from Nietzsche's self-defeating global genealogical suspicion — when he states that "[t]he philosophical pretention to truth is ideological. Justification is always suspect" (ibid., p. 103), and further, that "[w]hat is just cannot simply be what is justifiable" (ibid., p. 103). Even if Brassier were here to follow the great pessimist Schopenhauer's brilliant negative formulation of justice — that the "concept of *justice* is, like that of *freedom*, a negative concept [and, conversely, that] the concept of injustice is the positive one, and means the same thing as *injury* in the broadest sense"[10] — if Brassier continues to hold that the feelings of joy, beauty, and goodness are no valid criterion for our justifying justice,[11] then certainly neither is *injury*, for what difference could it all make to a nihilist who holds that we are *already dead?*

Nevertheless, Brassier does leave us with a remarkably salient question regarding the human drive for justice: *if the threat of total annihilation of consciousness from the universe doesn't light a fire under our asses, what will?*

Iain Hamilton Grant's Defence of Nature's Autonomy

> This World is not Conclusion.
> A Species stands beyond —
> Invisible, as Music —
> But positive, as Sound —
> It beckons, and it baffles —
> Philosophy —
> — Emily Dickinson[12]

According to Iain Hamilton Grant, the greatest injustice to reality in the history of philosophy is certainly *physiocide.*[13] That is, philosophers — especially of these last few hundred years — are guilty of "trying to murder nature".[14] Grant seeks to continue the legacy of F.W.J. Schelling, who "strikes at the ethical heart of all modern philosophy" (Grant, 2008, p. 159)[15] by prosecuting all such claims that nature is finished, that we humans have finally escaped nature through superior self-consciousness and science, and *that the end of nature has already taken place* — so that we are already functionally dead. Instead, Grant maintains that it is one of the precious few Absolutes we can glean about reality *that this is certainly not the case.* Reaching for a glass, he cheerfully says to a crowd, "I'm glad the universe isn't over, because then I wouldn't be able to have a sip of water. I have had a sip of water, therefore the universe isn't over."[16] Relatedly, the idea of *creation* has been abandoned by philosophers, scared of being confused with anti-naturalists, and since "holding a concept of creation is likely to expose us to accusations of theologism. Fine, I say!"[17] Grant finds a sensible defence of the concept, as each act, doubt, passing comet, and gust of wind bears witness to the fact that "[t]he creation of the world did not occur at the beginning of time, but occurs every day", as Marcel Proust once put it.[18]

Although the problem of "correlationism" hardly appears in Grant's work, it seems this is because he discerns this phenomena to merely be the new malnourished offspring of irresponsible parents more deserving of blame for this "murder of nature" — namely, eliminative *materialism* and *subjectivist idealism.* They have left the correlationist with an abyssal view of both the terms that haunt them — namely, *thought* and *being*. We find through Grant's work that an injustice has been done *to* the common correlationist — simply set up to trivialise the world they inherit. Only after sketching out this family feud can we proceed to Grant's resolution, where *thought and being* are not divorced, but reconciled in nurturing the creative sovereignty of the nature they share.

The Original Sin of Self-Centred Nihilism – The reader will already notice a sharp contrast from the fiercely *negative* philosophy just covered. Alternatively to Brassier's *annihilative procedure*, which radicalises dialectical logic to *do justice to Reason*, Grant pursues an unapologetically *positive* philosophy, which "offers a counterpoint to the eliminativist strategy in contemporary neurophilosophy" (ibid., p. 188), in order to do *justice to the Nature that produces reason in the first place.* For reasons that will become clear, it should be noted that this positive philosophy is not merely a comfort to the emotional needs of *one solipsistic bi-pedal species.* Contra Brassier, Grant argues that eliminative materialism cannot account for "nature beyond the epistemological concerns of the philosophy of science" (ibid., p. vii), and that such "dead-matter" accounts of nature cannot explain, for example, the abundant processes of *purposive organisation* (i.e., the production of mechanisms as such), as the only resources left are equiprobable noise or a mechanical closure that "threatens to result in, at best, Kantian or phenomenological constructivism,[19] and, at worst, completely nihilistic solipsism" (Dunham/Grant, 2011, p. 237).[20] Contrary to the notion that ideas are abstracted from the world as utter fictions, Grant points out that meanings and *ideas* are no less *causal* than neurons in structuring the world as it is.[21] To gain a complete and comprehensive view of reality, we cannot bulldoze the landscape of minds, meanings, and ideas found naturally occurring throughout nature. The sensuous mind stands as an exemplar of this dense wilderness, which can't be brushed away as artifice. So, although a rare theorist like Brassier certainly gets points for going beyond anthropocentric metaphysics, we find it comes at the expense of the *constructive* reality of Nature. Grant will go even a step further here, challenging the original dualism of *reality vs. ideality altogether*, holding rather to the synthesis that "[t]he irreducible organizational forms in question are *real* Ideas" (ibid., p. 249, emphasis added).

Reductive scientism is not the only way critical reason has been wielded as a weapon against the full scope of sensuous nature. Another culprit is the *legalistic logician.* Grant explains:

> [I]t's a common line with practically every philosopher of logic that logic does not inhabit the same world as logic is made of [...] It's a claim to exempt logic from nature insofar, in other words, nature is considered as a body of things, or as some mega-body, or as slime. (Grant, 2014, 16:00)

Doubling down on this dubious transcendence from the slime of reality, logicism follows scientism in scrubbing reality of *freedom,* which is mistaken as a violation of unbreakable laws, the *final system* that mind-as-nature slavishly obeys. These philosophies fail to comprehend the free and constructive aspects of reality, which is why "Schelling, by contrast, takes repeated pains to distinguish critical- from nature-philosophy" (Grant, 2008, p. 14), and why freedom is the "leading Idea" (ibid., p. 64) that a naturalist must account for: *a nature that produces the messy reality of genuine freedom.*

But an account of the reality of freedom is not easy, for as we contemplate this baffling phenomena — *the legislation of new laws and constitution of new realities* — we are pulled toward the other "parent" of correlationism — *the subjective Idealist* — who has been beating this one drum for ages: independent human freedom, with its unique powers to think, say, the ethical and universal, creates its own "second nature", and thus makes the rest of reality stand relatively *dead* or *enslaved* to its "Nature" in comparison. We fall near the conclusion that humankind must be the *Subjective Protagonist of Reality, Lord of Being,* or at least s*hepherd of beings*. Everything else — from microbes to far-off planets — become props on the human stage. Grant calls this common claim, which puts the ethical human world above and the world of mindless laws below, "Ethicism". And he immediately puts the highest warning on it, proclaiming that "[e]thicism is physiocide when it does not recognise dependence. Ethicism is synonymous therefore with *evil*, just because its claim is the end of Nature" (Grant, 2014, 15:00). Nature once more becomes a dumb and formless matter, but now simply placed under the feet of one *Supreme Life*.[22] Following Kant's precedent, these philosophies act as if this life "is no longer matter, but an entity of quite another kind, as if from another world" (Grant, 2008, p. 9). According to Grant, this "mutual exteriority of nature and freedom [...] remains the axis around which philosophy is organized" (ibid., p. 17). Mysticism, existentialism, phenomenology, and correlationism are all found guilty of placing the mind outside reality, as if there is made an ontological division between them in an "isolation of physics from metaphysics" (ibid., p. 5) — talk about theological residue. We might even say that this reduction of reality to a ground and game for humans was the *first* bad idea of Nature.

As we have just seen, Grant maintains that eliminativist materialism presents a hollow account of Ideas and freedom, and conversely, subjectivist idealism presents an impoverished account of nature's own creative powers outside the human circle. In order to finally overcome this primal opposition within philosophy, we need a theory capable of articulating *at once* the strange *nature of Freedom*, which exceeds all critical reductions, and the *freedom of Nature*, which overcomes the inflation of human subjectivity. The task is to reconcile freedom and science, "to unify realist parts and idealist wholes" (Dunham/Grant, p. 193), in *a speculative physics of everything.*

On Nature's Self-Legislation – Grant's excitement for this *Speculative Physics* is palpable: "I don't know about you, but the very idea of combining those two things seems an absolute recipe for heaven on Earth" (Collapse, 2007, p. 335). Toward this goal, he advises we start doing justice to the rich inheritance left for us, as we did not simply move from Kant to Meillassoux. Forefront in his mind are Plato and the Absolute Idealists, who have been brutally underestimated (on his account) as anthropocentric daydreamers and problematic forerunners to the correlationist dilemma by the likes of Brassier, but also by anthropocentric daydreamers and correlationists themselves. Grant alternatively discovers in these classic thinkers the beginnings of a working model of a fully *Realist-Idealist* philosophy — a model stretched infinitely far beyond the bounds of the correlationist circle and simultaneously suspending a bridge between the infamous analytic/continental divide no less. But such a novel philosophy could not be *artificially constructed*, and must rather be produced by the *authoritative voice of Nature herself.*

First, against any lingering claims that we humans, in particular, are *the* Special Subject of Reality, Grant simply reminds us that we did not give birth to ourselves, that Nature is not a reflection of human consciousness, but human consciousness a reflection of Nature, and further, "what we call reason is simply a play of higher natural forces unknown to us" (System of Philosophy, III, pp. 273–4; 2004). Second, against those who claim only a theological residue as the explanation for why reality slips from the grasp of reason, our improved naturalist must submit the abundant evidence that Nature is always *adding* more reality, at a rate faster than any second-hand snapshots, and even incorporates these without delay. In Grant's words, "nature maintains a manifest productive priority over its explainability" (Dunham/Grant, 2011, p. 280). From just these retorts, the Speculative Naturalist implicates the self-legislation of reality beyond human access. There *must* indeed be *some* transcendental subject, but it cannot be we rational humans alone. And any *complete* science of nature cannot merely chase down observable laws, but must finally get to the heart of legislation itself.[23] Slowly, we draw out Nature's jurisdiction beyond all laws and judgements.

To get a fuller picture, we turn to the promising reinterpretation of Plato *through* Schelling's Absolute Idealism, read as a misunderstood *naturalist*. But first, we must get over our allergy to idealism, as Schelling and Grant "intend to demonstrate the importance of metaphysical idealism to contemporary science" (ibid., p. 223). *Ideas* themselves will provide "the means by which 'we must think the emergence of the world'" (Grant, 2008, p. 27).[24] As Grant summarises, "Platonism gives the Idea alone the status of '*auto kath' auto*' the absolute, 'itself according to itself'" (ibid., p. 26–7),[25] and this self-legislation of the Absolute is the meaning of Plato's *immanent law*. Rather than the ideal being the way we transcend into *another world*, the ideal is the "self-augmentation of the real".[26] Far from the trivialising the correlationist's claim that our thoughts are inherently severed from nature, this naturalist-idealism challenges us to recognise *reality itself thinking through us*. We can observe this directly in the generation of ideas, not needing to wait, like Brassier, for human consciousness to become extinct to see the autonomy of reality. "[W]e reach the surprising conclusion that only a non-eliminative idealism is capable of the philosophy of matter" (ibid., p. 202), because "conceptual genesis and natural genesis become one and the same; or, in other words, nature autoproduces its self" (ibid., p. 19). In the simplest possible terms, the *concept* of creation is a genuine *instance* of creation. Perhaps the most astonishing consequence of this Speculative Physics has to do with the *material purpose* that Ideas serve in the cosmos, i.e., organisation. Here Grant refers to a proposed fourth law of thermodynamics that would incorporate Plato's insights into the Ideas — now conceived as a phase space through which Nature anticipates, selects, and indeed copies (e.g., genetically) — a free-constraining of the set of possibilities by means of preference for certain fates over others.[27] We find here a philosophy of *creative freedom as the novel legislation of the laws of nature,* with no separation of being and thinking. And perhaps fresher still is an aspect of such supra-human justice escaping the courtroom scenario for a much-needed breath of air, since a Nature that exceeds all law is not considered so much *lawless* as *innocent.* We may conceive this as the sovereignty of the goddess *Díkē,* as she freely, almost musically, draws all fates, directing all flows by immanent law. Or, in those familiar eschatological terms, alternatively to Brassier's damning *Revelations,* Grant proposes a brand-new secular vision of *Genesis.*

But Where Is Nature Leading? – We are left with one lingering problem threatening the speculatively *Just Nature* rendered by this "complete science of freedom", for if Nature is the singular sovereign and innocent Subject, then we are returned to something structurally akin to the Judeo-Christian problem of evil, or the inexplicable origin of injustice proper.[28] It appears that the problem haunting all *absolute idealisms* — their own noble capacity to incorporate conflicting and contradictory aspects of One Sovereign Entity — comes with the steep price of an oxymoronic philosophical (or mythologised as a theological) system. Nature (or God) becomes the victim, perpetrator, judge, jury, and executioner all in One. While the *correlationist circle* entraps us in our own symbolic abstractions, and the eliminativist entraps us within the changeless laws of logic or mechanics of matter, Absolute Idealism replaces these bounds with the grander metabolic circle of a *self-eating* Nature. Irrespective of the circumference, there remains a problem with all these unicyclical models of causation, for all unincorporated *particularity* is stripped of its sovereignty, naturally considered a necessary evil, an outlaw, the inexplicable corruption of nature's purity, or the sole "retardation" of its otherwise boundless prowess — at best a second-class citizen. In a sentence, *autonomous things* can only be *products, fictions,* or *injuries.* Grant's *positive* philosophy, in the end, can only diagnose injustice as the trivial *self-harm* of Nature's immortal body. We come away lacking the tools to meaningfully articulate the landscape of concerns, i.e., justice. As Heidegger asked of Schelling's system: "*is evil then really a being at all?*"[29]

What are the ethico-political consequences of a philosophy of automatically "Just Nature"? What are the stakes when injustice is essentially wiped from the situation? When regarding theories accused by this philosophy of "murdering Nature" — since, in reality, they *cannot* murder this Nature, and so, *no harm no foul* — even the Capital offense is pardoned with a tongue-lashing. Grant could perhaps be accused of *quietism,* save for a single article where he expresses support for playful and even postmodern experiments with political theory.[30] So, while Grant is to be commended for refreshing the project of a Speculative Physics of the future, planted beyond the correlationist's circle, and for attempting to explain the *self-legislation of reality*, when it comes to distinct concerns of value, his system (like Brassier's) ends up too unipolar (whether positive idealism or negative materialism) to simultaneously render a philosophy where justice and injury are *significantly distinct.* We will see it's quite a different story in the works of Harman and Meillassoux.

Graham Harman's Fair Trial for All Things

> And for all this, nature is never spent;
> There lives the dearest freshness deep down things;
> — G.M. Hopkins[31]

Among the speculative realists, Graham Harman's theory of everything — *Object-Oriented Ontology* (OOO) — is the simplest to summarise: "The concreteness of objects [...] refers to something so real that no description or definition ever does it justice" (Harman, 2005, p. 248). The original sin of philosophy, according to Harman, has been giving into the temptation *to get rid of objects.* Zipping his eyes from his index-cards to the crowd, he says, "I defend the integrity, the autonomy of objects from all qualities, all relations, and all possible uses that can be made of them."[32] The grand hopes of building some ultimate tribunal of reason or borrowing down to the infinite well of Nature's own justice are traded for a philosophy which prioritises the *justness of things in their own right.*

OOO has already had a popular influence on art, architecture, ecology, and virtually every sub-discipline of philosophy. It has likewise provoked a great deal of vitriol and suspicion. Harman seems to welcome the skirmishes, as he controversially holds — contra all other speculative realists — that idealism and materialism should not be reformed — rather that *they must be destroyed*.[33] For Harman, too many philosophies have been built upon these negative and positive variations of an all too seductive *fundamentalism*; either dissolving things down to their constituent parts (undermining), up to their socio-relational effects (overmining), or both extremes at once (duomining)[34] — as is notably the case with correlationisms. Such object-diminishing philosophies render a dreary landscape where "nature is a realm of ironclad deterministic law in which objective answers are always possible in principle, while culture is a zone of power struggles and arbitrary projections" (Harman, 2018, p. 57), usually placing Humans as *the* ontological division in the cosmos, crudely replacing the old theological duality of *Creator/creations* with *Humans/literally everything else.*

To break up these crude fundaments that have spoiled philosophy, Harman proposes a *flat ontology*, which we can also term a *principle of fairness*. Under this proposal, objects are not exiled as phantoms nor injuries to an otherwise seamless World, but rather all things are included, given a fair trial, and so (at least initially) treated equally. This already flies us far from Grant's worldview, where the freedom of the *parts* is swallowed up by the autonomy of the *whole*. Here, the *singular* qualification for autonomy is a thing's *mere irreducibility to any other* — each *is* a whole. It is no longer only the Human Subject nor Whole of Nature given the special recognition of sovereignty: the great problems of freedom and finitude belong to *all* things insofar as they are things at all. But in order to genuinely do justice to this proposed independence of things themselves, we must let all pretensions to absolute mastery and knowledge die their rightful death.

Justified Untrue Belief? – Unlike the others we have just covered, let us hit the most challenging critique of OOO right off the bat — why should we seek a justice we cannot *justify?* Despite OOO's enormous success in its battles against the common doxa of fundamentalist and subjectivist metaphysics, it has also run into a threat seeking to disqualify it as "real philosophy". The major accusation levelled is that OOO abandons science and critical justification wholesale,[35] slipping into an "epistemological anti-realism"[36] built on *groundless aestheticism,* one affording no rights to assert one claim truer than any other. As one might already have anticipated, these arguments are levelled primarily from the corner of Brassier's *Tribunal of Rationality.* Brassier writes, concerning OOO, "The denigration of rationality often serves as an alibi for those seeking to evade the obligation to justify their philosophical claims. But this is precisely the obligation that no philosopher can shirk" (Wolfendale/Brassier, postscript, 2014). Starkly posed: "that everything is real is uninformative". Indeed, it is certainly a core tenet of OOO's speculative *fairness principle* that *all objects* and so *all claims* be equally *included* — from outright lies to the earth beneath our feet. And Harman's OOO also claims that "[n]o one is actually in possession of knowledge or truth" (Harman, 2018, p. 6), for all theories of reality can only ever be *justified but nonetheless untrue* beliefs (ibid., p. 180). This all seems to bode in favour of the critic. But, upon deeper inspection, we find it is in fact a mirror image of Brassier's own philosophy of science — for in both philosophies, science gives us *improvable justifications,* but never arrives at *final truth.* For Brassier, this is because there is always a residual fiction to scrub out, while for Harman it is because things are never equal to any theory, model, or translation of them. OOO's *equal-openness to all objects* mirrors Brassier's own principle of *non-materialist materialism.* Harman even explicitly claims of his own system: "If this is 'materialism,' *then it is the first materialism in history to deny the existence of matter*" (Harman, 2002, p. 293). *Both* of these epistemological frameworks are "uninformative",[37] but this itself is a crucial aspect of their methodological machinery, as this *initial openness* to autonomous realities is not *meant* to be informative on its own, but rather flattens for the very *reception of information*. Harman may even counterattack that it is *Brassier* who is ultimately committed to a world of mere images, some mythic and some scientific, whereas OOO's epistemological wager is that *neither* of these are the reality in itself. So, paradoxical as it may sound, it is by admitting we *cannot* do things justice that we make the best initial move *toward* such a goal.[38] It is less accurate to say OOO *abandons* the gems of Justification and Truth than to say it demonstrates an inherent tension between the two, akin to the quanta-continua problems that haunt all physics and metaphysics, e.g., particle-wave, space-time, product-process, and being-becoming. For Harman, logics and sciences give us the improvably *justified untrue belief* we have just seen,[39] while it is the immediate experience of otherness as in metaphor and aesthetics (and philosophy, as we'll see) that secures cognitive importance as *unjustified* but *true* belief.[40]

It's hard to think of a better context to address the lingering accusation of OOO's "groundless aestheticism" — based as it is on the emphasis of an unjustifiable metaphysical importance in metaphorical cognition — than using it to unpack the original metaphor for causality itself: justice.

Díkē: The Original Metaphor for Justice – The literal meaning of Díkē (δίκη) was not originally a goddess but a "*watercourse embankment*", built to guide flows and prevent flooding. We see aspects of this primordial metaphor in all of the ancient Ionian theories of the cosmos and causation *(díkēphysis)* — from Thales' water-world to Heraclitus' eternal river and even Plato's own Great Divide between Ideal forms and sensuous flows. And the idea stretches back long before even these.[41] In ancient courtrooms, the term was used to describe judges "drawing a divided line" between guilt and innocence, true and false testimony.[42] The word "nomos" (from which we get *norm* and *law*) likewise meant "to divide".[43] What is important here, according to OOO's theory of metaphor, will not be found in the act of mining these concepts for their literal origin, but precisely in that so many discrete forms bloom from this one seed. Harman traces the origin of *Philosophia* to Socrates, pointing out exactly this:

> Western philosophy emerged [*after* the physicists][44] through Socrates' discovery that undermining is not a tenable method for revealing the nature of virtue, justice, friendship, or anything else. For what Socrates seeks is not a kind of knowledge. [He seeks] philosophia, [which] means the love of wisdom rather than the possession of it. (Harman, 2018, p. 47)

Metaphor provides OOO with a mode of cognition distinct from those pretending to access the final laws and constitution of things, as if all things could be written on the surface of a tablet. Metaphor is a form of access that brings the exceptional autonomy of a thing into view, the cognition of ulterior spacious depths, which *themselves* necessitate the analogical leaps. No abstraction, negative or positive, does justice to these depths. In other words, truth is a relative surface, while *reality* remains absolute depth. Harman here follows Heidegger's insight into *thinking:* "The reason we are not yet thinking is because we are not yet able to do justice to the emergence of things from concealment" (Harman, 2007, p. 149). This inescapable *allusiveness* or *withdrawal* of things is not merely a failure of the hungry human intellect, but a byproduct of the *finitude* of things, as they *must* translate one another into their own partial, sensuous terms. Thus, OOO offers an epistemological mode of *analogue truth* — beyond the self-justification that imprisons correlationism.

According to Harman, for too long we have been looking for the ultimate laws and legislation *behind* all things rather than for causation between things themselves. By clearing a path through all false fundaments (following the example of *allure*), OOO is better equipped to trace formative aspects back to discrete causes, rendering the *autonomy of the object* intelligible. OOO's model of *díkēphysis* locates the *essential division* between things and their relations — not in the far-fetched splits of Nature/Idea, nor Self/World. It is not only *We* nor *the Goddess of Justice herself* who draw the fates of things, but *all objects are the legislators of the cosmos*, carving it up and bearing laws around their contours.[45] In fact, for OOO, the withdrawal of things from any surface or appearance of them is *Space* itself, while *Time* spills, pours, and floods out of these embankments. He explains: "the fissure between objects and qualities reappears in every least crevice of the world" (Harman, 2005, p. 160).

Following the original philosophical justice (díkē) metaphor through the lens of OOO, we see a world where all realities have the hidden capacity to flood beyond precedent laws, knowledge, and even *physical mastery.* Harman's answer to the correlationist's scepticism is not in any absolute grasp, but in a *humility* that presumes the ungraspable reality of things. He maintains, "philosophy has great cognitive value even though it is not a form of knowledge" (Harman, 2018, p. 7), and would certainly agree with Einstein when he said, "Whoever undertakes to set himself up as judge in the field of truth and knowledge is shipwrecked by the laughter of the Gods." Using a similar metaphor, Harman writes: "Reality is the rock against which our various ships always founder, and as such it must be acknowledged and revered, however elusive it may be" (ibid., p. 6).

The Bonds of Mesotopia – But what does it mean to do justice to things themselves in the familiar ethico-political sense? Surely all things *cannot be valued and treated equally.* And perhaps a deeper question still: if things are actually all cut off from each other — and can only ever *fail* to do justice to one another — *how might there be any causation without injustice?* — wouldn't this lead us to the isolationist conclusion that relation *is* a cosmic injustice? Harman openly admits that relation is the *key problem* for OOO, and also the one with which objects themselves must reckon.[46] This is to be expected from a world that is nothing *but* a multitude of legislators, each with its own terms, limits, and powers. The reduction inherent to relation appears to be the penalty paid according to the ordinances of Time: "Causation in general is what allows one object to inflict blows on another, and causation is undeniably a form of violence, since it involves one thing touching the essence of another through the door of the inessential" (Harman, 2005, p. 219). Thus the more pressing questions might be: *What could make any relation worthwhile? What makes one object more worthy of attention than another?* More broadly, *is there any possible notion of justice within the relations of objects?*

The reader may already have intuited that there can be no final ethical nor political answers to these questions, according to OOO. It would appear Harman offers only a negative formulation of justice parallel to Brassier's, as what has yet to be seen is a vision of "positive" justice beyond the mere justness of things in their usual alienated or injurious trenches. But luckily, Harman has offered some positive aspects of finitude that claim a break from the usual violence, accidents, errors, injuries, and deaths. The most sensible place to start looking for such positive justice in OOO would be *in that which is concerned or injured in the first place*. Too commonly, the strictly negative account of finitude and causation outstrip sensual bonds, which, for Harman, is where a world of value opens up, where "an ethical vocation forms a new object in its own right, and not just an external interaction between two permanently separate entities" (Harman, 2018, p. 107). In fact, reaching deeper than even the enchanted theatricality of sensuality, "we might speak here of commitment" (ibid., p. 192). Finite and sensuous commitments carve up the world no less than ancient iron-clad law in OOO. Rather than genuine innocence, justice, love, or grandeur being overmined to an immortal Law of Nature, we recognise here that these have value precisely in their being *exceptional particulars*. Just as there can be no global genealogical reduction of all matter to one substratum, there also cannot be a global theological reduction of all values to one Subject. Harman suggests, "We do not merely desire an infinitely perfect and unattainable justice, but experience numerous bite-sized samples of justice in our everyday lives" (Harman, 2016). Indeed, he stresses throughout the book *Dante's Broken Hammer* that the symbiotic bonds of love (simply considered the smallest ethical unit) break the normal, negative situation where things are either cut off or violently reduce one another; "the object of love does not withdraw to an unbridgeable distance, but is already here in our midst" (Harman, 2016). These exceptional moments of bonding are behind the creation of new objects. Object-oriented ethics becomes here a growing encyclopaedia of the various wagers, commitments, and bonds between things, which create new autonomous objects.

This brings us to some concluding remarks on OOO's vision of justice. Living inescapably in a world full of conflicting passions, we find the world is neither laid on a pre-established train-track toward Utopia, nor is it helplessly swirling toward a purposeless Dystopia; rather, for OOO, the ethico-political landscape is always a mixed, plastic,[47] and ecological *Mesotopia*.[48] It is worth noting that, for this reason, Harman rejects radical politics in general.[49] Among the speculative realists, Harman is the only declared non-Marxist. It is a move that opens up accusations of a neoliberal "protection of the status quo".[50] No doubt, the ethics and politics of OOO so far have been predominantly descriptive rather than prescriptive, and, facing the inescapable horizon of genuine threats that OOO recognises, it would certainly be strange for philosophy to leave us empty-handed. Brassier would blame all this on OOO's distracting attempt to re-enchant the world, while Grant would blame it on OOO's disregard for the Absolute sovereignty all things share underneath, but the more powerful critique comes from the final speculative realist we are about to meet. Meillassoux will argue that there is no getting around our longing for a bigger picture of justice, untethered from *things as they presently are.*

Quentin Meillassoux's Hope for Cosmic Justice in the Future

> "Justice? You get justice in the next world, in this world you have the law."
> — William Gaddis[51]

The Speculative Realist who coined the term *Correlationism* is also the only one among the original four to write explicitly and extensively on the theme of justice. In the mere sixty-four published pages from his long-awaited opus, *L'Inexistence Divine,* Quentin Meillassoux mentions "*justice*" a total of 128 times.[52] The reader will find shortly that the entire body of his work drives toward this singular aim: the "hope for a justice worthy of the name" (Meillassoux/Harman, 2015, p. 234).

The Principle of Unreason – The first task Meillassoux sets forth in establishing this grand philosophy is to discern a new way of *justifying justification.* This task is made so difficult because the collective consensus in modern critical philosophy is that of correlationism: "*to think something absolute is to think an absolute for-us, and hence not to think anything absolute*" (Meillassoux, 2008, p. 51). The modern world has been washed clean of absolutes by a flood of scepticism, unleashed by Hume and Kant's profoundly sceptical and critical philosophies. When pressed under critique, we find all justifications for absolute Truth dissolve into self-justified dogma. But, although Meillassoux is concerned that this exodus from metaphysical dogma has only delivered us to a barren intellectual landscape, the problem is further doubled, because the correlationist's rational argument — which treats all claims about reality as "equally legitimate from the viewpoint of knowledge" (ibid., p. 47) — simultaneously enables a mutant form of *religious fanaticism.* In a now famous example, Meillassoux points out that the rational philosopher is left defenceless against the fundamentalist believer who claims the world is 6,000 years old, because the evidence of the *arche-fossil* — despite being dated back to a time prior to both life and consciousness — can only be claimed by the correlationist to be 6.4 billion years old *for-us,* immediately diminishing any literal scientific claim about reality itself. The paradox of our time is thus that "the more thought arms itself against dogmatism, the more defenceless it becomes before fanaticism" (ibid., p. 48). And worst of all, both the relativist and dogmatist are *leading the world nowhere.*

The way out of this terrible stalemate, Meillassoux argues, is to demonstrate an Absolute truth about reality itself, beyond whatever appears *for-us*. He sets out to locate this key truth within the insular correlationist argument itself, to unlock the *Great Outdoors* of thought. Due to the fact Meillassoux spends roughly 128 pages laying out this Absolute justification, we will only cover some of its major moments here. Throughout, he draws our focus to what the critical correlationist *correctly* holds: that regardless of whatever thought or content is presently given for us, reality-in-itself *really could be or become wholly otherwise.* The radical turn Meillassoux makes against the correlationist here is that this claim is no longer to be construed as *mere ignorance of what really is,* but rather a proof that contingency — the capacity for things to be or become otherwise than as they are given — is the *necessary facticity of being in the world.* He calls this demonstrable constant, deeper than all content given for us, the *Principle of Unreason.* Meillassoux demonstrates step-by-step how the correlationist is forced to concede *contingency* itself as the *sole* undeniable aspect of reality, which reason affords us. In his own words, "we can say that it is possible *to demonstrate the absolute necessity of everything's non-necessity.* In other words, it is possible to establish, through indirect demonstration, the absolute necessity of the contingency of everything" (ibid., p. 62).

We are about to see Foucault was quite right when he said, "Unreason is to reason as dazzlement is to daylight",[53] because, beyond successfully passing "through the correlationist circle — or at least to have broken through the wall" (ibid., p. 98), this justification, by way of a *positive unreason*, simultaneously opens an astonishing and horrifying new view onto the Absolute: "one unavoidable consequence [...] is that it asserts the actual contingency of the laws of nature" (ibid., p. 83).

Lawless Superchaos – If we simply reverse engineer the principle just discovered to its material singularity — i.e., from the "point of view" of reality itself — we begin to see precisely why no ultimate Law and Order of the cosmos has ever been found: the Absolute source of reality is a lawless "sovereign flux" (ibid., p. 69), making all things, laws, and even worlds contingent and so mortal. Meillassoux terms this reasonless *díkēphysis* of everything "super-chaos":

> We see something akin to Time, but a Time that is inconceivable for physics, since it is capable of destroying, without cause or reason, every physical law, just as it is inconceivable for metaphysics, since it is capable of destroying every determinate entity, even a god, even God. This is not a Heraclitean time, since it is not the eternal law of becoming, but rather the eternal and lawless possible becoming of every law. (Ibid., p. 64)

Bearing this strange new Absolute in mind, we apprehend that philosophies from the beginning have been running a fool's errand looking for a pre-established Order's eternal law responsible for all things. Meillassoux writes, "since the Greeks, one conception, and one only, of becoming, has always imposed itself upon us: time is only the actualisation of an eternal set of possibles, the actualisation of Ideal Cases" (Collapse, 2007, p. 71). He continues that even "modernity does not break with Greek metaphysics on one essential point: finite or infinite, the world remains governed by the law" (ibid., p. 71). The real problem with these views is the injury done to novelty, originality, emergence, and chance, as reality always pales in comparison with the *Ideal Forms* or *mechanical Laws* over the rainbow, while all immanence is pushed aside as an *accident* or *corrupted descendant* fallen from pre-established grace,[54] and *here* the *real-time* legislation of the cosmos is obscured. Alternatively, with *super-chaos* as our speculative origin, time is granted "the capacity to bring forth new laws which were not 'potentially' contained in some fixed set of possibles" (ibid., p. 72).[55] Meillassoux even assures us, "we have nothing to lose by moving from a causal to an acausal universe — nothing except enigmas" (Meillassoux, 2008, p. 92). Further, this view is more profoundly *rational* than, not only fanatical idealism, but "all positivism, all scientism, and all logicism [which] have a mystical, religious essence" (Meillassoux/Harman, 2015, p. 230), due to their being "burdened with superstitious belief in the perennial character of laws" (ibid., p. 237).

As a final nail in the coffin, Meillassoux presents his climactic arguments against all such absolute Laws, Orders, and Sovereign Entities in familiar theological terms. We can deduce from the Absolute we've grasped that there could never have been an Absolute *Entity* behind all things. This is not only due to the familiar Problem of Evil — where God's act of creating a world with injustice in it (and also not stopping it for whatever reason) renders Him ungodly — but also because "[i]f an infinitely perfect God were the source of advent, time would essentially be poor, since what followed this Origin could be no better than a diminishing of it" (ibid., p. 176). Time would in fact be impossible, eternally forestalled. Or rather, time only ever possibly occurs *because* there has never been an Absolute Sovereign Entity nor eternal state of cosmic justice in the past. Such an Absolute "would be tantamount to a 'black hole of differences', into which all alterity would be irremediably swallowed up" (Meillassoux, 2008, p. 70). And this Universal-Order could not withstand the emergence of *even a single creation* (let alone free agents), as this would irreparably injure its Absolute status, as *injustice anywhere is injustice everywhere.*[56] Thus, "philosophy amounts to an astonishment that God does not exist" (Meillassoux/Harman, 2015, p. 177). With *super-chaos* as the explanation, there is no longer a mystery, because everything exists *ex nihilo* and without reason.

But the story does not end on this anticlimax of chaos. According to our new Absolute, the fact that something has never occurred in the past *does nothing to outlaw its becoming in the future.* Anything is yet possible. Additionally, in a world where the only necessity is contingency, the advent of *any* law, form, life, or thinking being takes on a miraculous — *albeit not divinely pre-ordained* — character. It is on these grounds Meillassoux begins to build up his philosophy of Justice.

The Possible Becoming of Cosmic Justice – Consider for a moment the many ontological advances, the laws and layers that appear so carefully laid out around us, as the fabric of the material universe. Meillassoux pulls our focus to the odd lineage of Laws and Worlds produced thus far from raw super-chaos; unprecedented events he simply calls *advents.* From nothing, and without reason, there became the *First World* of particles, gases, and material laws. Then, a *Second World* of organic matter and its sensuous life. Finally, the leap into this *Third World* of reasoning beings, capable of thinking the world wholly other than as given. Naturally, Meillassoux begins to wonder about a still higher *Fourth World*; what could emerge as far above our present world as life from inanimate matter? A God? What could be further from Brassier's inevitable doomsday than the future becoming of Heaven?

But the first apparent problem is that this next World is not guaranteed and we must maintain it is *just as possible* that humans simply become extinct instead. Indeed, Meillassoux admits an "absence of any superior law capable of preserving anything, no matter what, from perishing" (Meillassoux, 2008, p. 53). Heaven, hell, extinction, or this world unchanged all appear equally likely. Why inquire into, let alone wager on, any one fate over another? And centrally, "How does a non-human real justify the requirement of justice? How does the world outside humans relate ontologically with human requirements? This is the primordial axis of philosophical questioning" (Meillassoux/Harman, 2015, p. 195). It is here we must examine closer the nature of this *latest advent* of thought: reason itself. Prior to thought, life traversed its world guided by sensuous anticipation of the world as it had already been given to it. But with the advent of reason, life begins to imagine worlds other than it senses, what has already been given to it, and thought itself *builds this virtual world.* Meillassoux defines human reason according to the advent of this capacity: to draw a line, a díkē, between life's quantifiable world of experienced potentials and thought's purely qualitative world of virtuality, which can imagine new laws, the breaking of present ones, and even unexperienced absolute potentials like God, super-chaos, or Ideals like the Good, True, and Beautiful. Most importantly here, Meillassoux will argue that this advent of virtual reason introduces the highest novelty conceivable from out of reasonless super-chaos: the advent of, finally, a concrete *World of Reason*. Reason affords, for the first time in being, the capacity to envision Absolutes wholly beyond the laws or injuries of the present world. This virtual aspect of reason is not to be dispelled as *mad myth*, but is rather like Marshall McLuhan's definition of art: an *anti-environment* to the present world.[57] The overarching point for Meillassoux is that it is *purely* up to us to *decide* this virtual possibility. Since literally *anything* (even a God) is yet *possible*, it is important once more to ask *what would be the greatest possibility*? He writes, "one can never extinguish the splendid desire that makes of humans something other than a clever beast or a lukewarm, mediocre individual" (ibid., p. 234), and goes on, "one cannot limit what humans want, because one cannot limit what a world can do" (ibid., p. 234).

A true "*World of Reason*" would not merely be one of *absolute knowledge* (as, in a speculative sense, we have already obtained here in principle), but rather *absolute Justice*. Only a limitless justice could hold this psychic centre of gravity, the heaviest attractor toward a higher phase of existence. Meillassoux claims that "humans are [...] defined by their relation to a fourth World, [as] the desire of humans torn between their present contingency and the knowledge of the eternal by which they reach the idea of justice" (ibid., p. 191). Although certainly *realities thus far* have all generated the higher state of being — *unlike a God* — without any foreknowledge, blueprint, mastery, and without *reason*, the advent of a World of Justice would retroactively give a World-first *literal* reason, even a *meaning*, to reality's struggling — a World where "[t]he requirement of justice is no longer reduced to an abstract principle deprived of all ontological basis" (ibid., p. 194). In the simplest possible terms, only *this* future possibility would give *reason* for reason and *justify* justice itself.[58] He writes:

> [T]he sole possible novelty surpassing humans just as humans surpass life would be the recommencement of the human. That is why the fourth World ought to be called the World of justice: for it is only the World of the rebirth of humans that makes universal justice possible, by erasing even the injustice of shattered lives. (Ibid., p. 190)

Again, any chance a World of Justice has of becoming is unknowable for us. Nonetheless, Meillassoux asserts it is simultaneously *decisive*, regarding which future we *desire*, and also whether or not we roll the dice on this possibility. He follows here very seriously the poet Mallarme's notion that "Every Thought emits a Roll of the Dice" — in other words, the chance is already *given* to thought.[59] It is as if "justice wants to come about" (ibid., p. 217). We ourselves are the introduction of *reason* and the longing for *justice* in reality, and so, for the first time, against all odds and laws, there is something like a *seed* or *kernel of reason* — a chance — already given to hold out hope for its becoming. He even insists, "[t]he World of justice can arise only on condition of following the world of thought in conformity with the active hope for it that is deployed beforehand" (ibid., p. 215). Taking seriously the divide between the past-tense *Laws of Potential* and the future-tense *Ideals of Virtuality*, we find that the subjective, ethical decisions we make are not at all reflections of the reality as it is, but *only* as we ideally would have it; rather, *it is a reflection of our own-most character*, whichever possibility we hope to become.[60] Accordingly, "[h]ope exchanges guarantee for possibility" (ibid., p. 231).

Meillassoux's philosophy of justice finally culminates in a renewed conception, study, and even ethical life of a fully secular *Philosophical Divinity — to believe in God because he does not exist.* The aim of this philosophy is ultimately to materialise the divine, "to give birth to God just as matter gives birth to life" (ibid., p. 231), as naturally, "[t]he goal of every philosophy must be the immanent inscription of values in being" (ibid., p. 195). Clearly, it is a philosophy liable to be confused both by dogmatic believers and sceptical atheists,[61] but this Justice-philosophy is really meant to serve as a *rival* to both. "For the atheist, God is a matter for the priest; for the philosopher, God is too serious a matter for the priests" (ibid., p. 230). It is because God does *not* yet exist that, if God were to become in the future, this One would finally be free from the ancient problem of Evil: cleansed of all responsibility for injustices, as it did not create them — only this World of Justice. He even goes as far as to accuse the religious believer: "[t]o say that God exists is the worst of blasphemies, for this amounts to saying that God reigns over the world in a sort of grand politics [...] It is to say that this world is as God has willed it" (ibid., pp. 235–6). But this philosophical divinity is also not a pure atheism — "has anyone ever seen an atheist believe in God?" (Ibid., p. 233). So while the dogmatist lives in the past and the sceptical relativist lives in the present, only the philosopher lives in the *future*, which is why a philosophical "justice is opposed not to the ignorant, but to the hopeless" (ibid., pp. 196–7). This link by faithfulness to the absolute virtual horizon of cosmic justice "makes each of us the possible forerunner of God, [which] I call the divine" (ibid., pp. 231–2). But Meillassoux emphasises that this link does not entail "a Promethean identification of humans with God" (ibid., p. 232), like in Brassier's philosophy, but rather "[w]e bear God in our wombs" (ibid., p. 231) and our lives of virtue, "of living an unselfish relation to other humans" (ibid., p. 194), which endows our being with an immortal Good, as if spilling its gold from the future into the present. Each "time I act with a view to justice, I renew the awaiting which alone gives meaning to the possible sudden advent of another world that would not simply be the repetition of a World of life or thought, but which would actually constitute the final World — the ultimate World of justice" (ibid., p. 216).

There is an implicit *Golden Rule* here, imbedded in Meillassoux's definition of virtual Reason as purely *more-than-calculative* thought, namely: *Do not hold back Heaven with your belief in, nor blame for, the present* — "to believe no longer means to have faith, and no longer to believe in the law. It is to hope for a justice worthy of the name" (ibid., p. 234). It is very difficult indeed to live out this distinction — that is, the distinction between the *realism of the given* and *idealism of the possible.* We usually get it wrong, mixing them, looking at the present world as if already guaranteed some hidden justice, or else we go looking at the future as if death is the only possibility. Clearly, both the atheist and the believer are found guilty on this point and *cannot hold the díkē* — i.e., they are guilty of artificially imposing the past as if a law against the future. Both are consequently entrenched in a diminished view of precisely what is good in humanity, "a sarcasm of humans toward humans, and thus a hatred of oneself" (ibid., p. 234). And this singular ethical error finds its closest theological counterpart in the infamous blasphemy against the *Holy Spirit,* from which all Good springs. Opposing both evils, we must fuse "light and warmth, meaning knowledge and hope" (ibid., p. 229). It would be no more ridiculous for us to now deny this hope for Absolute Justice than for our animal ancestors to have ignored the sensuous pangs of hunger, thirst, boredom, and fear — which certainly would've bore a cold and *colourless* world. Like them, *we cannot live merely according to what presently is.*

Beside any reflexive scepticism lingering about such a remote possibility, there are certainly major critiques of this grand philosophy of justice to briefly sketch here. First, Harman argues this is an insufficient account of *what already is,* disregarding the achievements and powers of things in preference for a super-chaos "*without reserve*" (ibid., p. 177). This too has political consequences, as we cannot hope to simply break all laws one day, but must rather work *with* all co-legislators of the universe toward our ends. Second, Brassier thinks "Meillassoux mortgages the autonomy of the in-itself to chronology"[62] and wrongly ascribes to humanity the sole *reason for reason*, whereas Brassier holds that objects *force* us to think. Similarly, Catherine Malabou argues this lineage of Worlds places humans too close to the centre of reality once again, easily becoming a justification for human-supremacy and ownership of the lower, i.e., the *given,* World.[63] Finally, in the spirit of Schelling, as renewed by Grant, we are led to wonder: if such a Fourth World of Justice were to emerge, if God finally emerged, would this itself not halt all creation thereafter? — be the end of all time? Does not Nature eternally *require* her chaos to go on? Despite these critiques, we are given the most profound challenge by Meillassoux's philosophy, compelled to seek a new principle for thought and life, for a critically justified realism and absolute-ideal justice *beyond all precedent.*

What Is to Come of These Speculative Justices?

> "If justice perishes, then it is no longer worthwhile for men to live upon the earth."
> — Kant[64]

> "If we do not maintain justice, justice will not maintain us."
> — Francis Bacon

Through the correlationist's rigorous destruction of Absolute justifications, which split the world into the singular strife between untrustworthy humans and unknowable matter, every claim defending a genuine *reality to justice* became at once liable to accusations of dogmatic self-justification. The concept of justice had been stripped down to its socio-economic desert bones, with only the mirage oases of myth for our minds to yearn for. speculative realisms, as we have seen, sought to unleash refreshing philosophies onto this desolate landscape, defending some *absolute reality;* realisms that could not be mistaken for yet another dry regressive scepticism or teary-eyed reactionary dogmatism. Instead, each conceived a non-human, non-mechanical, non-mystical autonomy, rejecting the default vision of reality as pre-established Selves, Laws, Gods, preferring explicitly autonomous objects (Brassier, Harman) or else material absolutes (Grant, Meillassoux) as *the sovereign legislators of the World.*

What had so far been left behind in the background of this revolutionary project was a direct answer to philosophy's originary question — *what is justice?* The straightest answer was found in the mere fragments of one unpublished work by just one of these original four speculative philosophers. Nevertheless, this article gathered up a provisional answer from each of these four on the *reality of justice*, independent of human thought. We saw this first in Brassier's commitment to the trials of critical judgement, no matter how demanding or self-wounding, in order to cut off the greatest injustice — *false justice.* Then, in Grant's defence of Nature's innocent and on-going self-legislation, which exceeds all particular thoughts, laws, and subjects. And we saw it in Harman's flat fairness across object-hood, recognising the autonomy of even the least of things. Finally, we saw it in Meillassoux's meticulous justification for a renewed ontological justice to become, literally beyond all odds (and beyond all laws, for that matter). Between them, we are presented with vastly divergent targets around the general aim of justice. We are told that justice is an unrealisable hope by Brassier, while Meillassoux insists it is absolutely possible to realise. Conversely, we are told by the other two that justice is always only *partially* realisable, either because Nature is considered a never-ending experiment with itself by Grant, or because things are found to never completely unify or directly relate. Correspondingly, each of these views can helpfully be portrayed by symbolic eschatologies; namely, Brassier's *Judgement-Day* extinction event, Grant's naturalised *Genesis*, Meillassoux's virtual advent of a *Kingdom of Cosmic Justice*, and Harman's arguably most realistic — or least un-theological — *Mesotopia.*

There is certainly a great deal to be worked out (and already being worked out) in creating syntheses and alternatives to these philosophies just covered, and, in tandem, new speculations regarding this re-configured theme of justice. But before we conclude with a brief survey of this expanding canon of SR, let us regard some important critics who stand near the gate. An important critic to note is co-founding member Ray Brassier himself, who now criticises SR essentially as a myth and image (as, admittedly, he criticises *most* things), citing chiefly its lack of explicitly and exclusively shared tenets. He notes, as evidence, that many analytic philosophers have already been hard at work, speaking of the thing-itself first and foremost — namely, David Lewis, Michael Devitt, David Armstrong, Timothy Williamson, and Theodore Sider. But touching closer to the nerve, Brassier has publicly expressed resentment for the crude popularity of the conference as a "movement" at all. He laments that, "[p]erhaps they [the original four thinkers] would have burgeoned in philosophically fruitful ways had they not been prematurely petrified by branding".[65] For the sake of argument, let us suppose for a moment that SR really *is* a mere rebranding of continental philosophy, as Brassier implicates. Among the other original three, such an object as a "brand" would likely not be so swiftly rejected, as each of their models factors in the quasi-causality of even *unreal* things, like symbols and cultural artefacts, whether in the form of attractive ideas (Grant), alluring sensual objects (Harman), or virtual possibilities (Meillassoux). Meanwhile, Brassier himself only seems capable of downplaying such things as myths, illusions, and ideologies. More to the point: could one not level this same argument — with equivalent weight — against philosophies since Plato re-branded Heraclitus' becoming and Parmenides' Being as his own theory of dual forms? Do not such philosophical movements more resemble movements in the arts (like impressionism, cubism, surrealism) than religious creeds or state constitutions? Not only have other philosophical movements been loose brandings between figures with vastly distinct approaches — from idealism and materialism to existentialism, phenomenology, and pragmatism —

but it is difficult to imagine what could make a given philosophical movement count as anything more than a loose and humble *re-framing* for this nihilist.[66]

The more threatening critique against our project with SR has come mostly from Hegelians like Slavoj Žižek; namely, that justice is an exclusively *human* concern. More precisely, that universal ideals like justice are unveiled only to beings with self-reflective reason, and no beings but humans possess this odd ontological position-across our entire empirical-historical horizon. Worse still for SR, not only do humans have this unique status, according to Žižek and scholar Catherine Malabou, the correlationist dilemma was already solved by Hegel, whose Absolute knowing consists precisely of the moment where reality realises itself through negative logic as itself. Related to our theme of autonomy, in this exulted moment of Absolute knowing, we supposedly grasp and expand reality's own freedom on the Whole. Žižek famously dramatises this paradoxical vision of autonomy as an atheist-Christian theology, where we fragile humans take the seat of God, only to be forced to contend with the difficult and confusing task of making it all into our *own* ideal image.[67] Malabou — in a move closer to SR than Žižek's system — illustrates this autonomy-increasing Knowing as rationality's negative access to the primordial void of open freedom itself,[68] which is, she holds, the reality deeper than both human subjects and material objects. But whether or not Hegel successfully succeeded beyond the correlationist circle into his proposed Living Whole is a matter for deeper debate elsewhere. We can here say with more confidence that at least the structure of Hegel's argument and its empirical effect on philosophical discourse has been *confusion*, *division* (sometimes cited as the first crack between analytic and continental traditions, as well as the popularity of left/right politics as such), and also has inspired a vast proliferation of thinker-centred correlationist ontologies. This is no reason to neglect Hegel's own work, as he did not have the luxurious freedom to challenge this larger ontological *re-framing* following Kant — that would have been un-dialectical, in fact. And this returns us to the lingering question around SR's own re-framing and response to the claim that justice is a concern exclusive to humans. First, in the negative sense, SR is a movement that attempts to reframe philosophy to exclude naive realisms and reactionary dogma as well as the *self-circling* meanderings of phenomenological examination, dumb-struck existentialism, and literary deconstruction; in a word, continental thought that had gone stale. Secondly, and more positively, it is a movement drawn toward beginning its models from the POV of reality. Thus, for SR, the question of justice simply must begin with concern for reality itself, despite the obvious and seemingly insurmountable difficulties in doing so. For while we humans may be the only ones *concerned* with justice, justice *concerns* more than humans. And only such a speculative metaphysics is in the position to ask what to do when dealing with — not iron physical laws, cloudy mental constructions, or the blurred lines between self/world in special knowings — but autonomous reality itself.

Let us now finally turn to survey a select few of the noteworthy advances being made by SR thinkers, especially those orbiting this central theme of justice. Because those following in the vein of Brassier have largely opted out of identification with SR (the most prolific follower being Peter Wolfendale, whose work has most notably consisted of a critical book against OOO), we will instead begin by covering those most proximal to Grant's nature-philosophy, developing concepts of Absolute becoming(s). In the richly political philosophy of Thomas Nail, we find a perfect mirror reversal of OOO in a universally *motion*-oriented ontology, inspired most profoundly by Lucretius' swerve, with its eye of justice turned toward reckoning with the unmasterable migration of everything.[69] In Manuel DeLanda's excessively humble "realist interpretation" of Deleuze, we find an author concerned with the most universal problems of *design* across human and non-human realities,[70] as well as an author who reads sentence-for-sentence further beyond the correlationist circle than any of the original four. And in the promising philosophy of information being developed by Cecile Malaspina, we face the correlationist problem in the midst of its exchange of terms, in "epistemological noise".[71] Additionally, in her emphatic revival of Gilbert Simondon's concept of "pure information" (i.e., any metastable state open to a certain measure),[72] we are implicitly afforded an alternative to the reining anthropic measure of autonomy (say, by Hegelian Absolute knowledge), as this new measure of autonomy, rendered by pure information, applies just as much to human dialectics as it does every other communication system there is. For both DeLanda and Malaspina, across the totality of these moving, flowing, noisy operations, we glimpse a shared recognition that reality is not any static law nor obedient slave, and so, for them, justice must be in *co-operation*; working *with* — neither against nor around — the autonomy of manifold becomings.

Next, let us cover the thinkers nearest by Harman's object-oriented ontology. Worthy of note here also are the valiant diplomatic efforts of Levi Bryant and Niki Young, who have effectively translated OOO into its some of its chief enemies' terms (Deleuzian and Derridean, respectively). Then, there is Timothy Morton's profoundly politicised — even supposedly Communist — expansion of OOO, emphasising an ecology of hyperobjects and suggesting that justice will be found in reckoning with alienation head on, handling the sheer ambiguity of other entities by growing in *kindness*.[73] And, as if by chance or something in the air, the French philosopher Tristan Garcia developed an encyclopaedic theory of things remarkably close to OOO before once hearing of it.[74] He hints that the consequent theory of justice, following his own ontology, is a "letting be".[75] And another worthy of note in this cul-de-sac is philosopher Charles William Johns, whose early work centred around articulating the irreducible autonomy of objects, but whose recent turn has found him attempting to reconcile Hegel and OOO. One remarkable aspect of this new enterprise is the surprisingly *grounded* concept of *relative Absoluteness*. In this theory, Johns asks us to speculate the Earth itself as our own Absolute, since it serves as both its own conditions and products (i.e., a measure of maximal autonomy). The Earth also qualifies due to being orders of magnitude more *dialectically elaborated* than any of those more automatic reductions of matters to, say, plasma by stars, or to empty information around black holes, and the Earth may even be more "dialectically absolute" than the World as a "Whole" — which, following the insights of OOO, may well turn out to be an indifferent abstraction anyway. The payoff of this new theory is that, in speculatively taking the Earth as our Absolute, we refresh the original meaning of *human being* (i.e., "*buried being*") from the point of view of this "Other" (ex-timate) reality itself, identifying even ourselves as *earthlings* first and foremost. In doing so, we at once step outside the correlationist circle, beyond the division of thought and world, while also explicitly addressing the root of Hegelian injustice in *alienation*. For all these thinkers parallel to OOO, justice is certainty no longer above all an abstract-logical concern, but the sincere concern for things themselves.

A friendlier group of neighbours to SR than the Hegelians are those who take the speculative metaphysician of creative process and radical empiricism, Alfred North Whitehead, as the primary precursor to its formation. Harman himself has named Whitehead's influence the most important of any twentieth-century philosopher, having been an early combatant against the bifurcation of nature/culture, with preference for treating human and non-human entities on a level ontological playing field. The most well-known process philosophies working parallel to SR include Isabelle Strenger's Cosmopolitics, aimed at a magical justice beyond the capabilities of religion and science to be achieved by a post-human pragmatism, and Bruno Latour's actor-network theory, which presents an irreductionist metaphysics where the prime measure of justice is *alliance*. Importantly for both philosophies, *pluralism* is no longer taken as expressing merely different *perspectives* on reality, but rather as ontologically different *realities* within the world. Two other Whiteheadians have offered disparate accounts of process philosophy's compatibility with SR: Steven Shaviro has provided a critique of SR as a largely redundant and politically blindfolded movement in light of the work already achieved by Whitehead, while more recently Hilan Bensusan has provided a vision of Whiteheadian philosophy called "indexicalism", which he finds perfectly compatible with, and even furthered by, the SR canon. For Bensuasan, the ethico-political aim is the head-spinning task of discerning *maximal importance* across a sheer *untotalisable totality*. The natural question "*how to discern maximal importance?*" leads us to the final Whiteheadian neighbour to consider, Matthew Segall. Known primarily for his work on psychedelic research, the origins of organisms beyond just the biological, and the ancient philosophical concept of World-Soul, he has begun galvanising thinking around planetary justice as a divine and on-going *cosmic adventure.*[76] Overlapping most proximally to Meillassoux, Segall follows Whitehead's own project of secularising the concept of God, finding that divinity cannot so hastily be dismissed, but instead needs to grasp those most attractive, alluring, and promising notions of more-than-human *importance*. Although, Segall maintains — contrary to Meillassoux's one-and-done commencement of God's emergence — that each epoch is given its own unique divine occasion for which to rise, touching and being touched by eternal objects (like Goodness, Truth, Beauty) or else failing to do so — either way, thus setting the stage for the next epoch. As Whitehead put it, there is never a final end to such creative procession, but rather there is "always an element of unrest. For sensitiveness to ideas means curiosity, adventure, change".[77] Toward this aim of realising our present epoch's divine moment, Segall suggests a remarkably concrete action: reset our time-systems and start a new global calendar set to Year Zero.[78] The specific contrast between Segall's coincidence of the occasional/eternal and Meillassoux's culmination of the eternal by the vanquishment of contingencies — these two immanent ontologies tilted toward the seizure of divinity — certainly deserves to be fleshed out to further detail.

Stepping back to view the larger tapestry still being woven by this speculative movement within the grander view of philosophical history, it is beginning to appear that SR is the most explicit return by contemporary thought to Western philosophy's original schemata of *díkēphysis.* Let us examine its primary aspects on this level. Alongside the extensively covered *physis of autonomy*, we have also seen the notion of *díkē as secular divinity* emerge among a significant portion of speculative realists. Picking apart this latter notion, clearly, we see the *secular* aspect signals the desired satiation of our invaluable sceptical faculties, our deep and cutting intellect — in a word, secularity satisfies our hunger for true *justification*. The divine aspect has shown itself here as a way of harassing, persuading, coordinating our collective sensual and virtual sensibilities, to satisfy the demands of ethics and aesthetics — this divinity signals the very hunger for real *justice*. It seems sensible, then, that any future for a *speculative realist justice* belongs to those focused on incorporating these two prevailing aspects. Following this trajectory, they will no doubt *begin* with that open, flat, negative or positive recognition of sovereign autonomy, as there is still fruit to be gathered by such ontologies, which begin below the prevailing formal and dialectical logics to show their messier *analogue* roots, whether as Nature, Earth, matter, forces, flows, occasions, operations, acts, noise, or objects. And after establishing a fair base, there are more conversations to be had around generating *harmonies* across analogue assemblages, alliances, co-operations (perhaps to be measured by a new notion of *soundness,* expressing the asymptotically divine coincidence of resonant autonomies and their integral bonds). Similarly, there are more conversations to be had around the tension between philosophies prioritising objects or objectives, as we try to paradoxically balance reckoning with the inescapable Mesotopia of the world *just as it is*, while also not losing hope for the World *as it ought to be.*

Most of the enterprises just covered are at once *grander* in scope than Plato's *Republic* and palpably more *grounded* than prevailing existential, formal-linguistic, and post-structural thought. It should be no wonder why speculative realism has been so radically influential, for SR has proposed a remedy to the *weightless feeling* haunting much of contemporary philosophy by novel absolutes with ecological gravitas. But, however rhetorically weighty or aesthetically exciting, and however abundantly this tilling of modern thought by SR has nourished novel philosophies around the world, the most important issue for us will be whether these philosophies mark a fresh imprint upon the world in a step toward cosmic justice, or as just another fantastical way for people to ramble on about reality-in-itself without adequate justification. The latter possibility is the greatest danger lying ahead for this movement; Brassier is right to warn.

As I finish writing this, I'm seeing breaking reports that Russia is invading Ukraine. There is no telling what will happen between the titanic powers now in conflict. Out of all realities, this is ours, and there is no exit but by dying. Most realistically, despite our most profoundly realistic reflections, you and I will find ourselves unromantically powerless once again in preventing the greatest injuries of our world. And yet, I hear a voice say, "all the more reason to try".

References

Aristotle. *The Complete Works of, Vol. I & II*, translated, Revised Oxford, edited by Jonathan Barnes. Princeton: Princeton University Press, 1984.

Auden, W.H. *Collected Poems*. Vintage, 1991.

Bacon, Francis. *The Works of Francis Bacon, Vol. II*. Complutense University of Madrid, 1753.

Badiou, Alain. Saint Paul: *The Foundations of Universalism*, translated by R. Brassier. Stanford: Stanford University Press, 2003.

Brandom, Robert. *A Spirit of Trust: A Reading of Hegel's Phenomenology*. Cambridge; London: Belknap Press of Harvard University, 2019.

Brassier, Ray. *Alien Theory: The Decline of Materialism in the Name of Matter*. University of Warwick, 2011.

Brassier, Ray. "Dialectics Between Suspicion and Trust". *Stasis*, Vol. 4 (2) (2016), pp. 98–113.

Brassier, Ray. "The Enigma of Realism". In *Collapse II*, pp. 15–54, edited by Robin McKay. London: Urbanomic, 2007.

Brassier, Ray. *Nihil Unbound: Enlightenment and Extinction*. New York: Palgrave Macmillan, 2007.

Brassier, Ray. "Nihil Unbound: Remarks on Subtractive Ontology and Capitalism". In *Think Again: Alain Badiou and the Future of Philosophy*. Continuum, 2004.

Brassier, Ray. "Prometheanism and its Critics". In *#Accelerate: The Accelerationist Reader*, edited by Robin Mackay and Armen Avanessian, pp. 467–487. Falmouth: Urbanomic, 2014.

Brassier, Ray. "The View from Nowhere". *Identities, Journal for Politics, Gender, and Culture* Vol. 8, No. 2 (2011), pp. 7–23.

Collapse: Journal of Philosophical Research and Development. "Speculative Realism". Falmouth: Urbanomic, 2007, pp. 306–449.

Cornell, Drucilla, Michael Rosenfeld, & David Gray Carlson (eds). *Deconstruction and the Possibility of Justice*. New York: Routledge, 1992.

DeLanda, Manuel. *Assemblage Theory*. Edinburgh: Edinburgh University Press, 2016.

Derrida, Jacques. "Force of Law: The 'Mystical Foundation of Authority'". In Cornell, Rosenfeld, & Carlson, *Deconstruction and the Possibility of Justice*, pp. 3–67.

Dickinson, Emily. *The Complete Poems of*. Boston; Toronto: Little, Brown, 1976.

Dunham, Jeremy, Iain Hamilton Grant, & Sean Watson. *Idealism: A History of a Philosophy*. Durham: Acumen Publishing, 2011.

Ferreira, J.R., D.F. Leão, & C.A. Martins de Jesus (eds). *Nomos, Kosmos, & Dike in Plutarch*. Coimbra University Press, 2010.

Freud, Sigmund. *The Basic Writings of Sigmund Freud*, translated by A.A. Brill. Penguin Random House, 1995.

Gaddis, William. *A Frolic of His Own*. Poseidon Press, 1994.

Garcia, Tristan. *Form and Object: A Treatise on Things*, translated by M.A. Ohm & J. Cogburn. Edinburgh: Edinburgh University Press, 2014.

Garcia, Tristan. *The Life Intense: A Modern Obsession*. Edinburgh: Edinburgh University Press, 2018.

Grant, Iain Hamilton. "All the principles of being and becoming: Schelling's ontogenetic hypothesis". *Rivista di Estetica* 74 (2020), pp. 22–38.

Grant, Iain Hamilton. "Creation". Lecture for *World Philosophy Day* at the University of the West of England, 2013. [0:02:58]

Grant, Iain Hamilton. "Everything is Primal Germ or Nothing Is: The Deep Field Logic of Nature". *Symposium* Vol. 19, Issue 1, Spring (2015), Schelling After Theory, pp. 106–124.

Grant, Iain Hamilton. *Philosophies of Nature After Schelling*. London; New York: Continuum, 2008.

Grant, Iain Hamilton. "Nature After Nature". Lecture for the *Nature After Nature Symposium* at Fridericianum, 2014.

Grant, Iain Hamilton. "Philosophy and the Natural History of Mind". Lecture for the *Human Experience and Nature, Royal Institute of Philosophy Conference*, UWE, Bristol, 2011.

Grant, Iain Hamilton. "Postmodernism and politics". In *The Routledge Companion to Postmodernism*, edited by Stuart Sim. p. 25.

Harman, Graham. "Autonomous objects". *New Formations*, 71 (2011), pp. 125–130.

Harman, Graham. *Bruno Latour: Reassembling the Political*. London: Pluto Press, 2014. Harman, Graham. *Dante's Broken Hammer: The Ethics, Aesthetics, and Metaphysics of Love*. London: Repeater, 2016.

Harman, Graham. "I Am Also of the Opinion that Materialism Must Be Destroyed". *Environment and Planning D: Society and Space* 28:5, (2010).

Harman, Graham. *Guerrilla Metaphysics: Phenomenology and the Carpentry of Things*. Chicago; La Salle: Open Court, 2005.

Harman, Graham. *Heidegger Explained: From Phenomenon to Thing*. Chicago; La Salle: Open Court, 2007.

Harman, Graham. "Malabou's Political Critique of Speculative Realism". *Open Philosophy*, Vol. 4, No. 1 (2021), pp. 94–105.

Harman, Graham. *Object-Oriented Ontology: A New Theory of Everything*. Penguin: Pelican, 2018.

Harman, Graham. *Speculative Realism: An Introduction*. Cambridge: Polity Press, 2018. Harman, Graham. *Tool-Being: Heidegger and the Metaphysics of Objects*. Chicago; La Salle: Open Court, 2002.

Harman, Graham. "Undermining, Overmining, and Duomining: A Critique". *ADD Metaphysics*, edited by Jenna Sutela, pp. 40–51. Aalto: Aalto University Design Research Laboratory, 2013.

Harman, Graham. "Zero-person and the psyche". In *Mind that abides: panpsychism in the new millennium*, edited by David Skrbina, pp. 253–282. Amsterdam: John Benjamins Publishing Company, 2009.

Heidegger, Martin. *Early Greek Thinking*, translated by D. F. Krell & F. A. Capuzzi. San Francisco: Harper & Row, 1975.

Heidegger, Martin. *Schelling's Treatise on the Essence of Human Freedom*, translated by J. Stambaugh. Athens; London: Ohio University Press, 1985.

Herodotus. *The Histories*, translated by A. D. Godley, Loeb Classical Library. Cambridge: Harvard University Press, 1920.

Hopkins, Gerard Manley. *Complete Poems*. Penguin Classics, 1953.

Johns, Charles William. *Object-Oriented Dialectics*. Mimesis International Press, 2022.

Johns, Charles William. "Different Correlations: A Heuristic Approach". In *Speculative Realism Now*. Bloomsbury, 2024.

Kant, Immanuel. *Critique of Judgment*, translated by W. Pluhar. Indianapolis: Hackett, 1987.

Kant, Immanuel. *Critique of Pure Reason*, translated by P. Guyer & A. Wood. Cambridge: Cambridge University Press, 1999.

Kant, Immanuel. *The Metaphysical Elements of Justice*, translated by J. Ladd. Indianapolis; London: Hackett Publishing, 1999.

Latour, Bruno. *Reassembling the Social: An Introduction to Actor-Network-Theory*. Oxford; New York: Oxford University Press, 2007.

Malabou, Catherine. "The future of Continental philosophy", lecture at European Graduate School, 2014.

Malabou, Catherine. *The Future of Hegel: Plasticity, Temporality and Dialectic*. London; New York: Routledge, 2004.

Malaspina, Cecile. *An Epistemology of Noise*. London: Bloomsbury Press, 2018.

Malaspina, Cecile. "Pure information: on infinity and human nature in the technical object". *Culture, Theory and Critique*, 60:3–4 (2019). Routledge, pp. 205–222.

Mallarme, Stephane. *The Collected Poems of*, translated by Winfield, H.M. Berkley: University of California, 2011.

McLuhan, Marshall, & McLuhan, Eric. *Laws of Media: The New Science*. Toronto: University of Toronto Press, 1988.

Meillassoux, Quentin. "Appendix: Excerpts from L'Inexistence Divine". In *Quentin Meillassoux: Philosophy in the Making*, translated by Graham Harman, second edition. Edinburgh: Edinburgh University Press, 2015.

Meillassoux, Quentin. *After Finitude*, translated by Ray Brassier. London; New York: Continuum, 2008.

Meillassoux, Quentin. "Potentiality and Virtuality". *Collapse II*, edited by Robin McKay, pp. 15–54. Oxford: Urbanomic, 2007.

Morton, Timothy. *Humankind: Solidarity with Nonhuman People*. Verso, 2017.

Nail, Thomas. *Being and Motion*. Oxford University Press, 2018.

Nietzsche, Friedrich. *The Gay Science: With a Prelude in Rhymes and an Appendix of Songs*, translated by W. Kaufman. New York: Random House; Vintage, 1974.

Plato. *The Republic*, translated by Jowett, B. London: Arcturus, 2018.

Schelling, F.W.J. *First Outline of a System of the Philosophy of Nature*, translated by K.R. Peterson. SUNY Press, 2004.

Schmitt, Carl. *The Nomos of the Earth in the International Law of the Jus Publicum Europaeum*, translated by G.L. Ulmen. Telos Press, 2006.

Schopenhauer, Arthur. Essays and Aphorisms. Penguin Classics, 2004.

Segall, Matthew. *Physics of the World-Soul: Alfred North Whitehead's Adventure in Cosmology*. SacraSage Press, 2021.

Whitehead, Alfred North. *Adventures of Ideas*. Free Press, 1967.

Wolfendale, Peter. *Object-Oriented Philosophy: The Noumenon's New Clothes*. Falmouth: Urbanomic, 2014.

Žižek, Slavoj. *The Fragile Absolute*. London; New York: Verso, 2009.

The author thanks Valerie Lighthart, Tsai-Yi Wu, Josh & Josh, Frances Dillon, David Martie, and his parents.

Notes

1 "As I Walked Out One Evening", *Collected Poems* (Vintage, 1991).

2 "Global genealogical reduction" is a phrase Brassier borrows from the work of Robert Brandom.

3 Freud, S. "The Question of Lay Analysis", midway through Chapter 5.

4 Brassier gives credit to Jean-François Lyotard for first raising this question.
5 Brassier does not, to my knowledge, point out this example — but I find it a natural addition to his case against Nietzsche.
6 Brassier, 2007, p. 237, 7.5: The trauma of life: Freud
7 See Brassier, R. "The View from Nowhere" (2011).
8 Note an intriguing parallel with St Paul's claim that all are made equal under the death of Christ. This is also relevant because Brassier happened to translate Badiou's excellent work *Saint Paul: the Foundation of Universalism* (Stanford, 2003).
9 Brassier states his faith that "[n]on-materialism is the transcendental encryption of materialist Decision in such a way as to render the latter undecipherable according to the epistemic codes furnished by World-Capitalism" (Brassier, 2011, p. 436). Although elsewhere he readily admits: "Integrated global capitalism is constitutively dysfunctional: it works by breaking down. It is fueled by random undecidabilities, excessive inconsistencies, aleatory interruptions [...] harnessing the uncomputible" (Brassier, 2004, p. 57).
10 Schopenhauer, A. *Essays and Aphorisms* (Penguin, 2004), p. 148. "On Law and Politics". Brackets added.
11 "Beauty, brilliance, preciousness, and vibrancy are aesthetic rather than cognitive qualifications" (Brassier, 2007, p. 188).
12 Poem 501, *Complete Poems* (Back Bay Books, 1976).
13 "Nature After Nature" lecture (2014). Timecode [0:15:00]. Abbreviated NANL from hereon.
14 [3:20] NANL
15 Grant, I.H. *Philosophies of Nature after Schelling* (Continuum, 2008).
16 [32:22] NANL
17 Grant, I.H. Lecture on "Creation" at the University of the West of England for World Philosophy Day 2013–14 [0:02:58].
18 Marcel Proust, *In Search of Lost Time, vol. 5: The Captive & the Fugitive*; (1923–1925).
19 Schelling accuses Kant of giving boundless authority to science's mechanical explanation of nature. See Grant, 2008, p. 14.

20 Note that *Idealism: the History of a Philosophy* (Routledge, 2014) is co-authored with Sean Watson and Jeremy Dunham, thus authorship for each quote from this book is ambiguous.

21 "Whereas the [reductive] realist starts from atoms and builds up, the idealist starts from structure and builds down" (Dunham/Grant, 2011, p. 208); brackets mine for contextual clarification.

22 Grant, 2008, p. 90.

23 "The justice, which science makes into a law, is at the same time the highest law of the world." Schelling, *Philosophische Einleitung in die Philosophie der Mythologie*, pp. xi, 492, trans. I.H. Grant in the paper "All the principles of being and becoming: Schelling's ontogenetic hypothesis", pp. 22–38.

24 Grant is partly quoting Schelling here.

25 Grant quoting Tim. 51a1.

26 Grant, I.H. "Everything is Primal Germ or Nothing Is. The Deep Field Logic of Nature"; Symposium: Canadian Journal of Continental Philosophy, 19 (1), pp. 106–124.

27 "The Platonic gene is like a phase space of the Idea, diagrammed in the genesis of matter" (Grant, 2008, p. 45).

28 A point that Martin Heidegger writes extensively about in his works on Schelling.

29 Heidegger, M. *Schelling's Treatise: On Essence Human Freedom.* (OSU, 1985); pp. 101.

30 To quote from the article's conclusion, "if the tools of the past — Marxism, the Enlightenment project, market liberalism and so on — have been tried and found wanting, then experiment is demanded. [...] What new modernity might yet dawn from postmodern politics?" Grant, I.H. "Postmodernism and politics" in *The Routledge Companion to Postmodernism* (2011).

31 "God's Grandeur", *Complete Poems* (Penguin, 1953).

32 Harman, G. "Objects, a Brief Description" lecture delivered to AA School of Architecture — 23 April 2007. Timecode [0:03:40].

33 See Harman, G. "I am Also of the Opinion That Materialism Must Be Destroyed", *Environment and Planning D: Society and Space.* 2010; 28 (5): pp. 772–90.

34 See Harman, 2018, p. 50.

35 OOO "becomes the alibi for a doctrine that wishes to spare itself the trouble of justification" (Wolfendale/Brassier, 2014, p. 435).

36 This is the driving thrust of Peter Wolfendale's massive book against OOO, *Object-Oriented Philosophy: The Noumenon's New Clothes*. Urbanomic, 2019; (OOP). For this term, see Wolfendale, 2014, p. 402.

37 Brassier, R. "Concepts and Objects", in *The Speculative Turn* (2011), p. 48. Note that this is the same argument he uses against philosophies of difference. The relevant question — Harman will agree — is rather what makes a difference. For both thinkers the answer is surprisingly the same: the autonomy of the object.

38 "We become philosophers rather than aggressive ideologues by always being under way towards discovering what everything is" (Harman, 2018, p. 136).

39 "Only philosophy, not physics, can do justice to physis" (Harman, 2007, p. 107).

40 Harman 2018, p. 180.

41 The word has shared hypothetical Proto-Indo-European roots [*dheigw — "to point", "to straighten"] with the Hebrew term for justice "tzedek" [קדצ] and the Sanskrit "dharmika" [धार्मक्यि] and "dehin" [देहनि्] which means "embodied", "walled", and also "soul". There is significant etymological overlap of this common root with the English terms "dig" "ditch", "digit", "dice", and "fix".

42 See Herodotus' *The Histories* (Cambridge, 1920).

43 Schmitt, C. *The Nomos of the Earth in the International Law of the Jus Publicum Europaeum* (Telos, 2006), p. 70.

44 The pre-Socratics are read here as classic underminers: "the pre-Socratics were tacitly committed to all four of the basic notions that OOO rejects: physicalism, smallism, anti-fictionalism and literalism" (Harman, 2018, p. 46).

45 Harman's fourfold tensions resemble "Heidegger's own concept of justice [which] holds its four constituent terms in a kind of permanent strife or instability" (Harman, 2007, p. 125).

46 Also known as the problem of vicarious causation. See Harman, 2005, p. 93.

47 See Harman, G. "Malabou's Political Critique of Speculative Realism" (2021).

48 "Everyone has to theorize utopia and dystopia all the time. Drama queens. We will actually end up with a mesotopia, as usual. Let's try to figure out how to make it a better one." Harman, G. https://twitter.com/DrZamalek/status/1451620875602563076

49 "Radical politics as we know it is an outgrowth of modern philosophy with its modern idealism, and hence is unlikely to survive much longer than modern philosophy itself" (Harman, 2018, pp. 145–6).

50 Even after agreeing with Harman that it is important to stay cautious of the extremes of political idealism and nihilism, there may be some bite to this claim against OOO. In its commitment to describing things just as they (presently) are Harman may be undermining ethics which involves the reality of others to aesthetics which only alludes to them. OOO may be stuck in the idea that things already possess the qualities essential to them, thus deflating the account for purposiveness.

51 *A Frolic of His Own* (Poseidon, 1994).

52 See Harman, G. Quentin Meillassoux (2011); Appendix — *L'Inexistence Divine* (The Divine Inexistence) [excerpts].

53 Foucault, M. *Madness and Civilization*, 1961, p. 109.

54 A prime example of course is Plato's Idea where "Justice is inscribed once more in being, as a harmony of elements in the midst of the Whole. […] The Cosmos depicts the justice that guides the celestial world: […] a course that is uninterrupted and devoid of conflict" (ibid., p. 104).

55 "In revealing the contingency of laws, reason itself teaches that becoming is ultimately without reason" (ibid., p. 176).

56 Meillassoux's treatment of the ancient problem of evil offers something like an ontological extrapolation of Martin Luther King Jr's famous proclamation, paraphrased here.

57 See McLuhan, M. *The Gutenberg Galaxy*.

58 "It is not a question here of some exorbitant conception of justice, but only of giving a precise exposition of it in its excessiveness, since justice is only such an extravagance towards the present world by which the human condition is specified" (ibid., p. 192).

59 "In this way, one can compare the free act to a throw of the dice. A throw of the dice never guarantees chance, but is that alone which makes chance possible" (ibid., p. 216).

60 When it comes to absolute Justice, "the universal is universal only when it makes no exceptions" (ibid., p. 192).

61 "Atheism diminishes humans and humiliates their projects, by deposing what it believes to be a simple myth" (ibid., p. 234).

62 Brassier, R. "Enigma", *Collapse*, 2007, p. 32.

63 Malabou, C. "The future of Continental philosophy" lecture at European Graduate School (2014) [0:27:00].

64 Kant, I. *The Metaphysical Elements of Justice* (*Die Metaphysik der Sitten*) [1797], 1996, remark E after paragraph p. 49.

65 Brassier, R. (Wolfendale, 2014, p. 414); brackets added. He has in mind mostly the work of Graham Harman, who did the lion's share of work expanding the "Speculative Realist" movement throughout academia and (relatively) popular culture.

66 Final point regarding branding and Brassier: it turns out being the Contrarian is also a sure-fire way to stand out on the market!

67 Žižek, S. *Fragile Absolute*, Verso, 2009.

68 Malabou, K. *The Future of Hegel*, 2004.

69 Nail, T. *Being and Motion*, 2018.

70 DeLanda, Manuel. *Assemblage Theory*. 2016.

71 See Malaspina, C. *An Epistemology of Noise*, 2018.

72 See Malaspina, C. "Pure Information", Routledge, 2019.

73 See Morton, T. *Humankind*. 2017.

74 See Garcia, T. *Form and Object: A Treatise on Things*.

75 See Garcia, T. *The Life Intense*, 2018.

76 Segall, M. "Evolutions of Consciousness: Toward a Future Human Commons" [27:00]

77 Whitehead, A. *Adventure of Ideas*, 1967, p. 83.

78 Segall, M. *Physics of the World-Soul*, 2021.

CHAPTER 6

INTERVIEWS

OBJECT-ORIENTED ONTOLOGY IN THE POST-PANDEMIC AGE: INTERVIEW WITH GRAHAM HARMAN

Abstract:
Graham Harman, the founder of the philosophical school Object-Oriented Ontology, is Distinguished Professor of Philosophy at the Southern California Institute of Architecture. He was recently named by *Academic Influence* as the world's eighth most influential philosopher during the decade 2010–2020. This interview is conducted by Dr Tsaiyi Wu at the *ICL* Young Scholar Forum (2021, Series No. 1): *International Comparative Literature in the Post-pandemic Age—the Path and Ethics of Dialogue*, hosted by the editorial office of *International Comparative Literature* (Shanghai Normal University). In this interview, Harman speaks in a first-person, sincere, and familiar voice on three different aspects that readers are eager to know: how Harman himself becomes a philosopher of international and interdisciplinary stature; how Object-Oriented Ontology addresses the ecological and ethical

issues of the post-pandemic age; and the formation of OOO as well as its conversation with contemporary scholarship.

Keywords: Graham Harman, Object-Oriented Ontology, Post-pandemic Age, Aesthetics, Ethics

Author[1]

Tsaiyi Wu is a lecturer at the Research Center of Comparative Literature and World Literature, Shanghai Normal University. Her fields of study include modernist literary and contemporary philosophy. Currently, she is most interested in inquiring the human conditions and human responsibility in the post-pandemic age.

Part I. Love and Hope of Doing Philosophy

WU: *What was the idea that made you fall in love with philosophy in the first place, and is that idea still relevant to your thinking now?*

Harman: My mother enrolled me for a couple of philosophy classes against my will, proving that she knew me better than I knew myself, as is often the case with mothers. One was a group reading of Plato's *Apology, Crito*, and *Phaedo*, conducted by a local professor when I was 14. I didn't like it. At that age, I thought it was just pious discussions of justice and virtue and similarly vague notions. In fact, it took a long time before I could appreciate Plato the way I do now. The second class was a night class at our high school and covered the philosophy of law: scenarios such as whether two survivors in a lifeboat were guilty of murder for eating a third person. Those sorts of case studies interested me a bit more than the Plato class had; I would have been 15 by then. But the lightning-strike came at 16. I spent one night ignoring my homework and reading the whole article on philosophy in our encyclopaedia set. This was different: the history of philosophy was presented as a sequence of daring speculative theories about reality as a whole. Sort of like the history of physics — which already intrigued me — but covering lots of topics that physics could never touch. That was it for me. I was hooked, and there has never been any doubt about the basic direction of my life since that moment. That's actually somewhat surprising, since prior to that moment I had been a sort of aimless and lazy teen with no clear sense of my future direction.

Wu: *What keeps your hope alive, in spite of our political nightmares and ecological crisis in the post-pandemic age? Do you feel we philosophers have a duty to hope?*

Harman: I have a tendency to find hope in precisely those things that make others feel hopeless. For instance, at one point in my twenties, I felt nervous about flying due to several consecutive instances of unnerving turbulence on recent flights. My instinctive way of dealing with this may strike some readers as grotesque, but I somehow knew it would work. Namely, I sat down and read the whole Wikipedia article about all of the commercial plane crashes in history. I read the death tolls and the established cause for each crash. The first thing I noticed is the rather small number of such crashes compared to the total number of commercial flights that have occurred. The second thing I noticed was that vanishingly few of those crashes were caused by anything resembling turbulence. To this day, I am utterly untroubled by any turbulence during a flight, no matter how severe.

When it comes to the ecological crisis, my way of thinking is analogous. First, I read the recent climate report. Where others saw it as cause for more horror as usual, I made sure to zero in on the small amounts of good news in the report. I would say there were three pieces of good news: (1) we do still have a legitimate chance of limiting the damage, even if 2 degrees Celsius of warming seems like an inevitable minimum; (2) it seems unlikely that the Antarctic ice shelf will all melt away, which I had previously assumed was inevitable; (3) the currents in the North Atlantic are unlikely to go completely haywire and turn Europe into a desert, which I had also thought to be inevitable. Yes, the Arctic and Greenland ice are doomed, and sea levels will continue to rise for centuries or millennia, no matter what we do. And human behaviour during the pandemic has often been so stupid that I no longer trust most of my fellow creatures to behave helpfully in connection with the climate. So, still plenty of bad news. But the situation could be worse.

And furthermore, I have become better at resisting the human tendency to exaggerate. People see bad climate news and they say things like, "We're screwed! We're all going to die!" No, we aren't all going to die. Like many exaggerations, these are designed to avoid facing the very large *finite* disaster we are going to face. It could well be that 80–90% of humans die over the course of a century. There will be horrible scenes of abandoning entire countries to their fate, and the local and regional collapse of societies, agricultural production, medical networks, and of basic humane behaviour. All of this is miserable enough. But it is extremely unlikely that the human species as a whole will perish. We will exist in smaller numbers, no doubt, and this planet may be a very unpleasant place for a long time. But such things have happened before, if for different reasons. There have been unimaginable scenes of terror, famine, extinction, and mass murder at various points in human history, and yet other humans have come afterward and found life worth living. We can be fearful for our own fate and the fate of the younger generations now with us, but the human species is likely to awaken to other dawns that are not yet visible. Speaking in catastrophic terms of "extinction" is a way of erasing the finite (if colossal) problems that actually face us.

Part II: OOO in the Post-Pandemic Age

Wu: *In the post-pandemic age, we feel at every moment the weight of objects on us: that of coronavirus, of extreme heat waves, floods and forest fires. Against this background, what does OOO have to offer us?*

Harman: Most of the prominent philosophies in the continental tradition these days are subject-oriented. Let me start by naming two thinkers with whom I am friendly and for whom I have a high intellectual regard as well: Catherine Malabou and Slavoj Žižek. I recently wrote articles about both of them concerning this very topic. Both have a very strong sense that change will come primarily from the human political imagination. Yes, Malabou and Žižek both have their realist moments: Malabou when she speaks of neuroplasticity as a partial constraint on human freedom, and Žižek when he insists (against Alain Badiou and Jacques Rancière) on the enduring importance of economics. But when push comes to shove, they both consider the human being as having immense powers to retroactively determine the character of reality itself.

It seems to me that this way of thinking about politics belongs squarely within the modern tradition and its idolisation of the cogito. What will that do for us in a world of novel deadly viruses and skyrocketing levels of carbon dioxide? It seems to me that this is the very moment to make an object-oriented turn in political theory. Fortunately, as almost always happens, this doesn't need to be invented from scratch by me: Bruno Latour has already done a great deal of the work, as I argued in a book on his politics published 7 years ago, and since then he has developed his political thinking further, while picking up and using my term "object-oriented politics" as well.

People still tend to analyse politics in terms of the spectrum between Left and Right, a purely modern distinction from the era of the French Revolution that hinges primarily on whether humans were good (Left) or evil (Right) in some imagined state of nature. But what if human nature is beside the point, since the political sphere is structured and stabilised mostly by inanimate objects? This is what Latour brings to the picture, and he is the contemporary author who influences my political thinking the most right now.

Wu: *OOO is known for its claim that "aesthetic is first philosophy", and argues that a literary metaphor can reveal the plenitude of the* *object, which we may experience through a sympathetic bond. If, in the past, one most intense sensuous experience might be going to a 3D movie theatre and watching a fantasy film, since the year of 2020 we are experiencing direct and dire assaults from reality. We have uncompromising physical experience with the object, of staying at home, of power outage due to the heat or snowstorms, of crowded hospitals, and undue deaths. I was wondering, would all these change your thinking about the real?*

Harman: To some extent, even existentialism was aware of this role of the real: I'm thinking of Karl Jaspers' notion of limit-situations (*Grenzsituationen*), such as accidents. A few years ago in Ankara, Turkey, I stumbled on the curb and landed head-first on the sidewalk. Blood was everywhere and I was soon in the emergency room getting stitches above my eye. The injury wasn't serious; there isn't even a scar remaining. But it was deeply disturbing to lose control of my basic physical well-being like that, and it left a melancholic mark on my thinking for several months. And of course, there are many traumas much bigger than that undergone by people every day.

Such trauma — including the long collective trauma we've all lived through during COVID — is one form of contact with the real, though I would hesitate to overemphasise its importance. I think this is the mistake made by Jacques Lacan, who reaches this impasse because he can only deal with the real at the point where it meets with and disrupts the symbolic order. He does this consciously, making a reasonable argument for it in his Seminar IV (2020). But this shows how Lacan is too much an heir of the modern era as well, even though we can still learn a great deal about the human psyche from his works.

What modernity finds it nearly impossible to think is the relation between two objects apart from any human observer, except by passing it to the natural scientists and letting them dictate to us what happens here. It is a part of the enduring legacy of Immanuel Kant, who converts any relation into how it is accessible to the relation between the world and human thought. It is the repeated mistake that prevents us from escaping the basic parameters of modern philosophy. Even my fellow speculative realist Quentin Meillassoux, a really talented thinker, falls into this perpetual trap: "If you speak about something, you speak about something that is given to you, and posited by you" (see Brassier et al., 2007, p. 409). But this overlooks the function of names as theorised by Saul Kripke (1980).

Perhaps more importantly, it fails to account for aesthetic experience as an encounter with that which is *not* really given, though somehow vaguely compelling. In this respect, I would say that Meillassoux, like Markus Gabriel — another very talented contemporary philosopher — is too much of a literalist (see Gabriel, 2015). But OOO is all about the limits of literalism (see Harman, 2018, pp. 59–102). Reality is no more convertible into accurate propositional content than a globe is transferrable onto a two-dimensional map. There will always be distortion of size, shape, or both when such transfer occurs. And — why not? — we can throw in a reference to quantum theory here as well. According to Werner Heisenberg, you can't know both the position and momentum of a particle; according to Niels Bohr, that's because it doesn't have them prior to measurement. Of course, that doesn't mean that there is no *particle* there prior to measurement, simply that some of its properties are relational rather than integral.

Wu: *OOO holds that human consciousness is not different "in kind" from other relationships to the world, nor different from, say, a sea turtle feeling its way toward the sea or the slow stretching of a plant toward the sun. But I found one point held by Žižek somewhat compelling: human consciousness alone possesses a "universal scope" of cognition. Why is it important for OOO to hold that this is not an ontological distinction in kind from other objects' relations to the world? Especially since, in the age of the pandemic and global warming, we must have this universal scope to make decisions and take actions?*

Harman: My question to Žižek is this: why jump straightaway to the word "universal"? It would be enough, I think, to say that humans are apparently able to take an interest in a huge number of things by comparison with other life forms, as far as I can tell. In fact, this is why I distrust the discourse of human "transcendence" as well as any nihilistic attitude. Right now, I can look up all the birds of India online and admire their colours and songs for hours on end. Someone on Twitter was joking recently that one weird thing about males in particular (this is certainly true of me, for example) is that we can spend a whole evening doing nothing but mentioning to each other the names of former athletes from our childhood and have the time of our lives in doing this. People are very interested in things like comic books, clothes, wines, Roman history, and so forth. As far as we know, animals don't have this vast range of possible interests and enthusiasm, and to that extent I agree with Žižek.

But why always this jump from very large to "universal" or "infinite"? Timothy Morton wrote a whole book, *Hyperobjects* (2013), about the fallacy of always jumping from very large finite numbers to infinity. This is the Hegelian in Žižek talking — the Hegel who redefines the infinite as something that is inherently graspable. But Žižek has no idea what it is like to be a dolphin, or an alien. The Sumerians would never have understood Georg Cantor's transfinite mathematics, so at least historically, we are limited. And no doubt we are limited by certain structural features of the human mentality, as Kant already held. And Žižek, as a Lacanian, is also biased in favour of a Lacanian conception of the unconscious, which removes anything possibly deep and mysterious from the unconscious and makes it an immanent series of gaps and mishaps in language. But in all likelihood, this is simply a structuralist bias on Lacan's part, and there is actually something deep and mysterious in the unconscious.

I'm not opposed to the idea that humans are special in certain ways. At the very least, since we are humans, we are special to ourselves. But I distrust the assumption, found commonly among both idealist philosophers and mathematicians (and Alain Badiou combines both of these) that humans have attained some radical stance of direct access to truth. There is still need for a philosophical anthropology that considers us as *anthropos*, a specific and limited sort of creature, not as being able to read the language of God in an equation.

Wu: *In the age of Anthropocene, we humans are responsible for the future of the planet, for the global warming due to our activities, and for this we must drastically change our ways of using energy to achieve carbon neutrality, etc. I wonder for OOO, which claims that we humans are ontologically not different from a grain of sand of the beach, how do you convince people of our responsibility for the Earth?*

Harman: OOO simply holds that we are not *ontologically* different from a grain of sand on the beach. Flat ontology is only a first step, one that helps us to reconfigure the modern bias that I call "onto-taxonomical". Onto-taxonomy is simply the notion that there are primarily two kinds of things in the cosmos: (1) human thought, and (2) everything else.[2] On its face, this seems like an absurd idea. But modern philosophers aren't idiots, of course. They make this distinction because we supposedly have direct access to what lies in human thought and only mediated access to everything else. This is not the place to argue in detail against this assumption; I mention it only to clarify what OOO opposes. Alfred North Whitehead was the rare post-Kantian dissenter who placed all relations on the same footing, and I take inspiration from his courage on this point (see Whitehead, 1978).

In any case, the way to convince people that humans are responsible for climate change *is not* to get them to endorse modern onto-taxonomy. In other words, it's not because modern philosophy begins with the *cogito* that one should be convinced of anthropogenic climate change. That has to come from the details of the climate record and the state of the art in atmospheric chemistry and climate science more generally. And of course, human responsibility for climate change does not mean that the *cogito* is responsible for climate change. Lots of non-human elements play a role, such as carbon dioxide, methane, nitrous oxide, rock weathering, Atlantic currents, possible volcanic sulphur dioxide emissions, and the like. But none of these other elements can be handled very well by a subject-oriented philosophy like the sorts that have been in vogue again since around the time of Jacques Derrida's death in 2004. (That was the point when Žižek and Badiou became the most prominent living continental thinkers, and when the philosophical fashions changed from post-subject and left-liberalism back to the subject and hardcore leftism. People sometimes forget that the fashions will move on again, someday.)

Part III. Dr Harman and Contemporary Scholarship

Wu: *The inaccessibility of things; the withdrawn-ness of things; the weird realism; the mystery of things; the allusion and allure; the gaps among the real objects, real features, sensual objects and sensual features; the ontography; the concept of hyperobjects; the active role of things…*

> *OOO has proved to be very productive in the field of literary analysis and criticism, and I myself have benefited tremendously from your ideas. As you have said, at an interval of 4 years, you have always been able to re-think your ideas and put forward something new. Then, do you have something new to offer us with regard to the availability of OOO to literary studies, some 10 years after you published "The Well-Wrought Broken Hammer: Object-Oriented Literary Criticism" in* New Literary History*?*

Harman: There is an article from a few years ago entitled "Poe's Black Cat", in which I try to add more detail to the methods of an object-oriented approach to literature (2019). But an even better answer to your question is that I took a detour away from literary studies into art and architecture, while still working on terms relevant to literature.

In recent years, the study of literature has witnessed a rehabilitation of "formalism", an idea that went out of fashion across the arts from the early 1960s onward. Caroline Levine and Anna Kornbluh are two of the scholars linked with this new formalism, and in a different way, Tom Eyers, who has an intellectualist and Marxist spin on the term.[3] Though I consider Eyers to be an anti-formalist in my sense, he's a very productive representative of the other side.

As I see it, both the traditional formalists and the anti-formalists take the same extreme position. Kant's *Critique of Judgment* (1987) can be viewed as the original text of aesthetic formalism, in the sense that he finds beauty to be irreducible to specific rules, to personal preferences, or to the prose meaning of an artwork, but treats it as something beyond all these, and governed solely by "taste". This is all very important, and I side with this sort of formalism over the anti-formalist method that simply allows people to assert the importance of whatever influences from outside the text happen to be their favourites. It is all too easy to claim the moral high ground and act as the representative of some moral or political truth that can then be used either to praise or denounce any given artwork on the basis of that truth. Alternatively, the anti-formalist can claim (in a disappointingly abstract spirit) that nothing can be considered apart from history, but then they go on to pick *particular* historical influences arbitrarily and explain the text away in terms of them. I always learn something from New Historicist criticism, but it almost always strikes me as arbitrary in this way.

For that reason, I will always prefer formalism to its opposite, however old-fashioned it may look at any given moment. But Kant made the mistake of identifying the autonomy of the artwork with one specific *kind* of autonomy: the mutual independence of the work and its human beholder — to use Michael Fried's (1998) famous term. As I argued in *Art and Objects*, and even more so in the forthcoming *Architecture and Objects*, the work need not be separated from the beholder. Quite the contrary: the work *needs* its beholder, and the work and its consumer form a new third object that must *itself* be cut off from its surroundings. So, there is a point of intersection with reader-response theory as well (see Iser, 1978).

The aesthetic unit, in other words, is a new object formed of the work and its reader, beholder, or listener. This is the autonomous real object in question in art, not either of the two terms taken in isolation. But this work also admits some elements that do come from the outside. We cannot understand Picasso without knowing that Cézanne is there too, as a silent dialogue partner. We cannot make any sense of Charles Dickens without knowing something about the Industrial Revolution, and perhaps the most obvious example is that *Uncle Tom's Cabin* would make little sense at all as science fiction: there actually had to be real American slavery for that book to have the impact it did. I would add biographical factors to the mix: Emily Dickinson's poetic idiosyncrasies have to be grasped partly in terms of her literary isolation and relative lack of critical feedback. So, the anti-formalists are obviously sometimes right. The mistake is when people leap to the philosophical conclusion that, since no work is purely an island, then every artwork is obviously part of a holistic web of cultural and economic relations and must be understood in terms of such a web.

But as I argued in *Immaterialism*, in the case of the Dutch East India Company, it is simply not true that everything affects everything else. A historical event that serves as a decisive influence on one writer might mean nothing at all to another. For any object — and for me, authors too are objects — a half-dozen or so important relations are the only ones in play.

What makes me the most suspicious of all, of course, is when one particular environmental influence is taken to be dominant over everything else. This might happen, for instance, if a Freudian critic were to take every piece of literature to be ultimately about the Oedipus Complex. But what I'm really thinking of is Marxism, which has a tendency to devour everything by blaming it all on capitalism. The great exemplar of this among American critics is

Fredric Jameson, who has obviously had a remarkably influential career (see Jameson, 1974). For my next piece of writing on literature, I'm thinking of explaining my disagreement with Jameson's (2016) interpretation of the great detective writer Raymond Chandler, who is not only one of my favourite writers, but also a fellow Los Angeles resident now that I've moved here.

Wu: *To most scholars,* Tool-Being: Heidegger and Metaphysics of the Objects *(2002) is the starting point of your OOO. Looking back, now it has been almost 20 years, do you have any comments on your early academic direction? What is the beauty of Heidegger that caught your attention? How did you create a philosophical school out of re-reading another philosopher? And have your ideas taken any twist and turns, in the past or now due to the pandemic?*

Harman: Like many young philosophers, I had an early interest in Nietzsche. What was unusual in my case, for an American, was an attraction to Spanish philosophy, which was initially a fluke based on the fact that my parents gave me Julián Marías' *History of Philosophy* as a Christmas gift when I was 16. Marías' teacher, José Ortega y Gasset (see Ortega y Gasset, 1975), became an intense interest of mine, and I have said before that his essay on metaphor — read as a freshman at age 18 or 19, a year before I got serious about Heidegger — was perhaps the most formative influence on what would become OOO. I read that essay in the college library in 1987, but only when writing *Guerrilla Metaphysics* in 2004 did I finally figure out the mechanics of how it worked. In other words, I was chewing on that essay for 17 years; it was always in the back of my mind, and I still think it is one of the most important works of twentieth-century philosophy.

Well then, back to Heidegger. He and Ortega are just 6 years apart in age, and others before me have noted some similarities between them. But I came to Heidegger along a different path. First, I was interested in Husserl, and distrusted Heidegger's darker tone and more tangled language. At age 17, I earned a few hundred dollars from agricultural labour one summer, a typical thing to do in Iowa. I used $35 or $40 of that money to buy a copy of *Being and Time* from a store in Iowa City, where the university is located. The first three times I tried to read it, I did not get very far, and always quit.

Then, in February 1988, as a sophomore, I was frustrated with a classroom discussion on logic. I walked into the campus bookstore after class and purchased Heidegger's *Metaphysical Foundations of Logic*, which didn't help me with my questions about logic, but did open up a fascinating new world of Heidegger, on the one hand, and G.W. Leibniz, his topic, on the other. I would go into empty classrooms alone at night, read that book for hours alone, and copy Heidegger's diagrams in chalk on the board. And of course, I also read the pages of that book that included the moving obituary for Max Scheler.

All of this left a deep impression. In short order, I read every work of Heidegger's that our library had in English, with a special fondness for "Vom Wesen des Grundes" in the English translation by filmmaker Terrence Malick; the copy in the college library still had my illicit marginal notes in pencil the last time I visited. I had had 4 years of high-school German, but didn't work very hard at anything in high school, and needed to start working on German seriously, which I did just to read Heidegger. I spent most of my twenties reading through all of his works in German, which became very easy after the first two volumes, since his vocabulary is so repetitive.

What always fascinated me most in Heidegger was the famous tool-analysis. Everyone else was fascinated too, and much had already been written on the topic. But all of it seemed to me to miss the point. People really seemed to think that Heidegger was analysing equipment in the literal sense, as if it were just one kind of entity among others, whereas it seemed to me to go well beyond that. Also, people seemed very impressed by the apparent distinction between theory and praxis, which seemed to me like a mere triviality. From these suspicions, there eventually grew the basic structure of *Tool-Being*, my doctoral dissertation and then (3 years later) first published book.

But in my life, it seems that everything happens slowly. My dissertation took too long to finish. I published nothing in philosophy until age 34, though I have since published at what someone called "industrial levels" of quantity. So, I've always had to be patient because things generally don't happen as quickly for me as they do for others. Also, many of my teachers didn't like the way I did things, so early on, I had to build up independent judgement and a hard outer shell as protection from indifference toward and occasional ridicule of my work. And all of this has served me well.

After publishing *Tool-Being*, I had the same experience as many first-time authors: a kind of prolonged depression, out of the sense that no one at all was reading it. All that work for nothing! But that was an illusion; many people were reading *Tool-Being* from the start, and it just took years for me to meet enough of them to realise it. Jon Cogburn even paid a few hundred dollars for his copy, analytic philosopher though he is. When I later met Bruno Latour, I would often hear him complain about how all his books were going into the garbage unread, which is completely absurd in his case: he has been cited over a quarter of a million times! But it seems to be a universal illusion of authors that no one is reading them. And readers have the opposite illusion: they assume that authors are being swarmed with attention over their books, when in fact, most of the time one is alone and doesn't hear back from readers even when they are actively reading.

As far as building up a philosophical school, that happened gradually. You might meet a few interesting people per year over the course of two decades. Occasionally, you might have a falling out with one of them, but then you meet others. If you just keep on working, you'll find your readers. You have to be a workhorse: sheer quantity of work is more important in building up a critical mass of ideas than some people want to think. Putting an idea in words, perhaps rewording it in multiple publications, is key to getting beyond that idea and formulating a better one.

As for your question about "twists and turns" in my ideas over the years, I find that I have a really transformative idea every 4 years or so. It's uncanny how regular that rhythm is. Usually, it's not provoked by an outside event like the pandemic, but there seems to be a 4-year minimum calendar time for me to work through and exhaust any given stage of ideas, and then the new stage quickly emerges from the previous one. It begins with subverbal intuitions that something is wrong, but eventually I find the words for it.

Wu: *I marvel at your unparalleled knowledge of the complexities of Latour's work. As we know, there was a famous public discussion between you and Latour at the London School of Economics in February 2008. Would you like to tell us the significance of this event? What does Latour's view on modernity, on science, and his political philosophy have in common, in conflict, and conversation with your own work? I was curious, also, why you like to call Latour "a prince" for the titles of your two introductory books on Latour:* Prince and Networks: Bruno Latour and Metaphysics, *and* The Prince and the Wolf: Latour and Harman at the LSE*?*

Harman: I'm perfectly willing to go out on a limb and call Latour the most important philosopher working today. This is not meant as an invidious remark against all of the other important philosophers I've had the privilege to know. But as I see it, the rut in which contemporary philosophy is largely stuck is that of "onto-taxonomy", and Latour is the one who grabs this bull by the horns with his critique of modernity (see Latour, 1993). We've had our differences over the years, and our warm periods and cool periods, but I can never repay the intellectual debt I owe to Latour. It is not only the importance of his ideas, but the fact that he took me seriously from our first meeting, when I was a 31-year-old fresh PhD. As a graduate student, one receives a lot of condescending behaviour from one's own professors, but Latour was at a completely different level, and nonetheless treated me like someone whose feedback on his work was valuable and important.

I greatly admire the sum total of his intellectual output, and I think it will only look more important as time passes. Our major difference is simple, and has led to actual unpleasant arguments at times: Latour has a relational conception of actors, while I incline toward the non-relational tradition of the thing-in-itself and the various substance philosophies from Aristotle through the Medievals through Leibniz.

As for the 2008 event at the LSE, all of the credit for setting it up goes to Peter Erdélyi, who is listed as one of the co-authors of *The Prince and the Wolf*, and whose Foreword to the book tells the whole history of the event (see Latour et al., 2005, pp. 1–20). I met Erdélyi when he was in the audience at a lecture I gave at Goldsmiths in 2007. We quickly became friends, and one thing led to another, until finally he pitched the idea to Latour of a conference to discuss my manuscript for *Prince of Networks* (2009).

As for the word "Prince", I started with the working title for the book of "King of Networks", which I had used as a lecture title years earlier in Chicago (see Harman, 2010). But then I started playing with *Prince* instead, partly because "Prince of Networks" had a nice resonance with the phrase "Prince of Darkness". Erdélyi chose the title *The Prince and the Wolf*, playing on my manuscript title, and on Latour's reference in the discussion to philosophers as wolves who won't leave him alone.

Wu: *While Object-Oriented Ontology is often characterised as a major part of the "the material turn" in the twenty-first century, you debate fiercely as to whether "object" or "relations" deserve a more fundamental ontological status. For you, New Materialism often reduces objects to either internal relations, such as what they are made of, or external relations, such as what they do; but neither can account for the* inexhaustibility *of the object as a conceptual unit.*

To challenge New Materialism as put forward by Jane Bennett, you have even once labelled your philosophical view as an Immaterialism, because an object does not need to be "inanimate, durable, nonhuman, or made of physical matter" in order to be qualified as an object

(Immaterialism 40). Despite your phenomenological affiliation, you would go against our intuition and claim that the Dutch East India Company is not an assemblage of entities and relations, nor a nodal point in the network of imperialism, but an "object" — because it cannot be exhausted by counting its component parts. I was wondering, what is the peculiar strength of this ontology, especially at our post-pandemic age? What do we gain when we say the pandemic is an object, vaccination is an object, or global warming is an object?

Harman: "Matter" gets my vote as the most superfluous concept in the history of philosophy. In Platonism, it plays the role of explaining how forms aren't accessible directly: when stamped in matter, forms become partly concealed and less perfect, and the matter that makes up our bodies tempts us with pleasures and pains and lures us away from the good and the true. It is a way of saying that forms themselves are incapable of poor transmission: from the place of the sky to our minds, matter is blamed for the noise in transmission. In recent times, matter plays the opposite role: the only reason my idea of a horse does not run and eat and reproduce like a real horse is that the latter somehow inheres in "dead matter", whereas my idea does not — or at least not in the same matter as the horse. Here again, the form itself is held to be blameless for any difference between how it acts in the horse and how it acts in my mind. A much better model, it seems to me, is to recognise that the form itself undergoes deformation when moving from one place to another. There is no transport without transformation, as Latour puts it, and some of the Scholastics touched on this point as well (see Latour, 2005, p. 39). By contrast, look at Meillassoux's faith (and it really is a matter of faith, not explicit argumentation) that we can gain the primary qualities of things by mathematising them (see Meillassoux, 2008). He too makes the assumption that we need something called "dead matter" as a substrate in which the primary qualities inhere, so that they can be safely extracted and brought into our minds without bringing things themselves into our minds. It is a remarkably traditional philosophical stance.

The other function performed by "matter" is to justify the standard folk-metaphysics, in which there is a difference between the free play of ideas in a mind and the often-painful bumping and bruising that occurs when we smash into things. So-called "matter" is supposed to explain this phenomenon: my idea of a fire doesn't hurt, but an actual fire causes severe burns. My argument is that this is because the idea of a fire and the actual fire do not have the same *form*. Our idea of fire is, at most, a loose visual sketch, the components of which are visual pixels or some other visual unit, whereas the fire itself is composed of chemical reactions with genuine emergent properties. We don't need the idea of "matter" to explain the difference between two things whose forms are already so different. But since this isn't our usual way of approaching the problem, present-day common-sense rebels, and people keep drifting back to the assumption that forms can either exist in matter or in our minds, and the former are things and the latter are ideas. If we oppose this as adamantly as it deserves, many other traditional philosophical ideas will quickly dissolve.

In the case of New Materialism, a couple of different things are going on. One sometimes hears the phrase "New Materialist Feminists", but not all of them highlight feminist issues in their writing, and not all of them are even women. I see at least two groups among the New Materialists. One group is inspired primarily by the philosophy of Gilles Deleuze. This includes not only Jane Bennett and Manuel DeLanda, to whom I feel intellectually close in certain ways, but also Rosi Braidotti, who has been more critical of OOO and speculative realism (see Bennett, 2010; DeLanda, 2016; Braidotti, 2002). Another group is represented primarily by Karen Barad. Barad isn't inspired by Deleuze, but by the Copenhagen Interpretation of quantum theory. I have a high regard for Barad's *Meeting the Universe Halfway* (2007), which is one of the most thorough theoretical works in the twenty-first-century humanities. But despite the term "agential realism" that she uses for her own work, I see her more as a full-blown idealist of the same order as Žižek. Much of this is intriguing and inspiring, but much of it also denigrates the importance of individual things. Even DeLanda, a valued friend, seems more interested in attractors and topological structures than in individuals per se, though we always have productive discussions about philosophy (see DeLanda and Harman, 2017).

In any case, let there be no mistake: OOO is in no way, shape, or form a kind of materialism. Latour is again a pioneer on this point, arguing that materialism is inevitably a form of idealism (see Latour, 2007).

Wu: *You began to work in the American University in Cairo in 2000. Since then, you travelled to more than sixty countries and finished ten books in less than 10 years. In* Bells and Whistles: More Speculative Realism *(2013), the introduction says from Brazil to Russia, and in Poland, France, Croatia, and India, you addressed "local philosophical concerns with the energy of a roving evangelist". As an American scholar, have you ever come across any Eastern object-oriented ideas? If yes, did they have any influence on you?*

Harman: Teaching in Egypt for 16 years was one of the best things that ever happened to me. I owe the country of Egypt at least as much as I owe Latour or my earlier mentor, Alphonso Lingis. In part, it was the chance to live in a place that was warm and sunny every day, which does wonders for the moods, as I'm learning again in Southern California. And in part, it was the fact that I felt a real affinity for the students in Cairo. But there was also my job situation at the American University, which initially looked impossible. AUC, in those days, had a system of tenure quotas per department and for the university as a whole. Philosophy was already *over* the quota; there had been an uncomfortable fight over which of the two previous candidates deserved a permanent job, and the solution was to give tenure to both of them. An easy solution, but it put newcomers like me in a situation where we apparently had no chance whatsoever of a permanent job. But there was a loophole: the Provost was empowered to confer tenure anyway in special cases, but you had to absolutely blow down the door with publications to have that opportunity. I wanted to stay in Egypt so badly that that's exactly what I did: published like hell, to the point that they could never say no. And it worked, though only after a dozen or so misadventures, a few backstabbing schemes against me, and a freak clerical mistake that delayed it all by a year and made me angrier than I have ever been in my life. If I ever write any memoirs, this will all make for an interesting chapter in the annals of academic pettiness.

But as for what you call Eastern ideas, it depends on your definition of East. In Cairo, I spent a good deal of time familiarising myself with the tradition of Islamic philosophy, mostly because I knew that our students would want to learn more about their own cultural history. In the process, I ran across the history of Islamic Occasionalism, which is referenced frequently in my books and articles (see Harman, 2016a). But I think of Islamic philosophy as Western rather than Eastern, since it has Greek roots and belongs to the tradition of Abrahamic religions just like Europe does, however ostracised Islam may be by the West today.

If, by Eastern idea, you mean Indian, Chinese, and the like, these traditions have always been an object of fascination for me, though I know them less well than the Islamic tradition. But I am teaching Classical Chinese Philosophy this semester, and plan to teach Indian philosophy a year from now. But first things first. Islamic philosophy belongs to the Western philosophy family, and needs to be reintegrated into the family quickly. In the case of India and China, it takes a bit more care to determine where the real points of overlap are. Not everything is equally related, and I am suspicious of the wish to jump *immediately* to a "global" sense of philosophy, if that means not recognising that some fusions and comparisons are easier than others.

References:

Barad, Karen. *Meeting the Universe Halfway: Quantum Physics and the Entanglement of Matter and Meaning*. Durham, NC: Duke University Press, 2007.

Bennett, Jane. *Vibrant Matter: A Political Ecology of Things*. Durham, NC: Duke University Press, 2010.

Braidotti, Rosi. *Metamorphoses: Towards a Materialist Theory of Becoming*. Cambridge, UK: Polity, 2002.

Brassier, Ray, Iain Hamilton Grant, Graham Harman, & Quentin Meillassoux. "Speculative Realism". *Collapse III*, (2007), pp. 306–449.

DeLanda, Manuel. *Assemblage Theory*. Edinburgh: Edinburgh University Press, 2016.

DeLanda, Manuel & Graham Harman. *The Rise of Realism*. Cambridge, UK: Polity, 2017.

Eyers, Tom. *Speculative Formalism: Literature, Theory, and the Critical Present*. Evanston, IL: Northwestern University Press, 2017.

Fried, Michael. "Art and Objecthood". In *Art and Objecthood: Essays and Reviews*, pp. 148–172. Chicago: University of Chicago Press, 1998.

Gabriel, Markus. *Fields of Sense: A New Realist Ontology*. Edinburgh: Edinburgh University Press, 2015.

Harman, Graham. *Tool-Being: Heidegger and the Metaphysics of Objects*. Chicago: Open Court, 2002.

Harman, Graham. *Guerrilla Metaphysics: Phenomenology and the Carpentry of Things*. Chicago: Open Court, 2005.

Harman, Graham. *Prince of Networks: Bruno Latour and Metaphysics*. Melbourne: re.press, 2009.

Harman, Graham. *Towards Speculative Realism: Essays and Lectures*. Winchester, UK: Zer0 Books, 2010.

Harman, Graham. *Bruno Latour: Reassembling the Political*. London: Pluto, 2014.

Harman, Graham. *Dante's Broken Hammer: The Ethics, Aesthetics, and Metaphysics of Love*. London: Repeater, 2016.

Harman, Graham. "A New Occasionalism?". In *Reset Modernity!*, edited by B. Latour & P. Weibel, pp. 129–138. Cambridge, MA: MIT Press, 2016a.

Harman, Graham. *Object-Oriented Ontology: A New Theory of Everything*. London: Pelican, 2018.

Harman, Graham. "Poe's Black Cat". In *Romanticism and Speculative Realism*, edited by C. Washington & A. McCarthy, pp. 217–235. London: Bloomsbury, 2019.

Harman, Graham. *Art and Objects.* Cambridge, UK: Polity, 2020.

Harman, Graham. "The Only Exit From Modern Philosophy". *Open Philosophy* 3, (2020), pp.132–146.

Harman, Graham. "Malabou's Political Critique of Speculative Realism". *Open Philosophy* 4, No. 1, (2021), pp. 94–105.

Harman, Graham. *Architecture and Objects.* Minneapolis: University of Minnesota Press, 2021.

Harman, Graham. "Žižek on the Retroactivity of the Real". In *Zizek Responds!: Writing Back to my Critics*, edited by Dominik Finkelde & Todd McGowan, London: Bloomsbury, 2023.

Heidegger, Martin. *The Essence of Reasons*, translated by T. Malick. Evanston, IL: Northwestern University Press, 1969.

Heidegger, Martin. *The Metaphysical Foundations of Logic*, translated by M. Heim. Bloomington, IN: Indiana University Press, 1984.

Heidegger, Martin. *Pathmarks, translated by W. McNeill.* Cambridge, UK: Cambridge University Press, 1998.

Heidegger, Martin. *Being and Time*, translated by J. Macquarrie & E. Robinson. New York: Harper, 2008.

Iser, Wolfgang. *The Act of Reading: A Theory of Aesthetic Response.* Baltimore: The Johns Hopkins University Press, 1978.

Jameson, Fredric. *Marxism and Form: Twentieth-Century Dialectical Theories of Literature.* Princeton, NJ: Princeton University Press, 1974.

Jameson, Fredric. *Raymond Chandler: The Detections of Totality.* London: Verso, 2016.

Kant, Immanuel. *Critique of Judgment*, translated by W. Pluhar. Indianapolis: Hackett, 1987.

Kornbluh, Anna. *The Order of Forms: Realism, Formalism, and Social Space.* Chicago: University of Chicago Press, 2019.

Kripke, Saul. *Naming and Necessity.* Cambridge, MA: Harvard University Press, 1980.

Lacan, Jacques. *The Object Relation: The Seminar of Jacques Lacan*, Book IV, translated by A.R. Price. Cambridge, UK: Polity, 2020.

Latour, Bruno. *We Have Never Been Modern*, translated by C. Porter. Cambridge, MA: Harvard University Press, 1993.

Latour, Bruno. *Reassembling the Social: An Introduction to Actor-Network-Theory*. Oxford: Clarendon, 2005.

Latour, Bruno. "Can We Get Our Materialism Back, Please?" *Isis* 98 (2007), pp. 138–142.

Latour, Bruno. *Facing Gaia: Eight Lectures on the New Climatic Regime*, translated by C. Porter. Cambridge, UK: Polity, 2017.

Latour, Bruno. *Down to Earth: Politics in the New Climatic Regime*, translated by C. Porter. Cambridge, UK: Polity, 2018.

Latour, Bruno, Graham Harman, & Peter Erdélyi. *The Prince and the Wolf: Latour and Harman at the LSE*. Winchester, UK: Zer0 Books, 2011.

Levine, Caroline. *Forms: Whole, Rhythm, Hierarchy, Network*. Oxford: Oxford University Press, 2015.

Marías, Julián. *History of Philosophy*, translated by S. Applebaum & C. Strowbridge. Mineola, NY: Dover, 1967.

Meillassoux, Quentin. *After Finitude*, translated by R. Brassier. London: Continuum, 2008.

Morton, Timothy. *Hyperobjects: Philosophy and Ecology After the End of the World*. Minneapolis: University of Minnesota Press, 2013.

Ortega y Gasset, José. "An Essay in Esthetics by Way of a Preface". In *Phenomenology and Art*, translated by P. Silver, pp. 127–150. New York: Norton, 1975.

Whitehead, Alfred North. *Process and Reality*. New York: Free Press, 1978.

Young, Niki. "Only Two Peas in a Pod: On the Overcoming of Ontological Taxonomies". *Symposia Melitensia* 17 (2021), pp. 27–36.

Notes

1 The interview is organised by Tsaiyi Wu, but questions are composed and collected collaboratively from a roundtable including Hong Chen (Shanghai Normal University), Weisheng Tang (Jiangxi Normal University), Qiqun Han (Nanjing Forestry University), Tsaiyi Wu (Shanghai Normal University), Micah Tewers (Artist & Independent Scholar), and Niki Young (University of Malta).

2 On the concept of "onto-taxonomy", see Harman, 2016, 2020; and Young, 2021.

3 See Caroline Levine (2015), Kornbluh (2019), and Eyers (2017).

CURRENT THEMES: AN INTERVIEW WITH RAY BRASSIER INTERVIEWED BY HILAN BENSUSAN & CHARLES JOHNS

1. *First, I would like to ask you about your philosophical trajectory since* Nihil Unbound. *It seems to me that you have gone a long way away from conceiving philosophy as an organon of extinction. Still, there is a political stance in favour of the enlightenment and prometheanism that seems common both to your book and your more recent work. What are the ruptures and the continuities that you see in your thinking since 2006?*

A fundamental rupture was realising that it is possible to integrate meaning, value, and purpose within a robustly scientific perspective without hypostatising them metaphysically or mystifying them through transcendence. This is Sellars' achievement. I used his contrast between manifest and scientific images as a framing device in *Nihil Unbound* but came to realise I had misunderstood it because I had not properly grasped his account of the relation between the normative and the natural, to which the manifest/scientific image distinction is intimately connected (although they are not equivalent).

Realising that Sellars' account of meaning and value is not susceptible to the objections besetting standard transcendental or metaphysical accounts led me to reconsider the cogency of the eliminativism that I thought strict naturalism implied. This realisation inspired my subsequent immersion in Sellars' work, which let me see three things. First, that Sellars' account of meaning as rule-governed social practice de-reifies it by decoupling its normative authority from the phenomenological primacy of *vouloir dire*, or "meaning to say" in the voluntaristic sense deconstructed by Derrida. Second, that while Sellars' account of meaning as rule-governed social practice de-reifies it, his insistence on articulating rule-following with pattern-governed behaviour re-inscribes the normative within the natural, so that while meaning is de-reified, it is not thereby rendered transcendent. Third, that this articulation of rules and patterns, or reasons and causes, underlies Sellars' attempt to reconcile the epistemic and alethic dimensions of truth, or truth as justification and truth as adequation. Sellars is thereby able to distinguish justification and adequation, or knowledge and the real, without having to oppose them in the manner of Badiou and Laruelle, the French thinkers who had served as tutelary figures for me during the writing of *Nihil Unbound*.

Sellars' critical articulation of immanence and transcendence, coupled with his critique of what he calls "the entire framework of givenness" — which pertain not just to phenomenology and empiricism but also to the residues of rationalism discernible in Badiou, Laruelle, and Meillassoux — led me back to Kant and Hegel, and ultimately to Marx. Here there is a line connecting my current work on Marx to the investigation initiated in *Nihil Unbound*. By excavating the social forms enveloping cognitive activity, Marx also articulates the cognitive and alethic dimensions of truth, or truth bounded by the resources of justification and truth as ground of those resources. This is the distinction between truth as discursive form and truth as form generating social practice. Meaning, value, and purpose as we know them are shaped by exchange, money, and property; social forms that are not consciously instituted but unconsciously constituted by what we do without knowing it.

Lukács reveals Marx's momentous philosophical import in this regard. Historical praxis articulates intelligible form and sensory content: it generates form beyond reflection and content beneath sensation. This is why Marx's thought harbours the solution to many of the issues I was grappling with in *Nihil Unbound*. Binding extinction is the work of historical praxis that ties cognition's formal superstratum to its sensory substratum. This is to say that extinction is not only an epistemic quandary, of the sort explored in *Nihil Unbound*, but a social predicament whose cognitive reckoning requires revolutionary transformation.

2. *Speculative realism — the movement, if that label applies — started 15 years ago. In retrospect, how do you assess the impact of the initial meetings and the unfolding these ideas had in the last years? Was it, in your judgement, a watershed in contemporary continental philosophy? Will it have implications on the way we do philosophy in the near future?*

I don't own the term: it belongs to whoever has found something of worth in it. I'm not sure what its impact has been, but I doubt it qualifies as a watershed; it seems to me its impact was very limited, at least as far as philosophy is concerned. What it was and what it implies will have to be worked out by whoever was inspired by it, whether positively or negatively.

3. *There has been a resurgence of interest in Hegel over the last 30 years or so, starting with some Sellarsian philosophers such as Brandom and McDowell, and more recently in continental debates in works like Malabou, Negarestani, and yourself. How do you see the reception of Hegel in the twenty-first century? Is there any political urgency that guides a coming-back to some of his texts?*

One could adduce many reasons for this resurgence. Here's a simple one: perhaps it has become harder to believe that a philosopher as difficult as Hegel is reputed to be could also have been as stupid as his detractors make out. Here's another, tracking closer to my own trajectory: the rejection of positivism and rationalism by Sellarsians and the rejection of the Nietzschean-Heideggerian premises of post-structuralism by Badiou and Laruelle jointly encourage a reappraisal of Hegel's step beyond Kantianism. But because this step culminates with Marx, the philosophical stakes of Hegel's legacy are indissociable from its political stakes.

No-one would be much exercised by Hegel's difficulty — at least no more than they are irked by that of Fichte or Schelling — were it not for the fact that he was a decisive influence upon Marx, much more so than Fichte or Schelling. Of course, there are liberal and conservative readings of Hegel. But the political urgency concerning the reception of Hegel is directly tied to the question of his influence upon Marx.

Marx is a Hegelian — a startlingly heterodox one, but a Hegelian nonetheless — and the attempt by Althusser and others to purge Marx of the stain of Hegel's influence seems to me entirely forlorn. I think the issue of Marx's peculiar "overturning" of Hegel is more important than debates about metaphysical or post-metaphysical readings of Hegel. Metaphysical readings risk turning Hegel into a sanctifier of the world as it is; post-metaphysical readings risk turning him into a satisfier of what should be. The Marxian reading is more interesting: it makes Hegel the harbinger of social revolution — transformation of the mode of production.

Postmodernists dismiss this as an antiquated relic of modernity. But what are the alternatives? Incremental reform? Piecemeal transformation? Molecular becomings? These are even less credible. Our catastrophic conjuncture — the capitaloscene — has rendered them obsolete. What is required is not anticapitalism or postcapitalism but communism, understood as thinking and acting at the level of the social totality. Calling this totality by its proper name — capitalism — is already a decisive political gesture. But possessing the conceptual resources to think this totality once one has named it is also imperative. This is the emergency that makes it necessary to re-engage with Marx and to re-examine his debt to Hegel.

4. *While at least some continental developments under the influence of speculative realism are sometimes accused of disconnecting with a political agenda (with all the perils of such a gesture), analytical philosophy has gone into a political turn since the work of Miranda Fricker. Why has analytical philosophy become concerned with political matters now? How do you see the imbrications of philosophy and politics in the future?*

I'm not sure analytic philosophy has undergone what you call "a political turn": this would imply it was previously apolitical, which I don't think is the case. Like all philosophy, analytic philosophy was always political, and not just in the tepid liberal sense: think of Russell's pacifism and anti-imperialism; the socialism of the Vienna Circle (and of the young Wilfrid Sellars); Hilary Putnam's Maoism; Michael Dummett's militant anti-racism; or even analytic Marxism.

Of course, underlying your statement is the perception that the successful institutionalisation of analytic philosophy went hand in hand with a studious depoliticisation of its fundamental concerns, especially those having to do with meaning, mind, existence, and knowledge. But this depoliticisation was a sham, and the epistemic virtues supposedly exemplified by the analytic tradition — faith in logic, hope in science, clarity in expression — were thinly veiled alibis for the political virtues of capitalist democracy.

The ostensible depoliticisation of analytic philosophy at the level of its self-image is a corollary of its increasing professionalisation. Once philosophy becomes a well-renumerated profession — like law, medicine, or engineering — the politics of its practitioners become the politics of a professional class. What you describe as analytic philosophy's "political turn", by which I take it you mean its increasing preoccupation with questions of discrimination, privilege, and bias with regard to race, gender, and sexuality, reflects the politics of a class. The privileging of the discursive domain as the primary locus of social contestation clearly indicates that this is not so much a "political turn" as the explicit manifestation of a political agenda already latent in academic professionalisation. The question is whether this agenda will impede or facilitate greater attentiveness to the social realities of class, property, and state, which underlie all these discursive issues.

As for the question of the future imbrication of philosophy and politics: I hope that contemporary philosophy is gradually exiting the long post-Marxist interregnum that has prevailed for the past 50 years and is beginning to rediscover the astonishing scope of Marx's theoretical and political achievements. Much of the continental philosophy that is supposed to have surpassed or superseded Marx is, to my mind, a regression to pre-Marxian positions. It is remarkable to what extent Marx's critique of the German ideologists (Bauer, Feuerbach, Stirner) still pertains to contemporary post-Marxist theory.

5. *Regarding the CCRU times, what do you think of its legacy after all those years? Do you think it helped shape how philosophy — or some areas within it — is done? Do you think it was a fruitful experience for you to have started from there?*

I need to clear up a misunderstanding: I was never a member of the CCRU. I knew them and attended some of their meetings at Warwick (along with other graduate students), but I was not actively involved. The core of the CCRU was Mark Fisher, Steve Goodman, Anna Greenspan, Nick Land, Suzanne Livingstone, Robin Mackay, and Luciana Parisi (I believe Sadie Plant left soon after its inception). As for the CCRU's legacy: Robin Mackay and Amy Ireland have spoken and written about it with great insight. Their work is an ongoing negotiation with this legacy.

6. *What is your opinion on the "new realisms" of Maurizio Ferraris and, to some extent, Lee Braver? Do you think this can be contextualised as a response to the main concerns found already in speculative realism, or is "new realism" a different discourse altogether?*

I don't know enough about the work of Ferraris and Braver to have an informed opinion. Whether "new realism" and "speculative realism" are the same depends on what one understands by "speculative realism". As I said above, I don't espouse the term, so I'm not sure what it means anymore. If it just means rejecting Kant's legacy to rehabilitate metaphysical realism, then perhaps they are the same. But this is not a promising avenue in my opinion.

7. *Returning to the theme of Hegelian philosophy today (its multiple appropriations), I have always been surprised to see very little, sincere political commentary on Hegelian notions of "necessity", "totality", and "the absolute". Do you think it is somewhat of a caricatured technique for Hegelians on the Left to dismiss these ideas and instead focus on contingency, the non-totalisable, and social relations/formations of knowledge (mainly focusing on revolution/s for example), or are these "antiquated" Hegelian/metaphysical concepts simply not applicable or denounced as intrinsically fascist at present?*

I disagree with the suggestion that there has been little or no serious analysis of the political valence of necessity, totality, and the absolute in Hegel. Sartre's *Critique of Dialectical Reason*, Gerard Lebrun's *La patience du concept*, and Gillian Rose's *Hegel contra Sociology* surely qualify as profound meditations on these themes. More recently, Todd McGowan's *Emancipation After Hegel*, Karen Ng's *Hegel's Concept of Life*, Martin Hägglund's *This Life: Secular Faith and Spiritual Freedom*, and numerous essays by Rocío Zambrana all constitute serious attempts to engage with these issues. One might not agree with their conclusions, but it would be churlish to question their sincerity.

It is also worth mentioning that the popular caricature of Hegel as paradigmatic totalitarian thinker is usefully debunked in Jon Stewart's collection, *The Hegel Myths and Legends*. In light of all this, I don't think it's plausible to suggest that contemporary left-Hegelians simply ignore the allegedly sinister connotations of necessity, totality, and the absolute, emphasising instead the supposedly benign values of contingency, untotalisability, and sociality. Rather, they point out — or should be pointing out — that these are two sides of the same coin: that necessity is contingent, totality is not-All, and the absolute is a nexus of social relations.

These are the coordinates of Marx's materialist recoding of Hegel. Capitalism is a system of social forms in which the logic of the concept is displaced and co-opted by a system of social reproduction conditioned by class struggle. Necessity, totality, and the absolute are conceptual ciphers for effective social processes. Thinking the effective reality of these processes requires recontextualising the logic of these concepts. This is why they cannot simply be dispensed with. Enthroning contingency, multiplicity, and relativity in their place occludes social reality and unwittingly fetishises the chaotic mutability of capital.

Of course, there are those who equate the Marxian-Hegelian injunction to think totality with "fascism" per se. But this accusation redefines the term to make it synonymous with the rejection of false immediacy, conveniently obscuring the fact that it was precisely the ideologues of pure immediacy (of life, force, becoming, etc.) who paved the way for European fascism. The eagerness with which contemporary reactionaries like Nick Land denounce necessity, totality, and the absolute in the name of contingency, multiplicity, and relativity should make one think twice about assuming that the former are intrinsically oppressive and the latter inherently liberating. Ultimately, however, this is really a debate about Stalinism. The critique of Hegelian Marxism by figures like Althusser was an attempt to salvage Marx by laying the blame for Stalinism at Hegel's feet. I don't think this attempt stands up to serious scrutiny. But it was conjuncturally necessary in the early 1960s if a certain strain of Marxist philosophy — interestingly distinct from Critical Theory, which did not disavow its Hegelian inheritance — was to survive the death of Stalinism. The question is whether philosophy retains the metaphysical prerogative of thinking the absolute — as being, becoming, life, contingency, etc. — at the cost of mystifying its social conditioning; or whether it retains its relevance by abrogating this traditional prerogative and acknowledging its conditioning by an absolute now realised in the social totality.

MARXISM AND ONTOLOGY: AN INTERVIEW WITH ALBERTO TOSCANO BY CONRAD HAMILTON

Currently a Term Research Associate Professor in the School of Communication at Simon Fraser University in British Columbia, Canada, he generously spent six months (June 2021-January 2022) doing an e-mail interview with East China's Normal University's Conrad Hamilton for this volume.

C.H: It's well-documented that you co-organised and moderated the Speculative Realism workshop at Goldsmiths in 2007. How did you get involved with that? Did you have any sense at the time of the subsequent attention the event would attract?

A.T: Ray Brassier and I overlapped in our doctoral work at the University of Warwick's Department of Philosophy in the late 1990s/early 2000s — it was at that time that we began to collaborate, first around the journal *Pli*,[1] and then in a more concerted manner, around the work of Alain Badiou — this led to the publication of the collection *Theoretical Writings* in 2004.

I suppose the germ of the workshop lay in some of the arguments rehearsed in our postface to that collection, "Aleatory Rationalism", and in the broader effort shared with some of our peers at Warwick to explore the potentialities of so-called "continental philosophy" beyond a post-Kantian and post-Heideggerian frame, which seemed to lead towards scientific scepticism or obscurantism, a pious relationship to the sempiternal tasks of philosophy, and an ethics of finitude that, *volens nolens*, defanged any robust conception of transformative politics.

So, while our attitude to Badiou's work was not that of disciples or proselytisers (we both wrote critically about the work from the start), we did feel that his polemical targets were the right ones. This encounter with Badiou's work had as its background the intellectual milieu in which we did our doctoral work, rather heavily marked by a materialist reading of Deleuze's (and Deleuze and Guattari's) work (shared with a number of our peers), which emphasised its Spinozist and Marxist aspects and minimised its Bergsonian ones, while opening channels of communication with debates in the philosophy of biology, cognitive science, and what we could call the heretical traditions of rationalism.

Ray also brought to this debate his engagement with the non-philosophy of François Laurelle. While this conference has retroactively accrued a weird nimbus of significance, it was a rather modest and somewhat improvised symposium, which aimed at bringing together what we thought were some significant if largely divergent strands in a broader move away from that post-Kantian and post-Heideggerian legacy (often associated at the time with the University of Essex, as the other site for continental philosophy in England, and associated with the likes of Jay Bernstein, Robert Bernasconi, Simon Critchley, and Peter Dews).

Ray and I knew of Meillassoux's work via Badiou and were struck by its lucidity, originality, and ambition, but especially by the way in which it really tried to dismantle the anthropological machine at the heart of the dominant strands of continental philosophy, to wit finitude. Iain Hamilton Grant came from an earlier generation of Warwick speculative materialism, so to speak, and had published in *Pli*, so we felt that his effort to revive Schellingian *Naturphilosophie* was another interesting avenue for the exit from Kantianism. Harman represented the possibility of breaking out of the deadlock of finitude and so-called correlationism from within a Heideggerian starting-point (Ray had appreciated his *Tool-Being*; I think *Guerrilla Metaphysics* was published the year before the symposium).

As for the name, rather than intended to anoint some kind of school, or give rise to a chimerical "movement", it was arrived at by Ray after consultation with the participants, as a designation capacious enough to keep to provide some kind of commonality for this discordant quartet of projects. Other terms were tested out: "Post-Critical Metaphysics" came up against Meillassoux's objections to metaphysics *tout court*, while speculative materialism (employed by Grant and Meillassoux) seemed to invite confusion, as many of the existing varieties of self-described continental materialism (libidinal, dialectical, historical, transcendental) could be regarded as bearing "correlationist" features. As Ray put it in correspondence at the time: "So I prefer 'speculative realism': the 'speculative' component immediately dispels [the] spectre of G.E. Moore like common-sense realism, while the 'realist' aspect distinguishes it at a stroke from the entirety of the continental tradition."

C.H: In Graham Harman's 2018 Speculative Realism: An Introduction, *he notes that you declined to present at the 2007 workshop "for reasons unknown" to him. Why did you choose not to participate? Do you think that was a missed opportunity in hindsight?*

A.T: The precise reasons are unknown to me too. I suppose I felt distanced enough from my own speculations about an exit from a certain Kantianism via the ontology of individuation — explored in my first book, *The Theatre of Production*[2] (which, while published in 2006, was basically, bar the preface and some relatively minor revisions, my 2002 doctoral dissertation) — not to feel compelled to bring that line of inquiry into the conversation.

The project on *Fanaticism* I'd already started was not germane, and I only saw the partial relevance of the problematic of real abstraction to this set of debates a little later (namely, in mining Colletti's Kantianism[3] versus Meillassoux for my talk at the second SR workshop[4]). I was also quite busy with helping to organise a conference at the Centre for the Study of Invention and Social Process (CSISP) on *Oil and Politics*.

I don't see it as a missed opportunity, namely because, very shortly after finishing my doctorate, I felt that a purely intra-philosophical engagement with these matters was of limited interest to me; that it was not the register in which I was inclined to work. The repudiation of correlationism also seemed increasingly jettisoning or subordinated critical theory or the critique of political economy as somehow "impure", with the attendant conservative return to the autonomy and sufficiency of philosophy as a sovereign site of speculation.

My concern with the political and systemic significance of "actually-existing" metaphysics in thinking through fanaticism and real abstraction also persuaded me that a purely philosophical interrogation (in which other domains of thought and practice would ultimately accrue an illustrative rather than constitutive role) was of limited import. If you'll allow me a *détournement* of Horkheimer's 1939 dictum on fascism: "If you don't want to talk about capitalism, then you had better keep quiet about metaphysics".*

C.H: Right, and you're touching on something else here — the fact you did decide to present at the 2009 follow-up SR workshop in Bristol, in lieu of Quentin Meillassoux. And it's interesting that, whereas in your answer to my first question you spoke of seeking an "exit from

* In his 1939 article "The Jews in Europe," Max Horkheimer stated that "if you do not want to talk about capitalism, you should keep quiet about fascism." Though he later renounced this quote, this has not stopped it from continuing to be widely cited.

Kantianism", in your 2009 essay — published later in The Speculative Turn *— you argue for "a qualified Marxian defence for weak Kantian correlationism".*

Of course, as the "qualified" part suggests, you're obviously not a vintage Kantian: if I understand your argument properly, it's beholden to the notion of real abstraction, according to which dualism, the correlationist circle, can be seen as issuing from the social reality of capitalism (as the commodity-form in Marx is itself dualistic, insofar as it imposes a division between exchange value and use value). But I guess what bothers me about this essay is the way you seem to go beyond this thesis, as if Kantianism will always be necessary for (Marxian) materialism, insofar as it permits us to think the extra-logical "idea of real exteriority in the material world".

I worry here that, if the latter is your point, you're going further than Marx in affirming the eternality of such a division — perhaps even further than Alfred Sohn-Rethel, from whom the concept of "real abstraction" as we use it today derives.[5] *Do you have any thoughts on this?*

A.T: This is a very thorny question, and one that I don't think I have a settled position about. My suspicion, which I was trying to explore and enrich in this parallax reading of Colletti and Meillassoux, is that some version of what the latter would present as "weak correlationism" is indispensable for a materialist dialectic.

Why? First of all, because to claim noetic access to the absolute, be it through some variant of intellectual intuition or by way of some kind of impersonal logical machinery, is to render impossible any check or correction or critique of the means of cognition whereby this absolute comes to be figured or constructed. I was struck in this respect by the way in which Colletti stresses the materialist repercussions of a Kant-derived notion of *real opposition*. (As I summarised in the piece you refer to: "The idea of real opposition, Kant's *Realrepugnanz*, is significant because it is only by upholding the principle of non-contradiction and the idea of real exteriority in the material world that materialism can avert being enveloped by an idealism for which the material world is merely an incarnation of a fundamentally inclusive and unlimited reason.")

I think a certain Lacanian-Marxist attention to the *Real*[6] (or, as in one of Žižek's recent books, "absolute recoil" in Hegel[7] — which of course can be read against Colletti, as in Comay and Ruda's wonderful book on the *Logic),** or indeed Adorno's articulation of a materialism of *non-identity* can also be thought of in this regard. Or, to turn to another Colletti (as well as to contemporaneous reconstructions like Lefebvre's or Lecourt's), Lenin's own epistemological polemics could be read in this *anti-speculative* vein. That is, of course, a different tack to take than the one which builds up from real abstraction (without forgetting that both Sohn-Rethel and Adorno wrote critiques of epistemology).

I very much doubt anything like a critique of ideology is possible *without* weak correlationism in the broader sense (which need not be Kantian, individualist, or subjectivist). I'm not entirely sure it is possible to "derive" correlationism from the level of abstraction of value-theory, or that the social reality of capitalism itself can be "read off" from the logic of value in the first place (this seems to be a pan-logicist *dérive* where we take the notion of capital as an automatic subject uncritically and then act as though it is this *Geist* that produces different "shapes" of capitalism and its attendant ideologies). That said, of course there is a deep entanglement between the emergence of modern philosophy (and thus of the theory of the subject and of correlationisms, etc.) and that of capitalism, but the periodisation and the causalities of this emergence are very over-determined (as manifest in how much about the nature of philosophical cognition, Sohn-Rethel *docet*, can already be outlined on the basis of "pre-capitalist" Ancient Greek thought).

C.H: Yes, I mean I gave a very schematic definition of real abstraction; there's plenty of complexity there. But I guess the question here really turns on access — specifically, what kind of epistemology (or reconstruction of epistemology, which becomes ipso facto *its own epistemology) is*

* Rebecca Comay and Frank Ruda, *The Dash—The Other Side of Absolute Knowing* (Cambridge: MIT Press, 2018).

appropriate to a Marxian materialism? And after the 2009 workshop, it seemed that you turned to Fredric Jameson's "cognitive mapping" as potentially containing the solution to this — as he states, as being akin to the "Lacanian Symbolic" in the way that it can connect the "Real" and the "Imaginary"[8] *(though I think this does leave the question open of whether alienation is inexorable or not). This is most notably the subject of your book with Jeff Kinkle,* Cartographies of the Absolute. *What prompted that shift?*

A.T: While I can definitely discern the connections you're drawing, I didn't at the time (nor do I necessarily now) see cognitive mapping as an *epistemological* move. While Jameson obviously retools a post-Kantian representational problematic — after all, the motivation of this map is to make possible "a situational representation on the part of the individual subject to that vaster and properly unrepresentable totality which is the ensemble of society's structures as a whole" (as he puts it in *Postmodernism*) — what drew me to his framing of the problem was first and foremost a question of what, to borrow the heading for his multi-book opus, soon to be completed, is a "poetics of social forms" — a task that seemed of paramount significance (not least because a lot of degraded maps were circulating at the time, as they do so even more now) in the wake of the 2007–08 crisis and its representational repercussions (from the rhetoric of the everyday to the art gallery to the Hollywood studio or streaming platform).

Cartographies, notwithstanding its "titular" absolute, is not a book consciously concerned — or if so, only obliquely — with the thorny theoretical questions you're posing. But I guess this goes back to the matter I raised earlier, regarding the irrevocably correlationist character of any ideology critique — even those which, like Althusser's, are threaded through a structuralist idiom that is in open battle against Kantianism[9] (even though it could be regarded by some as Kantianism's unwitting epigone[10]).

Maybe another way of approaching this would be to assume Jameson's avowal that cognitive mapping was just another formula for class consciousness, and ask to what extent the latter requires a positive epistemology or rather a destruction or critique in the name of some kind of recombinant praxis (or theoretical practice). In this regard, we've perhaps never really gone past the 1920s — of *History and Class Consciousness*, the battle at Davos between Heidegger and Cassirer,[11] Sohn-Rethel's first theoretical epiphany about real abstraction, Lefebvre's entry into philosophy, and the myriad efforts to celebrate or criticise "Lenin the philosopher".

C.H: As regards the operationalisation of a specifically proletarian kind of class consciousness within philosophy, I wouldn't disagree about the 1920s being the furthest horizon we've reached, so to speak — though this does leave us with the teleologically disjunctive question of Maoism[12] *and its attendant intellectual consequences (the concept of "overdetermination"*[13] *you mentioned being in part one, I think). But of course, we should remember that even philosophy that doesn't aspire to this — I hesitate to say bourgeois philosophy — can bestow us with the constituent elements for a Marxist synthesis.*

I want to give an example. In 2012's Seeing it Whole, *you criticise Latourian actor-network theory*[14] *for its "painstaking attention to traces, objects, and devices" at the expense of the "virtual and shadowy" (quoted from Latour)* agencies that have totalised the social field; its absence of a "social-theoretic" account of capitalism. But you also admit that useful observations can be derived if one "follow[s] the actors themselves", in Latour's parlance.*

And then, in 2015, we have Jason Moore's eco-socialist work Capitalism in the Web of Life, *which marries ANT and real abstraction (he cites you on the latter, in fact). In the sense that, whereas for Moore, the "Cartesian" Nature/Society divide arises due to the establishment of the law of value and capitalism, lurking behind this in*

* This quote from Latour appears in Toscano's 2012 essay "Seeing it Whole: Staging Totality in Social Theory and Art," and is cited from p. 166 of the 2002 English translation of *Reassembling the Social.*

nature is this sort of pluralistic, agential dispensation (which, of course, doesn't mean we can ignore the real effects of the Nature/Society dyad).

Do you see this sort of synthesis as having theoretical legitimacy? Moore has received a lot of criticism, from Andreas Malm,[15] *for instance.*

A.T: While I can certainly see how the research protocols of ANT or STS[16] can be brought into the ambit of Marxian problematics, or how work can be produced that brings these traditions of inquiry into fruitful cross-pollination (Tim Mitchell's *Carbon Democracy* comes to mind),* I think that Latour's work is indelibly marked by a recurrent and tendentious polemic against the very notion of totalisation, not to mention a conception of politics dead set against any revolutionary conception of social change (Ben Noys has compellingly traced, in *Persistence of the Negative*, the convergence with François Furet's reactionary "anti-totalitarianism"[17]).

I appreciate the scope and ambition of Moore's work, and have been very impressed by some of his ecological histories (especially the two-part essay in *Review* on Madeira, sugar, and the conquest of nature), but I find the speculative frame of *Capitalism in the Web of Life* problematic, as, notwithstanding its promising grounding in the historicity of capitalist abstraction, it seems at times to verge into a contemporary tendency *a priori* to treat monism (or the opposition to binaries and dichotomies) as in itself emancipatory, as though some ontologies were *ipso facto* more liberatory than others. I am not persuaded by this approach.

Without wholly endorsing Žižek's asseverations in his *Ticklish Subject*,[18] I do also think that there is something rather... lazy in the consensus around the evils of "Cartesian dualism". As we can glean from serious historical-philosophical inquiries (not least among them Negri's *Political Descartes*[19]), the relation between Descartes' philosophy, materialist intuitions and the politics of his time was a complex matter indeed — and "Cartesianism" has

* In *Carbon Democracy*, Mitchell agrees with Latour regarding the need to unsettle the distinction between the natural and the human but argues that this must be fought for at the level of collective life or politics.

often been considerably more emancipatory than other strands of philosophy — just compare Descartes and Hume on the nexus of anthropological difference, or "race", and intelligence (Chomsky has, of course, long defended the egalitarian virtues of a certain "Cartesian" understanding of language and cognition).

This is not to say I would endorse all the terms of Malm's polemic, nor his particular variant of "property dualism". As I tried to argue in an essay for the collection *Materialism and the Critique of Energy*[20] (which also includes a piece by Jasper Bernes touching on the Malm/Moore differend),* with a detour via Sartre's *Critique of Dialectical Reason*, the monism/dualism *aut-aut* might not fully do justice to the challenges that the "Capitalocene" poses to our conceptions of the negativity that inheres in human agency, especially in the tragic collective figure of (to quote Hegel) "oneself as an enemy".[21]

C.H: I'm tempted to go a bit further on this one. Because I was surprised when you criticised the supposition that "some ontologies [are] ipso facto *more liberatory than others". And I wondered whether you were referring solely to monism in this context.*

It seems to me that, if we take Marxism, for instance, it depends upon a handful of retroductively realised,[22] a posteriori *concepts — value, capital, whatever — that amount to a materialist ontology (to channel critical realism). But often, Marxists don't really acknowledge this aspect of their discourse. This makes it easy for others to dismiss criticisms of ontology by Marxists, which are directed outwards, on the grounds that they're in denial of their own ontological groundwork.*

While not a question of Marxism per se, we can see something similar in SR — Harman has critiqued Brassier for opposing himself to ontology from the vantage point of a science (or scientistic thinking) that still requires it. I don't find this critique totally satisfactory, although I do wonder if it doesn't point to a lack of ontological and methodological

* "The Belly of the Revolution: Agriculture, Energy, and the Future of Communism".

elucidation, present perhaps both in Brassier's early work as well as in that of many Marxist thinkers.

So, how do you see the relationship between ontology and Marxian materialism? Do you think something like Althusser's hypothesis of a trans-historical battle between materialist and idealist camps,[23] *for instance, is plausible?*

A.T: To repurpose Stuart Hall's critical remarks on Laclau's post-Marxism, though we can't say that there is "necessarily no connection" between, roughly, ontology and politics, we can advance that there is "no necessary connection".[24]

I find the notion that political strategies or even analyses are undermined by lacking an ontology or implying a "bad" one to be the kind of arrogant condescension advanced by "philosophers" who have little appreciation that politics is its own thought, with its own criteria and its own, so to speak, dignity. In effect, I remain convinced that there is something quite salutary in Badiou's gesture of "de-suturing" philosophy from its condition and rejecting an "expressive" link between ontology and politics in particular.

That is not to say that we cannot reconstruct and systematise something like, as you put it, a "materialist ontology" that innervates the categorial apparatus of the critique of political economy — I think this is a worthy enough pursuit, and indeed, one which I tried to make a small contribution to by foregrounding the whole problematic of real abstraction, precisely to stress that the parameters of such an ontology are not the sovereign purview of speculative philosophy and its noetic privileges, but are already forged "out there" in the seemingly banal materiality of our social relations and forms.

I appreciate, in this respect, the provocative stimulus of Sohn-Rethel's suggestion that philosophy "is money without its material attachments, immaterial and no longer recognisable as money". I think that, while it doesn't exempt us from inquiring into what a materialist ontology might be, this insight ruins the philosophical pretension that there we must seek a purely philosophical foundation *independent of capital* for our critique and our politics. I don't find the trans-historical *gigantomachia* plausible, not least because, as Paolo Virno nicely noted in a brief text called "The Two Masks of Materialism" (*Pli*, vol. 12) — likely informed by his own readings of Adorno and Sohn-Rethel — taking the problem of real abstraction seriously means that idealist (or transcendental) positions often provides a much better grip on the nature of social forms and conflicts under capitalist conditions that supposedly materialist ones.[25] (Or, as per Lenin's marginalia to Hegel: "Intelligent idealism is closer to intelligent materialism than stupid materialism." Dialectical idealism instead of intelligent; metaphysical, undeveloped, dead, crude, rigid instead of stupid.

In this regard, I prefer another framing formula from Althusser, which speaks to the notion of "no necessary connection" between ontology and the critique of political economy — namely, the one that, while there is no *philosophy of Marx* as such, the task of constructing a philosophy *for Marx* and for Marxism remains worthwhile.

C.H: Since we're talking about the relation between ontology and politics, maybe now is a good time to discuss the political agendas that emanated out of the SR conference itself (as opposed to e.g., Moore's slightly more heterodox approach).

I think it's clear that you lack enthusiasm for the sort of politics of actants advocated by Latour — and elaborated by Harman — insofar as it is unable to think social totality — that is, to confront the regnant status of capitalist abstractions. But the other side of the post-SR divide — I guess we could call it the Brasserian or "Promethean" side — has been defined politically above all by the "left accelerationism" of Srnicek and Williams (both of whom were bloggers during the brief SR-adjacent blogging boom, running Speculative Heresy *and* Splintering Bone Ashes *respectively). What do you think of their ideas?*

I know that some major left-wing philosophers have evinced scepticism. Éric Alliez and Maurizio Lazzarato, in their 2016 book Wars and Capital, *for instance, acerbically refer to it as productivism with a "techno beat". You seem to go in a similar direction in your essay from the same year — "The Promethean Gap" — when you call for making workers and the productive forces they use "visible to one another", rather than celebrating the "crushing of living labor for the sake of veritably titanic projects". You also suggest, I think, that the evocation of this grandiose modernising trajectory can serve as a substitute for more substantive engagement with mechanisms of political control — and, in this sense, can be read as a symptom of the left's doleful state. But as you never explicitly discuss the* #ACCELERATE Manifesto, *I'm wondering if you could be a little more direct…*

A.T: I think there's ultimately little commonality between Brassier's critique of the critique of Prometheanism and a "left accelerationism", which seems to me an unstable amalgam of leftovers from Landian *Schwärmerei* and an English nostalgia for techno-modernity — or, a tendentially Rightist reading of *Anti-Oedipus*[26] meets Harold Wilson 2.0 (theoretical anti-humanism plus *dirigiste* social democracy). I really don't find much to engage with in this material, which I think does not stand up to scrutiny when it is confronted with a critique of political economy that thinks seriously about the relationship between automation, technology, and the labour-capital relation — whether (and I'm intentionally mentioning two very different perspectives) we explore the serious limits of utopias of automated (post-)capitalism via Jason Smith's *Smart Machines and Service Work* or assume the dystopian potentialities of AI along the lines of Nick Dyer-Witheford, et al.'s *Inhuman Power.* Accelerationism's future seems a very threadbare one, little attuned to capital's uneven temporalities or, indeed, to its ecological contradictions.

C.H: Yes, well, I think a consistent refrain in your work is the need to start from the immanent political situation, rather than projecting fanciful aspirations onto it (you critique theories of communisation along similar lines, for instance). And in a way, you seem to be doing this now by confronting the subject of race, which — while always pertinent — has acquired more political visibility due to the rise of the (electoral) far-right. In your 2015 piece with Brenna Bhandar,[27] *you relate race to property via real abstraction. I found this interesting, since it reflects a residual ontological concern — yes, race is "socially constructed"; but on the other hand, the fact this "social construction" indexes to the operation of the economy means it has an ontological depth, so to speak (and it is maybe symptomatic of the limitations of our present-day political mapping that we all know race, gender, etc. is "socially constructed", but no one knows why). You told me you have a short book on fascism coming out with Verso. How will it add to this agenda?*

A.T: You're correct to discern in that *Radical Philosophy* article an effort to ground analysis of race in a specifically capitalist social ontology. While emphasising the richness, for instance, of Stuart Hall's refunctioning of both Althusser and Gramsci as analysts of the ideological work that "race" does, the articulation of real abstraction and real estate was indeed meant as a gesture towards a more materialist take on these questions.

In our introduction to an edited collection of Ruth Wilson Gilmore's work (*Abolition Geography*, Verso, 2022), Brenna and I tried to explore this further by unpacking Gilmore's contention that "race is a modality through which political-economic globalisation is lived" and her complementary framing of racism as itself a "process of abstraction". I think that this link between race and real abstraction can also be usefully tackled in terms of some of the elements towards a theory of antisemitism, advanced by members of the Institute for Social Research (Adorno and Leo Löwenthal, in particular) in the 1940s — an approach which, while remaining strikingly oblivious to racial formation in the US, can also be approached as a research programme into "racial capitalism".

As for my work-in-progress on late fascism, it will try to tie together some of these strands of research, namely by drawing on Black radical theorists of fascism (from George Padmore to Angela Y. Davis) to make a case for how fascism is intimately linked to the capitalist uses of race, as well as to specific histories of racism (especially in its settler-colonial varieties), but also by understanding theories of real abstraction as themselves integrally connected to the effort to theorise fascism — this is evident in the complicated intellectual relations between Adorno and Sohn-Rethel — and to theorise it as over-determined by a kind of hatred of the abstract, which is also a hatred of theory (as opposed to world-views, or more or less nebulous and esoteric figures of Thought, Tradition,* or Spengler's "ideas without words"†).

C.H: You also published two new books in Spanish recently. One of these — Una visión compleja. Hacía una estética de la economía (A Complex Vision: Towards an Aesthetics of the Economy, *Dec. 2020, Meier Ramirez) — is an essay collection consisting of three of your essays from the mid-2010s, around the time of* Cartographies*: "Seeing Socialism", "Photography Against the Flow: Abstraction and Logistics in Allan Sekula's Writings", and "The World is Already Without Us" (the book also includes an introduction and an interview with you, both attributed to Stephan Gruber and Mijail Mitrovic). The other —* La abstracción real. Filosofia, estética y capital (Real Abstraction: Philosophy, Aesthetics and Capital) *— I had a hard time finding out much about online, though apparently it was published by Palinodia*

* For the Italian far-right thinker Julius Evola, "Tradition" refers to eternal supernatural knowledge, premised upon authority, hierarchy, order, discipline and obedience. Himself influenced by the French esoteric intellectual René Guénon, Evola's work would eventually influence others, such as the Romanian historian of religion Mircea Eliade (and, later, the Russian 'anti-racist' fascism of Alexander Dugin).

† In his two-volume post-World War I work *The Decline of the West*, the German nationalist philosopher Oswald Spengler uses the term "ideas without words" to describe vital forces or creative concepts which are culturally derived, and that language can never adequately represent. It was later co-opted by the Italian socialist historian Furio Jesi, who applied it to explain the substitution of reasoned language for symbols or shopworn phrases characteristic of the far right (but that also can be found on the far left).

in May 2021. How did you end up putting out an essay collection in Spanish prior to English? And what does the latter text deal with?

A.T: The first of the two books was the idea of two Peruvian scholars and critics who had drawn for their own investigations on *Cartographies* and thought it could be worthwhile to collect together some of the essays written on the margins and the wake of that project. The interview is available in English on the Zer0 blog.[28] While I had input on the composition and title of the project (taken from Raymond Williams' reflections on Brecht), the initiative was theirs. The Palinodia book, which had been delayed by the pandemic but which should be published in Chile very soon, is a collection of all my extant writings on and around real abstraction with a short framing introduction. It was commissioned during an extended academic visit to Chile in 2017 (where I taught a couple of courses on critical theory, cognitive mapping, and real abstraction at the Pontificia Universidad Católica de Valparaiso, at the invitation of my friend Ricardo Espinoza Lolas) by Miguel Valderrama, editor at Palinodia and author, *inter alia*, of a very striking short book on Gramsci's reading of Dante in the *Quaderni.**

C.H: This is the tenth question, so we'll wrap up here. I wanted to ask you one last thing about the SR workshop. I was quite struck by a line in the 1970 essay "Structuralism and Its Successors" by the Italian Marxist Sebastiano Timpanaro, where he states that the hegemony of post-structuralism will continue until a new "socio-political situation" emerges. Because this is, in a way, what happened with SR—I think the workshop took place 16 days after the Federal Reserve declined to lower fed fund rates in response to early warning signs of economic recession. But SR, while a crucial stimulus to the struggle against idealism, didn't completely break with it: its opposition to correlationism was, as you put it yourself, based on "drawing ontological conclusions from logical intuitions" rather than confronting "extra-logical reality" (a deficiency

* Miguel Valderrama, *Coloquio sobre Gramsci* (Santiago: Palinodia, 2016).

that could be traced back to its influences: Badiou, Latour, etc.) And much as neoliberalism seems to hobble along post-2007 somehow, so too does a strong correlationism of the Heideggerian or Wittgensteinian type. Obviously, with COVID, we're faced with yet another socio-political situation. Do you think maybe there's a chance this time to operationalise a Marxian materialism within philosophy? And do you think re-interpreting the SR workshop with a mind to its failings can help us achieve this?

A.T: While I'm always keen to historicise, I wonder how much mileage we can get out of correlating that anti-correlationist moment with the fore-tremors of economic crisis — that said, as I suppose I tried to intimate in my short essay on Colletti and Meillassoux, the combination in the latter, and perhaps in many theoretical tendencies in the SR-nebula, to lean towards the absolute while treating the extra-cognitive character of reality as ultimately speculative, makes them ill-suited to a theoretical confrontation with the over-determination of thinking by capital.

Among the symptoms of this predicament is the combination, in someone like Meillassoux, of a formidable speculative intellect with a surprisingly impoverished and pre-Marxian theory of ideology. The multiple menaces, dislocations, and shocks that mark our present of "uneven and combined apocalypse" (to borrow the title of a book by Evan Calder Williams[29]) seem to give succour and stimulus to two opposed but ultimately complementary attitudes or — and I do mean it here in the pejorative sense — world-views: on the one hand, to seek new forms of stability in a kind of metaphysics of dwelling (I think this is the ideological background to those Wittgensteinian or Heideggerian positions); on the other, to go further in the direction of the destructuring of our social world, in the manic anticipation of some kind of saving conversion or event. The complementarity of these two dispositions, towards homeopathic re-embedding or radical dis-embedding, is perhaps best testified by the kind of ultra-Left Heideggerianism that marks the discourse of destituent power, with Agamben's unique synthesis of the Magus of Messkirch with Debord, Foucault, Benjamin, and Arendt playing a potent role as philosophical intercessor.[30]

It is a complementarity that I think is ultimately defined by a repudiation of strategy as a horizon for political thought. I think some of the theoretical interventions spurred by the conjuncture of the pandemic do demonstrate the vitality of the nexus of Marxism and philosophy, though whether they open up further dimensions for development of a distinct Marxist materialist philosophy, I'm not sure. I'm thinking of the critical reflections by Panagiotis Sotiris on democratic biopolitics,[31] of Toffanin and Finelli's critique of Agamben and Cacciari,[32] of Andreas Malm's recent books and the debates they've elicited.[33] While I haven't undertaken that work myself, I think there is potential in approaching "the moment of speculative realism" — with all due proportions and humility (it's not Cassirer versus Heidegger at Davos!) — as a "case" worth investigating for those who are still preoccupied by the question: what does it mean to be a materialist in philosophy?

Notes

1 A journal of philosophy edited and produced by members of the Graduate School of the Department of Philosophy at the University of Warwick.

2 In which Toscano argues — in a manner far more in concert with the goals of SR than his later work would be — for an "ontology of anomalous individuation", drawing above all from the work of Gilles Deleuze and Gilbert Simondon.

3 For Lucio Colletti, Marxism must adopt a Kantian theory of knowledge, lest it permit external reality to be subsumed by the all-encompassing Idea of Hegel (who for Colletti rejects both materialism and science).

4 In "Against Speculation, or, a Critique of the Critique of Critique", Toscano argues that Meillassoux's insistence that correlationism must be staved off also due to the way it licences "religious (or 'poeticoreligious') belief in the absolute" risks recapitulating a "conservative thesis",

according to which "relativistic proliferation of beliefs, beyond any horizon of legitimacy, is a form of de-Christianization".

5 In his 1970 text *Intellectual and Manual Labour*, Sohn-Rethel argues that the (Marxian) commodity-form — that is, the structure that envelopes products when they are offered for sale on a general market — is a *real abstraction. Real* in the sense that it corresponds with the physical exchange of commodities; an *abstraction* in the sense that the assignation of value to products has no empirical referent. From this, Sohn-Rethel proceeds to deduce the entirety of Western metaphysics — as well as Kantian epistemology — from this structure, which he sees as having endowed it with a quantitative conception of substance from the time of the Milesian school onwards.

6 For Lacan, the ontological absolute in-itself; "the essential object which is not an object any longer, but this something faced with which all words cease and all categories fail, the object of anxiety *par excellence*".

7 Though it originates in the work of Hegel, "absolute recoil", for Žižek, refers to the way that a term — once removed from the "relationship of reflection", in which it is determined by its opposite (difference by identity, appearance by essence, and so forth) — can determine itself. An example provided in the eponymous book is the way that India — while furnished with the idea of liberalism by British colonialism — paradoxically actualised it more authentically in the context of their independence.

8 In layman's terms, to furnish us with representations capable of mediating between higher order capitalist structures and a quotidian reality, in which they're often not apparent.

9 Althusser's "structural Marxism" — though this term itself is contentious — is anti-Kantian in that it rejects empiricism and representationalism in favour of a coherentist theory of knowledge, in which concepts give rise to other concepts (the way the notion of "quasars", for instance, has no basis in empirical representation).

10 "Unwitting epigone" in the sense, presumably, that it does not adequately chart the relation of thought to capitalism.

11 A 1929 debate held in Davos, Switzerland between the neo-Kantian Ernst Cassirer and Martin Heidegger. Considered significant for both

twentieth-century philosophy and politics, to a large extent it revolved around the question of whether humans are capable of acquiring (and acting upon) objective knowledge, with Heidegger defending a more relativistic position.

12 "Teleologically disjunctive" in the sense that — because China was not industrialised when the Chinese Communist Party was attempting to seize power, and thus did not have a large proletariat — Mao was forced to break with Marxist orthodoxy in order to forge a viable revolutionary strategy, concentrating his efforts on the construction of a peasant army.

13 The term "overdetermination" was used by Louis Althusser — under the influence of both Mao and Freud, and against the conventional notion of dialectical "contradiction" — to describe the theory that every element in the productive structure reflects and determines all the others.

14 For Latour, both human and non-human "actants" relate to each other via networks, the nature of which are obfuscated should one attempt to impose a nature/culture binary upon them.

15 The crux of Malm's critique of Moore is that the latter — by defining ecological crisis as "relative" and economically contingent — obscures the destruction of nature.

16 Science and technology studies — that is, the study of the historical and cultural contexts of science.

17 François Furet was a post-World War II historian of the French Revolution, who argued — among other things — that the French Revolution skidded into totalitarianism after 1792. His works typically focus more upon the political dimension of the French Revolution than social and economic analysis.

18 While Žižek rejects Descartes' view of the subject as the self-assured, "master and possessor of nature", he nevertheless argues against those — from Heideggerians to structuralists to new materialists — who wish to do away with the contradictory tension it imposes upon philosophy.

19 In which Negri argues that the Cartesian "I" provided the philosophical foundation for the conquest of reality by the bourgeois class.

20 "Antiphysis/Antipraxis: Universal Exhaustion and the Tragedy of Materiality".

21 Toscano's basic argument — which channels Sartre — is that, when nature becomes apparent to us, it does so as *anti-praxis*, or as the obverse of our own productive activities (as with the deforestation which wracked China over the past few centuries).

22 The method of "retroduction" in Bhaskar's critical realism refers to the way that ontological tendencies or powers are postulated so as to explicate events which one is attempting to understand.

23 In his famed *Materialism and Empirio-criticism*, Lenin frames philosophy as a tug of war between two mutually exclusive camps: that of materialism and that of idealism. While this idea was arguably abandoned by him during his 1914–15 studies of Hegel in favour of a less binary understanding, it nevertheless came to exert a considerable influence on Marxist thinkers due to its canonization under Stalin. One of these was Louis Althusser, who in the late 1960s argued that — because neither materialism nor idealism can be 'proven' at the level of first principles — the task of Marxist philosophy is to defend materialism (that is, the truth and adequacy of science) within the realm of philosophical debate. Later, in the 1980s, he would expand upon this motif, arguing that there exists an "underground current" of "aleatory materialism" that has served as a vector of resistance to idealism throughout the history of philosophy. This lineage includes Democritus, Epicurus, Lucretius, Machiavelli, Spinoza, Hobbes, Rousseau, Montesquieu, Heidegger, Wittgenstein, and — of course — Marx.

24 Whereas Ernesto Laclau's work has calcified into a political ontology, in which ideology is replaced with discourse and the distinctions between the economic, political, and ideological are neutralised, Hall has criticised this as a reductive, prefabricated framework.

25 In the essay, Virno's main argument is that — because our culture is conditioned by abstractions — the materialist must "*identify and describe a specific form on the basis of the type of knowledge which permeates it*", rather than resorting to "sensationism".

26 Deleuze's rejection of the idea that economic contradictions would give rise to communism was developed in a "rightist" direction by Nick Land, who eschewed the various leftist alternatives (e.g., plurivocal "left assemblages") postulated by Deleuze in favour of the view that only capitalism is capable of generating radical novelty.

27 "Race, real estate and real abstraction", in *Radical Philosophy* 194.

28 https://www.johnhuntpublishing.com/blogs/zer0/a-complex-seeing-toward-an-aesthetic-of-the-economy.

29 *Combined and Uneven Apocalypse: Luciferian Marxism*, published in 2011 by Zer0 Books.

30 The Italian philosopher Giorgio Agamben has controversially criticised the imposition of measures to contain the pandemic on the grounds that, following Schmitt, they are being used as a pretext to revive coercive state authority in the face of its containment by capital — and that they ultimately represent an inauthentic retreat from our inexorable finitude (an argument influenced by Heidegger).

31 For Sotiris, the pandemic raises the question of whether there can be a democratisation of anti-pandemial measures; a "biopolitics from below".

32 In which Finelli and Toffanin critique Agamben and Cacciari — both neo-Heideggerians — for critiquing the state of the pandemic from the standpoint of a nebulous "Elsewhere" that elides its material dimensions.

33 Malm has linked COVID-19 to the overarching climate crisis, declaring the need for greater militancy; an "ecological Leninism" that — due to anarchist reservations — stops short of the full assumption of state power.

zer0
books

CULTURE, SOCIETY, & POLITICS

Contemporary culture has eliminated the concept and public figure of the intellectual. A cretinous anti-intellectualism presides, cheer-led by hacks in the pay of multinational corporations who reassure their bored readers that there is no need to rouse themselves from their stupor. Zer0 Books knows that another kind of discourse — intellectual without being academic, popular without being populist — is not only possible but already flourishing. Zer0 is convinced that in the unthinking, blandly consensual culture in which we live, critical and engaged theoretical reflection is more important than ever before.

Bestsellers from Zer0 Books include:

Poor but Sexy
Culture Clashes in Europe East and West
Agata Pyzik
How the East stayed East and the West stayed West.
Paperback:978-1-78099-394-2 ebook: 978-1-78099-395-9

An Anthropology of Nothing in Particular
Martin Demant Frederiksen
A journey into the social lives of meaninglessness.
Paperback: 978-1-78535-699-5 ebook: 978-1-78535-700-8

In the Dust of This Planet
Horror of Philosophy vol. 1
Eugene Thacker
In the first of a series of three books on the Horror of Philosophy, *In the Dust of This Planet* offers the genre of horror as a way of thinking about the unthinkable.
Paperback: 978-1-84694-676-9 ebook: 978-1-78099-010-1

The End of Oulipo?
An Attempt to Exhaust a Movement
Lauren Elkin, Veronica Esposito
Paperback: 978-1-78099-655-4 ebook: 978-1-78099-656-1

Capitalist Realism
Is There No Alternative?
Mark Fisher
An analysis of the ways in which capitalism has presented itself as the only realistic political-economic system.
Paperback: 978-1-84694-317-1 ebook: 978-1-78099-734-6

Rebel Rebel
Chris O'Leary
David Bowie: every single song. Everything you want to know, everything you didn't know.
Paperback: 978-1-78099-244-0 ebook: 978-1-78099-713-1

Cartographies of the Absolute
Alberto Toscano, Jeff Kinkle
An aesthetics of the economy for the twenty-first century.
Paperback: 978-1-78099-275-4 ebook: 978-1-78279-973-3

Malign Velocities
Accelerationism and Capitalism
Benjamin Noys
Long-listed for the Bread and Roses Prize 2015, *Malign Velocities* argues against the need for speed, tracking acceleration as the symptom of the ongoing crises of capitalism.
Paperback: 978-1-78279-300-7 ebook: 978-1-78279-299-4

Babbling Corpse
Vaporwave and the Commodification of Ghosts
Grafton Tanner
Paperback: 978-1-78279-759-3 ebook: 978-1-78279-760-9

New Work New Culture
Work we want and a culture that strengthens us
Frithjof Bergmann
A serious alternative for humankind and the planet.
Paperback: 978-1-78904-064-7 ebook: 978-1-78904-065-4

Romeo and Juliet in Palestine
Teaching Under Occupation
Tom Sperlinger
Life in the West Bank, the nature of pedagogy and the role of a university under occupation.
Paperback: 978-1-78279-637-4 ebook: 978-1-78279-636-7

Color, Facture, Art and Design
Iona Singh
This materialist definition of fine art develops guidelines for architecture, design, cultural studies, and ultimately, social change.
Paperback: 978-1-78099-629-5 ebook: 978-1-78099-630-1

Sweetening the Pill
or How We Got Hooked on Hormonal Birth Control
Holly Grigg-Spall
Has contraception liberated or oppressed women?
Sweetening the Pill breaks the silence on the dark side of hormonal contraception.
Paperback: 978-1-78099-607-3 ebook: 978-1-78099-608-0

Why Are We the Good Guys?
Reclaiming Your Mind from the Delusions of Propaganda
David Cromwell
A provocative challenge to the standard ideology that Western power is a benevolent force in the world.
Paperback: 978-1-78099-365-2 ebook: 978-1-78099-366-9

The Writing on the Wall
On the Decomposition of Capitalism and its Critics
Anselm Jappe, Alastair Hemmens
A new approach to the meaning of social emancipation.
Paperback: 978-1-78535-581-3 ebook: 978-1-78535-582-0

Neglected or Misunderstood
The Radical Feminism of Shulamith Firestone
Victoria Margree
An interrogation of issues surrounding gender, biology, sexuality, work and technology, and the ways in which our imaginations continue to be in thrall to ideologies of maternity and the nuclear family.
Paperback: 978-1-78535-539-4 ebook: 978-1-78535-540-0

How to Dismantle the NHS in 10 Easy Steps (Second Edition)
Youssef El-Gingihy
The story of how your NHS was sold off and why you will have to buy private health insurance soon. A new expanded second edition with chapters on junior doctors' strikes and government blueprints for US-style healthcare.
Paperback: 978-1-78904-178-1 ebook: 978-1-78904-179-8

Digesting Recipes
The Art of Culinary Notation
Susannah Worth
A recipe is an instruction, the imperative tone of the expert, but this constraint can offer its own kind of potential. A recipe need not be a domestic trap but might instead offer escape — something to fantasise about or aspire to.
Paperback: 978-1-78279-860-6 ebook: 978-1-78279-859-0

Most titles are published in paperback and as an ebook. Paperbacks are available in traditional bookshops. Both print and ebook formats are available online.
Follow us at:
https://www.facebook.com/ZeroBooks
https://twitter.com/Zer0Books
https://www.instagram.com/zero.books